Principles of Macroeconomics

READINGS, ISSUES, AND CASES

Fourth Edition

A companion volume by Edwin Mansfield

Principles of Macroeconomics, *Fourth Edition*

Principles of Macroeconomics

READINGS, ISSUES, AND CASES

Fourth Edition

Edited by

EDWIN MANSFIELD

UNIVERSITY OF PENNSYLVANIA

W · W · NORTON & COMPANY · INC · NEW YORK · LONDON

Copyright © 1983, 1980, 1977, 1974 by W. W. Norton & Company, Inc.
ALL RIGHTS RESERVED.
Published simultaneously in Canada by George J. McLeod Limited, Toronto.
Printed in the United States of America.

Library of Congress Cataloging in Publication Data
Main entry under title:
Principles of macroeconomics—readings, issues, and
  cases.
  "Companion volume to: Principles of macroeconomics
Edwin Mansfield.   4th ed. c1983.
  1. Macroeconomics—Addresses, essays, lectures.
I. Mansfield, Edwin.   II. Mansfield, Edwin.   Principles
of macroeconomics.   4th ed.
HB172.5.P74   1983   339   83-8038

ISBN 0-393-95340-8

W. W. Norton & Company, Inc., 500 Fifth Avenue, New York,
    N. Y. 10110
W. W. Norton & Company Ltd., 37 Great Russell Street, Lon-
    don WC1B 3NU

1 2 3 4 5 6 7 8 9 0

Acknowledgments

Permission to use copyright materials from the following sources is hereby acknowledged.

"The Price System" by W. Allen Wallis. Reprinted by permission from *The Freeman*, July 1957. "The Economic Organisation of a P.O.W. Camp" by R. A. Radford from *Economica*, November 1945. Used with permission of the publisher. "Capitalism: An Irrational System" by Paul Baran and Paul Sweezy. Copyright © 1966 by Paul M. Sweezy; reprinted by permission of Monthly Review Press. "The Future of Capitalism" by Robert L. Heilbroner from *Business Civilization in Decline*, pp. 17–34. By permission of W. W. Norton & Company, Inc. © W. W. Norton & Company, Inc. "Our Blend of Democracy and Capitalism" by Arthur M. Okun from *Across the Board*, March 1979. Reprinted by permission of The Conference Board and the author. "The Government of the Economy" by George J. Stigler in A *Dialogue on the Proper Economic Role of the State*, 1963 (Selected Papers No. 7, The Graduate School of Business). Reprinted by permission of The Graduate School of Business (University of Chicago). "The Economic Role of Private Activity" by Paul A. Samuelson from A *Dialogue on the Proper Economic Role of the State*. Reprinted by permission of The Graduate School of Business (University of Chicago) and by the author. "Proposition 13 and Its Aftermath" by Anita Summers from *Business Review*. March/April 1979. Reprinted by permission of the Federal Reserve Bank of Philadelphia. "The Great Depression," reprinted from the September 1932 issue of *Fortune* magazine by special permission; © 1932 Time Inc. "Fiscal Policy and Economic Stabilization" from *Federal Tax Policy* by Joseph A. Pechman. © 1971 by The Brookings Institution. Reprinted by permission of the Brookings Institution. "Deficit, Deficit, Who's Got the Deficit?" Reprinted by permission from *National Economic Policy* by James Tobin. Copyright © 1966 by Yale University. "Economic Forecasting and Science" by Paul A. Samuelson. Reprinted by permission of the publisher, The University of Michigan, © 1965. "Is Monetary Policy Being Oversold?" Reprinted from *Monetary vs. Fiscal Policy* by Milton Friedman and Walter Heller. By permission of W. W. Norton & Company, Inc. © 1969 by The Graduate School of Business Administration, New York University. "Rules and Roles for Fiscal and Monetary Policy" by Arthur M. Okun from *Issues in Fiscal and Monetary Policy: The Eclectic Economist Views the Controversy*, published by the DePaul University Press. Reprinted by permission of the author and the publisher. "Open-Market Operations: A Case Study." Reprinted by permission of Paul Meek, Monetary Adviser, from *Open Market Operations*, published and copyrighted by the Federal Reserve Bank of New York, 1973. "Rational Expectations—Fresh Ideas That Challenge Some Established Views of Policy Making" by Clarence Nelson from *Annual Report*, 1977. Reprinted by permission of the Federal Reserve Bank of Minneapolis. "The Intelligent Citizen's Guide to Inflation" by Robert M. Solow. Reprinted by permission of the author from *The Public Interest*, No. 38, Winter 1975. © 1975 by National Affairs, Inc. "The Inflationary Bias in our Economy" by Arthur F. Burns. Reprinted by permission of the author from his address, "The Real Issues of Inflation and Unemployment," delivered at the University of Georgia, September 19, 1975. "The Case against Economic Growth" from *The Costs of Economic Growth* by E. J. Mishan. Reprinted by permission of Praeger Publishers, Inc. "The Limits to Growth" from *The Limits to Growth* by Donella H. Meadows, Dennis L. Meadows, Jorgen Randers, William W. Behrens III, a Potomac Associates Book, published by Universe Books, New York, 1972. "Is the End of the World at Hand?" by Robert M. Solow. Reprinted by permission from *Challenge*, published by International Arts and Sciences Press, Inc., White Plains, New York 10603 "Contribution of Research and Development to Economic Growth in the United States" by Edwin Mansfield, originally published in *Science*, Vol. 175, pp. 477–486, February 4, 1972. © 1972 by the American Association for the Advancement of Science. Reprinted by permission. "The Multinational Firm and Imperialism" from Paul A. Baran's *The Political Economy of Growth*. © 1957 by Monthly Review Inc., reprinted by permission of Monthly Review Press, "The New Protectionism" by Walter Adams. Originally published in *Challenge*, May–June 1973. Reprinted by permission of the publisher. "The Poor Nations" Reprinted from *The Rich Nations and the Poor Nations* by Barbara Ward. By permission of W. W. Norton & Company, Inc. © 1962 by Barbara Ward. "The Less Developed Countries: Observations and Implications" Reprinted from Simon Kuznets, *Population, Capital, and Growth*. By permission of W. W. Norton & Company, Inc. © 1973 by W. W. Norton & Co. Inc.

CONTENTS

PART TWO
UNEMPLOYMENT, NATIONAL OUTPUT, AND FISCAL POLICY

PART THREE
MONEY AND MONETARY POLICY

PART FOUR
INFLATION AND ANTI-INFLATIONARY POLICIES

PART FIVE
ECONOMIC GROWTH, PRODUCTIVITY, AND ENERGY PROBLEMS

PART SIX
INTERNATIONAL TRADE, FINANCE, AND THE LESS DEVELOPED COUNTRIES

PREFACE

to the Fourth Edition

This book is intended for use in courses in the principles of economics. It is designed as a supplement to, not a substitute for, a textbook presenting the principles of economics. Although meant to serve as a companion to my text, *Principles of Macroeconomics*, fourth edition (Norton 1983), it can be used with any standard textbook. It attempts to present a balanced blend of both theory and applications—and to do this within a reasonable length. Moreover, it provides a wide spectrum of views—conservative, liberal, and radical—concerning the important public policy issues of the day. The advantages of including spokesmen of various persuasions are obvious, for no single ideological group has a monopoly on economic truth, nor are economic issues cut and dried.

The papers contained in this volume cover the full range of macroeconomics. I have included some classic theoretical and policy papers, as well as papers that illustrate the measurement and empirical usefulness of theoretical constructs, and papers that provide interesting case studies. Throughout the book, articles are included that demonstrate the application and applicability of basic principles, either to problems of public policy or to private decision-making.

To keep the overall length of the volume within reasonable limits, some abridgment of selections has been necessary. I have tried, however, to present whole arguments rather than isolated snippets, as is done in some other readers. (For it is possible to so digest a piece that what remains is more shadow than substance.) I have also given precedence to current debates over older ones. The central problems of any economy are never settled once and for all; inevitably, they are more interesting to students when discussed in the present rather than the past tense.

I have taken special pains to keep this book at a level commensurate with the background and abilities of the typical student. Of course, there are advantages in including some articles that will appeal to the most capable, and I have done so. But the bulk of the selections can be read and comprehended by those of average competence. Fortunately, it is possible, I believe, to acquaint students with classic papers by the great names of present-day economics—Samuelson, Friedman, Stigler, Tobin, Heller, Wallich, Solow, and many others—without expecting them to perform intellectual feats beyond their capacities or training. Also, one can introduce them to the giants of the past—such as Adam Smith and Thomas Malthus—and focus their attention on the reports of government agencies and national commissions on vital current problems, without taxing their capacities unreasonably.

In this fourth edition, I have tried to alter the book's contents in the light of the reactions of the many instructors who have used the book in their courses. New articles have been included on federal budget deficits, the inflation process, indexation, the consumption tax proposal, changes in the world economy, financial innovation, and other topics. About one-fifth of the articles in this edition are new.

I would like to thank the many teachers who gave me the benefits of their experiences using the first, second, and third editions. Also, I would like to thank my wife for her help in assembling some of these materials.

E.M.

Principles of Macroeconomics

READINGS, ISSUES, AND CASES

Fourth Edition

PART ONE

Economics and the American Economy

The American economy is a mixed capitalistic system; and like any capitalistic system, it depends heavily on the price system. The advantages of the price system have long been recognized, as indicated by the opening item, which is an excerpt from Adam Smith's *The Wealth of Nations*. Smith argues that: "As every individual . . . endeavors as much as he can . . . to employ his capital [so that] its produce may be of greatest value," he is "led by an invisible hand" to promote the public interest. W. Allen Wallis's brief essay indicates how the price system solves the basic problems of what should be produced, how it should be produced, and who should receive the output. Even in prisoner-of-war camps during World War II, the price system sprang up, in a spontaneous way, to allocate the supplies of food and commodities received by prisoners. The next selection, by R. A. Radford, is a classic account of how the price system functioned behind enemy lines in World War II.

Marxists Paul Baran and Paul Sweezy, in the following article, make a sweeping indictment of capitalism on the grounds that the capitalistic division of labor has a dehumanizing effect on workers. Needless to say, their analysis would not be accepted by most American economists. Robert L. Heilbroner then analyzes the future of capitalism. In his view, "the next phase of capitalism must be an increasingly planned system, and the drift of business society will be toward a business-government state." This view, like that of Baran and Sweezy, is highly controversial.

Arthur M. Okun, in the next essay, points out that "the United States has built a society on two differing foundations. The capitalistic foundation attaches top priority to efficiency—operating through market incentives for getting the economic job done in the way that obtains the most useful output from our labor, capital, and natural resources. The democratic foundation, in

1

contrast, emphasizes egalitarian and humanitarian values of cooperation, compassion, and fraternity."

While the American economy is capitalistic, it is a mixed capitalistic system, which means that the government, as well as the price system, plays an important role in determining how society's resources are used, and for what purpose. No question is debated more hotly than the proper economic role of the government. Some, like George J. Stigler, are skeptical about the efficiency or effectiveness of the government, and favor a reduction in government controls over economic life. In his witty and provocative paper, Stigler asks that, despite the fact that "no method of displaying one's public spiritedness is more popular than to notice a problem and pass a law," close studies be made of the comparative performance of public and private enterprises to determine what activities can in fact be carried out more efficiently by government.

Paul Samuelson, on the other hand, is much less concerned about the growth of government intervention in economic matters. Although he agrees with Adam Smith about the undesirability of certain types of government intervention, he goes on to point out that Smith's "invisible hand" maximizes social welfare only if "the state intervenes to make the initial distribution of dollar votes ethically proper." In Samuelson's view, the price system, no less than the government, is a method of coercion; and he concludes that "there are no rules concerning the proper role of government that can be established by *a priori* reasoning."

During the late 1970s, there was considerable evidence of a taxpayer's "revolt," as illustrated by California's Proposition 13. Anita Summers describes some of the reasons for the taxpayer malaise.

1

The Invisible Hand of Free Enterprise

ADAM SMITH

Adam Smith, one of the giants of economics, was Professor of Moral Philosophy at the University of Glasgow. This piece comes from his great work The Wealth of Nations, *published in 1776.*

Every individual who employs his capital in the support of domestic industry, necessarily endeavours so to direct that industry, that its produce may be of the greatest possible value.

The produce of industry is what it adds to the subject or materials upon which it is employed. In proportion as the value of this produce is great or small, so will likewise be the profits of the employer. But it is only for the sake of profit that any man employs a capital in the support of industry, and he will always, therefore, endeavour to employ it in the support of that industry of which the produce is likely to be of the greatest value, or to exchange for the greatest quantity either of money or of other goods.

But the annual revenue of every society is always precisely equal to the exchangeable value of the whole annual produce of its industry, or rather is precisely the same thing with that exchangeable value. As every individual, therefore, endeavours as much as he can both to employ his capital in the support of domestic industry, and so to direct that industry that its produce may be of the greatest value, every individual necessarily labours to render the annual revenue of the society as great as he can. He generally, indeed, neither intends to promote the public interest, nor knows how much he is promoting it. By preferring the support of domestic to that of foreign industry, he intends only his own security; and by directing that industry in such a manner as its produce may be of the greatest value, he intends only his own gain, and he is in this, as in many other cases, led by an invisible hand to promote an end which was no part of his intention. Nor is it always the worse for the society that it was no part of it. By pursuing his own interest he frequently promotes that of the society more effectually than when he really intends to promote it. I have never known much good done by those who affected to trade for the public good. It is an affectation, indeed, not very common among merchants, and very few words need be employed in dissuading them from it.

What is the species of domestic industry which his capital can employ, and of which the produce is likely to be of the greatest value, every individual, it is evident, can, in this local situation, judge much better than any statesman or lawgiver can do for him. The statesman, who should attempt to direct private

3

people in what manner they ought to employ their capitals, would not only load himself with a most unnecessary attention, but assume an authority which could safely be trusted to no single person, to no council or senate whatever, and would nowhere be so dangerous as in the hands of a man who had folly and presumption enough to fancy himself fit to exercise it.

To give the monopoly of the home market to the produce of domestic industry, in any particular art or manufacture, is in some measure to direct private people in what manner they ought to employ their capitals, and must, in almost all cases, be either a useless or a hurtful regulation. If the produce of domestic can be brought there as cheap as that of foreign industry, the regulation is evidently useless. If it cannot, it must generally be hurtful. It is the maxim of every prudent master of a family, never to attempt to make at home what it will cost him more to make than to buy. The tailor does not attempt to make his own shoes, but buys them of the shoemaker. The shoemaker does not attempt to make his own clothes, but employs a tailor. The farmer attempts to make neither the one nor the other, but employs those different artificers. All of them find it for their interest to employ their whole industry in a way in which they have some advantage over their neighbours, and to purchase with a part of its produce, or with the price of a part of it, whatever else they have occasion for.

What is prudence in the conduct of every private family, can scarce be folly in that of a great kingdom.

If a foreign country can supply us with a commodity cheaper than we ourselves can make it, better buy it of them with some part of the produce of our own industry, employed in a way in which we have some advantage. The general industry of the country, being always in proportion to the capital which employs it, will not thereby be diminished, no more than that of the above-mentioned artificers; but only left to find out the way in which it can be employed with the greatest advantage. It is certainly not employed with the greatest advantage when it is thus directed towards an object which it can buy cheaper than it can make. The value of its annual produce is certainly more or less diminished, when it is thus turned away from producing commodities evidently of more value than the commodity which it is directed to produce. According to the supposition, that commodity could be purchased from foreign countries cheaper than it can be made at home. It could, therefore, have been purchased with a part only of the commodities, or, what is the same thing, with a part only of the price of the commodities, which the industry employed by an equal capital would have produced at home, had it been left to follow its natural course. The industry of the country, therefore, is thus turned away from a more, to a less advantageous employment, and the exchangeable value of its annual produce, instead of being increased, according to the intention of the lawgiver, must necessarily be diminished by every such regulation.

2

The Price System

W. ALLEN WALLIS

W. Allen Wallis is Under Secretary of State. This article appeared in The Freeman, *in 1957.*

Almost everyone says he's in favor of free enterprise but hardly anyone really is. Slogans like "Make free enterprise work" or "Preserve capitalism" are the usual rallying cries of all kinds of programs to impair freedom of enterprise. A lot of this is disingenuous.

These disingenuous slogans of the false friends of free enterprise don't bother me nearly as much as the fact that many real friends of free enterprise have hazy notions about how such a system is supposed to work. Even they fail to understand that most so-called "welfare" objectives can be achieved better by free enterprise than by collectivism. In debate they are too often easy pushovers for the collectivists.

I am continually impressed by the fact that most individualists and most collectivists are surprisingly close together in their general objectives of social welfare—elimination of poverty, reduction of inequality, and provision for hardship. The differences between the individualists and the collectivists are differences not in values but in technical analysis of the means of attaining these values.

For this reason, I shall make an attempt to picture in very broad strokes the basic mechanism of a free enterprise economy—to describe the way it should—and mostly does—work.

200 Million Individuals

Here in the United States is an area of about three million square miles containing 200 million people. Suppose you were asked how to organize these people to utilize the resources available to them for their material satisfactions. You can imagine you have a fairly detailed inventory of the natural resources of the country, of the people and their knowledge, energies, and abilities, and of their wants. Imagine that all these resources are as unorganized as a set of chessmen just poured out of their box and awaiting organization on the chessboard. Your problem is to organize the resources so that wants will be filled as well as possible.

5

Organization Problems

If you can get your head working at all in the face of so staggering a prospect, it will occur to you that one of the first things you are going to need is some way of establishing goals and measuring achievement. Which of the many things wanted are going to be produced, in what quantities, and with what priorities?

And after you establish these goals and priorities, you will need a method of assigning the various pieces of capital, the various natural resources, and the various people to particular activities. Each will have several alternative uses; you will need a method of coordinating the resources assigned to cooperate in each task.

Then, third, you will have to have some system for dividing the product among the people; who gets how much of what, and when?

Fourth, you will probably realize that for one reason or another your system will not work perfectly but will sometimes have overproduced some things and underproduced others. You will need some system of adjustment to these temporary shortages and abundances, until your method of measuring achievement and your method of allocating resources can get the basic situation corrected.

A fifth kind of problem you may worry about is that of providing for the expansion and improvement of your capital equipment and technological knowledge.

These five functions have to be provided for when you establish any organization, even a small and relatively simple one. When we consider the large and complex organization of an entire economy, what are some of the alternative ways of arranging for them?

Alternative Systems

The most obvious way to arrange things is the way an army does. You set up a commander or a general staff. They decide on goals, they decide who shall do what to attain them, they decide how to apportion the product, and they issue orders accordingly. Another method is that used in beehives and ant colonies in which caste and custom determine who does what. Things go on in the same way, generation after generation.

A third way is to introduce money and let each person decide which he will perform of the activities that others will pay for, and what he will buy of the things that others offer for money.

Under this system, goals are set by the money offers of individuals for goods and services. Resources are allocated to one activity or another by the desires of their owners for money income. Goods are distributed to individuals according to their willingness and ability to pay the prices. Thus prices become the crucial organizing element in such an economy. Indeed, this system is often called the "price system."

Efficient and Voluntary

The price system has two outstanding features. First, it is by all odds the most efficient system of social organization ever conceived. It makes it possible for huge multitudes to cooperate effectively, multitudes who may hardly know of each other's existence, or whose personal attitudes toward one another may be indifference or hostility. Second, it affords a maximum of individual freedom and a minimum of coercion. And since people can cooperate effectively in production even when their attitudes on other issues are hostile, there is no need for unity and conformity in religion, politics, recreation, and language—or even in patriotism and good will except in the very broadest sense.

Although one of the big features of the price system that commends it is the voluntary nature of individual actions, the system nevertheless exerts powerful inducements and even compulsions.

Guides to Action

A consumer who has it in mind to use up a lot of a scarce commodity highly prized by others is forced to forego consuming other commodities to an extent judged by others to be equivalent. A producer who tries to get more income than his services are judged by others to be worth is prevented from doing so by the freedom of buyers to buy elsewhere and of other sellers to underprice him. A business manager who tries to waste labor, capital, and raw materials is prevented from doing so because he will find himself taking in less money than he pays out. As long as he can make good the deficit, by giving up his own right to consume, this can continue; but when he can no longer make good—that is when he can no longer pay for the labor, capital, and raw materials—he is forced to stop wasting them just as firmly as if a cease and desist order were issued by a Federal Bureau of Efficiency. Maybe more firmly, for his congressman may be more influential with the federal bureau than with his creditors.

The freedom of the system produces inducements or compulsions for individuals to act efficiently in the general interest. It is not by any means true that each enterprise is free to do what it pleases. It is restricted by the freedom of consumers to buy elsewhere; of the owners of labor, capital, and raw materials to sell elsewhere; and of business managers to enter the same business in competition with it.

Price Communications

This freedom of others to compete for advantages is effective in checking individual self-aggrandizement because economic information is effectively disseminated by prices. Prices represent one of the most efficient communication devices ever invented.

Indeed, we might look on the problem of organization as hinging on communication. The problem is to bring to bear on each decision two very different kinds of information. On one hand, any decision depends on general, over-all economic data; for example, how much a certain product is wanted, and how abundant the resources are from which it could be made. On the other hand, it depends on minute special knowledge; for example, knowledge of peculiar abilities, of unused resources, of possible changes in ways of doing things.

Centralize or Disperse?

Now the problem is whether to transmit the detailed knowledge of special circumstances to a central agency, or to transmit the general information to the individuals who have the detailed knowledge. The detailed knowledge is too voluminous and nebulous for transmittal or for assimilation, and no one could know what parts should be selected. The general information, however, is summarized in prices.

Just that part of the general data that is relevant to an individual's decision is summarized in prices. If a price goes up, that tells him everything he needs to know to guide his action; he does not need to know why the price went up; the fact that it did go up tells him to try to use a little less or it tells him to produce more of the commodity, and how far to go in his efforts.

Not only do prices convey information on how an individual *should* act, but they provide at the same time a powerful inducement for him to do so.

An understanding of the theory of a price system is essential to any efforts to improve our economic organization or to any comparison of alternative modes of economic organization. To me, the most depressing thing about the prospects for a free society is not the hydrogen bomb, or international politics, or communist agitation; it is the fact that so very few have any understanding of economics.

3

The Economic Organisation of a P.O.W. Camp

R. A. RADFORD

This well-known article by R. A. Radford first appeared in Economica, in 1945, the last year of World War II.

Although a P.O.W. camp provides a living example of a simple economy which might be used as an alternative to the Robinson Crusoe economy beloved by the textbooks, and its simplicity renders the demonstration of certain economic hypotheses both amusing and instructive, it is suggested that the principal significance is sociological. True, there is interest in observing the growth of economic institutions and customs in a brand new society, small and simple enough to prevent detail from obscuring the basic pattern and disequilibrium from obscuring the working of the system. But the essential interest lies in the universality and the spontaneity of this economic life; it came into existence not by conscious imitation but as a response to the immediate needs and circumstances. Any similarity between prison organisation and outside organisation arises from similar stimuli evoking similar responses.

The following is as brief an account of the essential data as may render the narrative intelligible. The camps of which the writer had experience were Oflags

and consequently the economy was not complicated by payments for work by the detaining power. They consisted normally of between 1,200 and 2,500 people, housed in a number of separate but intercommunicating bungalows, one company of 200 or so to a building. Each company formed a group within the main organisation and inside the company the room and the messing syndicate, a voluntary and spontaneous group who fed together, formed the constituent units.

Between individuals there was active trading in all consumer goods and in some services. Most trading was for food against cigarettes or other foodstuffs, but cigarettes rose from the status of a normal commodity to that of a currency. Our supplies consisted of rations provided by the detaining power and (principally) the contents of Red Cross food parcels—tinned milk, jam, butter, biscuits, bully, chocolate, sugar, etc., and cigarettes. So far the supplies to each person were equal and regular. Private parcels of clothing, toilet requisites, and cigarettes were also received, and here

8

equality ceased owing to the different numbers despatched and the vagaries of the post. All these articles were the subject of trade and exchange.

The Development and Organisation of the Market

Very soon after capture people realised that it was both undesirable and unnecessary, in view of the limited size and the equality of supplies, to give away or to accept gifts of cigarettes or food. "Goodwill" developed into trading as a more equitable means of maximising individual satisfaction.

We reached a transit camp in Italy about a fortnight after capture and received one-quarter of a Red Cross food parcel each a week later. At once exchanges, already established, multiplied in volume. Starting with simple direct barter, such as a nonsmoker giving a smoker friend his cigarette issue in exchange for a chocolate ration, more complex exchanges soon became an accepted custom. Stories circulated of a padre who started off round the camp with a tin of cheese and five cigarettes and returned to his bed with a complete parcel in addition to his original cheese and cigarettes; the market was not yet perfect. Within a week or two, as the volume of trade grew, rough scales of exchange values came into existence. Sikhs, who had at first exchanged tinned beef for practically any other foodstuff, began to insist on jam and margarine. It was realised that a tin of jam was worth one-half pound of margarine plus something else; that a cigarette issue was worth several chocolate issues, and a tin of diced carrots was worth practically nothing.

In this camp we did not visit other bungalows very much and prices varied from place to place; hence the germ of truth in the story of the itinerant priest. By the end of a month, when we reached our permanent camp, there was a lively trade in all commodities and their relative values were well known, and expressed not in terms of one another—one didn't quote bully in terms of sugar—but in terms of cigarettes. The cigarette became the standard of value. In the permanent camp people started by wandering through the bungalows calling their offers—"cheese for seven" (cigarettes)—and the hours after parcel issue were bedlam. The inconveniences of this system soon led to its replacement by an Exchange and Mart notice board in every bungalow, where under the headings "name," "room number," "wanted" and "offered" sales and wants were advertised. When a deal went through, it was crossed off the board. The public and semipermanent records of transactions led to cigarette prices being well known and thus tending to equality throughout the camp, although there were always opportunities for an astute trader to make a profit from arbitrage. With this development everyone, including nonsmokers was willing to sell for cigarettes, using them to buy at another time and place. Cigarettes became the nonmal currency, though, of course, barter was never extinguished.

The unity of the market and the prevalence of a single price varied directly with the general level of organisation and comfort in the camp. A transit camp was always chaotic and uncomfortable: people were overcrowded, no one knew where anyone else was living, and few took the trouble to find out. Organisation was too slender to include an Exchange and Mart board, and private advertisements were the most that appeared. Consequently a transit camp was not one market but many. The price of a tin of salmon is known to have varied by two cigarettes in 20 between one end of a hut and the other. Despite a high level of organisation in Italy, the market was morcellated in this manner at the first transit camp we reached after our removal to Germany in the autumn of 1943. In this camp—Stalag VIIA at Moosburg in Bavaria—there were up to 50,000 prisoners of all nationalities. French, Russians, Italians, and Yugoslavs were free to move about within the camp: British and Americans were confined to their compounds, although a few cigarettes given to a sentry would always procure permission for one or two men to visit other compounds. The people who first visited the highly organised French trading centre, with its stalls and known prices, found coffee extract—relatively cheap among the tea-drinking English—commanding a fancy price in biscuits or cigarettes, and some enterprising people made small fortunes that way. (Incidentally we found out later that much of the coffee went "over the wire" and sold for phenomenal prices at black market cafés in Munich: some of the French prisoners were said to have made substantial sums in RMk.s. This was one of the few occasions on which our normally closed economy came into contact with other economic worlds.)

Eventually public opinion grew hostile to these monopoly profits—not everyone could make contact with the French—and trading with them was put on a regulated basis. Each group of beds was given a quota of articles to offer and the transaction was carried out by accredited representatives from the British compound, with monopoly rights. The same method was used for trading with sentries elsewhere, as in this trade secrecy and reasonable prices had a peculiar importance, but as is ever the case with regulated companies, the interloper proved too strong.

The permanent camps in Germany saw the highest level of commercial organisation. In addition to the Exchange and Mart notice boards, a shop was organised as a public utility, controlled by representatives of the Senior British Officer, on a no profit basis. People left their surplus clothing, toilet requisites, and food there until they were sold at a fixed price in cigarettes. Only sales in cigarettes were accepted—there was no barter—and there was no higgling. For food at least there were standard prices: clothing is less homogeneous and the price was decided around a norm by the seller and the shop manager in agreement; shirts would average say 80, ranging from 60 to 120 according to quality and age. Of food, the shop carried small stocks for convenience; the capital was provided by a loan from the bulk store of Red Cross cigarettes and repaid by a small commission taken on the first transactions. Thus the cigarette attained its fullest currency status, and the market was almost completely unified.

The Cigarette Currency

Although cigarettes as currency exhibited certain peculiarities, they performed all the functions of a metallic currency as a unit of account, as a measure of value and as a store of value, and shared most of its characteristics. They were homogeneous, reasonably durable, and of convenient size for the smallest or, in packets, for the largest transactions. Incidentally, they could be clipped or sweated by rolling them between the fingers so that tobacco fell out.

Cigarettes were also subject to the working of Gresham's Law. Certain brands were more popular than others as smokes, but for currency purposes a cigarette was a cigarette. Consequently buyers used the poorer qualities and the Shop rarely saw the more popular brands: cigarettes such as Churchman's No. I were rarely used for trading. At one time cigarettes hand-rolled from pipe tobacco began to circulate. Pipe tobacco was issued in lieu of cigarettes by the Red Cross at a rate of twenty-five cigarettes to the ounce and this rate was standard in exchanges, but an ounce

would produce thirty homemade cigarettes. Naturally, people with machine-made cigarettes broke them down and rerolled the tobacco, and the real cigarette virtually disappeared from the market. Hand-rolled cigarettes were not homogeneous and prices could no longer be quoted in them with safety: each cigarette was examined before it was accepted and thin ones were rejected, or extra demanded as a make-weight. For a time we suffered all the inconveniences of a debased currency.

Machine-made cigarettes were always universally acceptable, both for what they would buy and for themselves. It was this intrinsic value which gave rise to their principal disadvantage as currency, a disadvantage which exists, but to a far smaller extent, in the case of metallic currency—that is, a strong demand for nonmonetary purposes. Consequently our economy was repeatedly subject to deflation and to periods of monetary stringency. While the Red Cross issue of fifty or twenty-five cigarettes per man per week came in regularly, and while there were fair stocks held, the cigarette currency suited its purpose admirably. But when the issue was interrupted, stocks soon ran out, prices fell, trading declined in volume and became increasingly a matter of barter. This deflationary tendency was periodically offset by the sudden injection of new currency. Private cigarette parcels arrived in a trickle throughout the year, but the big numbers came in quarterly when the Red Cross received its allocation of transport. Several hundred thousand cigarettes might arrive in the space of a fortnight. Prices soared, and then began to fall, slowly at first but with increasing rapidity as stocks ran out, until the next big delivery. Most of our economic troubles could be attributed to this fundamental instability.

Price Movements

Many factors affected prices, the strongest and most noticeable being the periodical currency inflation and deflation described in the last paragraphs. The periodicity of this price cycle depended on cigarette and, to a far lesser extent, on food deliveries. At one time in the early days, before any private parcels had arrived and when there were no individual stocks, the weekly issue of cigarettes and food parcels occurred on a Monday. The nonmonetary demand for cigarettes was great, and less elastic than the demand for food: consequently prices fluctuated weekly, falling towards

Sunday night and rising sharply on Monday morning. Later, when many people held reserves, the weekly issue had no such effect, being too small a proportion of the total available. Credit allowed people with no reserves to meet their nonmonetary demand over the weekend.

The general price level was affected by other factors. An influx of new prisoners, proverbially hungry, raised it. Heavy air raids in the vicinity of the camp probably increased the nonmonetary demand for cigarettes and accentuated deflation. Good and bad war news certainly had its effect, and the general waves of optimism and pessimism which swept the camp were reflected in prices. Before breakfast one morning in March of this year, a rumour of the arrival of parcels and cigarettes was circulated. Within ten minutes I sold a treacle ration for four cigarettes (hitherto offered in vain for three), and many similar deals went through. By 10 o'clock the rumour was denied, and treacle that day found no more buyers even at two cigarettes.

More interesting than changes in the general price level were changes in the price structure. Changes in the supply of a commodity, in the German ration scale or in the makeup of Red Cross parcels, would raise the price of one commodity relative to others. Tins of oatmeal, once a rare and much sought after luxury in the parcels, became a commonplace in 1943, and the price fell. In hot weather the demand for cocoa fell, and that for soap rose. A new recipe would be reflected in the price level: the discovery that raisins and sugar could be turned into an alcoholic liquor of remarkable potency reacted permanently on the dried fruit market. The invention of electric immersion heaters run off the power points made tea, a drug on the market in Italy, a certain seller in Germany.

In August, 1944, the supplies of parcels and cigarettes were both halved. Since both sides of the equation were changed in the same degree, changes in prices were not anticipated. But this was not the case: the nonmonetary demand for cigarettes was less elastic than the demand for food, and food prices fell a little. More important however were the changes in the price structure. German margarine and jam, hitherto valueless owing to adequate supplies of Canadian butter and marmalade, acquired a new value. Chocolate, popular and a certain seller, and sugar, fell. Bread rose, several standing contracts of bread for cigarettes were broken, especially when the bread ration was reduced a few weeks later.

In February, 1945, the German soldier who drove the ration wagon was found to be willing to exchange loaves of bread at the rate of one loaf for a bar of chocolate. Those in the know began selling bread and buying chocolate, by then almost unsaleable in a period of serious deflation. Bread, at about forty, fell slightly; chocolate rose from fifteen; the supply of bread was not enough for the two commodities to reach parity, but the tendency was unmistakable.

The substitution of German margarine for Canadian butter when parcels were halved naturally affected their relative values, margarine appreciating at the expense of butter. Similarly, two brands of dried milk, hitherto differing in quality and therefore in price by five cigarettes a tin, came together in price as the wider substitution of the cheaper raised its relative value.

Public opinion on the subject of trading was vocal if confused and changeable, and generalisations as to its direction are difficult and dangerous. A tiny minority held that all trading was undesirable as it engendered an unsavoury atmosphere; occasional frauds and sharp practices were cited as proof. Certain forms of trading were more generally condemned; trade with the Germans was criticised by many. Red Cross toilet articles, which were in short supply and only issued in cases of actual need, were excluded from trade by law and opinion working in unshakable harmony. At one time, when there had been several cases of malnutrition reported among the more devoted smokers, no trade in German rations was permitted, as the victims became an additional burden on the depleted food reserves of the hospital. But while certain activities were condemned as antisocial, trade itself was practiced, and its utility appreciated, by almost everyone in the camp.

More interesting was opinion on middlemen and prices. Taken as a whole, opinion was hostile to the middleman. His function, and his hard work in bringing buyer and seller together, were ignored; profits were not regarded as a reward for labour, but as the result of sharp practices. Despite the fact that his very existence was proof to the contrary, the middleman was held to be redundant in view of the existence of an official Shop and the Exchange and Mart. Appreciation only came his way when he was willing to advance the price of a sugar ration, or to buy goods spot and carry them against a future sale. In these cases the element of risk was obvious to all, and the convenience of the service was felt to merit some reward. Particularly unpopular was the middleman with an element of monopoly, the man who contacted the ration wagon driver, or the man who utilised his knowledge of Urdu. And middlemen as a group were blamed for reducing prices. Opinion notwithstanding, most people dealt with a middleman, whether consciously or unconsciously, at some time or another.

There was a strong feeling that everything had its "just price" in cigarettes. While the assessment of the just price, which incidentally varied between camps, was impossible of explanation, this price was nevertheless pretty closely known. It can best be defined as the price usually fetched by an article in good times when cigarettes were plentiful. The "just price" changed slowly; it was unaffected by short-term variations in supply, and while opinion might be resigned to departures from the "just price," a strong feeling of resentment persisted. A more satisfactory definition of the "just price" is impossible. Everyone knew what it was, though no one could explain why it should be so.

As soon as prices began to fall with a cigarette shortage, a clamor arose, particularly against those who held reserves and who bought at reduced prices. Sellers at cut prices were criticised and their activities referred to as the black market. In every period of dearth the explosive question of "should nonsmokers receive a cigarette ration?" was discussed to profitless length. Unfortunately, it was the nonsmoker, or the light smoker with his reserves, along with the hated middleman, who weathered the storm most easily.

The popularity of the price-fixing scheme, and such success as it enjoyed, were undoubtedly the result of this body of opinion. On several occasions the fall of prices was delayed by the general support given to the recommended scale. The onset of deflation was marked by a period of sluggish trade; prices stayed up but no one bought. Then prices fell on the black market, and the volume of trade revived in that quarter. Even when the recommended scale was revised, the volume of trade in the Shop would remain low. Opinion was always overruled by the hard facts of the market.

Curious arguments were advanced to justify price fixing. The recommended prices were in some way related to the calorific values of the foods offered: hence some were overvalued and never sold at these prices. One argument ran as follows: not everyone has private cigarette parcels—thus, when prices were high and trade good in the summer of 1944, only the lucky rich could buy. This was unfair to the man with few cigarettes. When prices fell in the following winter, prices should be pegged high so that the rich, who had enjoyed life in the summer, should put many cigarettes circulation. The fact that those who sold to the rich in the summer had also enjoyed life then, and the fact that in the winter there was always someone willing to sell at low prices were ignored. Such arguments were hotly debated each night after the approach of Allied aircraft extinguished all lights at 8 P.M. But prices moved with the supply of cigarettes, and refused to stay fixed in accordance with a theory of ethics.

4

Capitalism: An Irrational System

PAUL BARAN and PAUL SWEEZY

Paul Baran and Paul Sweezy are two of America's best-known Marxist economists. This piece is taken from their book, Monopoly Capital, *published in 1966.*

Adam Smith saw in the division of labor the key to the wealth of nations, and he was of course right. Many before and after him saw a darker side, and they were right too. In Marx's words, "the division of labor seizes upon not only the economic but every other sphere of society and everywhere lays the foundation of that all-engrossing system of specializing and sorting men, that development in a man of one single faculty at the expense of all other faculties, which caused A. Ferguson, the master of Adam Smith, to exclaim: 'We make a nation of helots, and have no free citizens.'"

The great social critics of the nineteenth century, from Owen and Fourier through Marx and Engels, were all moved by a sense of outrage at this profoundly dehumanizing effect of the capitalist division of labor. And much as their visions of the good society differed, they all had one thing in common: conditions must be created to foster the development of whole human beings, "free citizens," in possession of all their faculties and capable of realizing their full potentialities. Some thought in romantic terms, of a return to a supposedly lost Golden Age. Others, of whom Marx and Engels were by far the most influential, saw the

solution in the maximum development through scientific and technological advance of the productivity of human labor. As Marx expressed it in a well known passage in the *Critique of the Gotha Program,* it would be only

> when the enslaving subordination of the individual to the division of labor, and with it the antithesis between mental and physical labor, has vanished; when labor is no longer merely a means of life but has become life's principal need; when the productive forces have also increased with the all-round development of the individual, and all the springs of cooperative wealth flow more abundantly—only then will it be possible completely to transcend the narrow outlook of bourgeois right and only then will society be able to inscribe on its banners: From each according to his ability, to each according to his needs!

Marx thought that such a high degree of labor productivity could be realized only in a "higher stage of communist society." We can now see that this was an illusion, that from the point of view of raising the productivity of labor, capitalism had a much greater potential than Marx, or for that matter contemporary bourgeois social scientists, imagined. The giant

13

corporation has proved to be an unprecedentedly effective instrument for promoting science and technology and for harnessing them to the production of goods and services. In the United States today the means already exist for overcoming poverty, for supplying everyone with the necessities and conveniences of life, for giving to all a genuinely rounded education and the free time to develop their faculties to the full—in a word for escaping from that all-engrossing system of specializing and sorting men of which Marx wrote.

In fact, of course, nothing of the sort has happened. Men are still being specialized and sorted, imprisoned in the narrow cells prepared for them by the division of labor, their faculties stunted and their minds diminished. And a threat to their security and peace of mind which already loomed large in Marx's day has grown in direct proportion to the spreading incidence and accelerated speed of technological change under monopoly capitalism.

> Modern industry never looks upon or treats the existing form of a production process as final. The technical basis of industry is therefore revolutionary, while all earlier modes of production were essentially conservative. By means of machinery, chemical processes, and other methods, it leads to continual changes not only in the technical basis of production, but also in the function of the laborer, and in the social combinations of the labor-process. At the same time, therefore, it revolutionizes the division of labor within the society, and incessantly transfers masses of capital and of work-people from one branch of production to another. Large-scale industry by its very nature therefore necessitates changes in work, variability of function, universal mobility of the laborer; on the other hand, in its capitalistic form, it reproduces the old division of labor with its ossified particularities. We have seen how this insurmountable contradiction robs the worker's situation of all peace, permanence, and security; how it constantly threatens, by taking away the instruments of labor, to snatch from his hands his means of subsistence, and, by suppressing his particular subdivided task, to make him superfluous. We have seen, too, how this contradiction works itself out through incessant sacrifices by the working class, the most reckless squandering of labor power, and the devastations caused by social anarchy.

To bring this statement up to date one need only add that the scale of industry has grown incomparably bigger during the past century, that with the advent of automation and cybernation its technical basis has become far more revolutionary, and that the suppres-sion of particular subdivided tasks has never taken place in so many areas of industry and with such startling speed. If it were not for the expansion of jobs in the so-called service sector of the economy (including government), the plight of the worker who must sell his labor power in order to earn his livelihood would indeed be desperate.

While the growth of the service sector has partially compensated for the job-destroying effects of modern technology, it and related developments have added a new dimension to the dehumanization of the labor process under capitalism. There is no need to repeat here what has been so much emphasized in earlier chapters, that a large and growing part of the product of monopoly capitalist society is, judged by genuine human needs, useless, wasteful, or positively destructive. The clearest illustration is the tens of billions of dollars worth of goods and services which are swallowed up every year by a military machine the only purpose of which is to keep the people of the world from solving their problems in the only way they can be solved, through revolutionary socialism. But it is not only those who man and supply the military machine who are engaged in an anti-human enterprise. The same can be said in varying degrees of many millions of other workers who produce, and create wants for, goods and services which no one needs. And so interdependent are the various sectors and branches of the economy that nearly everyone is involved in one way or another in these antihuman activities: the farmer supplying food to troops fighting against the people of Vietnam, the tool and die makers turning out the intricate machinery needed for a new automobile model, the manufacturers of paper and ink and TV sets whose products are used to control and poison the minds of the people, and so on and on and on.

"There is," Paul Goodman writes, "'nearly full employment' (with highly significant exceptions), but there get to be fewer jobs that are necessary and unquestionably useful; that require energy and draw on some of one's best capacities; and that can be done keeping one's honor and dignity." Goodman is certainly right to stress that his "simple objective fact" is important in explaining the troubles of young people in this society. But it is more than that: it is important in explaining the alienation from work, the cynicism, the corruption which permeate every nook and cranny of monopoly capitalism and which anyone with a sense of history cannot fail to recognize as characteristic features of a society in full decline.

5

The Future of Capitalism

ROBERT L. HEILBRONER

Robert L. Heilbroner is Norman Thomas Professor of Economics at the New School for Social Research. This article is taken from his book, Business Civilization in Decline, *published by W. W. Norton in 1976.*

Capitalism is drifting into planning. Is there anyone who would deny the fact? The problem is to interpret it, to place the drift in the perspective of a larger historic movement. It will be my major thesis that the political apparatus within capitalism is steadily growing, enhancing its power, and usurping functions formerly delegated to the economic sphere—not to undo, but to preserve that sphere. In the end, I think this same political expansion will be a major factor in the extinction of the business civilization.

Let us begin, then, by considering the present. Everyone agrees that business has contracted its place within society over the last fifty years, crowded out by a growing government presence. Hence our first task is to gain some understanding of this basic shift. Does the enlargement of the political apparatus of the state in itself mean that business civilization is declining? Need we go no further than a recognition of this change to concede that capitalism is disappearing?

This central problem has been discussed many times. I would like to bring some freshness to the issue by considering the matter in an impressionistic, but I think not unrealistic way, from the points of view of two New Yorkers, both conveniently named Smith, one a conservative businessman, the other a professor of radical leanings.

Arising early one morning, Conservative Smith glances at the headlines, which feature the Government's latest incursions into the economy (whatever they may be), and groans: They are out to destroy the business system. As he reads the details of these Government rulings and forays, he is moved to reflect on the invasion of Government into every facet of private life. Even his breakfast is touched by its ubiquitous presence—the orange juice container, the wrapper on his loaf of bread, the tin that holds his coffee, all bear descriptive labels imposed by Government decree.

Indeed, as he goes about his day, it seems to Smith that it is impossible to escape from the presence of Government. The taxi he takes to Pennsylvania Station charges a fare set by Government. The train he boards for Washington (Government city) is owned and operated by the Government. Once in Washington, Smith learns that a proposed merger in which his company is interested will be forbidden by a Government ruling. Telephoning the news to New York at rates set by a Government agency, he decides to return immediately, boarding an aircraft whose route, maintenance, equipment, operating procedures, and fare have all been Government-determined. On the trip home Smith figures how much of his year-end bonus will go to the Government in taxes, ruefully calculating the rate at 50 percent: how can a man make any money, he asks, when he works as much for the Government as for himself?

Home again, he relaxes in his apartment, whose construction was partly subsidized by Government, and idly watches a Government-licensed television station dutifully complying with a Government regulation to devote a portion of its prime time to public-interest broadcasting. His son, who attends a Government-supported university, comes in to borrow the family's car, which has been designed to meet certain Government specifications. Before retiring, Smith looks over his mail, which includes a bill from the Government for the Social Security payments he must make for his maid. Switching off the lights, for which he has been paying at Government-established rates, he settles into his bed, from whose mattress dangles the Government-decreed tag ("Do not Remove Under Penalty of Law"), and as he finally dozes off, he asks himself: "Is this still capitalism? God, no!"

This is the sort of scenario that delights the guardians of economic conservatism. But consider it again, this time from the viewpoint of our other Smith, of radical political leanings.

Shaking his head over the paper at breakfast (once again the Government has acted as a front for business), Smith also observes the compulsory labels on his foods, but reflects on how little faith one can repose in them, given the sorry record of the Food and Drug Administration's responsiveness to industry pressure. Paying his cab fare downtown, Radical Smith muses that the taxi industry is controlled by a public agency more ready to boost fares than to increase the number of licensed cabs. Boarding the Amtrak train, he recalls that the railroad was taken over by Government only as a last resort to shore up a sagging industry. Arriving in Government city, he is struck by the ease with which business executives communicate their views to the Government and the difficulty with which the "working man" communicates his views: could this be, he wonders, why the tax laws so outrageously favor the rich and propertied, why a national health insurance plan is still lacking, why wage incomes suffer but dividends rise, despite the worst depression since 1929?

During his rounds, Smith hears of the failure of his namesake to pull off the merger he was seeking. Radical Smith is not much impressed, because he knows that Conservative Smith's experience was the exception rather than the rule. Largely because of mergers, the top 100 industrial corporations today own a larger percentage of total corporate assets than did the top 200 industrial firms only twenty years ago. So, too, Smith is not so impressed by the Government regulation of the plane on which he flies home as by the fact that regulation has largely been used to suppress competition: not a single new trunk line has been authorized since regulation began in 1938. Again, Radical Smith does not worry about Conservative Smith's tax burden, because he knows that the top 1 percent of taxpayers (with incomes of roughly $50,000 and up) pay an average of only 26 percent of their total incomes, including capital gains, to the Internal Revenue Services. He would point out as well that the expensive apartment house in which the other Smith lives was built with money provided for "low-cost" housing that somehow got diverted into high-cost housing; that the safety specifications on Smith's car are generally regarded as inadequate, thanks to industry protestations; that the Social Security payments going to the maid are insufficient to support her above the poverty level, whereas the electric light rates established by Government were intended to provide utility companies with profits of about 10 percent on sales. "Is this capitalism?" asks Radical Smith. "Of course. What else?"

Thus both Smiths would impatiently dismiss the question "Is this capitalism?" although each would answer it differently. Nevertheless, I think it is useful to pose the question in all seriousness. For I am inclined to think that neither the stereotyped conservative nor radical conceptions of capitalism shed enough light on the economic and political reality that surrounds us, much less on the destination toward which we may be headed.

Let me begin with the conservative's picture of capitalism. Like the radical's, it is founded on what we might call a minimal structural definition: capitalism is an economic system in which the means of production—factories, farms, mines, etc.—are owned by private individuals or firms, and in which the primary method of distributing incomes is the competition of the marketplace. We shall have an opportunity later to discuss how useful this minimal definition is. But also like the radical, the conservative sees more in capitalism than a bare institutional structure. He also sees capitalism as a larger social system, but a social system with a particular (although usually unacknowledged) characteristic. This is its essentially static nature. By this the conservative does not rule out change, above all the change of economic improvement. But the change affects economic magnitudes and not social relationships. Capitalism is thus conceived as a dynamic economic process contained in a basically fixed social setting, especially with regard to its class differences.

We shall return to this vision of a fundamentally fixed society. But one disturbing trend bedevils the conservative's static conception of capitalism. It is the trend we have already noticed—the steadily growing presence of Government. From decade to decade, government looms ever larger in the economic framework. No wonder, then, that the conservative pictures the intrusion of government as disruptive—even subversive—of the stable social milieu that capitalism implies to him.

Has the steady entry of government meant the subversion of capitalism? Let us try to answer the question by dividing the long history of government intervention into three distinct, although overlapping, periods. The first can be traced back to colonial America and probably reached its heyday in the early to middle decades of the nineteenth century. This is the period when government intruded into the economy as a direct stimulus for economic expansion itself. It is the era during which federal and state money made possible the network of early roads, canals, and railroads (not to mention public schools) that played an important role in imparting the momentum of growth to the formative system. To be sure, it is difficult to measure exactly the contribution made by government, but it seems indisputable that undertakings such as the Erie Canal, the transcontinental railroads, or later the Panama Canal, were at least as important for the expansion of capitalism in their time as the federal highway system, the airline network, or the armaments industry have been for the growth of the economy in more recent times. Need I add that these examples testify that the role of the government as a propulsive force for economic expansion has certainly not come to an end?

A second period of government's relation to capitalism began after the Civil War, vastly accelerated during the New Deal, and is perhaps peaking in our own time. This is the phase during which the main form of government intervention appears in the proliferation of agencies such as the Interstate Commerce Commission, the Federal Trade Commission, the Federal

Reserve System, and the alphabet array that arose under Franklin Roosevelt to supervise the operation of agriculture, the securities industry, utilities, and the like.

What was the common element in this new insinuation of government power? I think most historians would agree that it was the regulation of markets. In one manner or another, the new agencies sought to bring order to markets in which the competitive process was threatening to bankrupt an industry (farming), or to undermine its reliability (banking), or to demoralize its operations (utilities). Indeed, one of the insights that radical historians have given us is the recognition of the role played by leading businessmen in actively promoting regulation in order to stave off the cut-throat competition and other evils they were unable to police by themselves. In 1911 Judge Elbert Gary, the arch-conservative head of the United States Steel Corporation, actually told a dumfounded Congressional Committee that "I believe we must come to enforced publicity and government control . . . even as to prices, and, so far as I am concerned . . . I would be very glad if we knew exactly where we stand . . . and if we had some place where we could go, to a responsible governmental authority, and to say to them, 'Here are our facts and figures . . . now you tell us what we have the right to do and what prices we have the right to charge.'"[1]

Whatever the responsibility of the business community in originating the legislation designed to control its own operations, there is little doubt that, once enacted, the regulatory laws were used to stabilize industrial operations. Here we can witness the long, solicitous history of ICC railroad rate-setting, or the aforementioned refusal of the CAB to license an additional competitive trunk line. This does not mean that businessmen have "liked" being regulated, or that regulation has not to some extent served the public as well as the private interest. But the history of regulation makes it difficult to contend that the power of government has been used to "destroy" any sector over which it was appointed to keep order. On the contrary, the evidence is overwhelming that regulation has been used mainly to protect the regulated sector against competition, from within or without, or to ameliorate abuses threatening to undermine it.

A third phase of government-business interaction opens with the New Deal and is still very much with us. This is the active use of central government's pow-

[1]Quoted in Gabriel Kolko, *The Triumph of Conservatism* (Glencoe, Ill.: The Free Press, 1963), p. 174.

ers to bring the economy to an acceptable level of employment, growth, and welfare.

Of all changes in business-government relations, this is probably the one most attended with feelings of "socialistic" betrayal on the part of conservatives. Indeed, in the late 1930s the Veritas Society was founded at Harvard University to expunge the teaching of Keynesian economics from the curriculum. I suspect that the Society is now defunct, for with the general embrace of Keynesian principles by the Republican Party there is no longer any respectable opposition to the use of the government's fiscal and monetary powers to counteract a deficiency in aggregate demand, or to bring individual incomes above some minimum poverty line. How conservative—how conserving of the business system—does not the New Deal look in retrospect!

But just as the dust has settled in this area of government intervention, it is stirred up in another, brought about by a condition that was quite unforeseen by Keynes—namely, the stubborn persistence of inflation despite the presence of a very high level of unemployment.

Many efforts have been made in various countries to control inflation—tightening the money supply, deliberately deflating the economy, applying wage and price controls, formulating a concerted "incomes policy." None has yet been successful. There seems to be a chronic and deep-seated pressure for rising prices built into the operations of contemporary capitalism—a pressure that resides ultimately in a changed balance of power between capital and labor, tilting the balance in favor of the latter.

Whatever the differences in the attempted cures for inflation, there is a marked common feature to the responses to the problem. *In one manner or another, public responsibility for the working of the system has been extended.* The economic aims of government have now been broadened to include the attainment of socially acceptable levels of price stability. Moreover, just because the various measures so far tried have not succeeded, I believe the reach of government intervention will be forced to expand still further, probably through controls that cover not only prices and wages, but also dividends and profits. If, as I shall contend, inflation is basically an endemic consequence of the operation of the economic mechanism, what possible remedy is there other than the assertion of a political will over the unwanted outcome of that mechanism?

This is a diagnosis that is today advanced by only a few economists and advocated by still fewer, John Kenneth Galbraith being a principal exception. But I believe the number of adherents for extended government intervention will grow if the underlying condition continues to be intractable to milder medicines, as has been the case to date in every capitalist nation. Moreover, despite the general distaste with which controls are viewed today, I presume it will not come as a surprise if I declare that their eventual imposition will be accepted as a measure needed to save, not to destroy, the business system.

Is the conservative wholly wrong, then, in his conception of capitalism? Clearly, I think he is indeed mistaken with regard to the "subversive" intent of government. Yet, oddly enough, I believe the conservative is right in his underlying picture of capitalism as a static social system. But it is not the institutional framework—and certainly not the business-state relationship—that is static. It is the social core of the system, its structure of privilege.

The most obvious and important form of this privilege is the continuous creation and allocation of a highly disproportionate share of income to two groups within capitalist society—those who own substantial quantities of property and those who man the command posts within the business world. Capitalism has always rewarded these strata generously. Going back to 1910, admittedly on the basis of somewhat shaky data, we find that the top 10 percent of income recipients, whose incomes were mainly derived from property and management, got just over one-third of the nation's total individual income. In recent years, the top 10 percent of family units received about 30 percent of all income. The change, if any, has been miniscule. Moreover, on the basis of much firmer data, it seems certain that the share of the top 10 percent has been unchanged since 1960.

Income statistics are deceptive, because changes in the tax laws cause high-income receivers to rearrange the manner in which they get income, exchanging outright compensation for capital gains, or causing large payments to be deferred into installments over future years. However, when examining more substantial data with respect to the ownership of wealth, we find that here too the irrefutable impression is one of stability rather than change. Estimates based on studies by Robert Lampman and others indicate that the share of private wealth held by the top 2 percent of all families declined from 33 percent in 1922 to 25 percent in 1949, but thereafter rose again to 32 percent in 1958. There is no evidence that the concentration of wealth has diminished since then.

The point of these well-known statistics is obvious. Despite fifty years of increased government intervention, supposedly "confiscatory" taxation, welfare statism, and the rest, nothing like a dramatic change has marked the distribution of income or wealth within American capitalism. This in no way denies that the system has generated a steadily rising standard of living for most of the population. But there remains a vast gulf between the quality of life of the "middle" classes—the 15 million-odd American families that enjoy, in the mid-1970s, incomes of more than about $10,000 but less than about $15,000—and the very small group of Americans—perhaps some 200,000 families in all—who enjoy an annual income of $100,000 or more. It is this stratum of privilege that capitalism protects, and whose persistence confirms, albeit from an unexpected angle, the conservative's view of capitalism as a system that grows but that does not fundamentally change.

Not surprisingly, the radical sees things from a diametrically opposite vantage point. Like the conservative, the radical also fastens on the pillars of private property and the market as the critical and distinctive institutions of capitalism. But unlike the conservative, who sees in these institutions the foundation for a static social system, the radical sees in them the source of a pervasive and ultimately irresistible dynamics.

In fact, to the radical the most striking attribute of capitalism is precisely its inherent tendency for revolutionary change, brought about by the irrepressible contradictions of its economic processes. The very problems that we have noted as generative of government intervention—the need to support and advance economic growth, the need to control markets, the need to assure a minimum of social provisioning, the need to repress inflation—appear to the radical as the outcome of the peculiar economic institutions and mechanisms of capitalism, and the intervention of government therefore appears to him to be part of the inherent self-preservative reaction of a system threatened with self-destruction.

I think the radical is essentially correct in this diagnosis. Nonetheless, I find a weakness in the radical view. It is a tendency to assume a subservience of the political apparatus to the economic interests of the system—a subservience that ultimately defines too narrowly the independent power of government or the independent shaping influence of social institutions.

As I have put it elsewhere, the radical view sees the economy as the engine and the government as the caboose in the evolution of capitalism—indeed, perhaps of all socio-economic systems. I believe the process is more accurately likened to a train in which there are two engines, one economic, one political, capable of pulling in different directions as well as coordinating their efforts.

Only such a conception, I think, can help us understand the extraordinary variety of institutions that we find when we survey the spectrum of countries with private property and market bases. How else are we to account for the differences between Japan, where the large corporations guarantee lifetime employment to their workers and where it is difficult to distinguish, at the apex, government from business, and the United States, where the indignities of unemployment are considered no part of a corporation's responsibilities and where government and business intermingle but preserve their respective identities? How shall we explain the severe taxation of upper-income groups in Norway with the easy enforcement of tax laws in Italy? How shall we understand the difference between Sweden, where the public sector, as such, is very small but the degree of public control over the economy is considerable, and France, where the public sector is formidable but its effectiveness small?

All these nations have economic structures that rest on private property and economic systems that depend on market forces. All display similar tendencies of instability, inflation, business concentration, and the like. But from nation to nation the degree and manner of public correction of these problems varies, largely as a consequence of differing capacities to create and maintain strong and effective political authorities willing to set themselves "against" as well as side by side with the business community.

This is a problem to which we shall return in due course. Here I wish to do no more than emphasize the existence of a political sphere whose composition, coherence, and will vary enormously from one capitalism to the next. The political engine in some capitalist economies is extremely powerful. In others it is weak. The defieiency of the radical view of capitalism lies in its failure to explain—or even to consider—this problem. The world of politics and power remains unexamined in the radical perspective, or worse, assumes the character of a passive accompaniment to changes in the economic structure. The tacit assumption is therefore that there can be no exercise of political power for ends that lie beyond those of the maintenance of privilege. The possibility that the very preservation of society may require changes that will profoundly alter the social relationships of capitalism or the still more heretical possibility that government may "detach" itself from the economic base and assert control for the ultimate purpose of preserving a system of political power are not part of the radical scheme of things. Yet it is precisely such tendencies that I think underlie the long-term evolution of the system, in ways that we shall examine in the chapters to come.

But [here] we are considering only the immediate future—the next ten years or so of capitalist history. Is it possible to venture a general prognosis for this period? From what I have written, it should follow that the relationship between business and state will be affected primarily by the nature and severity of the difficulties generated by the economic workings of the system. And here I think we can discern three kinds of difficulties, present in varying degrees in all capitalist economies:

1. *There is the continued propensity of capitalism to develop generalized disorders that require government intervention.* Inflation is only the latest of these "macro" problems. Depression persists as a dangerous social malady. At the very least, these ills require a continuation of the existing levels of public intervention. If, as I shall maintain, inflation is deeply rooted in the economic system, or if the deflationary "cure" for inflation becomes worse than the disease, then we can expect further intervention along the lines I have indicated.

2. *There is a tendency to develop serious localized disorders.* The near-breakdown of the mass transportation system in the United States, the near-collapse of the financial structure in Europe and the United States in the early 1970s, the near-insolvency of many cities at home and abroad, are all instances of recent "micro" failures within the economy. They have brought increasing government involvement in the rescue of the affected areas, for it is evident that railroads, large banks, or vital cities cannot go bankrupt without creating a vast wreckage. This is a consequence of an ever more tightly knit economic mechanism. I therefore suspect that the trend toward government ownership of unprofitable private activities, and responsibility for failing local public activities, will increase further in the future.

3. *There are the dangers imposed by a constricting environment.* During the past few years, we have become aware of the possibility of overrunning our resource base before technological remedies can be found. There is also a growing unease over the damage that unconstrained industrial expansion works on the life-carrying capabilities of the planet. These new elements add an imperious force for the monitoring, direction, and, if needed, forceful suppression of economic activity. Much has been written about these environmental challenges, and I shall refer to them many times. I shall therefore say no more at this stage than to point to their obvious implications with respect to the extension of the government's role within the economic system.

Thus the general prognosis for the immediate future seems very clear. The next phase of capitalism must be an increasingly planned system, and the drift of business society will be toward a business-government state.

6

Our Blend of Democracy and Capitalism: It Works, But Is in Danger

ARTHUR M. OKUN

Arthur M. Okun was a senior fellow of the Brookings Institution. He was Chairman of the Council of Economic Advisers under President Johnson. This article appeared in Across the Board *in 1979.*

In establishing a capitalistic democracy, the United States has built a society on two differing foundations. The capitalistic foundation attaches top priority to efficiency—operating through market incentives for getting the economic job done in the way that obtains the most useful output from our labor, capital, and natural resources. The democratic foundation, in contrast, emphasizes egalitarian and humanitarian values of cooperation, compassion, and fraternity.

Because our society rests on both of these foundations, we encounter creative tensions and uneasy compromises. As individuals, we attach different weights to the two sets of values, and we reach different conclusions on particular policy issues that define the scope of the marketplace and the scope of the political process. So, inevitably, we disagree and we debate. And the debates are often constructive. In the broad light of history, our nation has displayed remarkable ability to hammer out the needed compromises to balance the two value-systems. We have generally avoided big polarizing ideological debates that might have rocked our institutional structure off its democratic and capitalistic foundations. Yet, the threat of polarization has always lurked in the background, and at times has become a clear and present danger.

The polarizers seem particularly hard at work today. By grasping at either the market or democratic value system and ignoring the other, one can readily indict our society for grave defects and grievous crimes. Those who march under the banner of democracy point to the ugly features of capitalism. Our economic contests are motivated by greed and allow the winners to ride roughshod over the losers. There is less nutrition on the tables of many of our poor than in the garbage pails of our rich. Our egalitarian political rights are sometimes contaminated by the power bought by money.

Those who wave the banner of market efficiency see a different set of specters: high tax rates that choke off initiatives; expensive government programs that fail to accomplish their goals; and a maze of regulations that impose large economic costs and that constrain individual liberty.

There is some truth in both of these diagnoses, but both are distorted and partial views that lead to fundamentally wrong and dangerous prescriptions. One would set laudable humanitarian targets and cripple the productive capability essential to hit those targets. The other would probably strengthen our productive capability, but in a manner that could destroy our social cohesion. Despite the appeals of the polarizers, the vital center in American political and social attitudes typically prevails. These centripetal forces stem from the appreciation of the favorable features of both our capitalistic and egalitarian foundations, and from the recognition of their mutual limitations. I want to focus on some of the essential unifying principles that promote consensus—on the broadly shared ideas that help us to maintain our blend of democracy and capitalism.

The Market and The Government Need Each Other

At bottom, most Americans know that our government and our private economy depend on each other. Many of the government's functions in promoting and regulating activity in the marketplace are not controversial; indeed, some are conducted so routinely that they tend to be taken for granted. And the same general, implicit acceptance applies to many of the contributions that our private economy makes to the vitality of our democracy. An explicit recognition and examination of these critical interdependencies helps to put into perspective the adversary relationships and the conflicting issues between the state and the market. The best antidote to polarization is the joint recognition that the pursuit of our human values depends on harnessing materialism and "greed," and that the conduct of our market activity relies on the restrictive legal powers of the state and its "bureaucracy."

Strikingly, the government needs the marketplace in two distinct ways—one as a support and one as a counterweight. As a support for government in a capitalistic system, the private economy is the goose that lays the golden eggs. The markeplace finances the public efforts to educate our youth, protect our shores, and aid our poor. The material resources required to fulfill the objectives of the public sector come from the tax base of a healthy, progressive, private economy.

As a counterweight, the decentralization of power inherent in a private enterprise economy supplies the limitation of government that is essential to the survi-

val of democracy. It is a remarkable uniformity of history that a fully collectivized economy has never produced a single free election or one free press. And that uniformity is not merely an accident or a coincidence. A collectivized economy entrusts government officials with the command over all of society's productive resources. It is natural for them to exercise that enormous power, which allows them to deprive dissenters of their livelihoods and to keep the views of the opposition out of the press and off the airwaves. Why should they put up with democratic processes that threaten their own status and power?

On the other side, the marketplace depends critically on the government and on the exercise of its legal powers to make and enforce the rules of economic activity. The value of contracts, orders, promises to pay, and money itself, stems from the power of politicians and bureaucrats to penalize the violators of the rules of the market game.

Without the government as referee, there could be no game.

The property rights that are the essence of economic transactions are established and enforced by government in a way that necessarily restricts the actions of all citizens, not just those of the parties to a particular contract. Capitalism works only because the government authorizes the posting of millions of "keep-off" signs—not merely to thwart trespassing and theft in a narrow sense, but to establish ownership; to maintain trademarks, patents, franchises, and copyrights; and to clarify who has the right to sell any particular asset to someone else. The keep-off sign invokes the coercive power of the state: it prohibits some citizens from doing things that they would like to do. In enforcing such restraints, society draws a line between liberty and license, between legitimate access and trespass, between constructive and unconstructive freedoms. If our goals were truly maximum liberty in the sense of minimum coercion by the state, if we really wanted "laissez faire," we would have a wasteland of chaos rather than a marketplace of economic activity.

Because we want an efficient and progressive economy, we ask the government to intervene in behalf of the marketplace in many ways. As a specific example, consider the joint stock corporation. Upon this inanimate entity the government has bestowed powers and rights normally reserved for human beings—and one outstanding right, eternal life, that is denied to all humans. This political invention has been enormously constructive; it has promoted the development of industrial capitalism and raised the living standards of the masses. The recognition of the corporation as a humanoid creation of the state illuminates a number of specific issues. Isn't it reasonable to expect corporate behavior to conform to our social norms? Is it obvious that a special tax on corporate income is inappropriate "double taxation"?

The government supplies private enterprise with physical and social as well as legal infrastructure. Obviously, public highways and airports have been essential to the development of our industries that manufacture and use motor vehicles and airplanes. Less obviously, public education has contributed much of the human capital employed in private business and has helped to establish a common language and common culture, which have been vital to American economic progress. In short, the successful private entrepreneurs and the successful public officials in our society owe each other a great deal.

The Competitive Marketplace Is Generally the Best System for Organizing Production

Every day for the past two centuries, our economy (as well as those of other advanced Western countries) has confirmed the validity of Adam Smith's theory of the "invisible hand." The competitive marketplace transmits signals to producers that reflect the values of consumers, offering profits for the production of those goods whose value to consumers exceeds their cost to producers. Profitability becomes the magnet that pulls resources into their most productive uses. Thus, in the competitive marketplace, economic self-interest becomes an engine of social welfare.

The market is such an impersonal, decentralized system that its contributions often go unnoticed. We take for granted that the goods we want are generally available in the stores; we don't award prizes for the continual decline in real costs of production generated by incentives for efficiency. And we do not applaud the flow of new products and new services that raise our standards of living.

Yet, when competition works, it creates values for the consumer far greater than the wealth it bestows on successful entrepreneurs and their financial backers. Clearly, an enormous social surplus was created by the dramatic transformation of energy use that Thomas Edison masterminded. We should all wish for a latter-day Edison who might do as much in the energy field today; and the whole country would gain even if he became ten times as rich as the original Edison did.

To be sure, not every entrepreneurial success in the competitive marketplace represents a shared victory for the consumer. There are con games and rip-offs and deceptive marketing and fraudulent advertising. Because illegitimate business practices can poison the consumer's general confidence in the market, the government enhances the vitality of private enterprise when it can stamp out such practices. Beyond this range, we can all identify results of competitive marketing that seem regrettable and yet acceptable. In one class of such cases, firms operate not by serving the needs of consumers but by playing on their anxieties—for example, by making them worry about whether various parts of their bodies emit the "ideal" scent. I don't care for that smell in the marketplace, but I'd rather tolerate it than pass a law to deodorize it.

The main exceptions to the general presumption of competitive efficiency stem from the presence of vast economies of scale. Monopoly is the only way to capture the potential efficiencies of large-scale production in communication, in the transmission of gas and electricity, and in some areas of transportation. Yet, society simply cannot afford to entrust to a private monopolist the power to enforce scarcity and to collect a huge toll from the consuming public. So government intervention is required. The form of intervention chosen by the United States is different from that adopted by most other nations that regard themselves as capitalistic. They have generally nationalized these industries, while (with the exception of the Post Office) we have relied on the public-utility concept of regulation. The course we have chosen is complex, rigid, bureaucratic, and inelegant and imperfect in a hundred other dimensions. But when the defects of public-utility regulation are weighed against those of unfettered private monopoly and of nationalized operation, our strategy looks remarkably good.

Apart from economies of scale, all of the favorable implications of Smith's "invisible hand" depend on the presence of effective competition and are undermined by monopoly. For monopoly is the very antithesis of competition: it imposes a logic of scarcity rather than of productivity; it enforces rigidity rather than responsiveness, consumer exploitation rather than consumer sovereignty. Yet the very profit-seeking motives that make a competitive market tick also lead producers to try to eliminate competition by collusion, by blocking the entry of new competitors, or by gobbling up or squeezing out existing competitors. A century ago the United States wisely decided to outlaw the freedom to destroy competition, just as it had outlawed the freedom to break contracts and the freedom to trespass. For all its imperfections, our antitrust policy has served the marketplace well, and has enhanced our long-run economic performance relative to that of other countries that tolerated collusion and cartelization.

Antitrust policy is confronted by a serious dilemma when monopoly emerges from a competitive race in which one firm has been so much more efficient than others that it grew rapidly in size and market share. Obviously, our regulatory policies should not penalize exceptionally good performance. But, also obviously, even when market share is obtained legitimately and constructively, it can subsequently be abused by practices that block the entry of competitors. In general, the bigness that comes from competitive success can be tolerated as long as new competitors have access to the market. To offer a particular example, I cannot share the concern of consumer groups in the Washington metropolitan area who decry the dominance of two food chains in the grocery business. With a huge number of competitors and extreme ease of entry, their large share of the market strikes me as a testimonial that they are doing something right rather than as a reason for suspecting that they are doing something wrong.

The government's role in preserving competition and curbing monopoly must adapt to changing developments in the marketplace. One important development in the past generation has been the vastly expanded scope of foreign trade. On the one hand, as long as this country pursues a liberal import policy, the presence of effective foreign competitors should permit some relaxation of antitrust policy. On the other hand, the emergence of multinational and state-sponsored corporations introduces new problems and issues. Monopoly has recently raised its ugly head in world markets through the formation of OPEC, the governmentally organized, multinational oil cartel. The world price of petroleum set by OPEC is a politically determined monopoly price, not a market-determined competitive price. Under these circumstances, the oil price in the United States is bound to be determined by government officials; the only question is how much of a role will be played by sheiks and shahs and how much by American presidents and members of Congress. A host of valid criticisms can be leveled against U.S. energy policy of recent years, but the charge that our government has interfered with a "free market" is not one of them. OPEC is not what Adam Smith had in mind! And that invalid charge can only weaken the strong case that can be made in favor of greater profit incentives for U.S. energy production.

Our Democracy Should Mitigate Inhumane Penalties of the Market

The incentive system of the marketplace uses both a carrot and a stick, offering large rewards to the outstanding winners of the competitive race and imposing heavy penalties on some of the losers. The operation of the stick is often ugly—indeed, inhumane. The unmitigated verdict of the marketplace would condemn millions to deprivation. When our economy is depressed many skilled workers cannot find jobs. Even when our economy is prosperous there are not enough jobs to go around for the young and others who have not had the opportunity to develop skills. And there are never remunerative jobs for many with severe physical or emotional handicaps. Small farmers are exposed to serious deprivation at the whim of nature. Technological progress exacts its toll; as we recognize Edison's contribution, we must also recognize that it indirectly destroyed the livelihoods of many owners, workers, and investors in the kerosene lamp business.

The cases of serious deprivation cannot be accepted passively or justified complacently in a democratic society. Even if the "losers" are all beaten in fair races, we must ask what is a fair penalty for a loser in a fair contest. And, unlike the citizenry of ancient Rome, we do not consider it fair to throw him to the lions!

In a fundamental sense, moreover, the contests *cannot* be fair over the longer run. Vast disparities in results—living standards, income, wealth—inevitably spawn serious inequalities in opportunity that represent arbitrary handicaps and head starts. In an unmodified market-dominated society, poverty becomes a vicious circle. The children of the poor are handicapped in many ways—their nutrition, their education, their ability to get funds to start businesses and buy homes, and their treatment on many of the hiring lines for both private and public jobs. Any commitment to a reasonable degree of equality of opportunity requires some correction of the glaring inequalities of results that an unmodified marketplace would decree.

Even more fundamental, poverty cannot be ignored by a society that proclaims democratic values, insisting upon the worth of all its citizens and the equality of their political and social rights. Our commitment to freedom of speech, equality of suffrage, and equality before the law rests on a broader commitment to human values that is violated by the persistence of economic misery in an affluent society. I cannot imagine how a sane society could decide deliberately to guarantee every citizen a fair trial before a judge and jury, and at the same time permit some citizens to be condemned to death by the marketplace.

The record of history makes clear that capitalism has no built-in tendency to correct the problem of deprivation and poverty, even though such a self-correcting tendency was predicted by many early advocates of a free market. In a particularly ringing passage, John Stuart Mill proclaimed that he would be a communist if he believed that deprivation and misery were inherent in capitalism. For nearly a century thereafter, America waited for Mill's implied prediction to come true. Then the Federal government began to intervene systematically to correct major areas of economic deprivation, producing evidence that Mill may indeed have been right. Deprivation and misery need not be inherent in a democratic capitalistic society if it uses its budgetary resources to eliminate them. Today, one-third of our Federal budget is devoted toward that end, largely through a reshuffle of progressive taxes into benefit payments. If not for that reshuffle, the number of Americans living below the poverty line would be at least double the actual figure.

This is an area of particularly vexing trade-offs. No objective dollar price-tag can be placed on the benefit of reducing deprivation and misery; the valuation is a matter of individual judgment and ethical assessment, on which citizens will disagree. And, with few exceptions, efforts to shift resources to the poor and disadvantaged have their costs. As I like to put it, society can transport money from rich to poor only in a leaky bucket. The leakages are of two distinct types: direct administrative and compliance costs of the tax and transfer programs; and indirect economic costs of the distortions of incentives to work, save, invest, and innovate. The cost of the leakages must be balanced against the benefits obtained from what is left in the bucket. A program cannot be damned just because it has some leakage, nor can it be blessed simply because something is left in the bucket. Correcting deprivation and preserving economic efficiency are both desirable goals, which unfortunately sometimes conflict with each other. Of necessity, we must live with com-

promises between the two. We cannot aid low-income groups to the point of destroying the incentive system of the market that marshals the effort and economic activity to fill the bucket. Nor can we tolerate kids with empty stomachs, adults selling apples, and oldsters with begging cups in the name of a greater aggregate of real GNP. There are serious, legitimate grounds for debate and controversy among informed citizens about how much assistance should be provided and how it can be handled with minimum leakage. We need those constructive dialogues and debates, not ideological shouting matches, to formulate policies in this perplexing and crucial area.

The Government Must Look After the Interests of "Third Parties"

It is axiomatic that voluntary transactions in the marketplace are mutually advantageous to both the buyer and the seller—or else they would not be agreed upon by the two parties. But a transaction may harm some third parties whose interests are not reflected in the exchange decision. Only the political process can determine when the interests of third parties are sufficiently weighty to warrant protection.

In some cases the decision is easy. We would all object if our next-door neighbor sold his land for use as a garbage dump. And so zoning laws are enacted by which the government prevents indirect trespassing on our property rights. Similarly, we used the force of law to require vaccinations against smallpox, recognizing the strong interdependence of our exposure to contagious diseases. On the other hand, we do not require homeowners to grow pretty gardens, nor do we ban activities that increase the likelihood of catching and spreading colds. In these cases our guide is not a general principle for or against government intervention, but rather a pragmatic weighing of costs and benefits. When the government does not intervene, the value of the unregulated activity—and the freedom to engage in it—is preserved for the participants, but the costs imposed on the nonparticipants are accepted. Regulation or intervention obviously reverses the balance sheet.

The complex environmental decisions that confront us today in the effort to control dirty air, dirty water, and unwarranted noise are similar to those posed by the next-door garbage dump or messy garden. Indeed, it is not obvious that the new problem areas are more vexing, in principle, than those in public health and urban land-use that we now handle routinely. They evoke more controversy and divisiveness, in part because we have not shaken down our policies in these new areas, and in part because they are related to technological advances that are still fraught with uncertain consequences. Only recently has anyone had to worry about whether flourocarbons should go into our air, whether nuclear power plants should be located in our suburbs, or supersonic transports should land at our airports. But, currently, those decisions have to be made—one way or the other. If they are left to the marketplace, the impact on third parties will be ignored and only the benefits and costs to producers and direct consumers will be reflected.

If, however, third-party interests are considered through the political process, sometimes they will loom large enough to justify constraining the producers and consumers—thus increasing the scope of government regulation. If we continue to balance benefits and costs pragmatically, we must be prepared for some net increase in the range of third-party protections as a by-product of technological advance. I do not welcome that prospect, but I believe it must be faced by improving regulation and collective rule-making, and not by disregarding the impact of technologically created interdependencies on the public at large.

Government Actions Must Be Subjected to the Test of Efficiency

I have emphasized that the competitive market gets its job done, but I have also identified some of its shortcomings—spawning monopoly, imposing inhumane penalties, and disregarding the interests of third parties. Any correction of those shortcomings must come through the operation of the government. But to score a net gain, the public sector must execute its tasks well. The government's cure must not be worse than the market's disease. In fact, Federal, state, and local governments do carry out many of their traditional tasks with reasonable efficiency. But the record of performance on the additional tasks that the Federal government has undertaken in the 1960s and 1970s is disappointing.

One source of this disappointment was the veritable explosion of demands for new and complex services from the Federal government—improving neighborhoods, training the unskilled, cleaning up the air and

the water, and rooting out discrimination and objectionable lobbying practices. Starting without a background of experience or a base of technological knowledge for the pursuit of these goals, we understandably encountered serious problems in trying to do so much so fast.

Some of the frustrations were not just a matter of the pace, but rather reflected the nature of the public sector and the political decision-making process. The public administrator cannot tune in to the market's signals; he does not get the guidance of the bottom line and the feedback of customer demand that make executives of competitive private firms perform efficiently.

Furthermore, the government suffers as a producer of services from a decision-making process designed to be painstaking and deliberate. Checks and balances of powers, and procedures to ensure due process and accountability are features of the political process for good reasons. They protect us against fraud, conspiracy, and capriciousness. But they also deprive us of flexibility, experimentation, and responsiveness in public administration, and they make political decision-making a costly process.

In addition, as Charles Schultze has explained in *The Public Use of Private Interest*, the pursuit of efficiency in the public sector is impeded by the rule of "we do no direct harm." The political process is generally intended to compensate losers and hence must avoid inflicting losses on citizens. But if it cannot inflict losses, it cannot follow those dictates of efficiency that require exercise of the stick (as well as the carrot). As Schultze notes insightfully, the rule was intended to protect citizens from arbitrary exercise of the powers of government, but it now works in practice mainly to extend the sphere of detailed state control. In order to avoid harming any minority, the government is busily adjudicating all kinds of competing claims, maintaining programs that have either failed or outlived their usefulness, and shunning the use of reward-and-penalty incentives.

A final impediment to efficiency is the greater weight attached to the interests of producers than to those of consumers, particularly in the Congress. In part, this imbalance is a corollary of "do no direct harm"; in part, it stems from the greater wealth and power of producer groups; mostly, in my judgment, it reflects an asymmetry of information and motivation. Every sugar producer knows how his Congressman votes on sugar legislation, while 200 million sugar consumers neither learn the facts nor care deeply enough to evaluate their Congressman on this particular dimension of performance. In principle, this imbalance can be rectified by organized consumer groups, but these generally find issues of health and safety more exciting than those of price supports, tariffs and quotas, restrictive labor practices, or tax shelters.

I doubt that there would be much serious disagreement with my assessment of the shortcomings of government performance in executing its new tasks, or with my diagnosis of some of the contributing causes. But there is a highly significant controversy about the lessons to be learned from that record. Many conservatives see a confirmation of their convictions about how little the government can do constructively and a demonstration of the need to abandon some social goals. In contrast, to liberals and many centrists, the record is not only a keen disappointment but also a challenge for reforms to improve government efficiency. Those of us who take up that challenge realize that the tasks we set for government must be revised in light of what it can realistically accomplish at a price the taxpayer can afford. Our past experience should allow us to kill some proposals on the drawing board, to nurture a selected few with more managerial effort, to follow up with a careful evaluation of results, and to phase out the failures.

I see a number of recent, significant, if still incipient, movements toward reform of government efficiency. First, the process by which priorities are weighed in the Congress has been changed for the better by the new budgetary process. With the establishment of the two Budget Committees, and of the Congressional Budget Office, and the institution of joint resolutions on the budget, our legislators now are facing up to the reality that the whole must equal the sum of the parts in the Federal budget. Second, "sunset" legislation is a promising procedure; if fully implemented, it should ensure that Federal programs do not keep going indefinitely by inertia. Third, despite the unrealism of the implied notion that every dollar of every program can be assessed anew each year, zero-base budgeting may bestow upon us 95-percent-base budgeting, which would be a genuine improvement over the traditional standard of 100 percent. Fourth, the newly enacted reform of the Federal civil service should strengthen carrot-and-stick incentives for our career public administrators.

Many policy-oriented researchers have advanced proposals for applying market-type incentives in public programs designed to correct the shortcomings of the market itself. Schultze's book developed that theme in detail and offered many examples of ways that rewards and penalties could be invoked to make private self-interest serve public purposes more effectively. These include the initiation of fees and subsidies for the curbing of pollution, greater dependence on liability insurance to meet safety and health objectives, the introduction of subsidies to private employers for hiring and training the disadvantaged and the handicapped. Currently, our elected officials are taking seriously proposals to invoke penalties or rewards through the tax system to help break the stubborn, ongoing wage-price spiral. This group of policy innovations calls for the government to apply the carrot-and-stick approach of the marketplace, as a partial substitute for the traditional command-and-control approach of the political process.

Efforts to improve performance in the public sector face many obstacles. Clearly, there is no built-in tendency for the government to become efficient any more than there is for the market to become humane. Indeed, I have noted several ways in which the political process creates inherent limitations on the efficiency of government as a producer of complex services. If we apply benefit-cost analysis rigorously, we will in many cases decide to tolerate market imperfections, rather than trying to correct them through public policy. But many tasks in our capitalistic democracy are going to be executed by government for better or for worse, and our common interest requires that they be done better.

Throughout this essay I have skipped over our serious and intriguing substantive economic problems—inflation and unemployment, poverty and productivity—in order to focus on the problem of polarization. In my judgment, that is a greater threat to our system than any of these substantive problems. And the character of that threat has changed. A decade ago it came mainly from the left—typified by the middle-class youths who emerged from their sports cars to condemn our society for its materialism and greed, for oppressing the masses, and for plundering the planet. Today, in my view, the main threat comes from the extreme right—from those who issue a blanket indictment against all government regulation and intervention, who redefine poverty as the "freedom to fail," and who basically ignore the values of democracy. The worst enemies of U.S. capitalism are a handful of its ardent proponents, who prescribe fiscal-monetary policies that would produce mass unemployment, regulatory policies that would flagrantly violate the legitimate interests of third parties, and "reforms" of government programs that would put vivid pictures of economic misery back on the front pages. The consequences of their program would swing the pendulum of public opinion far to the left. Because I do not believe that we will adopt their program, I expect capitalism to survive and thrive in the United States. And I expect us to continue to pursue the goals of democratic capitalism, striving to make the verdict of the market more humane and the operation of our government more efficient.

7

The Government of the Economy

GEORGE J. STIGLER

George J. Stigler is Walgreen Professor of American Institutions at the University of Chicago. This article, together with the following one by Paul Samuelson, was published by the Graduate School of Business of the University of Chicago in 1963.

No doubt this is the best of all possible worlds, for the time being. But even in the best of possible worlds, a good many things happen that displease us. Without exception we are shocked when a tranquilizer is sold, and its use by pregnant women leads to tragic deformities in babies. We are all distressed when there is extensive unemployment and personal suffering. Most of us are displeased when a strike closes down a railroad or a port or the airlines. Some of us are deeply annoyed when the price of soybeans falls. A few of us are outraged when an increase is announced in the price of steel, but this particular few is not unimportant. And I, if no one else, am incensed with an industry that bribes assistant professors to be learned on TV quiz shows. Some of us full professors could have memorized the answers, and anyway it should be necessary to bribe a professor only to be stupid.

There was an age when social dissatisfaction was kept in the house. All evils were ancient evils, and therefore necessary evils which served at least to keep men humble and patient. This resignation to imperfection has almost vanished in modern times—the

hereafter in which all problems are solved has been moved up to two months after the next election. And government has become the leading figure in almost every economic reform. I propose to discuss what governments can do in economic life, and what they should do.

The question of what governments can do, what they are capable of doing, will strike many Americans, and for that matter most non-Americans, as an easy one. For it is a belief, now widely held and strongly held, that the government can, if it really puts its mind and heart to a task, do anything that is not palpably impossible. The government, we shall all admit, cannot really turn the number π into a simple fraction by legislative mandate, nor can a joint resolution of the houses of Congress confer immortality. But with a will, the government can see to it that fully 85 per cent of the male population, and a few women, are taught several infinite series for calculating π, and with a will, the government can prolong human life appreciably by suitable medical and social insurance programs.

An Article of Faith

This acceptance of the omnipotence of the state does not represent a generalization of experience; it is not a product of demonstrated effectiveness in bending events to the wise or foolish designs of policy. On the contrary, the belief is an article of faith, indeed an article of almost desperate faith. It is not an intrinsically absurd belief; there is no rigorous logical demonstration that the state cannot turn sows' ears into silken purses. There is also no logical demonstration that all men cannot become saints, but the number of saintly men has not yet risen to the level where the census makes it a separate statistical category.

Our faith in the power of the state is a matter of desire rather than demonstration. When the state undertakes to achieve a goal, and fails, we cannot bring ourselves to abandon the goal, nor do we seek alternative means of achieving it, for who is more powerful than a sovereign state? We demand, then, increased efforts of the state, tacitly assuming that where there is a will, there is a governmental way.

Yet we know very well that the sovereign state is not omnipotent. The inability of the state to perform certain economic tasks could be documented from some notorious failures. Our cotton program, for example, was intended to enrich poor cotton farmers, increase the efficiency of production, foster foreign markets, and stabilize domestic consumption. It is an open question whether twenty-eight years of our farm program have done as much for poor cotton farmers as the trucking industry. Again, the Federal Trade Commission is the official guardian of business morals, including advertising morals. I am reasonably confident that more would have been achieved if one of the F.T.C.'s forty-eight years of appropriations had been devoted to a prize for the best exposé of sharp practices.

That there should be failures of governmental policy is not surprising, nor will the failures lead us to a blanket condemnation of governmental activity in economic life. Invariable success, after all, is found in only a few places—one, by the way, being the recapitulation of the previous year by college presidents. What is surprising is how little we know about the degree of success or failure of almost all governmental intervention in economic life. And when I say how little we know, I expressly include the people whose business it should be to measure the achievements, the professional economists.

When we have made studies of governmental controls that are sufficiently varied in scope and penetrating in detail, we may be able to construct a set of fairly useful generalizations about what the state can do. But society will not wait upon negligent scholars before meeting what seem to be pressing issues. The remainder of my article cannot wait either, so I am driven to present what I consider plausible rules concerning feasible economic controls.

There is a great danger, as you well know, that the lessons one draws from experience will be those which one seeks. From 1940 to 1942 I worked for an agency that eventually became the Office of Price Administration. I ask you to be forgiving; I was young, and at least I was eventually eased out for opposing price controls.

What economic tasks can a state perform? I propose a set of rules which bear on the answer to the question, but I shall not attempt a full argument in support of them—it must suffice to give an illustrative case, a plausible argument. It must suffice partly because full proofs have not been accumulated, but partly also because I wish to have time to discuss what the state should do, which is considerably less than what it can do.

RULE 1: The state cannot do anything quickly.

It would be unseemly to document at length the glacial pace of a bureaucracy in double step. Suffice it to say that if tomorrow a warehouse full of provisions labelled *"For General Custer: Top Priority"* were found, no one would have to be told whether the warehouse was publicly or privately owned. That warehouse is still lost, but consider this report on the Federal Trade Commission by the Select Committee on Small Business of the House of Representatives:

From a large number of individual cases studied, one has been selected to indicate the tortuous movement of a case through the complicated mechanism of the Commission. The *Florida Citrus* case (Docket 5640), although in other respects reasonably typical, was chosen for three specific reasons: (1) It is one in which prompt action was highly desirable; (2) it involved no novel questions of law; and (3) it required no lengthy hearings before trial examiners, as all allegations of fact were admitted by the respondent. The chronology in this case in brief is as follows:

Apr. 23, 1946	*Docketing of the application for complaint.*
Sept. 30, 1947	*Recommendation that complaint*

be issued upon completion of investigation.

Jan. 23, 1948   *Approval of examiner's recommendation by chief examiner.*

Feb. 3, 1948   *Consideration by Commission and assignment to Commissioner for preliminary review.*

Oct. 13, 1948   *Recommendation of Commissioner that case be referred to Bureau of Litigation.*

Oct. 29, 1948   *Request to Department of Justice for certain information.*

Do   *Assignment to trial attorneys for review and recommendation.*

Dec. 15, 1948   *Report of trial attorney submitting draft of complaint.*

Dec. 21, 1948   *Memorandum to Commission by Chief of Division of Antimonopoly Trials that complaint be issued.*

Dec. 27, 1948   *Referral to Commissioner.*

Feb. 11, 1949   *Recommendation by Commissioner that complaint be issued.*

Feb. 18, 1949   *Complaint issued. Beginning of formal action.*

Apr. 11, 1949   *Filing of answer by respondents admitting allegations of fact.*

Sept. 8, 1949   *Granting of respondent's request for leave to file substitute answer.*

Oct. 10, 1949   *Filing of respondent's brief on questions of law.*

Oct. 18, 1949   *Filing of reply brief.*

Dec. 30, 1949   *Assignment to Commissioner.*

Jan. 10, 1950   *Reassignment to another Commissioner.*

June 30, 1950   *Recommendation of Commissioner that matter be referred to Bureau of Industry Cooperation. So ordered by Commission.*

So passed fifty months; I must in candor add that twenty-five months later an order was issued. A decent respect for due process lies behind some of the procedural delays, and poses a basic issue of the conflicting demands of justice and efficiency in economic regulation. But deliberation is intrinsic to large organizations: not only does absolute power corrupt absolutely; it delays fantastically. I would also note that initiative is the least prized of a civil servant's

virtues, because the political process allots much greater penalties for failure than rewards for success.

Size vs. Control

RULE 2: When the national state performs detailed economic tasks, the responsible political authorities cannot possibly control the manner in which they are performed, whether directly by governmental agencies or indirectly by regulation of private enterprise.

The lack of control is due to the impossibility of the central authority either to know or to alter the details of a large enterprise. An organization of any size—and I measure size in terms of personnel—cannot prescribe conduct in sufficient detail to control effectively its routine operations: it is instructive that when the New York City subway workers wish to paralyze their transportation system, they can do so as effectively by following all the operating instructions in literal detail as by striking.

Large organizations seek to overcome the frustrating problems of communication and command by seeking and training able executives, who could be described more accurately as able subordinates. But to get a good man and to give him the control over and responsibility for a set of activities is of course another way of saying that it is impossible for the central authorities to control the activities themselves. As the organization grows, the able subordinate must get able subordinates, who in turn must get able subordinates, who in turn must get able subordinates, who in turn—well, by the time the organization is the size of the federal government, the demands for ability begin to outstrip the supply of even mediocre genes.

I estimate, in fact, that the federal government is at least 120 times as large as any organization can be and still keep some control over its general operations. It is simply absurd to believe that Congress could control the economic operations of the federal government; at most it can sample and scream. Since size is at the bottom of this rule, two corollaries are:

1. *Political control over governmental activity is diminishing.*
2. *The control exercised by a small city is much greater than the control exercised over General Motors by its Board of Directors.*

Uniformity of Treatment

RULE 3: The democratic state strives to treat all citizens in the same manner; individual differences are ignored if remotely possible.

The striving for uniformity is partly due to a desire for equality of treatment, but much more to a desire for administrative simplicity. Thus men with a salary of $100,000 must belong to the Social Security system; professors in New York must take a literacy test to vote; the new automobile and the 1933 Essex must be inspected; the most poorly coordinated driver and the most skillful driver must obey the same speed limits; the same minimum wage must be paid to workers of highly different productivities; the man who gives a vaccination for smallpox must have the same medical credentials as a brain surgeon; the three-week-old child must have the same whiskey import allowance as a grown Irishman; the same pension must be given to the pilot who flew 100 dangerous missions as to the pilot who tested a Pentagon swivel chair; the same procedure must be passed through to open a little bank in Podunk and the world's largest bank in New York; the same subsidy per bale of cotton must be given to the hillbilly with two acres and the river valley baron with 5,000 acres. We ought to call him Uncle Same.

RULE 4: The ideal public policy, from the viewpoint of the state, is one with identifiable beneficiaries, each of whom is helped appreciably, at the cost of many unidentifiable persons, none of whom is hurt much.

The preference for a well-defined set of beneficiaries has a solid basis in the desire for votes, but it extends well beyond this prosaic value. The political system is not trustful of abstract analysis, nor, for that matter, are most people. A benefit of $50 to each of one million persons will always seem more desirable than a $1 benefit to each of 150 million people, because one can see a $50 check, and hence be surer of its existence. In fact, it is worth mentioning one corollary of Rule 4: no politician will worry much about anything that can't be photographed. Another corollary is: if Texas wants it, give it.

The suspicion of abstract theory is of course well-founded: most abstract theories recorded in history have been false. Unfortunately it is also an abstract theory, and a silly one, that says one should believe only what he can see, and if the human race had adhered to it we would still be pushing carts with square wheels.

You do not need to be told that someone is always hurt by an economic policy, which is only a special case of the basic economic theorem that there is no such thing as a free lunch. On the other hand, I do not say that all political lunches are priced exorbitantly.

RULE 5: The state never knows when to quit.

One great invention of a private enterprise system is bankruptcy, an institution for putting an eventual stop to costly failure. No such institution has yet been conceived of in the political process, and an unsuccessful policy has no inherent termination. Indeed, political rewards are more closely proportioned to failure than to success, for failure demonstrates the need for larger appropriations and more power. This observation does not contradict my previous statement that a civil servant must avoid conspicuous failure at all costs, for his failure is an unwise act, not an ineffectual policy.

The two sources of this tenacity in failure are the belief that the government must be able to solve a social problem, and the absence of objective measures of failure and success. The absence of measures of failure is due much more to the lack of enterprise of economists than to the nature of things. One small instance is the crop forecasting service of the Department of Agriculture. This service began shortly after the Civil War, and it eventually involved thousands of reporters and a secrecy in preparation of forecasts that would thwart Central Intelligence. It was not until 1917 that a Columbia professor, Henry Moore, showed that the early season forecasts were almost as good as flipping a coin, and the later season forecasts were almost as good as running a regression equation on rainfall. But as I have remarked, most public policies simply have not been studies from this viewpoint.

Let me emphasize as strongly as I can that each of these characteristics of the political process is a source of strength in some activities, as well as a limitation in other activities. If the state could move rapidly, contrary to Rule 1, and readily accepted abstract notions, contrary to Rule 4, our society would become the victim of every fad in morals and every popular fallacy in philosophy. If the state could effectively govern the details of our lives, no tyranny would ever have been overthrown. If the state were to adapt all its rules to individual circumstances, contrary to Rule 3, we would live in a society of utter caprice and obnoxious favoritism. If the state knew when to quit, it would never have engaged in such unpromising ventures as the American Revolution, not that I personally consider this our best war. But what are virtues in the preservation of our society and its basic liberties are not necessarily virtues in fixing the wages of labor or the number of channels a television set can receive.

These rules, and others that could be added, do not say that the state cannot socialize the growing of wheat or regulate the washing of shirts. What the rules say is that political action is social action, that political action displays reasonably stable behavioral characteristics, and that prescriptions of political behavior which disregard these characteristics are simply irresponsible. To say, after describing a social economic problem, that the state must do something about it, is equivalent in rationality to calling for a dance to placate an angry spirit. In fact the advantage is with the Indians, who were sure to get some useful exercise. The state can do many things, and must do certain absolutely fundamental things, but it is not an Alladin's lamp.

State's Proper Economic Role

I turn now to our subject, the proper economic role for the state.

A tolerably adequate discussion of this subject would involve a fairly detailed statement of the major values of American society, either as we think they are or as we think they should be. In the course of such a statement we would have to decide on the comparative importances of national defense, personal freedom, benevolence and humanitarianism, egalitarianism, and other civilized values.

After completing this large task, probably to no one person's satisfaction, we should then have to take up each of the incredibly numerous economic activities now undertaken by the state or currently proposed to it, and examine this activity in the light of these basic social values, of the probable capacity of governments to perform tasks, and of the detailed economic effects of the policies. This may be a suitable syllabus for a four-year course, but borders on the ambitious as a program for the remainder of this hour.

I therefore propose merely to sketch what I believe is the proper treatment of certain classes of important economic problems. Even a much wiser man would have to court the charge of dogmatism by so cursory a

treatment, but at least a basis will be provided for our subsequent discussion.

Class 1: Monopoly

The fear of monopoly exploitation underlies a vast network of public regulation—the control over the so-called public utilities, including the transportation and communication industries and banking institutions, as well as traditional antitrust policies. The proper methods of dealing with monopoly, in their order of acceptability, are three:

1. The maintenance or restoration of competition by the suitable merger prevention policies, which we now fail to use in areas such as rail and air transport, and by the dissolution of monopolies. The method of once-for-all intervention provides the only really effective way of dealing with monopoly.

It will be said that for technological reasons even a modest amount of competition is unattainable in many areas. I believe these areas are very few in number. Even when a community can have only one electric company, that company is severely limited by the long-run alternatives provided by other communities.

2. Where substantial competition cannot be achieved—and I do not ask for perfect competition—the entry into the field is often controlled by the state—for example the TV channels are allocated by the FCC. Here auctioning off the channels seems the only feasible method of capturing the inherent monopoly gains. The history of regulation gives no promise that such gains can be eliminated.

3. In the few remaining cases in which monopoly cannot be eliminated or sold to the monopolist, monopolies should be left alone, simply because there is no known method of effective control.

Class 2: Poverty

A community does not wish to have members living in poverty, whatever the causes of the poverty may be. The maximum level of socially tolerable poverty will vary with the society's wealth, so poor societies will stop short at preventing plain starvation, but Texans will demand, through the oil embargoes that Presidents Eisenhower and Kennedy found expedient to accept, also Cadillacs and psychiatrists in their minimum poverty budget. I consider treatment of poverty a highly proper function of the state, but would propose that it be dealt with according to two principles:

1. Direct aid should take the form of direct grants of money, and only this form. The present methods involve an unending chain of *ad hoc* grants in kinds: some subsidized housing, some subsidized medical care, some subsidized food, some rigging of selling prices of cotton and wheat, some lunches for children, and so on. Not only are many of these policies grossly inefficient, as when a farm support program hurts tenants and helps landowners or a minimum wage law leads to the discharge of the neediest workers, but also the policies impose gross limitations on the freedom of the poor. If the poor would rather spend their relief checks on food than on housing, I see no reason for denying them the right. If they would rather spend the money on whiskey than on their children, I take it that we have enforceable laws to protect children.

2. The basic problem of poverty from the social viewpoint, however, is not the alleviation of current need but equipping the people to become self-supporting. Here we have been extraordinarily phlegmatic and unimaginative in acquiring understanding of the basic problem of low productivity and in devising methods of increasing the skills and opportunities of the poor. The old English settlement laws sought to tie the poor to their native parish, and this utter perversity is presently approached by a relief and old age system which at times imposes marginal taxes in excess of 100 percent on earnings. We have become so single-minded in worshipping the curriculum of the good liberal arts college that we have only a primitive system of industrial training. We tolerate widespread restrictionism on entry by unions, when it is the excluded entrants we should be worrying about.

In fact, so-called liberal policies in this area often seem to me to be almost studied in their callousness and contempt for the poor. Many ameliorative policies assume that the poor are much poorer in intelligence than in worldly goods, and must be cared for like children. Few people ask of a policy: What will be the effects on the poor who are not beneficiaries? If we tear down a slum, and rehouse half the people better at public cost, the only response to a query about the other half will be—we must do this for them too. Much of our welfare program has the macabre humor of a game of musical chairs.

Class 3: Economic Distress

I define economic distress as experiencing a large fall in income, or failing to share in a general rise, but without reaching some generally accepted criterion of poverty—of course the two differ only in degree. Much of our farm program, our oil program, our protective tariff system, our regional development schemes, our subsidies for metals and soon for commuters, are so motivated. Here my prescriptions would be:

1. Compensation for losses in the cases in which the distress is clearly and directly caused by governmental policy.
2. Exactly the same kind of treatment of distress as of poverty in other respects: Direct grants in the short-run; policies to foster the mobility of resources in the long-run. I do not conceal the belief that many of these special aid programs are so indefensible that an open subsidy program could not survive.

Class 4: Consumer and Worker Protection

Since unpunished fraud is profitable, it must be punished. I doubt whether many people realize how strong are the remedies provided by traditional law, and in particular how effective the actions of people who have been defrauded. I am confident that research in this area would suggest methods of vastly increasing the role of self-policing in the economy.

It is otherwise with the alleviation of consumer incompetence: The belief is becoming strong that there is much fraud, or at least indefensible waste, that consumers are incompetent to discover. An illustration may be taken from the hearings on the "Truth in Lending" bill which Senator Douglas has been seeking:

The following actually took place on the weekend of February 5, 1960, in the city of Chicago. It was a chill winter's day when William Rodriguez wandered from movie house to movie house, his mind desperately seeking the illusions of the great silver screen.

Finally, the projectors were still and William once more walked the now silent streets. Before returning to his wife, Nilda, and their four children, he stopped at a drugstore to make a purchase. Then, as he slowly trudged through the rain and snow, he began to eat rat poison.

At 2:00 A.M., he reached home and told his wife what he had done. Nilda called the police who came to take her husband to the hospital. As they carried him into the street, a letter dropped from his pocket. The letter had been sent by a Chicago firm that had sold William a second-hand TV set on time. The set had broken down the day after he received it. The firm threatened to garnishee his wages if he did not pay some of the money he owed. William Rodriguez received the bill on Thursday. He had until Saturday, the day he died, to make payment.

William Rodriguez had two failings. He simply would not listen to advice if it meant giving up something for Nilda and the children. Further, he would always take anybody's word for anything when buying things. At the time of his death, William Rodriguez owed about $700. Part of his debt included a religious medal he had bought for his wife on Mother's Day. The medal cost William $30. It was later valued at 50 cents.

It even reached the point where William was charged for goods he never purchased. Once a stranger came to Nilda's door and left a bedspread. The stranger said it was for a neighbor and that he would pick it up the next day. He never came. Shortly thereafter, William's pay was garnisheed for $34.

Although his wages had been garnisheed three times previously, there was no judgment against William Rodriguez when he died. This time, though, he feared new garnishments might mean the loss of his job. And he knew, too, that even if he was not fired, the garnishments would mean endless hardship to his family.

I assume this tragic tale is true—what shall we do? My basic answer to this painful problem is: In order to preserve the dignity and freedom of the individual in my society, I shall if I must pay the price of having some fail wholly to meet the challenge of freedom. I find it odd that a society which once a generation will send most of its young men against enemy bullets to defend freedom, will capitulate to a small handful of citizens unequal to its challenge.

This basic position does not imply that we should accept the institutions of 1900, or 1963, or any other year, as ideal in the protection they have given to men against fraud and danger. We should be prepared to examine any existing institution, or any proposal for change, with an open mind.

We should not, however, accept dramatic episodes as a measure of need; we should not simply assume that there is a useful law for every problem; and we should not lazily accept remedies which take freedom from ninety-seven men in order to give protection to three.

I should add, since I introduced the question, that I am in favor of truth in lending, and also in borrowing, and in selling, and in campaigning for office, and in lecturing to Swarthmore students, but not in courtship. Senator Douglas' bill has my support the day he shows me, first, that it will achieve any significant results, and second, that these results are worth at least 10 percent of the social costs of enforcing the statute.

These classes do not exhaust the range of functions undertaken by modern states, but they will suffice to illustrate the positions that seem to me to best meet the values of our society and the known limitations on its political processes.

And now I close. I consider myself courageous, or at least obtuse, in arguing for a reduction in governmental controls over economic life. You are surely desirous of improving this world, and it assuredly needs an immense amount of improvement. No method of displaying one's public-spiritedness is more popular than to notice a problem and pass a law. It combines ease, the warmth of benevolence, and a suitable disrespect for a less enlightened era. What I propose is, for most people, much less attractive: Close study of the comparative performance of public and private economy, and the dispassionate appraisal of special remedies that is involved in compassion for the community at large. I would urge you to examine my views in the most critical spirit, if I thought it necessary; I do urge you to attempt the more difficult task of exercising your critical intelligence in an appraisal of the comfortable wishfulness of contemporary policy.

8

The Economic
Role of Private Activity

PAUL A. SAMUELSON

Paul A. Samuelson is Institute Professor at Massachusetts Institute of Technology. This article, together with the previous one by George Stigler, was published by the Graduate School of Business of the University of Chicago in 1963.

Introduction: Matter and Antimatter

Thoreau, disapproving of the Mexican War, would not pay his taxes and was put in jail for civil disobedience. His Concord neighbor, Emerson, went to visit him down at the hoosegow and called out: "Henry, what are you doing in there?" Thoreau replied, "Waldo, what are you doing out there?"

Illustrative of the same point was a conversation I had once with an economist for one of the great international oil companies. I was astonished to learn from him that their crews and engineers did not drill for oil in the Middle East. He explained the paradox as follows: "The Sheiks there are always anxious to make us sell immediately more oil than the market will bear; and they would take a dim view if we slackened on the job of exploration. So, we drill in the hope of getting dry holes, but follow a research procedure that will mark off for us where oil really is to be found."

By now you will have perceived my point. One way of approaching the question, "What is the proper role of Government?" is to ask, "What is the proper role of non-Government?" While you cannot be confident that the man who is most proficient in playing regular checkers (or tic-tac-toe) will also be best at playing "give-away" (or cot-cat-cit in which the loser is made to have three of his symbols in a linear array), conventional wisdom or logic does ensure that by finding the optimal role for nongovernment, you can thereby define the proper role for government. Not taking the bull by the horns should at least give us a fresh perspective on the animal.

Lincoln's Formula

Some people begin the discussion of a concept by telling you how it is defined in Webster's dictionary. I follow the other fork and quote Abraham Lincoln. You may remember that the fellow who ran against Kennedy in 1960 quoted Lincoln on the proper role of government. It went something like the following.

I believe the government should do only that which private citizens cannot do for themselves, or which they cannot do so well for themselves.

36

One would think this is supposed to be saying something. Let us try it in its converse form.

I believe the private economy should be left alone to do those activities which, on balance after netting out all advantages and disadvantages, it can best do.

Obviously what I have stated is an empty tautology. It is no more helpful than the usual answer from Dorothy Dix to a perplexed suitor that merely says, "Look into your own heart to see whether you truly love the girl. And then after you have made up your mind, I am sure it will be the right decision."

But are these mere tautologies? Do the two Lincolnesque statements say exactly the same thing? There is a certain literal sense in which they can be interpreted to be saying the same thing. But we all bring to the words we hear certain preconceptions and attitudes.

I think Lincoln meant to imply in his formulation that there is needed a certain burden of proof that has to be established by anyone who proposes that the government do something. The balance of advantage in favor of the government must be something a little more than epsilon or you should stand with the *status quo* of private enterprise.[1]

Why? Lincoln does not say. But he takes it for granted that his listeners will understand that "personal liberty" is a value for its own sake and that some sacrifice of "efficiency" is worth making at the optimal point where activity is divided so as to maximize the total net advantage of "efficiency *cum* liberty" and vice versa.

The second statement that I have formulated also carries certain connotations. At a first hasty reading, it might suggest to some that the burden of proof is put on or against any proposal for *laissez faire* and individualism. And so it would be naturally construed in 1963 Soviet Russia.

After a second and more careful reading, it is seen to contain certain weasel words of qualification—such as "on balance," "netting" and "advantages" and "disadvantages." So interpreted, it can be made consistent with any desired emphasis on liberty as well as efficiency. And yet, even when almost completely emptied of its meaningful content, my formulation is left with a subtle connotation. It says, there are no absolutes here. The subject is an open one—open for debate and open to compromise. At some terms-of-trade, efficiency can be traded off against liberty. (Of course, Lincoln has already implied *this*, but not quite so strongly.)

Overture to the Program

So much for introduction. My Act I has prepared the way for what is to follow. In Act II, I want to examine the conditions under which efficiency is realizable by free enterprise or *laissez faire*. This is familiar ground, but too familiar and needs reexamination.

Then in Act III, I want to raise some questions about the notion that absence of government means increase in "freedom." Is "freedom" a simply quantifiable magnitude as much libertarian discussion seems to presume? Let me give you a hint of the kind of thing I have in mind: Traffic lights coerce me and limit my freedom, don't they? Yet in the midst of a traffic jam on the unopen road, was I really "free" before there were lights? And has the algebraic total of freedom, for me or the representative motorist or the group as a whole, been increased or decreased by the introduction of well-engineered Stop Lights? Stop Lights, you know, are also Go Lights.

Then I shall conclude on what may seem a *nihilistic* note, but which I hope is actually a *liberating* one.

Technical Requirements for Competitive Optimality

Consider a society with limited resources. Let certain facts about technology be "known" (in varying degrees). Let there be more than one person, so that we can speak of society. Let people have their tastes and values. And if you like, let there be one or more sets of ethical beliefs in terms of whose norms various

---

[1]Actually most people will in fact tend to give the benefit of the doubt to the *status quo*—any *status quo*. In our day the government does many things it did not do in Lincoln's time. When one of these activities is brought open to question, its being the *status quo* could shift the burden of proof on to the man who wants to bring the activity back into the private domain. I doubt that Lincoln would have agreed with this interpretation; in good nineteenth-century fashion, he thought of private activity as *natural* unless the contrary was demonstrated.

situations can be evaluated and ordered.

What I have now specified is so terribly general. Yet already I have been guilty of tremendous idealization and abstraction in comparison with any real life situation.

To some observers, none of the above admits of quantification. It is all quality, quality, quality. There is a possible utopia; there are a variety of actualities; one contemplates these as a whole, and reacts to them. And that's it. Such observers, patently, have little use for economics or economists.

Many observers, however, will note that one grain of sugar is much like another and rather different from grains of salt or Norwegian sweaters. Quantification is, so to speak, rearing its idealized head. Then one notes that five fingers and one nose tend to go together, and by a long chain of not-too-cogent arguments there emerges *Cogito, ergo sum* rather than *Cogitamus, ergo sumus*. Now individualism has reared its single head. And if I—or should it be said "we"?—can coin an Irish Bull, there is almost an anthropomorphic fallacy in considering that individuals exist in the sense that atoms exist.

Now, to save time, we plunge into heroic assumptions.

1. *Each person's tastes (and values) depend only upon his separable consumptions of goods. I.e., there must be no "consumption externalities."*
2. *Strict constant-returns-to-scale prevails.*
3. *Perfect competition, in senses too numerous to list here, prevails.*
4. *The interpersonal distribution of property (inclusive of personal attributes) is ethically correct initially or is to be made so by ideal lump-sum transfers of a perfectly nondistorting type.*

Then, and only then, has it been rigorously proved that perfect competitive equilibrium is indeed optimal. So strict are these conditions that one would have thought that the elementary consideration that a line is infinitely thinner than a plane would make it a miracle for these conditions to be met. Real life optimality, or an approach to it, would seem to cry out—not merely for departure from *laissez faire*—but for never having been remotely near to *laissez faire*. Yet, you might almost say by accident, our world is not galaxies away from this thin line.

Lawrence J. Henderson, a distinguished physiologist and philosopher at Harvard in my day, saw far beyond Darwinian evolution in which selection led to individuals that possessed fitness for the environment.

He wrote a charming book on *The Fitness of the Environment*. For example, life as we know it depends critically on the peculiar properties that water happens to have (with, I believe, only ammonia as a possible substitute). How remarkable that one planet should have the temperature in that special range where water is liquid! This planet got selected for its suitability to sustain life.

I say how miraculous that Victorian England came anywhere near the homogeneity-of-the-first-degree production conditions that perfect competition truly needs. If all production functions were homogeneous of degree 2 or 3.14156 . . . —and why shouldn't they be?—George Stigler would be out of work; he would be a brewer or a Nobel Prizeman in physics.

And note this. We each belong to many circles: the U.S.A., the Elks, the Samuelson family, the office pool, etc. In almost none of these relationships is the organizing principle that of decentralized competitive pricing. Let Abraham Lincoln ponder over that one.

The Nature of Freedom

But enough of these technicalities. . . . Adam Smith, our patron saint, was critical of state interference of the pre-Nineteenth-Century type. And make no mistake about it: Smith was right. Most of the interventions into economic life by the State were then harmful both to prosperity and freedom. What Smith said needed to be said. In fact, much of what Smith said still needs to be said: Good intentions by government are not enough; acts do have consequences that had better be taken into account if good is to follow. Thus, the idea of a decent real wage is an attractive one. So is the idea of a low interest rate at which the needy can borrow. None the less the attempt *by law* to set a minimum real wage at a level much above the going market rates, or to set a maximum interest rate for small loans at what seem like reasonable levels, inevitably does much harm to precisely the people whom the legislation is intended to help. Domestic and foreign experience—today, yesterday, and tomorrow—bears out the Smithian truth. Note that this is not an argument against *moderate* wage and interest fiats, which may improve the perfection of competition and make businessmen and workers more efficient.

Smith himself was what we today would call a pragmatist. He realized that monopoly elements ran through *laissez faire*. When he said that Masters never gather together even for social merriment without plotting to raise prices against the public interest, he anticipated the famous Judge Gary dinners at which the big steel companies used to be taught what every oligopolist should know. Knowing the caliber of George III's civil service, Smith believed the government would simply do more harm than good if it tried to cope with the evil of monopoly. Pragmatically, Smith might, if he were alive today, favor the Sherman Act and stronger antitrust legislation, or even public utility regulation generally.

The Invisible Hand Again

One hundred percent individualists skip these pragmatic lapses into good sense and concentrate on the purple passage in Adam Smith where he discerns an Invisible Hand that leads each selfish individual to contribute to the best public good. Smith had a point; but he could not have earned a passing mark in a Ph.D. oral examination in explaining just what that point was. Until this century, his followers—such as Bastiat—thought that the doctrine of the Invisible Hand meant one of two things: (a) that it produced maximum feasible total satisfaction, somehow defined; or (b) that it showed that anything which results from the voluntary agreements of uncoerced individuals must make them better (or best) off in some important sense.

Both of these interpretations, which are still held by many modern libertarians, are wrong. They neglect Assumption 4 of my earlier axioms for nongovernment. This is not the place for a technical discussion of economic principles, so I shall be very brief and cryptic in showing this.

First, suppose some ethical observer—such as Jesus, Buddha, or for that matter, John Dewey or Aldous Huxley—were to examine whether the total of social utility (as that ethical observer scores the deservingness of the poor and rich, saintly and sinning individuals) was actually maximized by 1860 or 1962 *laissez faire*. He might decide that a tax placed upon yachts whose proceeds go to cheapen the price of insulin to the needy might increase the total of utility. Could Adam Smith prove him wrong? Could Bastiat? I think not.

Of course, they might say that there is no point in trying to compare different individuals' utilities because they are incommensurable and can no more be added together than can apples and oranges. But if recourse is made to this argument, then the doctrine that the Invisible Hand maximizes total utility of the universe has already been thrown out the window. If they admit that the Invisible Hand will truly maximize total social utility *provided the state intervenes so as to make the initial distribution of dollar votes ethically proper,* then they have abandoned the libertarian's position that individuals are not to be coerced, even by taxation.

In connection with the second interpretation that anything which results from voluntary agreements is in some sense, *ipso facto*, optimal, we can reply by pointing out that when I make a purchase from a monopolistic octopus, that is a voluntary act: I can always go without alka-seltzer or aluminum or nylon or whatever product you think is produced by a monopolist. Mere voluntarism, therefore, is not the root merit of the doctrine of the Invisible Hand; what is important about it is the system of checks and balances that comes under perfect competition, and its measure of validity is at the technocratic level of efficiency, not at the ethical level of freedom and individualism. That this is so can be seen from the fact that such socialists as Oscar Lange and A.P. Lerner have advocated channeling the Invisible Hand to the task of organizing a socialistic society efficiently.

The Impersonality of Market Relations

Just as there is a sociology of family life and of politics, there is a sociology of individualistic competition. It need not be a rich one. Ask not your neighbor's name; enquire only for his numerical schedules of supply and demand. Under perfect competition, no buyer need face a seller. Haggling in a Levantine bazaar is a sign of less-than-perfect competition. The telephone is the perfect go-between to link buyers and sellers through the medium of an auction market, such as the New York Stock Exchange or the Chicago Board of Trade for grain transactions. Two men may talk hourly all their working lives and never meet.

These economic contacts between atomistic individuals may seem a little chilly or, to use the language of wine-tasting, "dry." This impersonality has its good side. Negroes in the South learned long ago that their money was welcome in local department stores.

Money can be liberating. It corrodes the cake of custom. Money does talk. Sociologists know that replacing the rule of status by the rule of contract loses something in warmth; it also gets rid of some of the bad fire of olden times.

Impersonality of market relations has another advantage, as was brought home to many "liberals" in the McCarthy era of American political life. Suppose it were efficient for the government to be the one big employer. Then if, for good or bad, a person becomes in bad odor with government, he is dropped from employment, and is put on a blacklist. He really then has no place to go. The thought of such a dire fate must in the course of time discourage that freedom of expression of opinion which individualists most favor.

Many of the people who were unjustly dropped by the federal government in that era were able to land jobs in small-scale private industry. I say small-scale industry because large corporations are likely to be chary of hiring names that appear on anybody's blacklist. What about people who were justly dropped as security risks or as members of political organizations now deemed to be criminally subversive? Many of them also found jobs in the anonymity of industry.

Wheat Growers Anonymous

Many conservative people, who think that such men should not remain in sensitive government work or in public employ at all, will still feel that they should not be hounded into starvation. Few want for this country the equivalent of Czarist Russia's Siberia, or Stalin Russia's Siberia either. It is hard to tell on the Chicago Board of Trade the difference between the wheat produced by Republican or Democratic farmers, by teetotalers or drunkards, Theosophists or Logical Positivists. I must confess that this is a feature of a competitive system that I find attractive.

We have seen how a perfect model of competitive equilibrium might behave if conditions for it were perfect. The modern world is not identical with that model. As mentioned before, there never was a time, even in good Queen Victoria's long reign, when such conditions prevailed.

Whatever may have been true on Turner's frontier,[2]

the modern city is crowded. Individualism and anarchy will lead to friction. We now have to coordinate and cooperate. Where cooperation is not fully forthcoming, we must introduce upon ourselves coercion. When we introduce the traffic light, we have by cooperation and coercion, although the arch individualist may not like the new order, created for ourselves greater freedom.

The principle of unbridled freedom has been abandoned; it is now just a question of haggling about the terms. On the one hand, few will deny that it is a bad thing for one man, or a few men, to impose their wills on the vast majority of mankind, particularly when that will involves terrible cruelty and terrible inefficiency. Yet where does one draw the line? At a 51 percent majority vote? Or, should there be no actions taken that cannot command unanimous agreement—a position which such modern exponents of libertarian liberalism as Professor Milton Friedman are slowly evolving toward. Unanimous agreement? Well, virtually unanimous agreement, whatever that will come to mean.

The principle of unanimity is, of course, completely impractical. My old friend Milton Friedman is extremely persuasive, but not even he can keep his own students in unanimous agreement all the time. Aside from its practical inapplicability, the principle of unanimity is theoretically faulty. It leads to contradictory and intransitive decisions. By itself, it argues that just as society should not move from *laissez faire* to planning because there will always be at least one objector—Friedman if necessary—so society should never move from planning to freedom because there will always be at least one objector. Like standing friction, it sticks you where you are. It favors the *status quo*. And the *status quo* is certainly not to the liking of arch individualists. When you have painted yourself into a corner, what can you do? You can redefine the situation, and I predicted some years ago that there would come to be defined a privileged *status quo*, a set of natural rights involving individual

pecuniary costs and social costs. They call for intervention: zoning, fiats, planning, regulation, taxing, and so forth.

But too much diluteness of the gas also calls for social interfering with *laissez faire* individualism. Thus, the frontier has always involved sparse populations in need of "social overhead capital." In terms of technical economics jargon this has the following meaning: when scale is so small as to lead to unexhausted increasing returns, free pricing cannot be optimal and there is a *prima facie* case for cooperative intervention.

[2]Density of population produces what economists recognize as external economies and diseconomies. These "neighborhood effects" are often dramatized by smoke and other nuisances that involve a discrepancy between private

freedoms, which alone requires unanimity before it can be departed from.

At this point the logical game is up. The case for "complete freedom" has been begged, not deduced. So long as full disclosure is made, it is no crime to assume your ethical case. But will your product sell? Can you persuade others to accept your axiom when it is in conflict with certain other desirable axioms?

Not by Reasoning Alone

The notion is repellant that a man should be able to tyrannize over others. Shall he be permitted to indoctrinate his children into any way of life whatsoever? Shall he be able to tyrannize over himself? Here, or elsewhere, the prudent-man doctrine of the good trustee must be invoked, and in the last analysis his peers must judge—*i.e.*, a committee of prudent peers. And may they be peers tolerant as well as wise!

Complete freedom is not definable once two wills exist in the same interdependent universe. We can sometimes find two situations in which choice A is more free than choice B in apparently every respect and at least as good as B in every other relevant sense. In such singular cases I will certainly throw in my lot with the exponents of individualism. But few situations are really of this simple type; and these few are hardly worth talking about, because they will already have been disposed of so easily.

In most actual situations we come to a point at which choices between goals must be made: do you want this kind of freedom and this kind of hunger, or that kind of freedom and that kind of hunger? I use these terms in a quasi-algebraic sense, but actually what is called "freedom" is really a vector of almost infinite components rather than a one-dimensional thing that can be given a simple ordering.

Where more than one person is concerned the problem is thornier still. My privacy is your loneliness, my freedom to have privacy is your lack of freedom to have company. Your freedom to "discriminate" is the denial of my freedom to "participate." There is no possibility of unanimity to resolve such conflicts.

The notion, so nicely expounded in a book I earnestly recommend to you, Milton Friedman, *Capitalism and Freedom* (Chicago, 1962), that it is better for one who deplores racial discrimination to try to persuade people against it than to do nothing at all—but, failing to persuade, it is better to use no

democratic coercion in these matters—such a notion as a *general* precept is arbitrary and gratuitous. Its arbitrariness is perhaps concealed when it is put abstractly in the following form: If free men follow Practice X that you and some others regard as bad, it is wrong in principle to coerce them out of that Practice X; in principle, all you ought to do is to try to persuade them out of their ways by "free discussion." One counter-example suffices to invalidate a general principle. An exception does not prove the rule, it disproves it. As a counter-example I suggest we substitute for "Practice X" the "killing by gas of 5 million suitably-specified humans." Who will agree with the precept in this case?

Only two types would possible agree to it: (1) those so naïve as to think that persuasion can keep Hitlers from cremating millions; or (2) those who think the *status quo*, achievable by what can be persuaded, is a pretty comfortable one after all, even if not perfect. When we are very young we fall into the first category; when old and prosperous, into the second; perhaps there is a golden age in between. The notion that any form of coercion whatever is in itself so evil a thing as to outweigh all other evils is to set up freedom as a monstrous shibboleth. In the first place, absolute or even maximum freedom cannot even be defined unambiguously except in certain special models. Hence one is being burned at the stake for a cause that is only a slogan or name. In the second place, as I have shown, coercion can be defined only in terms of an infinite variety of arbitrary alternative *status quo*.

The precept "persuade-if-you-can-but-in-no-case-coerce" can be sold only to those who do not understand what it is they are buying. This doctrine sound a little like the "Resist-Not-Evil" precepts of Jesus or Gandhi. But there is absolutely no true similarity between the two doctrines, and one should not gain in palatability by being confused with the other.

Marketplace Coercion, or The Hegelian Freedom of Necessity

Libertarians fail to realize that the price system is, and ought to be, a method of coercion. Nature is not so bountiful as to give each of us all the goods he desires. We have to be coerced out of such a situation, by the nature of things. That is why we have policemen and courts. That is why we charge prices, which are high enough relative to limited money to limit consumption. The very term "rationing by the purse" illustrates the point. Economists defend such forms of rationing, but they have to do so primarily in terms of its efficiency and its fairness. Where it is not efficient—as in the case of monopoly, externality, and avoidable uncertainty—it comes under attack. Where it is deemed unfair by ethical observers, its evil is weighed pragmatically against its advantages and modifications of its structure are introduced.

Classical economists, like Malthus, always understood this coercion. They recognized that fate dealt a hand of cards to the worker's child that was a cruel one, and a favorable one to the "well-born." John Stuart Mill in a later decade realized that mankind, not Fate with a capital F, was involved. Private property is a concept created by and enforced by public law. Its attributes change in time and are man-made, not Mother-Nature-made.

Nor is the coercion a minor one. Future generations are condemned to starvation if certain supply-and-demand patterns rule in today's market. Under the freedom that is called *laissez faire,* some worthy men are exalted; and so are some unworthy ones. Some unworthy men are cast down; and so are some worthy ones. The Good Man gives the system its due, but reckons in his balance its liabilities that are overdue.

Anatole France said epigrammatically all that needs to be said about the coercion implicit in the libertarian economics of *laissez faire.* "How majestic is the equality of the Law, which permits both rich and poor alike, to sleep under the bridges at night." I believe no satisfactory answer has yet been given to this. It is certainly not enough to say, "We made our own beds and let us each lie in them."[3] For once Democracy

rears its pretty head, the voter will think: "There, but for the Grace of God and the Dow-Jones averages, go I." And he will act.

The whole matter of proper government policy involves issues of ethics, coercion, administration, incidence, and incentives that cannot begin to be resolved by semantic analysis of such terms as "freedom," "coercion," or "individualism."

A Final Law

At the end I must lay down one basic proposition.

There are no rules concerning the proper role of government that can be established by a priori reasoning.

This may seem odd to you: for to state the rule that there are no rules may sound like a self-contradiction, reminiscent of the breakfast cereal box that contains an exact picture of itself . . . of itself . . . of itself. . . . However, no Bertrand Russell theory of types is involved here. For, my proposition—call it Samuelson's Law if you like—does not claim to be established by Reason, but merely to be a uniformity of experience. Whose experience? My experience, and that of every (I mean, almost every) man of experience.

If I am wrong it will be easy to prove me wrong: namely, by stating one valid nontrivial proposition about the proper role of government derived by cogent *a priori* reasoning alone. After I have digested, it, I shall have no trouble in eating my own words.

---

[3]If one disagrees with Malthus and France and thinks that we all had equal opportunities and *have* made the beds we are to lie in, our judgment of *laissez faire* improves—as it should. But note it is because of its fine welfare results, and *not because the kind of freedom embodied in it is the end-all of ethics.*

9

Proposition 13 and its Aftermath

ANITA A. SUMMERS

Anita Summers is a faculty member at the Wharton School of the University of Pennsylvania. This article appeared in the Business Review *of the Federal Reserve Bank of Philadelphia in 1979.*

In the first phase of the great tax reform flurry that began sweeping across the country last year, the banner headlines went to California's Proposition 13. Now they're going to a state-initiated constitutional amendment to limit the Federal budget; and many states are on the lookout for ways to respond to tax protests in their own capitals. Clearly, the accelerated pressure to reform reflects a general discontent.

While proposals for tax capping at the Federal level introduce a complex of issues connected with the use of Federal fiscal policy for economic stabilization, issues are far from being resolved even at the state and local level. Proposition 13 and several of its progeny reflect a confusion of the objectives of budget capping with those of fiscal reform. Restraining the size of government (and its associated tax burden), reducing government inefficiency, and reforming state and local taxes are distinct objectives. Each of them has an agenda that is appropriate to it alone and not to the others. But Proposition 13 and its variants have failed to keep them separate.

In practice, the size of state and local budgets will not be controlled best by any one constitutional or legislative action, and the fairness of the property tax will not be improved simply by lowering it. Responsible reformers who share the concerns of the taxpayers will want to consider many measures.

What Underlies The Current Discontent

Why have the past few years seen so much concern with reform of state and local government fiscal affairs? In part because growth rates of real income have been declining while the tax burden has been increasing. This combination of trends has focused attention on the total tax burden, on efficiency in government, and on the incidence of the major taxes. More particularly, it has led to protests against having government spend as large a portion of total income as it does and against the very visible property tax.

Income, Taxes, and Big Government

Recent assaults on the size of government and the level of taxation undoubtedly reflect the squeeze on

43

family budgets. Real personal disposable income increased about 50 percent from 1957 to 1967 but only about 32 percent from 1967 to 1977. People have perceived and reacted to this shift in trends but without fully appreciating that it arises from different factors. The slower growth of real income in recent years reflects a combination of escalating inflation, a substantial number of recession years, and sluggish growth in productivity.

Against this background of slow growth in real income, the more rapid real tax growth—51 percent from 1957 to 1967 and 38 percent from 1967 to 1977—stands out sharply. This tax growth reflects several factors. First, the United States has become increasingly concerned about social justice since World War II. Legislation and major court decisions, for example, reflect the increased emphasis on income redistribution as a policy criterion in the public sector. And this emphasis has translated into growth in Social Security, unemployment compensation, welfare, medical care, education, and many other income transfers and public services—or, in other words, into growth in government expenditures, which are supported from tax revenues. Second, those who want certain government expenditures can lobby more easily than those who want lower taxes: those who want ramps for the handicapped on street corners, for example, can coalesce to lobby for the budget allocation, but those who don't want to pay the, say, 10 cents extra in taxes needed to finance these accommodations, are too diffused to resist them effectively. Third, government decision-making, which in principle is based on cost-benefit calculations, often underestimates the cost of new programs. And fourth, rewards in the public sector tend to favor those who manage larger entities over those who produce more services with less resource input.

For all these reasons, government expenditures, and the taxes associated with them, have expanded. As the growth in real income has declined, the protest against this expansion has become more urgent.

Distaste for the Property Tax

A good deal of protest lights on the very visible property tax. In a period of rapidly rising property values, the property tax is a conspicuous target. The rising property value is not very visible (unless the property is sold), but the rise in the property tax bill has to be faced every year. Moreover, though the property tax has diminished from about 80 percent of all state and local taxes at the turn of the century to about 45 percent in the 1960s and about 35 percent now, it remains a major tax in the United States. Out of every $1 thousand of personal income, $123 goes to state and local taxes, $45 of which is paid in property taxes. The property tax is a perennial target. Public finance texts criticize it, the urban poor rail against it, Center City businessmen condemn it, and those who have retired on fixed incomes abhor it. Why so much criticism?

In a nonagricultural economy such as ours, *the property tax does not closely reflect the value of public services received by the property owner* (there is no evident relation of the value of fire protection services to the value of property, for example); and *the value of property is not a very good indicator of the owner's ability to pay*. A match-up of tax payments with value of services and ability to pay is a standard criterion for a good tax. So the property tax might appropriately be faulted on these grounds.

The property tax has been attacked also for its *regressivity*—its tendency to take a smaller percentage of income from those whose incomes are higher. And it can be regressive, but not for the reasons traditionally cited.

Until recently, people argued that since an increase in the property tax increases the cost of housing, and since lower income persons spend a larger portion of their income on housing, the burden of the property tax is heavier on them. In recent years, however, economists have become more sophisticated at tracking through the real incidence of taxes. They now recognize more fully that taxes may not fall only on homeowners who write checks to the tax collector and that, in the case of the property tax, part of the burden will be borne by all those who own interest-earning capital. Since the rich own more such capital than the poor, the tax incidence has some progressive portion. And, further, when economists look at the ratio of the value of housing to lifetime income, rather than to a single year's income, they find that this ratio is about the same for all income groups. While there is more evidence still to be gathered on the incidence of the property tax, the notion that the property tax is regressive seems highly questionable—provided, of course, that it's administered properly.

The property tax, however, generally is *not* administered properly. In most places, *assessments are not levied uniformly and are not kept up to date*. Assessment lag has the effect of producing higher assessment ratios in areas where market values have declined (inner city sections, for example) and lower assessment ratios in areas where market values have risen (affluent residential sections). So, while the property tax doesn't have to be regressive, in certain places it turns out to be so. The protests of the poor may not be supported in the public finance text, but they are supported in the urban assessor's records.

The plight of the *fixed-income owner* also has received a good deal of attention. The classic case is that of the person who retires to live on a fixed income in a house whose value has risen substantially since the time of purchase. The capital appreciation can't be realized unless the house is sold, but the property taxes rise to reflect that appreciation. The individual's current income doesn't allow for living in the house, but the value of the asset does. Should such a person have to sell his house? The view of fixed-income homeowners, and of others whose income is temporarily depressed, is really one of vocal and strong opposition to rising tax bills in relation to unrealized gains in housing value. But the opposition lights on the property tax as a whole rather than on any of its remediable defects.

The property tax, then, has been the most conspicuous target of anger in the tax protest because of its visibility and because of the accessibility to the taxpayers of those who levy it. Further, it doesn't bear a close relation to services received, it is administered in a way which converts it into a regressive tax, and it falls harshly on the fixed-income homeowner.

Mixed in with these concerns about the incidence of this major local tax are political concerns about the size and efficiency of government and more generalized concerns about the burden of taxation at a time when growth rates of real income are declining. The confluence of these factors produced Proposition 13 and its progeny—state and local budget reform initiatives throughout the country.

Proposition 13 and Its Progeny

'Proposition 13' has become almost a generic term for any legislative proposal designed to hold down expenditures, restrain revenues, or reduce the property tax. Actually, of course, Proposition 13 is a tax-capping amendment to the California constitution which was passed overwhelmingly by almost 65 per-

cent of the voters. Variants of this proposal appeared on ballots in a number of states last November, and though none has reached the voting stage in Pennsylvania, several are being considered here. All in all, very few states have accepted Proposition 13's variety of assault on the property tax, but some have opted for considerably broader types of restraint.

California

Although the rhetoric of the Proposition 13 campaign reflected a desire to respond to all the underlying issues—a government become too big and operating too inefficiently, a total tax burden grown too heavy, and an allocation of the tax burden become too inequitable—the weight of the amendment itself fell on the much-maligned property tax.

The concern about the size of government and its associated tax burden was reflected in the restraints imposed on state and local tax increases. As a result of the amendment, state increases are permitted only on a two-thirds vote of the state legislature, and enactments of new taxes by local governments require a two-thirds vote of the electorate. The absence of any automatic growth allowance makes it virtually certain that some enactments will occur. But, most important, it imposes no criteria for selecting which services will be curtailed. And it suggests no incentives to achieve restraint by operating with greater efficiency. The concern that government has gotten too big does not mean that every service is regarded as too big. Yet Proposition 13 does nothing to identify which services should be axed. Indeed, the only attempt to be specific is the targeting of, not an expenditure item, but a tax: the legislature is prohibited from enacting any new property taxes (new ad valorem or sales taxes, for example).

The property tax is hit forcefully in the California amendment, reflecting, in addition to the notion that taxes are too high, the notion that property taxes allocate the burden inequitably: Proposition 13 places a ceiling on property taxes at 1 percent of market value as of March 1, 1975, with a few exceptions; it limits increases in assessed valuation to 2 percent per year, unless two-thirds of the voters subsequently decide otherwise; and it prohibits full reassessment except when property is sold. Every which way, the property tax as a source of revenue is checked.

The problems with legislating such a severe attack on one form of taxation are many, and they are only beginning to unfold. For one thing, rolling the tax base back three years means that current taxes do not reflect the relative shifts in market values that have occurred since the base date. If, for example, the demand for housing in one area has become much greater than the demand in another, the increase in the market value in the high-demand area will escape capture arbitrarily. Placing a fixed ceiling on the percentage annual increase in assessed valuation from a prior base period implies a continuation of this distortion into the indefinite future. Also, allowing full reassessment only at time of sale sets up a direct financial inducement to stay put, though no one suggested during the campaign that limiting residential mobility was included in the amendment's intent or that it ought to be a policy objective at any level of government. And it means that residential property owners will pay a higher percentage of the property tax than businesses, since businesses move less often—again, not part of the original intent of the amendment. Finally, and ironically, the same taxpayers whose vote for Proposition 13 was a vote against Big Government now have demanded rent controls (already set up in Los Angeles and Beverly Hills) because their rents have continued to rise even with the enactment of Proposition 13!

What has happened in California is that the full force of taxpayer discontent has fallen on the property tax. Proposition 13's broad restraints on raising taxes do attack the issue of the total burden. But its other provisions fail to address the property tax incidence issues that people are really concerned with.

Other States

A few states, notably Nevada and Idaho, adopted proposals very similar to Proposition 13; and Alabama, Missouri, and Massachusetts placed strong restraints on the property tax. These states are likely to develop the same set of problems that California has experienced since last July. Fortunately, though, most other states that voted on budget capping did not mix it up with property tax reform. They registered their distaste for large governments and high taxes, but they also recognized the need for some growth factor and did not single out one tax as a target. Arizona passed an amendment to limit state expenditures to 7 percent of personal income; Hawaii and Texas tied growth in state expenditures to economic growth in the state; and Prince George's County in Maryland, along with the states of Michigan, North Dakota, South Dakota, and Illinois all moved in a similar direction. None of the legislative initiatives, however, took on the issues of government productivity and selection criteria for curtailing expenditures.

Pennsylvania

Pennsylvania differs from California in many ways, so that the buildup of pressures about the size of the total tax burden and the incidence of the property tax has not been as intense. The market value of housing has not risen as much as in California; the property tax is not relied on as heavily ($62.71 per $1 thousand of personal income in California; in contrast with $29.95 in Pennsylvania); for some time, local governments have been able to use nonproperty taxes in Pennsylvania; and there is a circuit breaker law here which refunds property tax payments to those with low incomes and to the elderly. In addition, the Pennsylvania state government is not sitting on a budgetary surplus, and its constitution, unlike California's, does not permit the use of the initiative process for putting questions on the ballot.

Many proposals have been made in this state that address one or another of the underlying concerns. Some try to provide more tax relief to the elderly and those with low incomes. Some try to limit property tax revenue á la Proposition 13. And some try to limit the total amount of state and local spending (which would require a constitutional amendment).

Thus the pressure to pass capping legislation or property tax reform is weaker in Pennsylvania than in many other places because the property tax is relatively low, other more elastic local taxes are used more extensively, and the procedures involved in placing ceilings on revenues and expenditures are more intricate. When and if Pennsylvanians cap or reform taxes, or do both, they should be able to benefit from the experience of other states and be able to choose legislation which attacks the problems surrounding the property tax and the size of state and local budgets more satisfactorily than does Proposition 13.

Sensible Approaches to Capping and Reform

To control the size of government, to improve government efficiency, and to reform the property tax are clearly expressed concerns of the American taxpayer. But no one agenda will meet all three of these. Responsible action involves considering several policies to meet the several concerns.

Controlling the Size of State and Local Government Budgets.

The most rational approach to budget control would involve careful cost-benefit analyses of all expenditure lines to develop appropriate selection criteria for the services to be curtailed most severely or eliminated entirely. In recent years, cost-benefit analyses have become much more common at the Federal level, but they still are relatively rare at the state and local level. Even where they are done, the political process does much to alter what the calculations suggest. The result is that all across the country we are feeling a dissatisfaction with the size of the total burden and, therefore, a desire to limit that total burden.

If, indeed, the total is what is to be limited, then the expenditure side of the budget is the one to focus on. Overspending is the objectionable activity; revenue collection only provides the means to carry out spending plans. By concentrating on the expenditure side, the major causes of increased spending can be eliminated and the real choices can be emphasized. And those choices have to do mainly with services provided by government. At the state and local levels, taxes go almost entirely for public services. Limiting expenditures means limiting those services, and this trade-off should be spelled out explicitly in tax limitation proposals.

Clearly, if a decision is made to cap expenditures, the use of *some sort of broad measure of economic activity as the anchor seems appropriate* in calculating the level of the cap. Growth in personal income in a state and growth in gross state product have been suggested as measures. (In some states, limiting growth in expenditures to inflationary growth has been proposed. This, of course, would not allow any growth in the economic base of the state to be translated into growth in public services.) In addition to tying expenditure growth to a broad measure, *consideration should be given to using an average over several years of the measure.* Few citizens would want state and local expenditures to fluctuate as sharply, as rapidly, and in the same direction as annual fluctuations in economic activity.

But, beyond adopting an overall ceiling, *rational control of expenditures involves improving productivity in the public sector.* Everyone is for it, but it doesn't happen. And it is unlikely to happen without merit rewards, in the form of merit salary increments, for clear evidence of improved output from the same input. Awareness that a Streets Commissioner has received a merit increase because his department has taken care of more potholes this year with the same number of men and trucks as last year, for example, is likely to do much more for public-sector productivity than exhortation would. Use of the many analytical tools available to improve service delivery probably would be stimulated by the likelihood of tangible rewards. As it stands now, the tools are available but not the rewards for using them.

The desire to limit the size of state and local budgets has been expressed clearly in this country over the last few years. It is to be hoped that this expressed voter preference will not be confused with concern for property tax reform, but that it will be met by a combination of responsible measures—relating expenditure growth to a several-year average of a broad measure of economic growth for the region and providing real incentives to improve productivity in the public sector.

Reforming the Property Tax

Inner city residents, business, and the elderly all complain about overly high property taxes. But the property tax would be made much more palatable if a number of new procedures were adopted. *Maintaining uniform assessments through frequent and regular revaluation of property* would eliminate the relatively high assessment ratios borne by those who live in areas where property values are growing relatively smaller and would meet much of the concern with the tax on the part of the urban poor. *Reducing the extensive amount of property exempted from the property tax,* much of which clearly is not being used for the public interest, would reduce the percentage of the tax that business has to pay. The concerns of the elderly, those on fixed incomes, and those who are suffering from temporary income squeezes might be met best by *allowing deferral of tax liabilities* until a later date—date of sale for the elderly and for those on fixed incomes, a set date in the future for other homeowners. Circuit breaker laws give relief, but they give relief to the rich as well as the poor, which is costly in terms of tax revenues.

All of these changes could help relieve concerns about the inequities of the property tax and redeem its much-maligned reputation. Simply rolling back the assessed valuations, California style, does not alter these inequities, which arise from defects in the procedures used to administer the property tax. Altering the procedures is the right medicine for the illness.

Summary

The taxpayer malaise that has reached to all levels of American government in the last few years reflects several overlapping concerns. People have a generalized dissatisfaction with the size of government, with its associated tax bruden, and with its waste and inefficiency; and they are concentrating their dissatisfaction in a frontal attack on the highly visible property tax. But meeting these several concerns will require a menu of policy approaches. Controlling the over all magnitude of state and local budgets calls for broad-based ceilings and productivity incentives. Re-shaping the distributional effects of the property tax calls for making assessments uniform, for regularizing revaluations, and for reviewing exemptions and deferrals of tax liabilities.

If, in this state, we confuse these issues, we may put a cap on our state and local budgets, but the way those budget dollars are raised and spent will not reflect attainable levels of efficiency and equity for fiscal management. In brief, Proposition 13 should not be Pennsylvania's role model. H.L. Mencken once said that "for every human problem there is a solution which is simple, neat, and wrong." This dictum applies to fiscal reforms as well as to other human affairs!

PART TWO

Unemployment, National Output, and Fiscal Policy

Unemployment is one of the most frightening words in the English language, and for good reason. It results in terrible costs to the unemployed worker and his or her family, as well as substantial costs to society in the form of output forgone. In 1946, the Congress passed the Employment Act, which said that the government had the responsibility "to promote maximum employment, production, and purchasing power." The opening selection, by the Council of Economic Advisers, describes the events leading up to the passage of the Act, as well as the measures taken by the government to promote full employment during the 1950s and early 1960s. The next selection, taken from a 1932 issue of *Fortune* magazine, describes what the Great Depression was like to those in the midst of it; later accounts, no matter how dramatically written, fail to give so vivid a feel for the plight of the unemployed, and of the nation as a whole.

In the decades since the Depression, economists have developed reasonably sophisticated theories of how the government's power to spend and to tax can be used to stabilize the economy at close to its full employment level. Joseph Pechman, in the following article, describes the impact of government spending and taxation, and discusses the use of the full-employment budget as a guide to fiscal policy. He concludes that: "When private demand is low and the economy is operating below capacity, taxes are too high relative to expenditures. In these circumstances, the ratio should be reduced—by cutting taxes, by raising expenditures, or by doing both. Conversely, when demand is too high, taxes should be raised or expenditures reduced, or both."

James Tobin, in the next selection, tries to clarify the true nature of the federal debt, and points out that: "The federal government will not succeed in cutting its deficit by steps that depress the economy, perpetuate excess capacity, and deter business firms from using outside funds."

Economic models are used by decision-makers in both the public and private sectors of the economy to forecast short-term changes in gross national product. In the next selection in this part, Paul A. Samuelson discusses how well economists can do as forecasters, and concludes that, although they may not be as good as one would like, they "are better than anything else in heaven and earth at forecasting aggregate business trends—better than gypsy tea-leaf readers, Wall Street soothsayers and chartist technicians, hunch-playing heads of mail order chains, or all-powerful heads of state. This is a statement based on empirical experience." It is also a very important reason for studying economics.

Finally, Walter Salant describes the explosion of economic information in the past fifty years. As he points out, "The enormous increase in the sheer quantity of economic information has been accompanied by great improvements in the reliability of estimates and in the speed with which they have become available."

10

The Employment Act of 1946: Background and Impact

COUNCIL OF
ECONOMIC ADVISERS

The following article comes from the 1966 Annual Report of the Council of Economic Advisers. It marked twenty years of experience with the Employment Act.

The Act and Its Background

The legislation of 1946 set forth the following declaration of policy:

> The Congress declares that it is the continuing policy and responsibility of the Federal Government to use all practicable means consistent with its needs and obligations and other essential considerations of national policy, with the assistance and cooperation of industry, agriculture, labor, and State and local governments, to coordinate and utilize all its plans, functions, and resources for the purpose of creating and maintaining, in a manner calculated to foster and promote free competitive enterprise and the general welfare, conditions under which there will be afforded useful employment opportunities, including self-employment, for those able, willing and seeking to work, and to promote maximum employment, production, and purchasing power.

In making this declaration, the Congress recognized that the billions of independent spending and saving decisions of a free economy could well result in levels of total demand either short of full employment or in excess of productive capacity. Furthermore, it took the view that Government policies could play a constructive role in improving the stability and balance of the economy.

The Act was a product of the experiences of the Great Depression and World War II. The Depression shook but did not destroy the faith in an automatic tendency of the economy to find its proper level of operation. In the early 1930s, public works and other antidepression programs were justified as temporary "pump priming," to help the private economy get back on its track after an unusual and catastrophic derailment. And the departure from orthodox fiscal principles was made with regret and without complete consistency. The Government expenditures explicitly designed to combat depression necessarily increased budget deficits; but this implication was veiled by financing these outlays through an "extraordinary" budget. Meanwhile, taxes were raised, and salaries and housekeeping expenditures cut in the regular budget, thereby reducing the overall stimulation of Government measures.

The relapse of the economy in 1937 into a sharp decline from a level still far below full employment

51

gave rise to conflicting interpretations. To some, it proved that pump priming and Government deficits had undermined the confidence of the business community and thereby only worsened the situation. Others, however, concluded that it pointed to the need for larger and more sustained fiscal and monetary actions to revive the economy. In drawing this conclusion, economists were buttressed by the writings of J. M. Keynes, who offered a theoretical explanation of the disastrous depression. The Keynesian conclusions received additional support during World War II because they offered a satisfactory explanation of why the high deficit-financed defense expenditures of that period not only wiped out unemployment but went beyond to create inflationary pressures.

Memories of the disastrous 1930s were very much in the public mind as World War II was drawing to an end. Many active proponents of "full employment" legislation in 1945 and 1946 feared a relapse into depressed levels of economic activity like those of the 1930s, once military spending ended. They looked toward Federal public works spending as a peacetime replacement—at least, in part—for the wartime defense outlays.

The opponents of "full employment" legislation had several reservations and objections. Some feared that it would mean a statutory blessing for perpetual budgetary deficits, soaring public expenditures, and massive redistribution of income from upper to lower income groups. There were doubts that Government actions could and would on balance raise employment; and there were fears that these actions would lead to regimentation and would jeopardize the free enterprise system. The proponents of legislation, on the other hand, argued that the Act would merely provide a setting essential to the proper functioning of the free enterprise system because a depressed economy heightened social tensions, discouraged innovation and initiative, dulled competition, and undermined confidence.

The legislation which finally emerged from this discussion wisely abstained from diagnosing depression as the disease and public works as the cure, but instead concentrated on establishing the principle of continuing Government responsibility to review and appraise economic developments, diagnose problems, and prescribe appropriate remedies. And it placed major responsibility squarely upon the President, who was asked to discuss his execution of that responsibility in an Economic Report to be transmitted to the Congress at the start of each year.

The Act also established two agencies—the Council of Economic Advisers in the Executive Branch and the Joint Committee on the Economic Report (later named the Joint Economic Committee) of the Congress—with interrelated but separate responsibilities. These institutions have each filled a vital and previously missing role in their respective branches of Government—they have provided a coordinated overview of the economic impact of the entire spectrum of Government tax, expenditure, monetary, and other acitvities. To maintain the emphasis on advice and coordination, the Joint Economic Committee was not given any substantive legislative responsibility nor the Council any policy-executing duties. Both agencies have participated actively in the counsels of Government; both have conscientiously striven for a thoroughly professional economic competence and approach in their respective reports and recommendations; and both have contributed to the public understanding of economic issues.

Today's economic policies reflect the continuing impact of the Employment Act in all the years since its inception. And our accumulating experience is certain to be reflected in the policies of the future. This paper reviews the development of policy during the 1950s and early 1960s and outlines the present relationship between economic analysis and economic policy.

Avoiding Depressions and Booms

The Congress proved wise in its decisions to state goals broadly and to concentrate on continuing review, analysis, and proposals, since the specific problems that actually arose were somewhat different from those which many supporters of the Employment Act had anticipated.

Although an important part of the impetus for the Employment Act derived from the prolonged depression of the 1930s and the resulting fear of stagnation in the American economy, this problem did not prove to be the primary challenge to economic policymaking under the Act. Indeed, immediately after World War II, excess-demand inflation proved to be the key problem. Subsequently, policy was focused on the age-old problem of limiting the size and duration of cyclical swings. Only much later and in a much different and milder form did stagnation arise as a live issue.

Thus, much of our experience under the Act

consisted of policy actions to combat recession—lest it turn into depression—and to contain excess demand pressure—lest it generate inflationary boom.

Combating Recessions

A series of relatively short and mild recessions required Government attention in the postwar period. The problem of cyclical declines was not unexpected by the framers of the Employment Act, nor was it new to the American economy. In the period between 1854 (the beginning of the business cycle annals of the National Bureau of Economic Research) and World War II, we had experienced twenty-one periods of recession or depression. Our postwar record is blemished by four additional periods of contracting economic activity—1948–49, 1953–54, 1957–58, and 1960–61.

Compared with the previous cyclical record, the postwar recessions have been far shorter, considerably milder, and substantially less frequent. Postwar recessions ranged in duration from eight to thirteen months; the average duration of previous declines had been twenty-one months, and only three had been shorter than thirteen months in length. Measured by the decline in industrial production from peak to trough, postwar recessions ranged in magnitude from 8 percent to 14 percent. By comparison, in the interwar period, the declines ranged from 6 to 52 percent; three of the five contractions exceeded 30 percent and only one was less than the 14 percent maximum of the postwar period. During the past twenty years, the economy has spent a total of forty-two months, or 18 percent of the time, in periods of recessions, far less than the 43 percent applicable to the 1854–1939 era.

This improvement in the postwar record of the economy was aided by the deliberate discretionary steps taken by the Government to modify the impact of business downturns and thereby to prevent cumulating declines into depression. The speed and force of these actions—in both the fiscal and monetary areas—varied among the recessions. Thus, in 1949 little new fiscal action was taken, partly because inflation was viewed as a key problem even during the decline, and partly because Government measures taken the previous year were expected to have a considerable impact on the economy: the tax reductions of 1948 were supplying large refunds, and large expenditure increases were forthcoming under the recently enacted Marshall Plan. The Federal Reserve did act to reduce reserve requirements in a series of steps during the spring and summer of 1949, reversing a two-year rise in short-term interest rates.

In 1953–54, as military outlays declined and aggregate activity retreated, the principal expansionary influence came from previously scheduled reductions of corporate and personal income taxes. But some new action was taken to reduce excise taxes and to speed up expenditures. All three major instruments of monetary policy—reserve requirements, the discount rate, and open market operations—were used to encourage the expansion of credit-financed expenditures. Meanwhile, the Administration planned larger fiscal steps that might be taken if the recession seemed likely to be prolonged. Significantly, in 1954, the bipartisan character of expansionary fiscal policies was established for the first time, as the Republican Administration of President Eisenhower adopted measures that had previously been linked to the New Deal and Keynesian economics.

In 1958, the recession was considerably deeper than its two postwar predecessors and both the Eisenhower Administration and the Congress were more vigorous in taking action. An important concern of earlier years—that business confidence might be disturbed by Government recognition of a recession—seemed insignificant since the sharp recession was obvious to all.

Several important measures were taken. The benefit period for unemployment compensation was temporarily extended. Grants to States under the Federal highway program were enlarged and accelerated, and other programs in the budget also were expanded or rescheduled to provide an earlier stimulative effect. The Government also acted to spur housing activity by financial operations in the mortgage market and by altering terms on Government-guaranteed home mortgages. The important measures were launched near, or after, the trough of the recession. Thus, in retrospect, policy helped most to strengthen the early recovery rather than to contain or shorten the recession. Nevertheless, in view of the general recognition that the Government would be running a substantial deficit in any case, these additions to Federal outlays were a significant reflection of changed attitudes toward the role of fiscal policy.

Monetary policy also played a constructive role in the 1957–58 recession, once the monetary authorities moved to ease credit three months after the peak in economic activity. Thereafter, Federal Reserve actions contributed to a revival in housing and other investment by promoting a sharp reduction in interest rates, both short- and long-term.

The first fiscal measures to deal with the 1960–61 recession were taken with the inauguration of President Kennedy in January 1961, when the recession had just about run its course. Nevertheless, improvements in the social insurance system, rescheduling of Federal expenditures, and expanded programs (including defense and space) were an important stimulus to the recovery during 1961. In contrast to the delay in taking fiscal measures, the Federal Reserve reversed a tight money policy early in 1960, prior to the downturn.

Not all discretionary changes in taxes or expenditures have contributed to economic stability. Indeed, some steps taken to pursue national security or social goals had destabilizing economic impacts, which were not always appropriately offset. Previously scheduled payroll tax increases took effect in 1954, 1959, and 1962, and drained off purchasing power in recession or in initial recovery. In 1953, defense outlays declined and triggered a recession before offsetting expansionary policies were adopted.

On the whole, discretionary fiscal and monetary actions made a distinct positive contribution in limiting declines. Even more important in this respect was the strengthened inherent stability of the postwar economy.

In large measure, this can be traced simply to the greater size of the Government relative to the total economy: that is, the increased importance of Government expenditures—both purchases of goods and services and transfer payments. Government outlays do not participate in the downward spiral of recession; because of its borrowing capacity, the Federal Government—unlike businesses and households—can maintain its spending in the face of declining income receipts. Although State and local governments do not have equal immunity from the need to tighten their belts, they have been able to maintain their growing spending programs relatively unaffected during the mild postwar recessions. Social insurance and national defense have added especially to the postwar totals of Federal outlays. State and local outlays have been rising rapidly in an effort to catch up with neglected needs and to keep up with the desires of a wealthier society for improved public services.

The contribution to the stability of the economy resulting from a high level of Government expenditures, insulated from revenue declines, has been augmented by the cushions to private purchasing power provided by the built-in fiscal stabilizers.

When private incomes and employment decline, purchasing power is automatically supported by both a decline of Federal revenues and an increase in unemployment compensation payments. Transmission of the virus of deflation is thus impeded. During postwar recessions, the progressive Federal personal income tax has not had to demonstrate its full stabilizing effectiveness because of the mildness of dips in personal earnings. There have, however, been sharp declines in corporate incomes; the Federal Treasury has shared about half of the drop in profits, thereby helping to bolster dividends and to cushion cash flow, and hence investment outlays.

A number of improvements in our financial structure were developed in the 1930s to assure that financial collapse and declines in economic activity would not generate a vicious downward spiral as they did after 1929. These important financial mechanisms include Federal insurance of private deposits; the separation of commercial and investment banking functions; the Federal Reserve's increased ability to provide banks with reserves in time of crisis; and the joint work of the Federal Reserve and the Securities and Exchange Commission to reduce harmful speculation in the stock market. The very existence of these structural changes has contributed to stability by improving confidence.

With the help of the more stable structure of the economy, recessions in the postwar era have been limited to declines in investment spending (and, in 1953–54, Federal outlays). Consumer incomes have not declined significantly, and hence households have maintained their spending in recession. With the nearly two-thirds of GNP represented by consumer expenditures insulated from decline and with a solid foundation of public outlays, declines in private investment have not cumulated. In contrast, the Great Depression generated a decline of consumer outlays of 40 percent from 1929 to 1933, and the shrinkage of consumer markets aggravated and reinforced the collapse in investment spending.

Why might monetary policy be a more flexible tool than fiscal policy

11

"The Great Depression"

FORTUNE

This article comes from the September 1932 issue of Fortune *magazine. Published at the bottom of the Great Depression, this is a vivid account of the nation's plight at that time.*

Dull mornings last winter the sheriff of Miami, Florida, used to fill a truck with homeless men and run them up to the county line. Where the sheriff of Fort Lauderdale used to meet them and load them into a second truck and run them up to *his* county line. Where the sheriff of Saint Lucie's would meet them and load them into a third truck and run them up to *his* county line. Where the sheriff of Brevard County would *not* meet them. And whence they would trickle back down the roads to Miami. To repeat.

It was a system. And it worked. The only trouble was that it worked too well. It kept the transients transient and it even increased the transient population in the process. But it got to be pretty expensive, one way or another, if you sat down and figured it all out—trucks and gas and time and a little coffee. . . .

That was last winter.

Next winter there will be no truck. And there will be no truck, not because the transients will have disappeared from Miami: if anything, there will be more blistered Fords with North Dakota licenses and more heel-worn shoes with the Boston trademark rubbed out next winter than there were last. But because the sheriff of Miami, like the President of the United States, will next winter think of transients and unemployed miners and jobless mill workers in completely different terms.

The difference will be made by the Emergency Relief Act. Or rather by the fact that the Emergency Relief Act exists. For the Act itself with its $300,000,000 for direct relief loans to the states is neither an adequate nor an impressive piece of legislation. But the passage of the Act, like the green branch which young Mr. Ringling used to lay across the forks of the Wisconsin roads for his circus to follow, marks a turning in American political history. And the beginning of a new chapter in American unemployment relief. It constitutes an open and legible acknowledgment of governmental responsibility for the welfare of the victims of industrial unemployment. And its ultimate effect must be the substitution of an ordered, realistic, and intelligent relief program for the wasteful and uneconomic methods (of which the Miami truck is an adequate symbol) employed during the first three years of the depression.

There can be no serious question of the failure of those methods. For the methods were never seriously capable of success. They were diffuse, unrelated, and unplanned. The theory was that private charitable organizations and semipublic welfare groups, established to care for the old and the sick and the indigent, were capable of caring for the casuals of a worldwide economic disaster. And the theory in application meant that social agencies manned for the service of a few hundred families, and city shelters set up to house and feed a handful of homeless men, were compelled by the brutal necessities of hunger to care for hundreds of thousands of families and whole armies of the displaced and the jobless. And to depend for their resources upon the contributions of communities no longer able to contribute, and upon the irresolution and vacillation of state legislatures and municipal assemblies long since in the red on their annual budgets. The result was the picture now presented in city after city and state after state—heterogeneous groups of official and semiofficial and unofficial relief agencies struggling under the earnest and untrained leadership of the local men of affairs against an inertia of misery and suffering and want they are powerless to overcome.

But the psychological consequence was even worse. Since the problem was never honestly attacked as a national problem, and since the facts were never frankly faced as facts, people came to believe that American unemployment was relatively unimportant. They saw little idleness and they therefore believed there was little idleness. It is possible to drive for blocks in the usual shopping and residential districts of New York and Chicago without seeing a breadline or a food station or a hungry mob or indeed anything else much more exciting than a few casuals asleep on a park bench. And for that reason, and because their newspapers played down the subject as an additional depressant in depressing times, and because they were bored with relief measures anyway, the great American public simply ignored the whole thing. They would still ignore it today were it not that the committee hearings and the Congressional debate and the Presidential veto of relief bills this last June attracted their attention. And that the final passage of the Emergency Relief and Construction Act of 1932 has committed their government and themselves to a policy of affirmative action which compels both it and them to know definitely and precisely what the existing situation is.

It should be remarked at this point that nothing the federal government has yet done or is likely to do in the near future constitutes a policy of *constructive* action. Unemployment basically is not a social disease but an industrial phenomenon. The natural and inevitable consequence of a machine civilization is a lessened demand for human labor. (An almost total elimination of human labor in plowing, for example, is now foreseeable.) And the natural and inevitable consequence of a lessened demand for human labor is an increase of idleness. Indeed the prophets of the machine age have always promised an increase of idleness, under the name of leisure, as one of the goals of industry. A constructive solution of unemployment therefore means an industrial solution—a restatement of industrialism which will treat technological displacement not as an illness to be cured but as a goal to be achieved—and achieved with the widest dispensation of benefits and the least incidental misery.

But the present relief problem as focused by the federal Act is not a problem of ultimate solutions but of immediate palliatives. One does not talk architecture while the house is on fire and the tenants are still inside. The question at this moment is the pure question of fact. Having decided at last to face reality and do something about it, what is reality? How many men are unemployed in the U. S.? How many are in want? *What are the facts?*

Twenty-five Millions

The following minimal statements may be accepted as true—with the certainty that they underestimate the real situation:

(1) Unemployment has steadily increased in the U.S. since the beginning of the depression and the rate of increase during the first part of 1932 was more rapid than in any other depression year.

(2) The number of persons totally unemployed is now at least 10,000,000.

(3) The number of persons totally unemployed next winter will, at the present rate of increase, be 11,000,000.

(4) Eleven millions unemployed means better than one man out of every four employable workers.

(5) This percentage is higher than the percentage of unemployed British workers registered under the compulsory insurance laws (17.1 percent in May, 1932, as against 17.3 percent in April and 18.4 percent in January) and higher than the French, the Italian,

and the Canadian percentages, but lower than the German (43.9 percent of trade unionists in April, 1932) and the Norwegian.

(6) Eleven millions unemployed means 27,500,000 whose regular source of livelihood has been cut off.

(7) Twenty-seven and a half millions without regular income includes the families of totally unemployed workers alone. Taking account of the numbers of workers on part time, the total of those without adequate income becomes 34,000,000 or better than a quarter of the entire population of the country.

(8) Thirty-four million persons without adequate income does not mean 34,000,000 in present want. Many families have savings. But savings are eventually dissipated and the number in actual want tends to approximate the number without adequate income. How nearly it approximates it now or will next winter no man can say. But it is conservative to estimate that the problem of next winter's relief is a problem of caring for approximately 25,000,000 souls.

These figures . . . are based upon estimates. For nothing but estimates exists. No heritage from the fumbling of the last three years is more discouraging than the complete lack of statistics. The Director of the President's Organization on Unemployment Relief, Walter S. Gifford of the American Telephone & Telegraph Co., was forced to acknowledge before a subcommittee of the Senate in January, 1932, that he did not know, nor did his organization know, how many persons were out of work and in need of assistance in the U.S. nor even how many persons were actually receiving aid at the time of his testimony. And more recently the Commissioner of Labor Statistics, Ethelbert Stewart, generally recognized as the government's foremost authority on unemployment, has been allowed to lose his office at the most critical period in American unemployment history because, according to press accounts, the Secretary of Labor, Mr. Doak, was irritated by the Commissioner's correction of one of his overoptimistic statements.

Fortunately, however, the more important estimators agree among themselves and the total of 25,000,000 may fairly be accepted.

But it is impossible to think or to act in units of 25,000,000 human beings. Like the casualty lists of the British War Office during the Battle of the Somme, they mean nothing. They are at once too large and too small. A handful of men and women and children digging for their rotten food in the St. Louis

dumps are more numerous, humanly speaking, than all the millions that ever found themselves in an actuary's column. The 25,000,000 only become human in their cities and their mill towns and their mining villages. And their situation only becomes comprehensible in terms of the relief they have already received.

That is to say that the general situation can only be judged by the situation in the particular localities. But certain generalizations are possible. Of which the chief is the broad conclusion that few if any of the industrial areas have been able to maintain a minimum decency level of life for their unemployed. Budgetary standards as set up by welfare organizations, public and private, after years of experiment have been discarded. Food only, in most cases, is provided and little enough of that. Rents are seldom paid. Shoes and clothing are given in rare instances only. Money for doctors and dentists is not to be had. And free clinics are filled to overflowing. Weekly allowances per family have fallen as low as $2.39 in New York with $3 and $4 the rule in most cities and $5 a high figure. And even on these terms funds budgeted for a twelve-month period have been exhausted in three or four. While city after city has been compelled to abandon a part of its dependent population. "We are merely trying to prevent hunger and exposure," reported a St. Paul welfare head last May. And the same sentence would be echoed by workers in other cities with such additions as were reported at the same time from Pittsburgh where a cut of 50 percent was regarded as "inevitable," from Dallas where Mexicans and Negroes were not given relief, from Alabama where discontinuance of relief in mining and agricultural sections was foreseen, from New Orleans where no new applicants were being received and 2,500 families in need of relief were receiving none, from Omaha where two-thirds of the cases receiving relief were to be discontinued, from Colorado where the counties had suspended relief for lack of funds . . . from Scranton . . . from Cleveland . . . from Syracuse. . . . But individual localities present their own picture.

New York City

About 1,000,000 out of the city's 3,200,000 working population are unemployed. Last April 410,000 were estimated to be in dire want. Seven hundred and fifty thousand in 150,000 families were receiving emergency aid while 160,000 more in 32,000 families were waiting to receive aid not then available. Of these latter families—families which normally earn an average of $141.50 a month—the average income from all sources was $8.20. Of families receiving relief, the allowance has been anything from a box of groceries up to $60 a month. In general, New York relief, in the phrase of Mr. William Hodson, executive director of the New York Welfare Council, has been on "a disaster basis." And the effects have been disaster effects. It is impossible to estimate the number of deaths in the last year in which starvation was a contributing cause. But ninety-five persons suffering directly from starvation were admitted to the city hospitals in 1931, of whom twenty died; and 143 suffering from malnutrition, of whom twenty-five died. While visiting nurses and welfare workers report a general increase in malnutrition, and the clinics and medical relief agencies are so overcrowded they can give adequate relief to no one, although 75 percent of persons applying to one relief agency had some form of illness. Housing is, of course, with the general lowering of standards and the doubling-up of families, worse even than it was during the boom. Relief expenditures for 1930 were something over $6,000,000; for 1931, more than $25,000,000; and for the first four months of 1932 over $20,000,000, or $5,000,000 per month. But large as this latter figure is it must be compared with the wage and salary loss by reason of unemployment, which is at least $100,000,000 per month. The need, even with static unemployment figures, is cumulative, and $75,000,000 for the next twelve months is a low estimate.

Philadelphia

The situation in Philadelphia was described by its Community Council in July, 1932, as one of "slow starvation and progressive disintegration of family life. . . ." "Normal" unemployment in Philadelphia is 40,000 to 50,000. In April 1931, 228,000 or 25.6 percent of the city's normally employed were unemployed, and 122,000 or 13.7 percent were on part time. Of the city's 445,000 families with employable workers, 210,000 had workers unemployed or on part time, about one in four had no worker employed on full time, and 12 percent had no worker employed.

Even the average person unemployed had been out of work for thirty-seven weeks and had had only a little over one week of casual or relief work during the period. By December, 1931, the number of unemployed had reached 238,000 with 43,000 families receiving relief and 56,000 families in which no one was at work. And by May, 1932, the total of unemployed was 298,000. In the following month the Governor of the state estimated that 250,000 persons in Philadelphia "faced actual starvation." Over the state at large the same conditions held. In June, 1931, 919,000 or 25 percent of the normally employed in the state were unemployed, according to the "secret" report then submitted to the Governor, and the number had risen to 1,000,000 by December and to 1,250,000 in August, 1932. One hundred and fifty thousand children were in need of charity. Malnutrition had increased in forty-eight counties—27 percent of school children being undernourished (216,000 out of a school population of 800,000). New patients in the tuberculosis clinics had doubled. And the general death rate and disease rate had risen. Only nine counties were well organized. Fifty-five gave cause for grave concern and nineteen were listed as distressed counties in dire need. Moreover, relief allowances have steadily dropped. Last December 43,000 of the 56,000 families in Philadelphia where no one was employed were receiving relief at the rate of $4.39 per week for families averaging 4.8 persons. By May the number of families receiving relief had risen to 55,000 and the amount of relief had dropped to $4.23, of which $3.93 was for food, being two-thirds of the minimum required for health. No provision is made for rents and the result is that the landlords of Philadelphia, like the landlords of the country at large, are compelled to choose between throwing their tenants into the streets or providing from their own pockets the shelter required. Outside of Philadelphia the weekly grant to a family is $3 or less in thirteen counties, and $3 to $4 in six more, while in some of the small steel towns it may be even lower. Funds in the counties are either exhausted or will be exhausted before November.

Detroit

Relief in Detroit was originally upon a boom-time, boom-extravagance basis with gross incompetence in the administration of funds, an embezzlement of

$207,000, and doles of silk stockings and cosmetics. The resultant imminent bankruptcy forced a contraction of expenditures, and relief in May, 1932, with a greatly increased need, was only $859,925 as against $2,088,850 in January, 1931. There were 223,000 unemployed last November in the city and 410,000 in the state. In January the city was caring for 48,000 distressed families. This number was cut to 22,000 in April and relief was given at the rate of fifteen cents per day per person. In July under pressure of further shortage a further cut of 5,000 families totaling 20,000 persons was determined. Aid was to be denied to ablebodied persons who had been public charges for a year or more whether work was available for them or not, and childless couples and small families with no definite ties in Detroit were to be forced to leave the city. The resultant relief roll was expected to be 17,757 families, of whom 7,000 were dependent because of age or illness. The great majority on relief are laborers but Detroit also carries or has carried forty-five ministers, thirty bank tellers, lawyers, dentists, musicians, and "two families after whom streets are named." Riots, chiefly employment riots, have been fairly common with bloodshed in at least one. And enormous breadlines and the like are daily sights. No adequate statistics on public health in Detroit exist but it may safely be assumed to be at least as low as New York's.

Chicago

Unemployed in Chicago number somewhere between 660,000 and 700,000 or 40 percent of its employable workers while the number for the state at large is about one in three of the gainfully employed. About 100,000 families have applied down to July for relief in Cook County. The minimum relief budget has been $2.40 per week for an adult and $1.50 per week for a child for food, with $22 to $23 per month to a family. But these figures have since been cut to $2.15 weekly for a man, $1.10 for a child. And persons demanding relief must be completely destitute to receive it. Rents are not paid by the relief agencies and housing is, in certain sections, unspeakably bad. While the situation of city employees is tragic. Teachers in May, 1932, had had only five months cash for the last thirteen months, 3,177 of them had lost $2,367,000 in bank failures, 2,278 of them had lost $7,800,000 in lapsed policies, 805 had borrowed $232,000 from loan sharks at rates adding up to 42 percent a year, and 759 had lost their homes. (The city at one time undertook to sell for tax default the houses of its employees unable to pay taxes because of its own default in wages.) It is estimated that $35,000,000 will be spent in 1932 for an inadequate job and that an adequate job would cost $50,000,000.

12

Fiscal Policy and Economic Stabilization

JOSEPH PECHMAN

Joseph Pechman is Director of Economic Studies at the Brookings Institution. The following article is taken from his book Federal Tax Policy, *published in 1971.*

During most of the nation's history, federal budget policy was based on the rule that tax receipts should be roughly equal to annual government expenditures. Declining receipts during a business contraction called for an increase in taxes or a reduction in expenditures, while surpluses that developed during periods of prosperity called for lowered tax rates or increased expenditures. This policy reduced private incomes when they were already falling and raised them when they were rising. By aggravating fluctuations in purchasing power, the policy of annually balanced budgets accentuated economic instability.

In the 1930s, new concepts of budget policy emerged that emphasized the relationship of the federal budget to the performance of the economy. Adjustments in federal expenditures and taxes were to be made to reduce unemployment or to check inflation. Budget surpluses were to be used to restrain private spending during prosperity, deficits to stimulate spending during recessions. But variations in government expenditures were expected to play a more active role than tax rate variations in counteracting fluctuations in private demand.

The view today is that private demand can be stimulated or restrained by tax as well as expenditure changes. Higher taxes and lower government expenditures help to fight inflation by restraining private demand; lower taxes and higher expenditures help to fight recession by stimulating private demand. Fiscal policy was actively used in the decade of the 1960s to promote economic stability, with results that exceeded expectations on some occasions (for example, when taxes were cut in 1964) and fell below expectations on others (for example, when the Vietnam war surtax was imposed in 1968).

Fiscal economics is based on national income analysis as it has developed over the past thirty-five years. The essence of this analysis is that the level of expenditures depends on total output or gross national product (GNP), which in turn depends on the total spending of consumers, business, and government. At any given time, there is a level of output that is consistent with full employment of the nation's supply of labor (except for seasonal, and a small amount of frictional, unemployment). This level is called *potential* or *full employment GNP* (Figure 1). The major objectives of fiscal policy are to stabilize the economy at full employment, maintain price stability, and promote economic growth and efficiency.

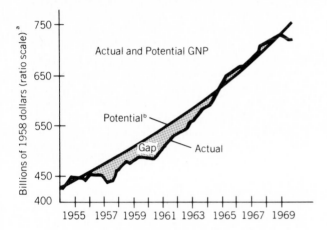

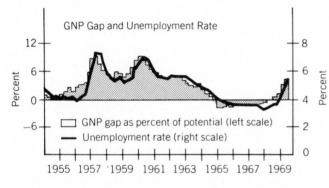

Sources U.S. Department of Commerce and Council of Economic Advisers.

aSeasonally adjusted annual rates.

bTrend line of 3-1/2 percent through middle of 1955 to 1962 IV, 3-3/4 percent from 1962 IV to 1965 IV, 4 percent from 1965 IV to 1969 IV, and 4.3 percent from 1969 IV to 1970 II.

Unemployment as percentage of civilian labor force; seasonally adjusted.

FIGURE 1. Gross National Product, Actual and Potential, and Unemployment Rate, 1955–70

Stabilization Policy

The federal government exerts great influence on total spending, and hence on output, through its expenditure and tax policies. It alters total spending directly by varying its own spending, or indirectly by raising or lowering taxes. If expenditures are increased or taxes lowered, the spending of higher incomes by the recipients requires additional output, which in turn generates still more income and spending; and the cycle repeats itself. The cumulative increase in GNP is, therefore, a multiple of the initial increase in government expenditures or reduction in taxes. Correspondingly, reductions in expenditures or increases in taxes reduce GNP by a multiple of the initial action.

Impact of Expenditure and Tax Changes

The process of income and output creation through fiscal policy may be illustrated by the following hypothetical examples. Assume that out of each dollar of GNP, 25 cents is taken in federal taxes, and the remaining 75 cents goes to consumers and business. Assume also that consumers and business together spend 80 percent of any additional income they receive.

If the government increases its purchases by $10 billion, private income before tax will initially rise by the same amount. Tax revenues will be $2.5 billion higher, and private disposable income will rise by $7.5 billion, of which consumers and business will spend $6 billion. This additional spending will generate another increase in income, with $1.5 billion going to taxes and the remaining $4.5 billion to consumers and business. Of this latter amount, consumers and business will spend $3.6 billion, which will generate still another round of income and spending, and so on. The total increase in GNP (including the initial $10 billion of government purchases) will amount to $25 billion ($10+ $6+ $3.6+ . . .). This is a multiplier of 2.5 times the original increase in spending.

Consider what will happen if, instead of increasing expenditures, the government reduces taxes by $10 billion. Consumers and business will again spend 80 percent of the higher after-tax incomes, or $8 billion. This will generate the same amount of additional private income, of which consumers and business will receive $6 billion and spend $4.8 billion, and so on. The total increase in GNP will be $20 billion ($8+ $4.8+ . . .), or two times the original tax cut. The difference between the multipliers in the two illustrations reflects the differences in first-round effects of the expenditure and tax changes: in this round output is raised by the entire amount of the expenditure increase, but by only 80 percent of the tax reduction.

If expenditures and taxes are increased simultaneously by the same amount, the effects of these two actions will not cancel one another because, dollar for dollar, expenditures have a more potent effect on the economy than do tax changes. For example, given the assumptions in the previous illustrations, if a tax increase of $10 billion were enacted together with a $10 billion increase in government spending, the former would reduce GNP by $20 billion, while the latter would stimulate a $25 billion increase, leaving a net increase of $5 billion. In other words, an increase in expenditures that is fully financed by an increase in taxes will on balance increase the GNP. (This theorem assumes that the change in spending resulting from an increase or decrease in private disposable income will be the same regardless of the source of the income change and that investment and other economic behavior will not be influenced by the government's action. The multipliers used are illustrative only; estimates of the multipliers vary greatly.)

The effect of changes in government expenditures and taxes on the size of the government's deficit depends on the increase in GNP generated by the fiscal stimulus and on tax rates. In the previous examples, federal taxes were assumed to account for about 25 percent of an increment to GNP. Thus, the increase in GNP would raise tax receipts by $6.25 billion if expenditures were increased by $10 billion (0.25 × $25), causing an increase in deficit (or a reduction in surplus) of $3.75 billion. If taxes were reduced by $10 billion, the increase in GNP would raise tax receipts by $5 billion (0.25 × $20), causing a $5 billion increase in the deficit. If expenditures and taxes were raised simultaneously by $10 billion, the increase in GNP would raise tax receipts by $1.25 billion (0.25 × $5) and *reduce* the deficit (or increase the surplus) by that amount.

Monetary policy also plays an important role in stabilization policy. Suppose the federal government increases expenditures or reduces taxes. As GNP increases, individuals and business firms will need additional cash to conduct their business affairs. If the money supply fails to increase, the greater demand for cash will drive up interest rates. The higher interest rates will tend to reduce residential construction, business investment, and state-local construction, thus offsetting at least some of the effect of the initial increase in spending. Fiscal policy thus requires an accommodating monetary policy if it is to be fully effective, but the precise combination of monetary and fiscal measures necessary to obtain any desired response is not known.

Built-in Stabilizers

In addition to discretionary changes in taxes and expenditures (that is, deliberate government actions to vary taxes or the rate of expenditures), the fiscal system itself contributes to stabilization by generating automatic tax and expenditure adjustments that cushion the effect of changes in GNP. These *built-in stabilizers* moderate the fall in private income and spending when GNP declines and restrain private income and spending when GNP rises. They are automatic in the sense that they respond to changes in GNP without any action on the part of the government.

The two major groups of built-in fiscal stabilizers are: (1) taxes, in particular the federal individual income tax; and (2) transfers, such as unemployment compensation and welfare payments.

Among taxes, the federal individual income tax is the leading stabilizer. When incomes fall, many individuals who were formerly taxable drop below the taxable level; others are pushed down into lower tax brackets. Conversely, when incomes rise, individuals who were formerly not taxed become taxable, and others are pushed into higher tax brackets. Under the 1964 act rates, federal individual income tax receipts (excluding the Vietnam war surcharge) automatically increased or decreased by about 14 or 15 percent for every 10 percent increase or decrease in personal income. Since consumption depends on disposable personal income, automatic changes in receipts from the individual income tax tend to keep consumption more stable than it otherwise would be.

Variations in receipts from the corporation income tax are proportionately larger than variations in individual income tax receipts, because profits fluctuate widely over a business cycle. The variation in corporate profits is a major nonfiscal stabilizer in the economic system. When economic activity slows down, profits fall in absolute terms and as a percentage of GNP, thus absorbing much of the impact of the reduction in incomes. During a cyclical recovery, profits rise much faster than do other kinds of income. Corporation taxes vary almost directly with profits, and they assist corporations to absorb the impact of declining incomes during the downswing. During the upswing, rising tax liabilities tend to restrain the growth of corporation incomes. The effect of variations in corporation tax liabilities on dividends is relatively small because corporate managers try to keep dividends in line with long-term earnings.

Fluctuations in investment are probably reduced to some extent, but the precise effect is unknown.

On the expenditure side, the major built-in stabilizer is unemployment compensation. Insured workers who become unemployed are entitled to benefits for up to twenty-six weeks in most states. Benefits for an additional thirteen weeks are paid throughout the nation when the national unemployment rate is 4-1/2 percent for three consecutive months, and in any state when the state unemployment rate increases by 20 percent over the average of the two preceding years and is at least 4 percent. These payments help to maintain consumption as output and employment fall, even though the recipients are not participating in production. As incomes go up and employment increases, unemployment compensation declines. Other transfer payments (old-age insurance, public assistance, and the like) also tend to vary inversely with changes in GNP.

It is possible to calculate the effect of built-in stabilizers on the federal surplus, as distinct from the discretionary actions of the government. Because of the built-in stabilizers, the actual surplus or deficit reflects the prevailing levels of income and employment, as well as the government's fiscal policy. Figure 2 shows how the effect of the built-in stabilizers may be separated from the discretionary changes.

Each line in the figure shows the surplus or deficit

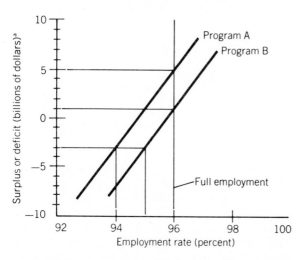

Source: Adapted from *Economic Report of the President, January 1962*, p. 79.

aNational income accounts basis.

FIGURE 2. Effect of Level of Activity on Federal Surplus or Deficit

that would be realized at various levels of employment under two different budget programs, A and B. For simplicity, it is assumed that the tax system is the same, but that expenditures are $4 billion higher under Program B. (The surplus is, therefore, $4 billion lower, or the deficit is $4 billion higher.) The lines slope upward, indicating that as employment and income increase, the deficits become smaller or the surpluses larger. The effect of the built-in stabilizers is given by the slope of each line: the greater the slope, the larger the impact of the built-in stabilizers on the surplus or deficit. As is shown in Figure 2, both programs have the same built-in stability features because the tax systems are identical. However, an actual deficit of $3 billion is realized when employment is at 94 percent of the labor force under Program A and 95 percent under Program B. Clearly, Program B is more expansionary than Program A. Differences between programs will also be due in practice to differences in tax rates; in such cases, the lines would not be parallel, but the slope of each line would still measure the built-in flexibility of each program.

The Full Employment Surplus

The degree of stimulation provided by fiscal policy is popularly regarded as a function of the *current* budget surplus or deficit (that is, the budget is considered to be restrictive when it is running a surplus and expansionary when it is in deficit). It should be clear from Figure 2 that actual surpluses or deficits are poor guides for evaluating fiscal policy because they include the effects of both automatic and discretionary fiscal actions.

The economic effects of two fiscal programs may be compared by examining the surplus or deficit at any given level of employment. By convention, the comparison is made at full employment, which is assumed to be when 96 percent of the labor force is employed. Defined in this way, the "full employment surplus" is $5 billion under Program A in Figure 2 and $1 billion under Program B. The difference of $4 billion reflects the assumed difference in expenditures. In practice, the differences are due to differences in taxes as well as expenditures.

There are two types of budget statements in current use—the official *unified budget* and the *national income accounts budget*. The full employment surplus is usually computed on a national income accounts basis, but it can be adjusted to the definitions in the unified budget.

The budget program that is appropriate at a given time depends upon the strength of private demand for consumption and investment goods. When private demand is high, a large full employment surplus is called for; when private demand is weak, a small full employment surplus, or even a full employment deficit, is required. Efforts to achieve a larger surplus or a lower deficit than is consistent with full employment would depress employment and incomes. If the budget called for too small a full employment surplus, total demand would be too high, and prices would rise.

Another characteristic of the full employment surplus is its tendency to increase with the passage of time and the growth of the economy. With the growth of the labor force, the stock of capital, and productivity, potential federal receipts also rise. At current tax rates and assuming full employment, federal receipts increase by about $18 billion a year. Thus, the full employment surplus will creep up by about $18 billion each year, or about 1.6 percent of potential GNP in 1971, unless the government takes steps to prevent it.

This upward creep in the full employment surplus has been called the *fiscal dividend* or the *fiscal drag*. It

THE TWO BUDGETS

The official budget statement of the federal government is the *unified budget,* which is an instrument of management and control of federal activities financed with federally owned funds. This budget includes cash flows to and from the public resulting from all federal fiscal activity, including the trust funds, and the net lending of government-owned enterprises. Thus, the unified budget provides a comprehensive picture of the financial impact of federal programs, but it does not measure their contribution to the current income and output of the nation. For this purpose, economists make use of the statement of receipts and expenditures in the official national income accounts, often called the *national income accounts budget.*

Like the unified budget, the national income accounts budget includes the activities of trust funds and excludes purely intragovernmental transactions (for example, interest on federal bonds owned by federal agencies) which do not affect the general public. However, there are significant differences between the two in timing and coverage. The national income accounts budget includes receipts and expenditures when they have their impact on private incomes, which is not necessarily when the federal government receives cash or pays it out. This adjustment involves putting receipts (except those from personal taxes) on an accrual basis and counting expenditures when goods are delivered rather than when payment is made. The adjustment for coverage excludes purely financial transactions because these represent an exchange of assets or claims and not a direct addition to income or production.

There are substantial differences in the size of surpluses or deficits between the two accounts, and even in their movements (Figure 3). In recent years, the national income accounts budget has shown the smaller deficit (or larger surpluses).

FIGURE 3. Federal Deficits and Surpluses, Two Budget Concepts, Fiscal Years 1954–70

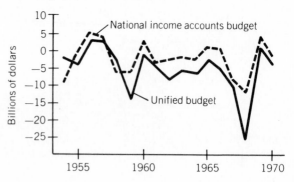

is identified as a *dividend* when used to describe the elbow room available in the federal budget to finance higher federal expenditures without raising tax rates. During the early 1960s, the fiscal dividend was large enough to finance tax rate reductions as well as expenditure increases. More recently, with continued high commitments for defense, the fiscal dividend has not been adequate to provide fully for urgently needed domestic social programs.

The automatic increase in federal receipts that accompanies economic growth is also called the *fiscal drag* because it acts as a retarding influence on the economy unless it is offset by rising expenditures or tax reductions. This terminology was in vogue in the early 1960s, when government expenditures were not rising fast enough to absorb the automatic growth in tax receipts.

According to current estimates, the federal budget would have been in surplus in every quarter between mid-1955 and mid-1965, had full employment been maintained (Figure 4). However, the actual budget showed a deficit during most of the period, reflecting the disappointing performance of the economy. It was only after the full employment surplus was sharply

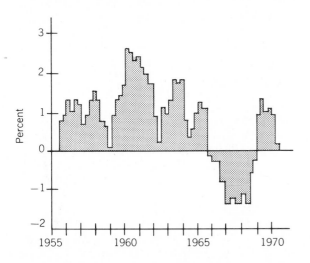

Sources: Arthur M. Okun and Nancy H. Teeters, "The Full Employment Surplus Revisited," in *Brookings Papers on Economic Activity* (1:1970), pp. 104–05; Teeters, "Budgetary Outlook at Mid-Year 1970," in *Brookings Papers on Economic Activity* (2:1970), p. 304 (adjusted to exclude the corporate financial adjustment).

FIGURE 4. Full Employment Surplus as a Percentage of Potential Gross National Product, National Income Accounts Basis, 1955–70

reduced in 1964 to stimulate the economy that employment began to move toward 96 percent of the labor force, which is regarded by most people as the minimum acceptable level. This experience illustrates the principle that planning for a budget surplus, without regard to the strength of private demand, may produce unsatisfactory rates of employment and output and create budget deficits besides.

The rapid build-up of military expenditures for the Vietnam war quickly wiped out the full employment surplus beginning in mid-1965, the deficit on a full employment basis averaging 0.5 percent of potential GNP in 1966, 1.4 percent in 1967, and 0.9 percent in 1968. This was the period when prices rose at an unacceptably rapid rate. The full employment budget was restored to a surplus position in early 1969, reflecting the effect of the Vietnam war surtax and the strict limitations that were placed on domestic federal programs. The sharp increase in fiscal restraint, combined with an extremely tight monetary policy, helped to bring about a slowdown and then a decline in the real GNP beginning in the fourth quarter of 1969. Unfortunately, by this time the inflation had been converted to a "cost-push" type of inflation, and prices continued to rise at an excessive rate even in the face of the decline in real GNP.

Although it is the most convenient single measure of restrictiveness or ease in the federal budget, the full employment surplus must be used with considerable care. In the first place, the degree of fiscal restraint needed at any given time depends on the strength of private demand. The same full employment surplus that may be appropriate for one period may not be appropriate for another. Second, differences in the level and composition of expenditures and taxes have an important bearing on the significance of the full employment surplus. For example, an increase in the full employment surplus resulting from a reduction in government expenditures on goods and services would be more restrictive than would a tax increase of the same amount. Third, the restrictiveness of a given *amount* of surplus, say, $10 billion, would be much greater in a $750 billion economy than in a $1,000 billion economy. In making comparisons over time, the full employment surplus should be expressed as a percentage of potential GNP (see Figure 4). Finally, there is no simple way to adjust the full employment surplus for the effect of price increases. Most calculations of the full employment surplus remove the effect of the built-in response of the federal budget to a business recession, but do not remove the built-in response of the budget to inflation. For these reasons, the meaning of the full employment surplus is likely to be unambiguous only during relatively short periods when changes in expenditures and taxes, and in the rate of growth of prices, are relatively small. Analysis of the fiscal impact of the budget over long periods requires more detailed information than the full employment surplus provides by itself.

Expenditure versus Tax Adjustments to Promote Stability

Both expenditure and tax rate changes can be used for stabilization purposes. While it is true that expenditure changes have somewhat larger multiplier effects, they are not necessarily preferable to changes in tax rates. In the first place, government expenditures should be determined on the basis of long-run national needs and not of short-run cyclical considerations. The controlling principle is that government outlays should not exceed the level where the benefit to the nation's citizens of an additional dollar of expenditures would be the same in public and private use. It is hardly likely that this point would shift sharply in one direction or the other during such short periods as a business contraction or even during an inflation. Second, considerations of economic efficiency argue against large short-run variations in expenditures. For example, it would be wasteful to slow down construction of a road or hydroelectric facility, once construction has begun, in the interest of reducing aggregate spending. Third, there may be a long time lag between a decision to undertake an expenditure and its effect on output and employment. When recessions are relatively brief—as they have been since the end of World War II—the impact of a decision to make an expenditure change often is not felt until recovery is under way. However, during periods of rapidly rising defense expenditures, such as occurred during the Korean and Vietnam wars, a slowing down or deferment of some government programs usually becomes necessary to keep total demand from outstripping the productive potential of the economy.

Among the various taxes, the individual income tax is the best suited for stabilization purposes. Under the withholding system for wages and salaries, changes in tax rates can be made effective in a matter of days and can also be terminated quickly. In most cases, the effect of a tax change on a worker's take-home pay is indistinguishable from the effect of a change in his gross weekly wage. Corporation income tax changes are not likely to have significant effects on investment if it is known, or expected, that they will be of short duration. Consumption tax changes may have a perverse effect in the short run; the expectation of a reduction may delay spending, and the expectation of an increase may accelerate spending. Nevertheless, once they become effective, consumption tax changes are at least as powerful as income tax changes in stimulating or restraining consumer demand.

Some economists believe that consumption depends on income that is expected to be received regularly and is not much affected by temporary or transitory changes in income. On this hypothesis, temporary income tax changes would have relatively little impact on consumption. Most economists believe that a temporary income tax change would have some effect on consumer spending, although they agree that it would be less powerful than a permanent tax change. Income tax changes also operate with a lag, because consumers do not alter their consumption immediately in response to changes in disposable income.

Tax changes are often assumed to have the largest effect on consumption if they are confined to the lower income classes. This view presupposes that poor people spend proportionately more out of any additional dollars they may receive than do the rich. There is no evidence, however, to confirm or deny this assumption. For policy purposes, it is probably satisfactory to assume that the incremental consumption rate is fairly high throughout most of the income distribution. This would suggest that, if the distribution of the tax burden is considered equitable by the large majority of taxpayers, tax rates could be moved up or down uniformly for stabilization purposes under a simple formula, such as an equal percentage change for all taxpayers.

Tax rate changes are sometimes criticized on the ground that they are too small to exert a significant economic effect. With sixty-five million taxpayers, a $13 billion individual income tax cut would be equivalent to an average increase in take-home pay of only $4 a week per taxpayer, a negligible amount in comparison with the total GNP of $1,000 billion. The comparison is erroneous, however, because it compares weekly and annual income flows. A $13 billion tax cut would amount to more than 1 percent of the GNP, whether expressed on a weekly, monthly, or annual basis, Because tax changes have a multiplier effect, a tax cut of this magnitude would provide a substantial stimulus to the economy. The deviation from full employment GNP, which tax cuts are intended to narrow, is usually less than 5 percent.

Tax adjustments can be used to restrain as well as to stimulate demand and are therefore important policy instruments for counteracting inflation. It may be impractical, if not impossible, to cut back government expenditures when inflation threatens. About half of federal expenditures are for defense, foreign aid, education, and research and development, which should not be altered for short-run reasons. Much of the remainder of the federal budget provides assistance to low-income persons, who are particularly hard-pressed during an inflation. Moreover, the inflationary pressures may have been due to an increase in government spending for defense or war purposes. In these circumstances, tax increases must be used to withdraw excess purchasing power from the income stream.

The time required for the legislative process to be completed is the major obstacle to prompt use of tax changes for stabilization purposes. Congressional consideration of major tax legislation may take as long as eighteen months. Proposals have been made to give the President authority to make temporary changes in individual income tax rates, or to speed up congressional procedures for action on presidential recommendations. However, Congress has not seriously considered such plans.

Automatic Budget Rules

It is now widely understood that following a policy of annually balanced budgets would accentuate business fluctuations. But many people continue to believe that it is unwise to rely exclusively on discretion to guide budget decisions. Discretionary policy depends heavily on forecasting techniques that are still subject to error. There is also a fear that removing budgetary restraint would lead to excessive federal expenditures. To avoid these pitfalls, attempts have been made to formulate rules that would reduce the element of judgment in budget decisions without impairing economic growth and stability.

The best known plan is the *stabilizing budget policy* of the Committee for Economic Development (CED), a nonprofit organization of influential businessmen and educators. Under this policy, tax rates would be set to balance the budget or yield a small surplus at full employment. Tax rates would remain unchanged until there was a major change in the level of expenditures. Reliance would be placed on the built-in stabilizers to moderate fluctuations in private demand.

The CED plan would operate successfully, however, only if full employment could be achieved with a balance or a small surplus in the federal budget. Moreover, the CED plan does not offer a systematic method for raising additional revenues if federal expenditures should rise by more than the amount of the automatic growth in tax receipts, or of lowering taxes if federal expenditures should rise by less than the amount of the automatic growth in tax receipts. With federal expenditure needs rising rapidly and recession still a considerable threat to economic stability, it would be both hazardous and unwise to keep tax rates unchanged for long periods.

A second type of plan—which would aim at helping to solve the fiscal drag problem—would provide for individual income tax rates to be reduced each year by a given amount, say 1 percentage point (which would reduce income tax receipts by about $4 billion a year at 1971 income levels), with the $14 billion remaining from the fiscal dividend of approximately $18 billion to be used for increasing federal expenditures. Presumably, the plan would begin with a surplus or deficit consistent with full employment. The difficulty with this approach is that it would freeze the allocation of increased federal receipts between tax reduction and increased expenditures. Periods when it would have been desirable to cut tax rates by a fixed amount or a fixed percentage each year have been rare in the nation's history.

A third approach to an automatic budget policy would be to build into the budget a formula that would trigger upward or downward changes in tax rates when certain predetermined economic indices are reached. For example, legislation might provide for a 1 percentage point reduction in income tax rates for every increase of 0.5 percent in unemployment above 4.5 percent of the labor force, or an increase of 1 percentage point for every rise of·2 points in a general price index, such as the consumer or the wholesale price index. While this type of formula would add to the effectiveness of the built-in stabilizers if the changes were correctly timed, no one index or set of indices could be used with confidence to signal an economic movement justifying tax action.

It is evident that budget policy cannot be based on a rigid set of rules. Nevertheless, the search for budget rules has greatly improved public understanding of the elements of fiscal policy. Great emphasis is placed on the automatic stabilizers for their cushioning effect on private disposable incomes and spending. Recognition of the capacity of the federal tax system to generate rising revenues has alerted policy-makers to the need for making positive decisions to determine the relative social priorities of public and private expenditures, so that the appropriate amounts can be allocated to tax reduction and to higher government expenditures. Unfortunately, the political advantages of an immediate tax reduction tend to be more attractive than the long-run benefits of new or improved government programs. Thus, the Tax Reform Act of 1969 included net tax reductions, phased in over a period of years, which amount to $8 billion a year (at 1975 income levels), even though the remaining fiscal dividend was acknowledged to be inadequate to finance urgently needed federal programs.

Policies to Promote Economic Growth

Fiscal policies are useful in promoting long-run economic growth as well as short-run stability. The objective of growth policy is to provide relatively full employment for the labor force and industrial capacity, at stable prices. Growth may be disappointing for two reasons: the resources of the economy may not be employed up to their full potential because the economy is in recession or is being artificially held down to combat inflationary pressures, or the rate of growth of potential output at full employment may be too low. The policies required under these circumstances differ, although they are often confused.

Achieving Full Employment and Stable Prices

The major contribution that fiscal policy can make to economic growth is to help keep total demand roughly in line with the productive potential of the economy. An economy operating at less than full employment is one in which potential GNP is larger than the total of actual spending by consumers, business, and government. The remedy for this deficiency is to increase private or public spending through fiscal and monetary stimulation. Conversely, when total demand exceeds the capacity of the economy to produce goods and services, the remedy is to curtail private or public spending through fiscal and monetary restraint.

Although the basic principles of stabilization policy are clear, they have been difficult to apply in practice.

Failure to absorb the normal growth in revenues will produce successively higher full employment surpluses, which may hold actual output below the economic potential of the economy. The high levels of unemployment and the large gap between potential and actual GNP in the late 1950s and early 1960s (see Figure 1) were caused largely by excessively restrictive fiscal policies that arose in this way. On the other hand, too large a growth in government expenditures relative to normal revenue growth may produce excess demand, which in turn leads to rising prices. The inflation that began in mid-1965 was triggered by the large rise in Vietnam war expenditures, which were superimposed on an economy already operating at close to full employment. A 10 percent surtax on individual and corporation income taxes was enacted in the summer of 1968, but this was about three years after the decision to escalate the war had been made.

It now seems clear that it will always be difficult to maintain full employment in a modern industrial economy and keep price increases within acceptable limits. Since the end of World War II, prices have shown a tendency to rise in the United States, even when total spending has been below potential GNP. Many economists believe that this dilemma can be resolved only by supplementing fiscal and monetary policies with some form of wage-price or "incomes" policy to keep wage increases roughly in line with the average growth in productivity of the economy as a whole, and to prevent price increases that are not justified by cost increases. Under such a policy, prices would decline in industries with above-average productivity increases and rise in industries with less-than-average productivity increases, but the average of all prices would be stable. These principles were established by the Council of Economic Advisers in 1962 as voluntary "guideposts" for wage and price behavior. The guideposts had the strong backing of Presidents Kennedy and Johnson and appeared to have some effect in restraining wage and price increases (a judgment that some professional economists dispute) until mid-1965, when the rapid build-up of military expenditures for the Vietnam war upset the balance between supply and demand. No country has yet devised a workable incomes policy under conditions of full employment, and the search continues.

Experience has shown that the major effect of inflation on growth is felt when the attempt is made to restore balance in the economy. Inflation distorts the distribution of the national income among different groups. Each group tries to protect itself against erosion of its share through wage or price increases or government transfer payments. Such pressures continue to be felt long after excess demand has been removed by fiscal and monetary restraint. Thus, without an effective incomes policy, it may be possible to halt inflation only at the cost of high unemployment and slow growth for relatively long periods. It is, of course, much less costly in social and economic terms to avoid inflation in the first place.

Raising the Growth Rate

If full employment is maintained, the rate of economic growth will depend on the ability of the economy to raise the rate of growth of potential output. The factors affecting potential output are the size of the labor force, the length of the average workweek and workyear, and productivity (output per man-hour). Productivity depends on the size of the capital stock, the quality of human resources, the attitudes and skills of management, the efficiency of resource use, and the amount of technological progress. Most of these factors are influenced to some extent by government expenditure and tax policy, but the influence is most direct and quantitatively most important with respect to the rate of national investment in both physical and human resources.

To increase the rate of growth, the rate of national investment must be raised to a permanently higher level and held there for a long period of time. The federal government can contribute toward increasing the investment rate through fiscal policy in three ways: (1) it can adopt a policy of budget surpluses when the economy is operating at full employment; (2) it can increase investment in physical and human capital directly through its own expenditures; and (3) it can adopt tax measures that provide incentives for private saving and investment.

SAVING THROUGH BUDGET SURPLUSES. The key to an understanding of growth policy is the relation between saving and investment. As measured statistically, national saving is the difference between national output and the amounts spent by consumers and government; private investment is also that part of the national product that is not consumed or used for government purposes. Thus, national saving is equal to private investment. In effect, through saving, the nation sets aside the resources needed for private investment purposes; otherwise the resources would be used to produce goods and services for consumers and government.

When the federal government runs a budget surplus, it adds its own saving to that generated by the private economy. When the budget is in deficit, national saving is reduced. Since increased saving and investment are needed to raise the growth rate, the federal government can stimulate a higher growth rate by running budget surpluses at full employment. Moreover, the larger the surplus at full employment, the larger the potential contribution to growth.

This growth strategy can be implemented only if there is sufficient investment demand in the private economy to use up the saving generated in the federal budget. If private demand for investment is too low, the federal surplus will generate unemployment rather than more growth. In other words, the full employment surplus must be just large enough to offset the deficiency in private saving. If there is more than enough private saving for the existing investment demand, the budget should be in deficit even at full employment.

An important ingredient of any strategy to increase the rate of private investment is monetary policy. Easy money provides ready access to credit and lowers the cost of borrowing for investment purposes by reducing interest rates. Tight money restrains the growth of credit and raises interest rates. Therefore, the best policy to promote private investment would combine a budget surplus with easy money. In implementing such a policy, it is important to avoid taxes that impair investment incentives.

In practice, the extent of monetary ease that a nation can afford is limited by balance-of-payments considerations. If interest rates are driven down too far, private capital will leave the country to take advantage of higher interest rates abroad. In extreme cases, the outflow of funds may require devaluation of the nation's currency to restore international equilibrium. When interest rates must be kept up for balance-of-payments reasons, fiscal policy must be easier (that is, the surplus must be lower or the deficit higher) to prevent a drop in demand and employment.

INCREASING INVESTMENT DIRECTLY. It is not generally realized that investment is undertaken by government as well as by private firms. Outlays for education, training of manpower, health, research and development, roads, and other public facilities are essential elements of national investment. Such outlays are not substitutable for private investment, or vice versa.

Education and research expenditures are perhaps the most important components of national investment, yet most of these expenditures are paid for by government (primarily state and local in the case of education, and primarily federal in the case of research). There is no basis for prejudging how total investment should be distributed between the public and private sectors, and it is important to avoid doctrinaire positions about one or the other. Both types of investment contribute to the nation's economic growth.

Public investment is financed directly by government through the tax system. If private demand is strong, the appropriate policy for growth would be to raise enough tax revenues to pay for needed government investment as well as to leave an additional margin of saving for private investment.

INCREASING SAVING AND INVESTMENT INCENTIVES. Given the aggregate level of taxation, the tax structure can be an important independent factor in determining the growth potential of the economy. The tax structure may encourage consumption or saving, help to raise or lower private investment in general or in particular industries, stimulate or restrain the outflow of investment funds to foreign countries, and subsidize or discourage particular expenditures by individuals and business firms. Most tax systems, including that of the United States, have numerous features specifically intended to promote saving and investment. For example, the federal income taxes provide liberal depreciation allowances, full offsets for business losses against other income over a period of nine years, averaging of individual income for tax purposes over a period of five years, and preferential treatment of capital gains. A 7 percent credit against corporation and individual income taxes was used to stimulate investment between 1962 and 1969. These and other provisions will be discussed in later chapters.

The "Debt Burden"

Effective use of fiscal policy to promote the full employment and growth objectives is hindered by public concern over a growth of the national debt. There is widespread fear that a long succession of annual deficits and a resulting rise in the national debt will impose dangerously heavy burdens on later generations. There is also concern about the economic burden of interest payments.

Growth of the national debt can impose a burden on future generations if it interferes with private capital formation. In this respect, there is a difference between debt created under conditions of excessive unemployment and debt created under conditions of full employment.

In a situation of substantial unemployment, an increase in the public debt can finance deficits that government uses to purchase goods and services directly or to provide transfer payments. Since there are unemployed resources, the goods and services acquired by government or by the recipients of transfer payments do not take the place of goods and services that might otherwise have been produced. If accompanied by the appropriate monetary policy, the debt increase can be absorbed without impeding the flow of funds into private capital formation. In fact, private investment will rise as a result of the stimulus that arises from a higher level of economic activity. The community is better off when the expenditures are made; and later generations will also benefit to the extent that the expenditures increase private and public investment in human or physical capital that will yield future services.

The situation is more complicated if the economy is at full employment. In this setting an increase in government expenditures that leads to a deficit (or reduces a surplus) in the federal budget cannot increase total output. This means either that prices will rise or that offsetting tax increases or monetary restraint will be required. If inflation is to be avoided, the necessary restraint must reduce consumption or investment. If the impact is on consumption, taxpayers will have in effect exchanged a collective good or service for current consumption. If the impact is on private or public investment, later generations will be worse off to the extent that the rate of growth of productive capacity has been reduced.

Since the federal government usually runs surpluses when the economy is at full employment (see Figure 4), there is little likelihood that the federal debt added in peacetime will be burdensome in an economic sense. Deficits incurred to restore or maintain full employment raise output and employment and actually increase the resources available to current and later generations.

The existence of the national debt does mean that interest must be paid to holders of the debt, and tax rates are therefore higher than they would be without the debt. The transfer of interest from general taxpayers to bondholders is a burden on the economy if the taxes levied to pay interest on the debt reduce saving or lower economic efficiency. (If the government debt is paid back by a per capita tax—which has no effect on economic incentives—and the market for bonds is competitive, the debt is exactly equivalent to the tax receipts and therefore does not impose a burden on future generations.) In any case, the debt burden in the United States must be small because net interest payments represent a relatively small proportion of federal expenditures (6 percent in 1969). Moreover, the ratio of net federal debt to the GNP has been declining since the end of World War II (Figure

5), and interest payments on the net debt, which fell markedly in the early postwar years, have amounted to only slightly more than 1 percent of GNP since the early 1950s. The growth of the economy over this period has kept the burden of the debt in relation to total production from rising, even though the interest rates at which debt can be issued have shown a rising trend over the entire period.

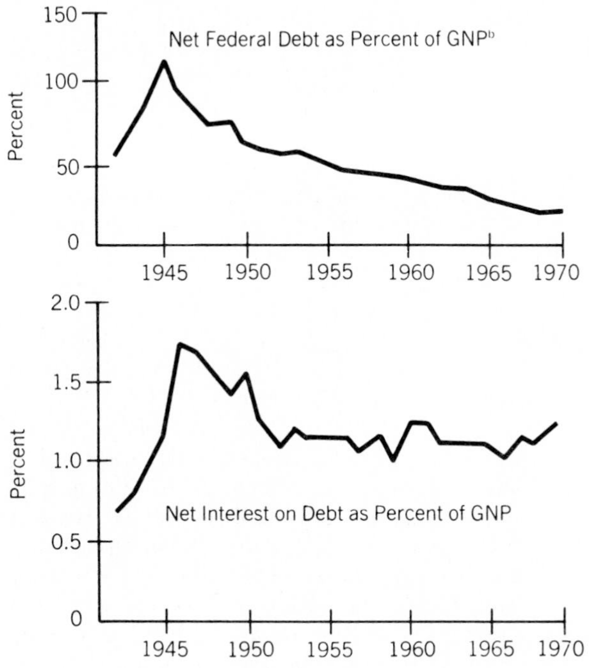

Sources: Net federal debt: *Economic Report of the President, February 1970*, p. 255. Net interest: 1946–69: Interest payments to the public shown in *The Budget of the United States Government*, various years, or supplied (for 1967–69) by the U.S. Bureau of the Budget, less Federal Reserve bank earnings on U.S. government securities by fiscal years (supplied by Board of Governors of the Federal Reserve System); 1942–45: Estimated from data in *Federal Reserve Bulletins*. Gross national product: *Survey of Current Business*, July 1970, pp. 8, 17; *The Budget of the United States Government, Fiscal Year 1971*, p. 593; and *The Budget of the United States Government, Fiscal Year 1969*, p. 544.

Net federal debt is debt held outside U.S. government investment account and Federal Reserve banks. Interest on net federal debt is total interest payments to the public less interest earned by Federal Reserve Banks.

Net federal debt at the end of calendar years divided by fiscal year gross national product.

FIGURE 5. Relation of Net Federal Debt and Net Interest on Debt to the Gross National Product, Fiscal Years 1942–69

13

Deficit, Deficit, Who's Got the Deficit?

JAMES TOBIN

James Tobin is Sterling Professor of Economics at Yale University. This article was first published in The New Republic *in 1963.*

For every buyer there must be a seller, and for every lender a borrower. One man's expenditure is another's receipt. My debts are your assets, my deficit your surplus.

If each of us was consistently "neither borrower nor lender," as Polonius advised, no one would ever need to violate the revered wisdom of Mr. Micawber. But if the prudent among us insist on running and lending surpluses, some of the rest of us are willy-nilly going to borrow to finance budget deficits.

In the United States today one budget that is usually left holding a deficit is that of the federal government. When no one else borrows the surpluses of the thrifty, the Treasury ends up doing so. Since the role of debtor and borrower is thought to be particularly unbecoming to the federal government, the nation feels frustrated and guilty.

Unhappily, crucial decisions of economic policy too often reflect blind reactions to these feelings. The truisms that borrowing is the counterpart of lending and deficits the counterpart of surpluses are overlooked in popular and Congressional discussions of government budgets and taxes. Both guilt feelings and policy are based on serious misunderstanding of the origins of federal budget deficits and surpluses.

American *households* and *financial institutions* consistently run financial surpluses. They have money to lend, beyond their own needs to borrow. Figure 1 shows the growth in their combined surpluses since the war; it also shows some tendency for these surpluses to rise in periods of recession and slack business activity. Of course, many private households have financial deficits. They pay out more than their incomes for food, clothing, cars, appliances, houses, taxes, and so on. They draw on savings accounts, redeem savings bonds, sell securities, mortgage houses, or incur installment debt. But deficit households are far outweighed by surplus households. As a group American *households* and *nonprofit institutions* have in recent years shown a net financial surplus averaging about $15 billion a year—that is, households are ready to lend, or to put into equity investments, about $15 billion a year more than they are prepared to borrow. In addition, *financial institutions* regularly generate a lendable surplus, now of the order of $5 billion a year. For the most part these institutions—banks, savings and loan associations, insurance companies, pension funds, and the like—are simply intermediaries which borrow and relend the public's money. Their surpluses result from

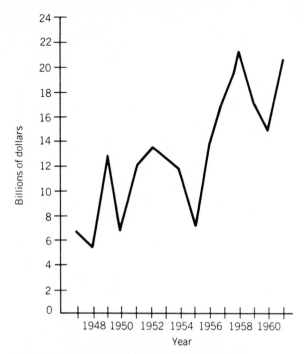

Source: Board of Governors of the Federal Reserve System

FIGURE 1. **Financial Surpluses of Consumers, Non-profit Institutions, and Financial Institutions, 1947–61.**

the fact that they earn more from their lending operations than they distribute or credit to their depositors, shareowners, and policyholders.

Who is to use the $20 billion of surplus funds available from households and financial institutions? *State and local governments* as a group have been averaging $3–4 billion a year of net borrowing. Pressures of the expanding populations of children, adults, houses, and automobiles, plus the difficulties of increasing tax revenues, force these governments to borrow in spite of strictures against government debt. *Unincorporated businesses,* including farms, absorb another $3–4 billion. To the rest of the world we can lend perhaps $2 billion a year. We cannot lend abroad—net—more than the surplus of our exports over our imports of goods and services, and some of that surplus we give away in foreign aid. We have to earn the lendable surplus in tough international competition. Recent experience shows clearly that when we try to lend and invest too much money abroad, we either have to borrow it back or else pay in gold.

These borrowers account for $8–10 billion. The remainder—some $10–12 billion—must be used ei-

ther by *nonfinancial corporate business* or by the *federal government.* Only if corporations as a group take $10–12 billion of external funds, by borrowing or issuing new equities, can the federal government expect to break even. This is, moreover, an under-statement of what is required to keep the federal debt from rising, for the federal government itself provides annually $3 to $4 billion of new lending; the Treasury would have to borrow to finance these federal lending programs even if the government absorbed no *net* funds from the economy. It is *gross* federal borrowing that offends the conservative fiscal conscience, whether or not the proceeds are used to acquire other financial assets.

The moral is inescapable, if startling. If you would like the federal deficit to be smaller, the deficits of business must be bigger. Would you like the federal government to run a surplus and reduce its debt? Then business deficits must be big enough to absorb that surplus as well as the funds available from households and financial institutions.

That does not mean that business must run at a loss—quite the contrary. Sometimes, it is true, unprofitable businesses are forced to borrow or to spend financial reserves just to stay afloat; this was a major reason for business deficits in the depths of the Great Depression. But normally it is businesses with good profits and good prospects that borrow or sell new shares of stock, in order to finance expansion and modernization. As the President of American Telephone and Telegraph can testify, heavy reliance on outside funds, far from being a distress symptom, is an index and instrument of growth in the profitability and worth of the corporation. The incurring of financial deficits by business firms—or by households and governments for that matter—does not usually mean that such institutions are living beyond their means and consuming their capital. Financial deficits are typically the means of accumulating nonfinancial assets—real property in the form of inventories, buildings, and equipment.

When does business run big deficits? When do corporations draw heavily on the capital markets ? The record is clear: when business is very good, when sales are pressing hard on capacity, when businessmen see further expansion ahead. Though corporations' internal funds—depreciation allowances and plowed-back profits—are large during boom times, their investment programs are even larger.

Figure 2 shows the financial deficits or surpluses of corporate business and of the federal government since the war. Three facts stand out. First, the federal government has big deficits when corporations run surpluses or small deficits and vice versa. Second, government surpluses and business deficits reach their peaks in periods of economic expansion, when industrial capacity is heavily utilized, as in 1947–48, 1951–52, and 1956–57. Third, the combined deficit of corporate business and the federal government is greater now than in the early postwar years; this is the counterpart of the upward trend in available surpluses shown in Figure 1.

Recession, idle capacity, unemployment, economic slack—these are the enemies of the balanced government budget. When the economy is faltering, households have more surpluses available to lend, and business firms are less inclined to borrow them.

The federal government will not succeed in cutting its deficit by steps that depress the economy, perpetuate excess capacity, and deter business firms from using outside funds. Raising taxes and cutting expenses seem like obvious ways to balance the budget. But because of their effects on private spending, lending, and borrowing, they may have exactly the contrary result. Likewise, lowering taxes and raising government expenditures may so stimulate private business activity and private borrowing that the federal deficit is in the end actually reduced.

This may seem paradoxical, and perhaps it is. Why is it that the homely analogy between family finance and government finance, on which our decisive national attitudes toward federal fiscal policy are so largely based, misleads us? If John Jones on Maple Street is spending $8,700 a year but taking in only $8,000, the remedy is clear. All Mr. Jones need do to balance the family budget is to live resolutely within his income, either spending some $700 less or working harder to increase his earnings. Jones can safely ignore the impact of either action on the incomes and expenditures of others and the possible ultimate feedback on his own job and income. The situation of the President on Pennsylvania Avenue, spending $87 billion a year against tax revenues of $80 billion is quite different. Suppose that he spends $7 billion less, or tries through higher tax rates to boost federal revenues by $7 billion. He cannot ignore the inevitable boomerang effect on federal finances. These measures will lower taxpayers' receipts, expenditures, and taxable incomes. The federal deficit will be reduced by much less than $7 billion; perhaps it will even be increased.

Incidentally, many of the very critics who are most vocal in chiding the government for fiscal sin advocate policies that would make fiscal virtue even more

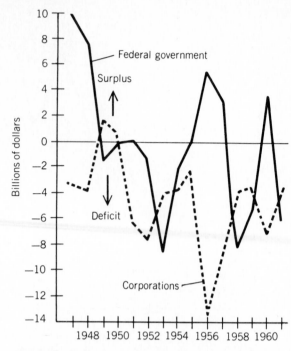

Source: Board of Governors of the Federal Reserve System

FIGURE 2. Net Financial Surpluses and Deficits of the Federal Government and of Nonfinancial Corporations, 1947–61

elusive. They want to keep private borrowing in check by the use of tight credit policies and high interest rates. They want to increase corporations' *internal* flow of funds by bigger depreciation allowances and higher profit margins, making business still less dependent on external funds to finance investment, even in boom times. When these apostles of sound finance also tell the government to shun external finance, have they done their arithmetic? If everyone is self-financing, who will borrow the surpluses?

The nation is paying a high price for the misapplied homely wisdom that guides federal fiscal policy. The real toll is measured by unemployment, idle capacity, lost production, and sluggish economic growth. But fiscal conservatism is also self-defeating. It does not even achieve its own aim, the avoidance of government deficits. Federal fiscal and monetary policies consciously and unashamedly designed to stimulate the economy would have sufficient justification in economic expansion itself. But they might well "improve" the federal budget too—by inducing business to use the private surpluses that now have no destination other than a rising federal debt.

14

Economic Forecasting and Science

PAUL A. SAMUELSON

Paul A. Samuelson is Institute Professor at Massachusetts Institute of Technology. This paper appeared in the Michigan Quarterly Review *in 1965.*

If prediction is the ultimate aim of all science, then we forecasters ought to award ourselves the palm for accomplishment, bravery, or rashness. We are the end-product of Darwinian evolution and the payoff for all scientific study of economics. Around the country, students are grinding out doctoral theses by the use of history, statistics, and theory—merely to enable us to reduce the error in our next year's forecast of GNP from $10 billion down to $9 billion.

Just as ancient kings had their soothsayers and astrologers, modern tycoons and prime ministers have their economic forecasters. Eastern sorcerers wore that peaked hat which in modern times we regard as a dunce's cap; and I suppose if the head fits, we can put it in.

Actually, though, I am not sure that the ultimate end of science is prediction—at least in the sense of unconditional prediction about what is likely to happen at a specified future date. Students are always asking of professors, "If you are so smart, how come you ain't rich?" Some of our best economic scientists seem to be fairly poor forecasters of the future. One of our very best economists, in fact, couldn't even correctly foresee the results of the last election. Is it legitimate to ask of a scholar: "If you are so scientific and learned, how come you are so stupid at predicting next year's GNP?"

I think not, and for several different reasons. In the first place, a man might be a brilliant mathematician in devising methods for the use of physicists and still be a very poor physicist. Or he might be a genius in devising statistical methods while still being rather poor at conducting statistical investigations. Let us grant then at the beginning, that a person might be poor himself at *any* predictions within a field, and still be a useful citizen. Only we would then call him a mathematician—rather than simply a physicist, statistician, or economist.

The late Sir Ronald Fisher, for instance, was a genius, as we all gladly acknowledge. And perhaps he did good empirical work in the field of agronomy and applied fertilizer. But I must say that his work on genetics—in which he blithely infers the decline of Roman and of all civilizations from the dastardly habit infertile heiresses have of snatching off the ablest young men for mates, thereby making them infertile—seems awfully casual statistical inference to me. And I can't think Fisher covered himself with immortal glory at the end of his life when he doubted that cigarette smoking and inhaling has anything to do with reducing longevity.

Yet even a good economist or physicist may be a bad predictor—if we want simply an ability to forecast the future. My old teacher, Joseph Schumpeter, was by anyone's admission a pretty good economist. But I would certainly not have trusted him to predict next year's income or tomorrow's stock market. His vision was focussed to a different distance. He could tell you what was going to happen to capitalism in the next fifty years, even though he often had to ask his wife twice for the time of day. Of course, the inability to predict well does not thereby make a man a better economist. Schumpeter would not have been soiled if he had been able to make shrewd guesses about the near future.

A good scientist should be good at *some* kind of prediction. But it need not be flat prediction about future events. Thus, a physicist may be bad at telling you what the radioactivity count in the air will be next year, but be very good at predicting for you what will be the likely effects on air pollution of a given controlled experiment involving fissionable materials. If he is a master scientist, his hunches about experiments never yet performed may be very good ones.

Similarly, a good economist has good judgment about economic reality. To have good judgment means you are able to make good judgments—good predictions about what will happen under *certain specified conditions*. This is different from having a model that is pretty good at doing mechanical extrapolation of this year's trends of GNP to arrive at respectable guesses of next year's GNP. Time and again your naive model may win bets from me in office pools on next year's outcome. But neither of us would ever dream of using such a naive model to answer the question, "What will happen to GNP, compared to what it would otherwise have been, when the Kennedy-Johnson massive tax cut is put into effect?" The mechanical, naive model does not have in it, explicitly, the parameter tax rates. And if we insist upon differentiating the result with respect to such a parameter, we will end up with a zero partial derivative and with the dubious conclusion that massive tax cuts cannot have any effect on GNP. The model that I use, which is perhaps very nonmechani-

cal and perhaps even non-naive, may be bad at predicting unconditionally next year's GNP, and still be very good at answering the other-things-equal question of the effect of a change in tax rates or in some other structural parameter of the system.

What I have been saying here can be put in technical language: to make good year-to-year predictions, you need not necessarily have accomplished good "identification" of the various structural relations of a model. And conversely, to be a scientist skilled in making predictions about various hypothetical structural changes in a system, you do need to have what Haavelmo, Koopmans, and others call "identification," of the type that is by no means necessarily contained in models that perform well in ordinary predictions.

Is it possible to have everything good?—to be able to make good annual predictions as well as good predictions of identified structural relationships? The best economists I have known, in the best years of their lives, were pretty good at making just such predictions. And that is what I call good judgment in economics.

Obviously, they have to be men of much experience. In the last analysis, empirical predictions can be made only on the basis of empirical evidence. But it is an equal empirical truth that the facts do not tell their own story to scientists or historical observers, and that the men who develop top-notch judgment have an analytical framework within which they try to fit the facts. I should say that such men are constantly using the evidence of economic time series; the evidence of cross-sectional data; the evidence of case studies and anecdotes, but with some kind of judgment concerning the frequency and importance of the cases and instances. And they are even using conjectures of the form, "What if I were no smarter than these businessmen and unionists? What would I be likely to do?"

We all know the great statistical problems involved in the small samples economic statisticians must work with. We have few years of data relevant to the problem at hand. Maybe the data can be found by months or by quarters; but since there is much serial correlation between adjacent monthly data, we can by no means blithely assume that we have increased our degrees of freedom twelvefold or more by using monthly data. Nature has simply not performed the controlled experiments that enable us to predict as we should wish.

This means that the master economist must piece together, from all the experience he has ever had, hunches relevant to the question at hand.

If science becomes a private art, it loses its characteristic of reproducibility. Here is an example. Sumner Slichter, from 1930 to his death in the late 1950s, was a good forecaster. Dr. Robert Adams of Standard Oil (New Jersey), comparing different methods of forecasting, found that "being Sumner Slichter" was then about the best. But how did Slichter do it? I could never make this out. And neither, I believe, could he. One year he talked about Federal Reserve policy, another year about technical innovation. Somehow the whole came out better than the sum of its parts. Now what I should like to emphasize is that the private art of Sumner Slichter died with him. No less-gifted research assistant could have had transferred to him even a fraction of the Master's skill. And thus one of the principal aims of science was not achieved—namely, reproducibility by any patient person of modest ability of the empirical regularities discerned by luck or by the transcendental efforts of eminent scholars.

The models of Klein, Goldberger, Tinbergen, and Suits have at least this property. Take away Frankenstein and you still have a mechanical monster that will function for awhile. But unlike the solar system, which had to be wound up by Divine Providence only once, any economic model will soon run down if the breath of intelligent life is not pumped into it. When you see a 7094 perform well in a good year, never forget that it is only a Charlie McCarthy; without an Edgar Bergen in the background it is only a thing of paint and wood, of inert transistors and obsolescing matrices.

How well can economists forecast? The question is an indefinite one, and reminds us of the man who was asked what he thought about his wife, and had to reply, "Compared to what?"

When I say that as an economist I am not very good at making economic forecasts, that sounds like modesty. But actually, it represents the height of arrogance. For I know that bad as we economists are, we are better than anything else in heaven and earth at forecasting aggregate business trends—better than gypsy tea-leaf readers, Wall Street soothsayers and chartist technicians, hunch-playing heads of mail order chains, or all-powerful heads of state. This is a statement based on empirical experience. Over the years I have tried to keep track of various methods of forecasting, writing down in my little black book what people seemed to be saying before the event, and then comparing their prediction with what happened. The result has been a vindication of the hypothesis that there is no efficacious substitute for economic analysis in business forecasting. Some maverick may hit a home run on occasion; but over the long season, batting averages tend to settle down to a sorry level when the more esoteric methods of soothsaying are relied upon.

What constitutes a good batting average? That depends on the contest. In baseball these days, .300, or 300-out-of-1,000, is very good. In economic forecasting of the direction of change, we ought to be able to do at least .500 just by tossing a coin. And taking advantage of the undoubted upward trend in all modern economies, we can bat .750 or better just by parrotlike repeating, "Up, Up." The difference between the men and the boys, then, comes between an .850 performance and an .800 performance. Put in other terms, the good forecaster, who must in November make a point-estimate of GNP for the calendar year ahead, will, over a decade, have an average error of perhaps one percent. And a rather poor forecaster may, over the same period, average an error of 1-1/2 percent. When we average the yearly results for a decade, it may be found that in the worst year the error was over 2 percent, compensated by rather small errors in many of the years not expected to represent turning points.

In a sense this is a modest claim. But again I must insist on the arrogance underlying these appraisals. For I doubt that it is possible, on the basis of the evidence now knowable a year in advance, to do much better than this. It is as if Nature does not even begin to toss the dice upon which next year's fate will depend by November of this year. There is then nothing that the clever analyst can peek at to improve his batting average beyond some critical level.

I do not mean to imply that this critical level is fixed for all time. Once our profession got new surveys of businessmen's intentions to invest, of their decisions as to capital appropriations, and of consumers' responses to random polling, the critical level of imprecision was reduced. In all likelihood, the critical level of uncertainty is a secularly declining one. But is its asymptote (for forecasting a year ahead, remember) literally zero? I do not know how to answer this question. Although it may seem pessimistic to give a negative answer, I am tempted to do so. For remember, you cannot find what is in a person's mind by interrogation, before there is anything in his mind. That is why preliminary surveys of the McGraw-Hill type, taken in October before many corporations have made their capital-budgeting decisions, are necessarily of limited accuracy—which does not deny that they are of some value to us.

The imprecision inherent in forecasting raises some questions about the propriety of making simple point-estimates. If you twist my arm, you can make me give a single number as a guess about next year's GNP. But you will have to twist hard. My scientific conscience would feel more comfortable giving you my subjective probability distribution for all the values of GNP. Actually, it is a pain in the neck to have to work out the whole probability distribution rather than to give a single point-estimate. But satisfying one's scientific conscience is never a very easy task. And there is some payoff for the extra work involved.

For one thing, just what does a point-estimate purport to mean? That is often not clear even to the man issuing it. Do I give the number at which I should just be indifferent to make a bet *on either side,* is forced to risk a large sum of money on a bet whose side can be determined by an opponent or by a referee using chance devices? If that is what I mean in issuing a point-estimate, I am really revealing the *median* of my subjective probability distribution. Other times estimators have in the back of their minds that over the years they will be judged by their mean-square-error, and hence it is best for them to reveal the *arithmetic mean* of their subjective distribution.

I have known still others who aimed, consciously or unconsciously, at the mode of their distribution—sometimes perhaps using the modal value of forecasts among all their friends and acquaintances as the way of arriving at their own mode. Warning: the distribution of all point-estimates issued from a hundred different banks, insurance companies, corporations, government agencies, and academic experts is usually more bunched than the defensible *ex ante* subjective probability distribution any one of them should use in November. This is illustrated by a story I heard Roy Blough once tell at a Treasury meeting. He said: "Economic forecasters are like six eskimos in one bed; the only thing you can be sure of is that they are all going to turn over together." Blough is right. In a few weeks time one often sees all the forecasts revised together upward or downward.

The difference between median, mean, and mode is not very significant if our expected distributions are reasonably symmetrical. But often they are not: often it will be easier to be off by $15 billion through being too pessimistic rather than too optimistic. Making your soothsayer provide you with a probability range may seem to be asking him to be more pretentiously accurate than he can be. But that is not my interpretation: using the language of arithmetical probability is my way of introducing and emphasizing the degree of uncertainty in the procedure, not its degree of finicky accuracy. There is a further advantage of using probability spreads rather than single point-estimates. One of the whizziest of the Whiz Kids in the Pentagon told me that they get better point estimates from Generals and Admirals if they make them always give high and low estimates. Before, you could never be sure whether some conservative bias or discount was not already being applied to data. Henri Theil of Rotterdam has studied how well forecasters perform and has found a similar tendency toward conservative bias in economic forecasters.

Suppose we think that GNP is likely to rise, say by $30 billion. If we issue the forecast of a rise of $20 billion, we shall certainly have been in the right direction. And we shall be in the ball park with respect to general magnitude. Why be hoggish and try for better? Particularly since GNP might go down, and then you would be standing all alone out there in right field, more than $30 billion off the mark. "Better be wrong in good company, than run the risk of being wrong all alone" is a slogan that every Trustee knows to represent wisdom for his actions.

But here I am talking about science, not about gamesmanship for the forecaster. Gamesmanship introduces a whole new set of considerations. Many forecasters, particularly amateurs, don't really care whether they turn out to be wrong or by how much they turn out to be wrong. They want to tell a good story. To amateurs it usually does not matter by how much you are wrong. The only prize is to be at the top. In science and in real economic life, it is terribly important not to be wrong by much. To be second-best year after year in a stock-portfolio competition would be marvelous for a mutual fund manager, and especially where the first-place winners are a shifting group of crapshooters who stake all on one whim or another.

As an economic scientist, I take economic forecasting with deadly seriousness. I hate to be far wrong. Every residual is a wound on my body. And I'd rather make two small errors, than be right once at the cost of being wrong a second time by the sum of the two errors. The reason is not vanity—because forecasting serves a purpose: each dollar of error costs something in terms of corporate or national policy: and if the "loss function" or "social welfare function" is a smooth one in the neighborhood of its optimum, it will be the square of the error of forecast that gives a rough measure of local error.

If we use mean-square-error as our criterion of fit, I think it will be found that forecasters have another persistent bias, namely a tendency to be too pessimistic. This is different from the conservatism that makes forecasters shade both their upward and downward forecasts below the true magnitude. Why is there this downward bias? First, because it is never easy to know where next year's dollar is going to come from, and many forecasters try to build up their total by adding up the elements that they can see. There is a second, perhaps more defensible, reason for erring on the downward or pessimistic side in making a forecast. The social consequences of unemployment and underproduction may be deemed more serious than those of over-full-employment and (mild) demand inflation. I once shocked the late John Maurice Clark at a meeting in Washington by saying, "Although the chance of a recession next year is only one-third, for policy purposes we should treat it as if it were two-thirds." He thought that a contradiction in terms. But in terms of his colleague Wald's loss-function concept, I could make sense of my statement by postulating that each dollar of deflationary gap had social consequences more serious than each dollar of inflationary gap.

Often a forecaster is forced to give a single point-estimate because his boss or consumers cannot handle a more complicated concept. Then he must figure out for himself which point-estimate will do them the most good, or the least harm. Years ago one of the publishing companies used to have every staff member make a prediction of the sales each textbook would enjoy. If people tried to play safe and guess low figures, the President of the company would penalize them for having too little faith in the company's sales staff and authors. (Incidentally, the sales manager used to come up with the least inaccurate predictions, odd as that may sound.)

A good speech should tell the audience something that it already knows to be true. Then having gained their good approval for soundness, it should tell them something they didn't previously know to be true. I don't know whether I have been able to complete the second part of this recipe, but I want to add a third requirement for a good speech. It should call attention to some problem whose true answer is not yet known. Let me conclude, therefore, by raising an unanswered question.

Naive models based upon persistence, momentum, or positive serial correlation do rather well in economics as judged by least-square-error of predictions. An extreme case is one which merely projects the current level or the current direction of change. Yet such models do badly in "calling turning points." Indeed, as described above, such naive models are like the Dow System of predicting stockmarket prices, which never even tries to call a turning point in advance and is content to learn, not too long after the fact, that one has actually taken place.

Forecasters regard models which merely say, "Up and up," or "more of the same," as rather dull affairs. When I once explained to editors of a financial magazine that one disregarded this continuity only at one's risk, they said: "Professor, that may be good economic science, but it's darn dull journalism." But are we forecasters here to have a good time? Dullness may be part of the price we must pay for good performance. More than that? Are we here to cater to our own vanity? One hates to be wrong; but if one's average error could be reduced at the cost of being more often wrong in direction, is that not a fair bargain?

I don't pretend to know the answer to these questions. But they do have a bearing on the following issue. Often an economist presents a model which he admits does worse than some more naive model, but which he justifies for its better fit at the turning points. Is this emphasis legitimate? That question I leave open.

Is policy action most important at the turning points? Is policy action most potent at the turning points? Is a correct guess about turning points likely to lead to correct guesses for the next several quarters? And if so, why doesn't this importance of accuracy of the turning points already get duly registered in the minimum-squared-error criterion? The whole notion of a turning point would be changed in its timing if we shifted, as many dynamic economies in Europe have to do, to changes in direction of trend-deviations rather than changes in absolute direction as insisted on by the National Bureau. Does this lack of invariance cast doubt on the significance of turning points?

Finally, is it possible that public preoccupation with

economics is greatest at the turning point and that we are essentially catering to our own vanity and desire for publicity when we stress accuracy at such times?

I promised to end up with a question, and I find by count that I have ended up with seven. I guess that is what practical men must expect when they invite an academic theorist to give a lecture.

But for all that, to the scientific forecaster I say, "Always study your residuals." Charles Darwin, who lived before the age of Freud, made it a habit to write down immediately any arguments *against* his theory of evolution, for he found that he invariably tended to forget those arguments. When I have steeled myself to look back over my past economic forecasts in the London *Financial Times*, they have appeared to be a little less prescient than I had remembered them to be. Janus-like, we must look at the past to learn how to look into the future.

After I had made some innocent remarks like this in my 1961 Stamp Memorial Lecture at the University of London, I ran into Professor Frank Paish, himself one of England's best economic forecasters.

"Great mistake ever to look back," he quipped, "you'll lose your nerve."

This is almost precisely what the great Satchel Paige of baseball said. "Never look backward. Somebody may be gaining on you."

Like Sir Winston, I bring you blood, sweat, and tears. The way of the scientific forecaster is hard. Let Lot's wife, who did look back, be your mascot and guide. What Satchel Paige didn't mention is that "they may be gaining on you anyway." Know the truth—and while it may not make you free—it will help rid you of your amateur standing.

15

The Explosion of Economic Information

WALTER S. SALANT

Walter S. Salant is Senior Fellow Emeritus at the Brookings Institution. This article is part of a compendium of papers submitted to the Joint Economic Committee of Congress, November 28, 1980.

One of the most dramatic changes during the past fifty years has been the vast expansion of information about virtually all the national economies.

Consider the United States. In 1929 we had monthly data on foreign trade, industrial production, wholesale prices, and retail food prices. But a comprehensive index of consumer prices was available only semiannually. Estimates of employment and payrolls (but not hours worked) were available, but for manufacturing only. Inventory figures were available, but for department stores only; retail sales also, but only for department stores, chain stores, and mail order houses. Federal government receipts and expenditures were known for short periods, but those of state and local governments were not. Commercial banking statistics for all banks were also collected and published, but regularly only for the ends of June and December, plus one or two other dates during a year if the appropriate authorities called for them. Weekly data for commercial banks were available, but only for banks that were members of the Federal Reserve System. The data that were available varied greatly in quality, and the more comprehensive series were published too long after the dates to which they related to be useful for decisions about short-period policy.

There were no official data on unemployment. Private estimates were diverse and crude, and became available only long after the period to which they related. The figures we now use for unemployment during the Great Depression were not available at the time; they were estimated only much later. There were no comprehensive data on national income and product or on most of its components until 1934, when Simon Kuznets's estimates for 1929–1932 were published. There were no comprehensive data on wholesale trade, services, or construction activity, except employment data at ten-year intervals.

In nearly all other countries even less information was available fifty years ago, with the possible exceptions of Germany, the Netherlands, and some of the Scandinavian countries. For some advanced countries it was not possible, even in the early postwar years, to get national income and product estimates for several preceding years. In 1929 official estimates of annual national income were provided in only four countries (Australia, Canada, the Soviet Union, and

Greece), and private estimates had appeared for twelve others. Moreover few if any of these estimates were current. By 1955 estimates were available for eighty or more countries. Now, for nearly all countries, the reporting is regular and frequent, and for most countries it includes estimates of both output and expenditure by sectors of the economy. Such estimates, once regarded by officials in most countries as of merely academic interest, have become central to the planning of fiscal and other policies.

The enormous increase in the sheer quantity of economic information has been accompanied by great improvements in the reliability of estimates and in the speed with which they have become available. This change in the quantity, quality, and timeliness of economic information has been an important change in the past fifty years. Perhaps policies are not wiser, but policy-makers are certainly better informed.

Macroeconomic Theory and Policy

Information is of course only one aspect of knowledge, and this is as true about economics as about any other field of knowledge. Facts without a theoretical framework in which to put them are useless, merely raw materials that cannot result in a product unless there is a means of fabrication, which, in the field of knowledge, we call theory. In the part of it that we call macroeconomic theory, which is concerned with what determines aggregate output, employment, and the general price level, the last fifty years have seen a revolution as important as the one in information.

This revolution has occurred, broadly speaking, in two stages. The first, associated with Keynes's 1936 book *The General Theory of Employment, Interest and Money*, reached a certain point and then ceased to develop. The second, which took off some fifteen years ago and is now still going on, is interpreted by some as refutation and rejection, by others as modification, and by still others as mere elaboration of his theories. It is not necessary, for the purposes of this paper, to enter into a discussion of which view of the relation of current theoretical developments to Keynes's views is correct. It is largely the first of the two stages of the revolution in theory that during the past fifty years has influenced the thought of opinion leaders and the public about what can be done to avoid or remedy widespread depression and unemployment, and has thereby affected the operation of the world economy. About the second stage, it suffices to say that it mod-

ifies crude Keynesian views about policy in ways that are important.

To appreciate the extent of the first stage of change, one has to be old enough to remember—or to have read enough of the economic literature of the 1920s and early 1930s to know—that although there were then some highly developed theories of the business cycle, there existed no theory of what determines aggregate output and employment that was consistent with prevailing long-run theories. The situation at that time was well summarized more than two decades ago by Professor Tibor Scitovsky:

> Let us bear in mind that before the *General Theory* unemployment was regarded as the result of friction, temporary disequilibrium, or the monopoly power of labor unions. This meant that the business cycle had to be explained within a theoretical framework that made no allowance for variations in employment and income. It also meant that business cycle policy had to be formulated without the benefit of a conceptually satisfactory measure of prosperity, such as the level of income or output or employment. . . .
> . . . The great majority of economists settled down to a kind of schizophrenia. They believed in and taught a logically elegant price theory; and at the same time they adhered to a monetary and business cycle theory that was sometimes good, sometimes bad, but always incompatible with their price theory.

The combination of better information and better theory was probably only one of several factors that made economic performance in nearly all market economies after World War II better than that of the decades before the depression of the 1930s: less instability and more rapid rates of growth in output in most countries. I have no doubt that other factors—more obscure and, so far as I know, mainly not identified—have also played a role. But the quality of economic advice now given to policy-makers is, in most if not all countries, considerably more sophisticated than that given fifty years ago, although it is not always right and, whether right or wrong, is not always taken.

I hasten to make clear that in referring to better economic performance I am not ignoring the difficulties that nearly all nations are facing in the form of inflation. Its persistence in recent years, even when aggregate demand is not excessive or is actually declining, has made "stagflation" a household word. It has baffled the economics profession as well as policy-makers and has brought economists into disagreement and low repute. It may appear outrageous, therefore, for anyone to assert that we know more about macroeconomics than we did fifty years ago. Insofar as the assertion relates to our understanding of how the economy works rather than the success of policy, it might be defended on the ground that in many situations economists are agreed as to what needs to be done but that their prescriptions are politically unacceptable. I do not press that proposition, however. Even if true, it is less relevant to the changes that have occurred over the past fifty years than another justification of the assertion: the present problem of stagflation is unprecedented and, insofar as it is not the result of the sharp oligopoly-created rise in the price of oil, it is, in my opinion, at bottom largely a reflection of the gradual development over the postwar years of a widespread public expectation of more or less constant, or at least only moderately interrupted, prosperity and continuing growth of real incomes, which political leaders in democratic countries are unwilling to disappoint.

Why have these expectations developed? The commitments of governments to maintain high employment would not, alone, have led to the expectations that have developed. I attribute those expectations to the experience of substantial stability over several decades. A generation has grown up that has had no other experience. It assumes, whether tacitly or explicitly, that it lives in an ever-expanding economy and that, whenever growth tends to be interrupted, governments will try and will succeed in preventing or minimizing the interruption.

This assumption is probably now in the process of being undermined, but its development over the postwar decades has led to greater demands on governments in nearly all countries. These demands in turn have led nearly all countries to build into their economies a greater number of devices to protect one or another social group and industry, as was noted earlier in the discussion of inflexibilities. The increased downward inflexibility of prices has prevented increases in some prices from being offset by decreases in other prices, giving an upward tilt to the general price level. The failure of price levels to fall in turn has led to widespread expectations of indefinitely continuing inflation, in contrast to the world of fifty years ago, when it was known that price levels could rise for several years at a time but when it was believed, correctly, that they could also fall. In that world there was no precedent in developed countries for continuing peacetime inflation at the rates nearly all of them have experienced in the past decade and a half. The point I wish to make is that, although the persistence

of stagflation is a failure of recent and current economic policy, it does not imply that we have learned nothing about macroeconomic policy in market economies, or that most or all of what we thought we had learned is wrong.

True, much of what we thought we had learned needs to be modified. Some common beliefs that all economists once rejected out of hand as popular fallacies are now thought by many to have become justified by institutional changes, and others are at least suspected of having some validity in the conditions now prevailing. (One example is the idea that even an unchanging degree of monopoly can cause a continuing rise of prices. Another is that a rise in nominal interest rates is pro-inflationary. Economists now recognize that it may have less anti-inflationary effect and more pro-inflationary effect than they once thought, because any effect it has in constraining demand has less downward effect on the price level than it formerly did, while, at least in the United States, the weight given to interest rates in the consumer price index and the effect of changes in that index in raising money wages make it more inflationary than it once was, so that its effect may, on balance, be inflationary.) But some ideas about macroeconomic policy that we had come to think wrong and best forgotten, including some that are now enjoying a revival, are still wrong. The foundation of the current stagflation problem is in large part the success in coping with a major earlier problem. Here, as in other fields of endeavor, success in solving one problem has bred another.

The development of stagflation has led to the second stage of change in the development of views about macroeconomic theory and policy. That stage is now far from completed and the process of change is accompanied by great diversity of opinion. The new developments in theory modify what came to be accepted theory by displacing its assumption that producers and consumers expect the general price level to fall, or at least not to rise, when substantial unemployment exists. Instead, expectations have been introduced explicitly into the theory of what determines aggregate demand for output. The other major new element is the consideration being given to factors that determine supply, which had previously been neglected. (By "supply" economists do not mean merely the quantity of output offered for sale, but the functional relation between the quantity and price of output. Thus economists regard a rise in the price at which an unchanged quantity of goods or services is offered as a decrease in supply; this generally implies that a smaller quantity would be offered at the initial price.) This new attention to the factors determining supply takes into account the expectations of producers and consumers, and it also includes other factors that were neglected by the theory that was so widely held until recently. Examples of such supply factors are, in addition to expectations about future market conditions, the costs of transactions and the costs that buyers and sellers incur in searching for the best offers and bids.

Thus there is now again much controversy and some confusion about macro theory and policy. This confusion is in some ways reminiscent of the situation that existed fifty years ago. But there are important differences. Aside from the fact that the number of professionally competent people trying to think their way through these problems is much larger, and that thanks to work done during the past fifty years their general level of competence is much greater, they share a common framework of thought and, I believe, are coming to general agreement about what points are at issue. Thus the intellectual debate is being conducted at a much higher level of sophistication. And, largely owing to the unprecedented growth and stability of the postwar years, the standards of economic performance that the people of the world expect their economies to attain are much higher. I believe that this fact and the better information, which makes us more aware of failures as well as successes, are responsible for most of our economic problems and frustrations.

PART THREE

Money and Monetary Policy

Changes in the quantity of money have an important effect on total spending and the price level. The resurgence of interest in monetary policy in recent years is due in no small measure to the work of Milton Friedman. In the opening selection, Friedman describes the evidence that, in his opinion, supports his views concerning the way in which money influences the economy. He draws on his own studies of monetary history as well as recent empirical findings by the Federal Reserve Bank of St. Louis. Concluding that one cannot predict economic events well enough to adopt a discretionary monetary policy, Friedman argues in favor of a rule specifying that the money supply should increase at a fixed rate.

Walter W. Heller is skeptical of many of Friedman's conclusions. In the next selection, he begins by saying that he and other Keynesians agree that money matters, but that they do not accept Friedman's postulate that money alone matters; consequently, they would supplement monetary policy with fiscal policy. Heller asks questions like: "Which money-supply indicator do you believe? . . . Don't observed variations in monetary time lags and velocity cast serious doubt on any simple relation between money supply and GNP? Can a rigid monetary rule find happiness in a world beset with rigidities and rather limited adjustment capabilities? That is, is the rigid Friedman rule perhaps a formula made in heaven, which will work only in heaven?"

Arthur M. Okun takes an eclectic view. He begins by saying that "When economists write textbooks or teach introductory students or lecture to laymen, they happily extol the virtues of two lovely handmaidens of aggregate economic stabilization—fiscal policy and monetary policy. But when they write for learned journals or assemble for professional meetings, they often insist on staging a beauty contest between the two. And each judge feels somehow obliged to decide that one of the two entries is just an ugly beast. My remarks here are in the spirit of bigamous devotion rather than invidious comparison. Fiscal policy and monetary policy are both beautiful; we need them both and we should treat them both lovingly."

Carl Christ agrees with those who feel that the money supply should increase at a "slow, steady rate of 3 or 4 percent per year, come what may." Roger Guffey, president of the Federal Reserve Bank of Kansas City, discusses the proposal that the Federal Reserve be made a part of the Treasury. He concludes that "Most national observers would agree that tampering with Federal Reserve independence is fundamentally unwise."

The next paper, published by the Federal Reserve Bank of New York, is an interesting case study of how open market operations are actually carried out by the Fed.

The next paper, taken from the 1977 *Annual Report* of the Federal Reserve Bank of Minneapolis, presents a description of the rational-expectations view of monetary policy. According to this view, "Monetary policy cannot systematically stimulate the economy to lower unemployment rates." The rational-expectations view is relatively new and highly controversial. Only time will tell how much influence it will have.

In the final paper, Lyle Gramley, a member of the Federal Reserve Board, describes recent financial innovations and their effects on monetary policy. He points out that "Financial innovation in the United States . . . has raised questions about the appropriate definition of money . . . and the mechanism by which monetary policy affects economic activity."

16

Monetary vs. Fiscal Policy

MILTON FRIEDMAN

Milton Friedman is at the Hoover Institution of Stanford University. This article comes from his dialogue with Walter W. Heller, Monetary vs. Fiscal Policy, *published in 1969.*

The key source of misunderstanding about the issue of monetary policy, in my opinion, has been the failure to distinguish clearly what it is that money matters for. What I and those who share my views have emphasized is that the quantity of money is extremely important for nominal magnitudes, for nominal income, for the level of income in dollars—important for what happens to prices. It is not important at all, or, if that's perhaps an exaggeration, not very important, for what happens to real output over the long period.

I have been increasingly impressed that much of the disagreement about this issue stems from the fact that an important element in the Keynesian revolution in economics was the notion that prices are an institutional datum determined outside the system. Once you take that view, once you say that prices are somehow determined elsewhere, then the distinction between nominal magnitudes and real magnitudes disappears. The distinction between magnitudes in dollars and magnitudes in terms of goods and services is no longer important.

That is why the qualifications we have always attached to our statements about the importance of money tend to be overlooked. We have always stressed that money matters a great deal for the development of nominal magnitudes, but not over the long run for real magnitudes. That qualification has tended to be dropped and a straw man has been set up to the effect that we say that money is the only thing that matters for the development of the economy. That's an absurd position, of course, and one that I have never held. The real wealth of a society depends much more on the kind of institutional structure it has, on the abilities, initiative, driving force of its people, on investment potentialities, on technology—on all of those things. That's what really matters from the point of view of the level of output. But, how many dollars will that be valued at? When you ask that question, that's where money matters.

Let me turn more directly to the questions: Is fiscal policy being oversold? Is monetary policy being oversold? I want to stress that my answer is yes to both of those questions. I believe monetary policy is being oversold; I believe fiscal policy is being oversold. What I believe is that fine tuning has been oversold. And this is not a new conclusion. It so happens that the facts haven't been inconsistent with them, and, therefore, we haven't had to change them over time.

Just this past week I came across a paper I gave to

the Joint Economic Committee in 1958. I would like to quote from that paper some sentences which expressed my view at that time, and which still express my view today, on the issue of fine tuning, rather than on the separate issues of monetary and fiscal policy.

I said: "A steady rate of growth in the money supply will not mean perfect stability even though it would prevent the kind of wide fluctuations that we have experienced from time to time in the past. It is tempting to try to go farther and to use monetary changes to offset other factors making for expansion and contraction. . . . The available evidence . . . casts grave doubts on the possibility of producing any fine adjustments in economic activity by fine adjustments in monetary policy—at least in the present state of knowledge. . . . There are thus serious limitations to the possibility of a discretionary monetary policy and much danger that such a policy may make matters worse rather than better."

I went on: "To avoid misunderstanding, it should be emphasized that the problems just discussed are in no way peculiar to monetary policy. . . . The basic difficulties and limitations of monetary policy apply with equal force to fiscal policy."

And then I went on: "Political pressures to 'do something' in the face of either relatively mild price rises or relatively mild price and employment declines are clearly very strong indeed in the existing state of public attitudes. The main moral to be drawn from the two preceding points is that yielding to these pressures may frequently do more harm than good. There is a saying that the best is often the enemy of the good, which seems highly relevant. The goal of an extremely high degree of economic stability is certainly a splendid one. Our ability to attain it, however, is limited; we can surely avoid extreme fluctuations; we do not know enough to avoid minor fluctuations; the attempt to do more than we can will itself be a disturbance that may increase rather than reduce instability. But like all such injunctions, this one too must be taken in moderation. It is a plea for a sense of perspective and balance, not for irresponsibility in the face of major problems or for failure to correct past mistakes."

That was a view that I expressed ten years ago, and I do not believe that the evidence of the past ten years gives the lie to that view. I think that the evidence of the past ten years rather reinforces it, rather shows the difficulties of trying to engage in a very fine tuning of economic policy. I would emphasize today even more than I did then my qualifications with respect to monetary policy because thanks fundamentally, I

think, to the difficulties that have been experienced with fiscal policy and to the experience of other countries, there has been an enormous shift in opinion.

Walter Heller says we all know that money matters; it's only a question of whether it matters very much. His saying that is, in itself, evidence of the shift in opinion. Before coming up here today I reread the reports of the Council of Economic Advisers that were published when he was chairman of the Council. I do not believe that anybody can read those reports and come out with the conclusion that they say that money matters significantly. While there was some attention paid to money in those reports, it was very limited.

There has been a tremendous change in opinion on this subject since then. And I am afraid that change may go too far. I share very much the doubts that Mr. Heller expressed about the closeness of the monetary relations. There is a very good relation on the average. But the relation is not close enough, it is not precise enough, so that you can, with enormous confidence, predict from the changes in the money supply in one quarter precisely what's going to happen in the next quarter or two quarters later.

Indeed, that's the major reason why I'm in favor of a rule. If I thought I could predict precisely, well then, to go back to the statement I quoted from, I would be prepared to make fine adjustments to offset other forces making for change. It's precisely because we don't know how to predict precisely that you cannot in fact use monetary policy effectively for this purpose. So I emphasize that my basic view is that what has been oversold is the notion of fine tuning.

Yet, fiscal policy has, in my view, been oversold in a very different and more basic sense than monetary policy. I believe that the rate of change of the money supply by itself—and I'm going to come back to those two words "by itself"—has a very important effect on nominal income and prices in the long run. It has a very important effect on fluctuations in nominal and real income in the short run. That's my basic conclusion about changes in the stock of money.

Now let's turn to fiscal policy. I believe that the state of the government budget matters; matters a great deal—for some things. The state of the government budget determines what fraction of the nation's income is spent through the government and what fraction is spent by individuals privately. The state of the government budget determines what the level of our taxes is, how much of our income we turn over to the government. The state of the government budget has a considerable effect on interest rates. If the federal government runs a large deficit, that means the government has to borrow in the market, which raises the demand for loanable funds and so tends to raise interest rates.

If the government budget shifts to a surplus, that adds to the supply of loanable funds, which tends to lower interest rates. It was no surprise to those of us who stress money that enactment of the surtax was followed by a decline in interest rates. That's precisely what we had predicted and what our analysis leads us to predict. But—and I come to the main point—in my opinion, the state of the budget by itself has no significant effect on the course of nominal income, on inflation, on deflation, or on cyclical fluctuations. . . .

I'd like to call your attention to some [evidence] relevant to the particular issue of the potency of fiscal and monetary policy. Some sixteen years ago, I wrote an article that compared the Civil War to World War I and World War II. The particular question I asked was, "Do you get a better understanding of what happened to prices during those three wars by looking at what was happening to monetary magnitudes, or by looking at what was happening to fiscal magnitudes?" The answer was completely unambiguous. And nobody has since produced any evidence contradicting that analysis. It turns out that you get a very clear, straightforward interpretation of price behavior in those three wars by looking at monetary magnitudes; you do not get an explanation by looking at fiscal magnitudes.

Anna Schwartz and I have studied the relation between monetary magnitude and economic magnitudes over the course of a hundred years, roughly a century. During that period, fiscal policy changed enormously. At the beginning of that period, the government budget was negligible. In the period since World War II, the government budget has been mammoth. And yet we found roughly the same kind of a relationship between monetary and economic magnitudes over the whole of that one-hundred-year period.

If fiscal policy were playing a dominant influence, it should have introduced more variability . . . into the relation between money and income in the later part than in the earlier; but as far as we can see, it's a homogeneous universe.

Third, some years back David Meiselman and I published a study directed specifically at the question, "Do monetary magnitudes or autonomous expenditure magnitudes give you a better interpretation of the movements in nominal income over short periods of time?" That article produced a great controversy and a large number of replies and counterreplies. It's a matter of biblical exegesis to trace through the thrusts and counterthrusts of that controversy though I am sure it would be good for all your souls to do so. But one thing that came out of that controversy is that everybody agreed that the monetary magnitudes did have an important and systematic influence. The complaint that was made against us was that we had gone too far in denying that the autonomous magnitudes exerted an influence.

The most recent study is one by the Federal Reserve Bank of St. Louis in which they have related quarter-to-quarter changes in GNP to changes in monetary totals over prior quarters and also to changes in governmental expenditures and taxes. They have been very thorough. Anything that anybody suggested to them which might be wrong with what they initially did, they have tried out. As a result, they have tried out many of the possible permutations and combinations. They have tried the high-employment budget and they have tried other budget concepts. But I'll refer to their findings about the high-employment budget.

What they have done is to try to see whether the monetary or the fiscal magnitudes play a more consistent and systematic role in explaining the course of GNP change over the period 1952 to 1968.

Let me quote their summary conclusion. They say: "This section tested the propositions that the response of economic activity to fiscal actions relative to monetary actions is (I) larger, (II) more predictable, and (III) faster."

Let me repeat this more explicitly. The proposition they tested was that the response of economic activity to fiscal action was larger, more predictable, and faster than the response of the economy to monetary action. "The results of the tests," they say, "were not consistent with any of these propositions. Consequently, either the commonly used measures of fiscal influence do not correctly indicate the degree and the direction of such influence, or there was no measurable net fiscal influence on total spending in the test period." To put it in simpler terms, what they found—far from there being a proven efficiency of fiscal policy—was that, as a statistical matter, the regression coefficients of the high-employment budget surplus or deficit, if the monetary variables are held constant, were not statistically significant.

17

Is Monetary Policy Being Oversold?

WALTER W. HELLER

Walter W. Heller is Regents' Professor of Economics at the University of Minnesota. During 1961–64, he was Chairman of the Council of Economic Advisers. This article comes from his dialogue with Milton Friedman, Monetary vs. Fiscal Policy, *published in 1969.*

My intent today is neither to praise nor to bury that towering iconoclast Milton Friedman, for to praise him and his works would absorb far too much of my limited time, and to bury him is, in a word, impossible.

At the outset, let's clarify what is and what isn't at issue in this discussion of fiscal-monetary policy. When we do this, I'm afraid that the lines may not be drawn quite as sharply as the journalists, who love a fight and drama, would have us believe with their headlines like "Is Keynes Defunct?"

The issue is *not* whether money matters—we all grant that—but whether *only* money matters, as some Friedmanites, or perhaps I should say Friedmanics, would put it. Or really, whether only money matters *much*, which is what I understand Milton Friedman to say—he is more reasonable than many of the Friedmanites.

It's important in this connection, too, to make clear that the economic policy of the 1960s, the "new economics" if you will, assigns an important role to *both* fiscal and monetary policy. Indeed, the appropriate mix of policies has often been the cornerstone of the argument. It was, for example, early in the 60s,

when we feared that tight money might stunt recovery, might thwart the expansionary impact of the 1962–64 income tax cuts. It was again, in 1966, when in strongly urging a tax increase, we put heavy emphasis on avoiding the ill effects of imposing too much of the burden of restraint on Federal Reserve policy. It was once again, in 1967–68, when we sought the surtax in considerable part to insure against a repetition of the monetary crunch of 1966. And it will be in the future, when full employment surpluses in the federal budget may be the only defensible way to buy the monetary ease that commitment to rapid economic growth implies. In short, to anyone who might fear that the "new economics" is all fiscal policy, the record offers evidence, and the new economists offer assurance, that money *does* matter.

With that straw man removed, we can identify the real monetary issues with which the monetarists confront us: First, should money supply be the sole or primary guide to Federal Reserve policy? Should it, at the very least, be ranged side by side with interest rates and credit availability in the Fed's affections? Second, should we rely on the Federal Reserve authorities to

90

adapt monetary policy flexibly to changing economic events and to shifts in fiscal policy, or should we instead not only enthrone money supply but encase it in a rigid formula specifying a fixed increase of 3, 4, or 5 percent a year?

Again, in the fiscal field, the issue is not *whether* fiscal policy matters—even some monetarists, perhaps in unguarded moments, have urged budget cuts or tax changes for stabilization reasons. The issues are *how much* it matters, and how heavily we can lean on discretionary changes in taxes and budgets to maintain steady economic growth in a dynamic economy: Is the close correlation of activist fiscal policy and strong expansion—which has brought our economy into the narrow band around full employment—a matter of accident or causation?

Pervading these operational issues is a basic question of targets, as yet not answered in any conclusive way by either analysis or evidence. Should the target be, as the Phillips Curve analysis suggests, somewhat less unemployment in exchange for somewhat more price creep? Or is this trade-off illusory, as the adherents of the classical real-wage doctrine are now reasserting? To hark back to words and men of the past—is a little inflation like a little pregnancy? Or was Sumner Slichter prophetic when he said that if we wanted to live with steady full employment and brisk growth, we also had to—and could—live with a little chronic inflation, with a price creep of 2 percent or so a year?

Summing up the key operational issues, they are: Should money be king? Is fiscal policy worth its salt? Should flexible man yield to rigid rules? You will note that I purposely cast these issues in a show-me form to put both the monetarists and the new economists on their mettle.

Let me review with you the factors that say "stop, look, and listen" before embracing the triple doctrine that only money matters much; that control of the money supply is the key to economic stability; and that a rigid fixed-throttle expansion of 4 or 5 percent a year is the only safe policy prescription in a world of alleged economic ignorance and human weakness and folly.

Turning to doubts, unresolved questions, and unconvincing evidence, I group these into eight conditions that must be satisfied—if not completely, at least more convincingly than they have been to date—before we can even consider giving money supply sovereignty, or dominance, or greater prominence in economic policy. These conditions center on such questions as: Which money-supply indicator do

you believe? Can one read enough from money supply without weighing also shifts in demand and interest rates—that is, don't both quantity *and* price of money count? Don't observed variations in monetary time lags and velocity cast serious doubt on any simple relation between money supply and GNP? Can a rigid monetary rule find happiness in a world beset with rigidities and rather limited adjustment capabilities? That is, is the rigid Friedman rule perhaps a formula made in heaven, that will work only in heaven?

The first condition is this: the monetarists must make up their minds which money-supply variable they want us to accept as our guiding star—M_1, the narrow money supply, just currency and bank deposits; M_2, adding time deposits; or perhaps some other measure like the "monetary base?" And when will the monetarists decide? Perhaps Milton Friedman has decided; but if he has, his disciples do not seem to have gotten the word.

Let me give you an example. M_1 (the money stock) was all the rage. It spurted for four months in a row, from April through July. But when that slowed down, most of the alarmists switched horses to M_2 (money plus time deposits), which quite conveniently began rising sharply in July. And listen to the latest release from the St. Louis Federal Reserve Bank—the unofficial statistical arm of the Chicago School—which very carefully throws a sop to all sides: "Monetary expansion since July has decelerated as measured by the money stock, accelerated as measured by money plus time deposits, and remained at about an unchanged rate as measured by the monetary base. As a result, questions arise as to which monetary aggregate may be currently most meaningful in indicating monetary influence on economic activity." Precisely.

It doesn't seem too much to ask that this confusion be resolved in some satisfactory way before putting great faith in money supply as our key policy variable.

Second, I would feel more sympathetic to the money-supply doctrine if it were not so one-track-minded about money stock—measured any way you wish—as the *only* financial variable with any informational content for policy purposes.

If we look at 1967 *only* in terms of the money stock, it would appear as the easiest-money year since World War II. M_1 was up 6 percent, M_2 was up 12 percent. Yet there was a very sharp rise in interest rates. Why? Probably because of a big shift in liquidity preference as corporations strove to build up their protective liquidity cushions after their harrowing experience the previous year—their monetary dehydration in the credit crunch of 1966. Again, the behavior of interest rates is vital to proper interpretation of monetary developments and guidance of monetary policy. Interest rates are endogenous variables and cannot be used alone—but neither can money stock. Either interest rates or money stock, used alone, could seriously mislead us.

The point is that a change in the demand for money relative to the supply, or a change in the supply relative to demand, results generally in a change in interest rates. To insist that the behavior of the price of money (interest rates) conveys no information about its scarcity is, as Tobin has noted, an "odd heresy."

Third, given the fluctuations in money velocity, that supposedly inexorable link between money and economic activity has yet to be established. We should not forget this, however sweet the siren song of the monetarists may sound. We should not forget the revealing passage from that monumental Friedman-Schwartz volume, *A Monetary History of the United States,* that makes my point:

> . . . the observed year-to-year change in velocity was less than 10 percent in 78 out of 91 year-to-year changes from 1869, when our velocity figures start, to 1960. Of the 13 larger changes, more than half came during either the Great Contraction or the two world wars, and the largest change was 17 percent. Expressed as a percentage of a secular trend, velocity was within the range of 90 to 110 in 53 years, 85 to 115 in 66 years. Of the remaining 26 years, 12 were during the first 15 years, for which the income figures are seriously defective, and 17 during the Great Contraction and the two wars.

Clearly, velocity has varied over time—some might say "greatly," others "moderately." Let me sidestep a bit and say, for purposes of this discussion, "significantly."

What Friedman and Schwartz report about the behavior of velocity suggests that there are other factors—strangely, such fiscal actions as tax cuts or budget changes come to mind—that influence the level of economic activity. Velocity has changed, as it were, to accommodate these other influences and will go on doing so, I have no doubt, in the future.

The observed changes in velocity underscore the broader point I was hinting at a moment ago: The Friedman-Schwartz study did not find anything like a near-perfect correlation—a rigid link—between money and economic activity. And such correlation as they did find was based on complex and often quite arbitrary adjustments of their raw data.

Fourth, it would help us if the monetarists could narrow the range on *when* money matters. How long *are* the lags that have to be taken into account in managing monetary policy? Here, I quote from Professor Friedman's tour de force, *A Program for Monetary Stability:*

> In the National Bureau study on which I have been collaborating with Mrs. Schwartz we found that, on the average of 18 cycles, peaks in the rate of change in the stock of money tend to precede peaks in general business by about 16 months and troughs in the rate of change in the stock of money to precede troughs in general business by about 12 months. . . . For individual cycles, the recorded lag has varied between 6 and 29 months at peaks and between 4 and 22 months at troughs.

So the Friedman-Schwartz study found a long average lag, and just as important it would seem, a highly variable lag. But why this considerable variance? No doubt there are several possible answers. But again, the most natural one is that the level of economic activity, or total demand for the nation's output, is influenced by variables other than the stock of money—possibly even by tax rates and federal spending and transfer payments!

Suppose I told you that I had checked and found that in repeated trials, it required from 100 to 300 feet for a car going so and so many miles an hour to stop. That is quite a range. But would you be surprised? I think not. You would simply remind me that the distance it takes a car to stop depends, among other things, on the condition of the road surface. If I had allowed for the condition of the road surface, I would not have ended up with such a wide range of stopping distances.

Just so. If Professor Friedman and Mrs. Schwartz had taken account of other variables that influence total demand, or if they had estimated the lag of monetary policy using a complete model of the U.S. economy, they would not have found the lag of monetary policy to be quite so variable. Again, then, one correctly infers that their findings are quite consistent with fiscal policy mattering, and mattering a great deal.

Professor Friedman has also used this finding of (a) a long average lag, and (b) a highly variable lag in support of his plea for steady growth of the money supply. With so long an average lag, the argument goes, forecasters are helpless; they cannot see twelve or fifteen months into the future with any accuracy. And even if they could, they would be at a loss to know how far ahead to appraise the economic outlook. But I doubt that he can properly draw this inference from his finding of a long and highly variable lag.

It seems to me misleading to estimate a discreet lag as the Friedman-Schwartz team did. It's reasonable to suppose, given the research findings of other investigators, that the effect of a change in monetary policy cumulates through time. To begin, there's a slight effect; and as time passes, the effect becomes more pronounced. But insofar as the feasibility of discretionary monetary policy is at issue, what matters *most* is whether there is some near-term effect. If there is, then the Federal Reserve can influence the economy one quarter or two quarters from now. That there are subsequent, more pronounced, effects is not the key question. These subsequent effects get caught, as it were, in subsequent forecasts of the economic outlook, and current policy is adjusted accordingly. At least this is what happens in a non-Friedmanic world where one enjoys the benefits of discretionary policy changes.

Lest I leave any doubt about what I infer from this: if there is a near-immediate effect from a change in policy, then discretionary monetary policy does not impose an unbearable burden on forecasters. For six or nine months ahead, they can do reasonably well. But given the too-discreet way Friedman-Schwartz went about estimating the lag of monetary policy, I see no way of determining the shape of the monetary policy lag. Until they know more about the shape of this lag, I don't see how they can insist on a monetary rule.

Fifth, I'd be happier if only I knew which of the two Friedmans to believe. Should it be the Friedman we have had in focus here—the Friedman of the close causal relationship between money supply and income, who sees changes in money balances worked off gradually, with long lags before interest rates, prices of financial and physical assets, and, eventually, investment and consumption spending are affected? Or should it be the Friedman of the "permanent-income hypothesis," who sees the demand for money as quite unresponsive to changes in current income (since current income has only a fractional weight in permanent income), with the implied result that the monetary multiplier is very large in the short run, that there is an immediate and strong response to a change in the money stock?

Sixth, if Milton's policy prescription were made in a

frictionless Friedmanesque world without price, wage, and exchange rigidities—a world of his own making—it would be more admissible. But in the imperfect world in which we actually operate, beset by all sorts of rigidities, the introduction of his fixed-throttle money-supply rule might, in fact, be destabilizing. Or it could condemn us to long periods of economic slack or inflation as the slow adjustment processes in wages and prices, given strong market power, delayed the economy's reaction to the monetary rule while policy makers stood helplessly by.

A seventh and closely related concern is that locking the money supply into a rigid rule would jeopardize the U.S. international position. It's quite clear that capital flows are interest-rate sensitive. Indeed, capital flows induced by interest-rate changes can increase alarmingly when speculators take over. Under the Friedman rule, market interest rates would be whatever they turned out to be. It would be beyond the pale for the Fed to adjust interest rates for balance-of-payments adjustment purposes. Milton has heard all of this before, and he always has an answer—flexible exchange rates. Parenthetically, I fully understand that it's much easier to debate Milton in absentia than in person! Yet, suffice it to note that however vital they are to the workings of his money-supply peg, floating exchange rates are not just around the corner.

Eighth, and finally, if the monetarists showed some small willingness to recognize the impact of fiscal policy—which has played such a large role in the policy thinking and action underlying the great expansion of the 1960s—one might be a little more sympathetic to their views. This point is, I must admit, not so much a condition as a plea for symmetry. The "new economists," having already given important and increasing weight to monetary factors in their policy models, are still waiting for signs that the monetarists will admit fiscal factors to theirs.

The 1964 tax cut pointedly illustrates what I mean. While the "new economists" fully recognize the important role monetary policy played in facilitating the success of the tax cut, the monetarists go to elaborate lengths to "prove" that the tax cut—which came close to removing a $13 billion full-employment surplus that was overburdening and retarding the economy—had nothing to do with the 1964–65 expansion. Money-supply growth did it all. Apparently, we were just playing fiscal tiddlywinks in Washington.

It seems to me that the cause of balanced analysis

and rational policy would be served by redirecting some of the brilliance of Friedman and his followers from (a) single-minded devotion to the money-supply thesis and unceasing efforts to discredit fiscal policy and indeed all discretionary policy to (b) joint efforts to develop a more complete and satisfactory model of how the real world works; ascertain why it is working far better today than it did before active and conscious fiscal-monetary policy came into play; and determine how such policy can be improved to make it work even better in the future.

In a related asymmetry, as I've already suggested in passing, some Friedmanites fail to recognize that if fiscal policy actions like the 1964 tax cut can do no good, then fiscal policy actions like the big budget increases and deficits associated with Vietnam can also do no harm. Again, they should recognize that they can't have it both ways.

Now, one could lengthen and elaborate this list. But enough—let's just round it off this way: if Milton Friedman were saying that (as part of an active discretionary policy) we had better keep a closer eye on that important variable, money supply, in one or more of its several incarnations—I would say well and good, by all means. If the manifold doubts can be reasonably resolved, let's remedy any neglect or underemphasis of money supply as a policy indicator relative to interest rates, free reserves, and the like. But let's not lock the steering gear into place, knowing full well of the twists and turns in the road ahead. That's an invitation to chaos.

18

Fiscal and Monetary Policy: An Eclectic Analysis

ARTHUR M. OKUN

Arthur M. Okun was a senior fellow at the Brookings Institution. He was Chairman of the Council of Economic Advisers under President Johnson. This article is taken from his paper in Issues in Fiscal and Monetary Policy, *published in 1971.*

When economists write textbooks or teach introductory students or lecture to laymen, they happily extol the virtues of two lovely handmaidens of aggregate economic stabilization—fiscal policy and monetary policy. But when they write for learned journals or assemble for professional meetings, they often insist on staging a beauty contest between the two. And each judge feels somehow obliged to decide that one of the two entries is just an ugly beast. My remarks here are in the spirit of bigamous devotion rather than invidious comparison. Fiscal policy and monetary policy are both beautiful; we need them both and we should treat them both lovingly.

The General Eclectic Case

In particular, both fiscal and monetary policy are capable of providing some extra push upward or downward on GNP. In fact, if aggregate stimulus or restraint were all that mattered, either one of the two tools could generally do the job, and the second—whichever one chose to be second—would be redundant. The basic general eclectic principle that ought to guide us, as a first approximation, is that either fiscal or monetary policy can administer a required sedative or stimulus to economic activity. As every introductory student knows, however, fiscal and monetary tools operate in very different ways. Monetary policy initially makes people more liquid without adding directly to their incomes or wealth; fiscal policy enhances their incomes and wealth without increasing their liquidity.

In a stimulative monetary action, the people who initially acquire money are not simply given the money; they must part with government securities to get it. But once their portfolios become more liquid, they presumably use the cash proceeds to acquire alternative earning assets, and in so doing they bid up the prices of those assets, or equivalently, reduce the yields. Thus prospective borrowers find it easier and less expensive to issue securities and to get loans; and investors who would otherwise be acquiring securities may be induced instead to purchase real assets such as capital goods. Also, because market values of securi-

95

ties are raised, people become wealthier, if in an indirect way, and may hence increase their purchases of goods and services. Thus many channels run from the easing of financial markets to the quickening of real economic activity.

A stimulative fiscal action is appropriately undertaken when resources are unemployed; in that situation, an action such as expanded government purchases, whether for good things like hospitals or less good things like military weapons, puts resources to work and rewards them with income. The additional cash received by some people is matched by reduced cash holdings of those who bought government securities to finance the outlay. But the securities buyers have no income loss to make them tighten their belts; they voluntarily traded money for near money. In contrast, the income recipients become willing to spend more, and thus trigger a multiplier process on production and income. So, while fiscal and monetary routes differ, the ultimate destination—the effect on national product—is the same, in principle.

Indeed, the conditions under which either fiscal tools or monetary tools, taken separately, have zero effect on GNP are merely textbook curiosities rather than meaningful possibilities in the modern U.S. economic environment. For stimulative monetary policy to be nothing more than a push on a string, either interest rates would have to be just as low as they could possibly go, or investment and consumption would have to show zero response to any further reduction in interest rates. The former possibility is the famous Keynesian liquidity trap, which made lots of sense in describing 1936, but has no relevance to 1971. With prime corporations paying 8 percent on long-term bonds, interest rates are still higher than at any time in my lifetime prior to 1969. There is plenty of room for them to decline, and, in turn, for states and localities, home-buyers and consumer installment credit users, as well as business investors, to be encouraged to spend more by lower costs of credit.

The opposite extreme, impotent fiscal policy, is equally remote. Fiscal policy must exert some stimulative effect on economic activity (even when the monetary policy makers do not accommodate the fiscal action at all) unless the velocity of money is completely inflexible so that no economizing on cash balances occurs. Though the money supply does not rise in a pure fiscal action, spending will tend to rise unless people are totally unable or unwilling to speed up the turnover of cash. And money holders do economize on cash to a varying degree—they do so

seasonally and cyclically, and they do so dependably in response to changes in the opportunity cost of holding money. The holder of zero-yielding cash is sacrificing the opportunity to receive the going interest rates of earning assets. The higher interest rates are, the more he sacrifices; and hence, economic theory tells us, the more he will economize on his holdings of cash.

And the facts confirm the theory. The negative relationship between the demand for money and the rate of interest is one of the most firmly established empirical propositions in macroeconomics. So a pure fiscal stimulus produces a speedup in the turnover of money and higher interest rates, and more GNP.

The fact that people do economize on cash balances in response to rises in interest rates demonstrates the efficacy of fiscal policy. Anybody who reports that he can't find a trace of fiscal impact in the aggregate data is unreasonably claiming an absolutely inflexible velocity of money—a vertical liquidity preference function—or else he is revealing the limitations of his research techniques rather than those of fiscal policy.

A few other artful dodges, I submit, make even less sense. Try to defend fiscal impotence on grounds of a horizontal marginal efficiency schedule—that means investment is so sensitive to return that even the slightest interest variation will unleash unlimited changes in investment demand. Or make the case that people subjectively assume the public debt as personal debt and feel commensurately worse off whenever the budget is in deficit. Or contend that businessmen are so frightened by fiscal stimulation that their increased demand for cash and reduced investment spoils its influence. Or use the argument that Say's law operates even when the unemployment rate is 6 percent. It's a battle between ingenuity and credulity!

The eclectic principle is terribly important, not because it answers any questions, but because it rules out nonsense questions and points to sensible ones. It warns us not to get bogged down in such metaphysical issues as whether it is really the Fed that creates inflation during wartime. Every wartime period has been marked by enormous fiscal stimulus, and yet that fiscal fuel-injection could have been neutralized by some huge amount of pressure on the monetary brakes. In that sense, the Fed could have been sufficiently restrictive to offset the stimulus of military expenditures. Anyone who chooses to blame the resulting inflation on not slamming on the monetary brakes, rather than on pumping the fiscal accelerator, can feel free to exercise that curious preference. Take another example: Did the expansion following the tax cut in 1964–65 result from monetary policy? Of course it did, the eclectic principle tells us. If the Fed had wished to nullify the expansionary influence of the tax cut, surely some monetary policy would have been sufficiently restrictive to do so. There is no unique way of allocating credit or blame in a world where both tools can do the stabilization job.

Side Effects as the Central Issue

So long as both tools are capable of speeding up or slowing down demand, the decisions on how to use them and how to combine them must be made on the basis of criteria other than their simple ability to stimulate or restrain. Nor do we typically get any help by considering *how much* work monetary or fiscal tools do, because usually the right answer is, "as much as needed," providing the shift in policy is large enough. In more formal terms, two instruments and one target produce an indeterminate system.

Of course, there are two basic targets of stabilization policy: price stability and maximum production. But the two tools will not serve to implement those two goals simultaneously. A pen and a pencil are one more tool than is needed to write a letter, but the second tool can't be used to mow the lawn. In the same way, fiscal and monetary policy can both push up aggregate demand or push down aggregate demand, but neither can solve the Phillips curve problem. Subject to minor qualifications, the fiscal route to a given unemployment rate is neither less nor more inflationary than the monetary route to that same unemployment rate.

We can have the GNP path we want equally well with a tight fiscal policy and an easier monetary policy, or the reverse, within fairly broad limits. The real basis for choice lies in the many subsidiary economic targets, beside real GNP and inflation, that are differentially affected by fiscal and monetary policies. Sometimes these are labeled "side effects." I submit that they are the main issue in determining the fiscal-monetary mix, and they belong in the center ring.

Composition of output. One of the subsidiary targets involves the composition of output among sectors. General monetary policy tools, as they are actually employed, bear down very unevenly on the various sectors of the economy. Homebuilding and state and local capital projects are principal victims of monetary restraint. Although the evidence isn't entirely conclusive, it suggests that monetary restraint discriminates particularly against small business. In the field of taxation, we agonize about incidence and equity. The same intense concern is appropriate in the case of monetary restraint and, in fact, increasing concern is being registered in the political arena. In the 1969–70 period of tight money, many efforts were made to insulate housing from the brunt of the attack. But the impact on homebuilding was still heavy. Moreover, there is considerable basis for suspicion that these actions defused—as well as diffused—the impact of monetary restraint. A more restrictive monetary policy, as measured in terms of either monetary aggregates or interest rates, is required to accomplish the same dampening effect on GNP if the sectors most vulnerable to credit restraint are shielded from its blows.

The concern about uneven impact may be accentuated because, in 1966 and again in 1969–70, monetary restraint hit sectors that rated particularly high social priorities. But that is not the whole story. Any unusual departure of monetary policy from a "middle-of-the-road" position may lead to allocations that do not accord with the nation's sense of equity and efficiency. For example, in the early sixties, it was feared that a very easy monetary policy might encourage speculative excesses in building because some financial institutions would be pressured to find mortgage loans in order to earn a return on their assets.

In the last few years, some economists—most notably, Franco Modigliani—have argued that monetary policy may have a significant impact on consumption through its influence on the market value of equity securities and bonds in addition to its more direct impact through the cost and availability of installment credit. In my view, the jury is still out on this issue. On the one hand, it's easy to believe that a huge change, say, $100 billion, in the net worth of the American public, such as stock market fluctuations can generate, could alter consumer spending in relation to income by a significant amount like $3 billion, even though that change in wealth, is concentrated in a small group at the very top of the income and wealth distribution. On the other hand, previous empirical work on this issue came up with a nearly unanimous negative verdict. In 1966 and 1969, however, the timing of stock market declines and the sluggishness in consumer demand seemed to fit fairly well with the hypothesis. One would like to believe the wealth hypothesis because it would suggest that monetary policy has broad and sizable effects on consumption, especially on that of high-income consumers; monetary restraint would then be revealed as less uneven and less inequitable. But before embracing that judgment, one should wait for more decisive evidence.

Interest rates and asset values. Another major consideration in monetary policy is its effects on interest rates and balance sheets. Some economists may argue that the only function of interest rates is to clear the market and the only sense in which rates can be too high or too low is in failing to establish that equilibrium. Every Congressman knows better! Interest rates are a social target. That is the revealed preference of the American public, reflected in the letters it writes to Washington and the answers it gives to opinion polls. And this is no optical illusion on the part of the citizenry. They have the same good reasons to dislike rising interest rates that apply to rising prices—the haphazard, redistributive effects. And they are concerned about *nominal* interest rates just as they are concerned about prices. It is not clear that such major groups as businessmen or workers are particularly hurt or particularly helped by tight money (or by inflation), but the impacts are quite haphazard in both cases. The resulting lottery in real incomes strikes most Americans as unjust.

The largest redistributive effect of tight money, like that of inflation, falls on balance sheets rather than income statements. People care about their paper wealth and feel worse off when bond and equity prices nose dive. Even though society is not deprived of real resources when security prices drop, it is hard to find gainers to match the losers. Although Alvin Hansen stressed the social costs of distorted, fluctuating balance sheets in the 1950s, this issue gets little attention from economists. But it never escapes the broader and keener vision of the American public.

Financial dislocation. A restrictive monetary policy may also have important, dislocating effects on the financial system. The key function of a financial system is to offer people opportunities to invest without saving and to save without investing. If people want risky assets, they can acquire them beyond the extent of their net worth; if they wish to avoid risk, they can earn a moderate return and stay liquid. The trade of funds between lovers of liquidity and lovers of real assets produces gains to all. "Crunch" and "liquidity crisis" are names for a breakdown in the functioning of the financial system. Such a breakdown deprives people of important options and may

permanently impair their willingness to take risks and to hold certain types of assets. To the extent that very tight money curbs an inflationary boom by putting boulders in the financial stream, a considerable price is paid. And to the extent that extremely easy money stimulates a weak economy by opening the flood gates of speculation, that too may be costly.

Balance of payments. The pursuit of a monetary policy focused single-mindedly on stabilization goals would have further "side effects" on the balance of payments, to the extent that it changes international interest rate differentials and hence influences capital flows. There are strong arguments for fundamental reforms of the international monetary system—especially more flexible exchange rates—that would greatly reduce this concern. But those reforms are not on the immediate horizon; nor is the United States prepared to be consistently passive about international payments. Meanwhile, the external deficit casts a shadow that cannot be ignored in the formulation of fiscal-monetary policies.

Growth. A final consideration in the mix of stabilization tools is the long-run influence of monetary policy on the rate of growth of our supply capabilities. An average posture of relatively easy money (and low interest rates) combined with tight fiscal policy (designed especially to put a damper on private consumption) is most likely to produce high investment and rapid growth of potential. That becomes relevant in the short run because the long-run posture of monetary policy is an average of its short-run swings. If, for example, the nation relies most heavily on monetary policy for restraint and on fiscal policy for stimulus, it will unintentionally slip to a lower growth path. The contribution of extra investment to growth and the value of the extra growth to a society that is already affluent in the aggregate are further vital issues. Recently, enthusiasm for growth-oriented policies has been dampened by the concern about the social fallout of rapid growth and by the shame of poverty, which calls for higher current consumption at the low end of the income scale. Nonetheless, the growth implications of decisions about the fiscal-monetary mix should be recognized.

In the light of these considerations, there are good reasons to avoid extreme tightness or extreme ease in monetary policy—even if it produces an ideal path of real output. Tight money can be bad medicine for a boom even if it cures the disease, just as amputation of the hand is a bad remedy for eczema. The experience of 1966 provides an object lesson. Judged by its performance in getting GNP on track, the Federal Reserve in 1966 put on *the* virtuoso performance in the history of stabilization policy. It was the greatest tight-rope walking and balancing act ever performed by either fiscal or monetary policy. Single-handedly the Fed curbed a boom generated by a vastly stimulative fiscal policy that was paralyzed by politics and distorted by war. And, in stopping the boom, it avoided a recession. To be sure, real GNP dipped for a single quarter, but the unemployment rate did not rise significantly above 4 percent; the 1967 pause was as different from the five postwar recessions, including

1970, as a cold is different from pneumonia. Moreover, inflation slowed markedly in the closing months of 1966 and the first half of 1967. What more could anyone want? Yet, you won't find the 1966 Fed team in the hall of fame for stabilization policy. In the view of most Americans, the collapse of homebuilding, the disruption of financial markets, and the escalation of interest rates were evils that outweighed the benefits of the nonrecessionary halting of inflation. The Fed itself reacted by refusing to give an encore in 1967–68, accepting renewed inflation as a lesser evil than renewed tight money.

19

A Critique of U.S. Monetary Policies

CARL CHRIST

Carl Christ is Professor of Economics at Johns Hopkins University. This article comes from his testimony before the Senate Banking Committee in 1975.

The Fed's Short-Run Policies

The Federal Reserve's short-run monetary policy behavior has not changed fundamentally in 30 years. Federal Reserve action has been too much and too late, with respect to the money stock and business cycle fluctuations. In recession after recession, the Federal Reserve has allowed the growth rate of money stock to decline, and in every major recession, including this one, the actual level of the money stock has been allowed to decline. This aggravates recession at the very best.

In recovery after recovery, the Federal Reserve has allowed the growth rate of the money stock to become substantially greater than it was in the previous recession and substantially greater than the 3 or 4 percent a year that would be consistent with price-level stability in the long run. This accelerates the recovery, but it makes it necessary to choose at the completion of the recovery between increased inflation on the one hand and a subsequent recession on the other hand.

The size of the decline allowed by the Federal Reserve in the growth rate of the money stock from a re-

covery period to the subsequent recession is typically between 3 and 6 percentage points on the annual growth rate.

For example, from early 1972 to mid-1974, the Federal Reserve allowed the money stock to grow at an annual rate of 7.4 percent. Then from June 1974 to January 1975, as the recession grew, the Federal Reserve allowed an average growth rate in the money stock of only 1.4 percent, which is 6 percentage points less than during the previous recovery.

We know that an increase in the rate of growth of money stock stimulates the economy and that a decrease in the rate of growth of the money stock depresses the economy, with a lag of about six to eighteen months. Since presently available methods cannot accurately and reliably predict the timing and severity of a recession six to eighteen months ahead, the Federal Reserve cannot use monetary policy effectively to prevent recessions that arise from nonmonetary causes.

If the Federal Reserve waits to increase the growth of the money stock until it is clear there is recession, as in February 1975, there is a grave risk that by the time

100

the effects of that increase come to fruition there will be no further need to combat recession, and indeed by that time the problem is likely to be inflation.

That is why so many economists have urged that the Federal Reserve increase the money stock at a slow, steady rate of 3 or 4 percent a year, come what may. It would avoid the "too much, too late" kind of mistake that the Federal Reserve has been making for thirty years and more, and it would avoid inflation too.

The Fed's Long-Run Policies

The Federal Reserve's long-run policy, unlike its short-run policy, has changed substantially over the last thirty years, and the change has been for the worse, toward inflation.

From the end of World War II until 1962 the Federal Reserve kept the growth rate of the money stock at about 2 percent a year, and prices rose at about that same rate. From 1962 to 1966, the Federal Reserve allowed the money stock to grow more rapidly, and the price level began to increase more rapidly in 1966.

From the end of 1966 to mid-1974 the Federal Reserve allowed the money stock to grow at a much more rapid rate, at an average of about 7 percent a year from 1972 to 1974. The price level responded by continuing to increase more rapidly too.

The inflation we have had since 1966 is the direct result of the more rapid increase in the money stock that the Federal Reserve has allowed to take place since 1962. The sad truth about the past is that the inflation was totally unnecessary. The happy truth about the future is that we need not continue it. What is required is that the Federal Reserve return to a long-run average growth rate of the money stock in the neighborhood of 3 to 4 percent a year.

Now, the short-run stabilization problem and the long-run inflation problem are independent of each other except in periods of transition from one long-run rate of inflation to another. The Federal Reserve can choose whatever long-run average rate of inflation it wants, positive, negative, as from 1864 to 1896, or zero, by choosing the appropriate long-run growth rate for the money stock.

The cyclical behavior of real output and employment will be essentially unaffected by the choice as to a long-run inflation rate once the economy has adjusted to that choice.

The Federal Reserve could improve its short-run and long-run policy in the absence of ability to predict the timing and severity of cycles six to eighteen months ahead, by maintaining a growth rate of the money stock nearly constant, at something like 3 or 4 percent a year.

There is an interaction problem between the stabilization problem and the inflation problem if the long-run inflation rate is being changed from one rate to another. An increase in the rate of growth of the money stock will increase the average rate of inflation, and in the two or three years that are required for people to adjust their expectations to the new rate of inflation there will be a temporary increase in real output and employment, but that will disappear when the new inflation rate is built into people's expectations. The experience of 1966–1975 confirms this.

Therefore, in order to maintain a permanently higher level of real output and employment by means of monetary policy, an ever-increasing rate of inflation, without limit, would be needed. We do not want to go the way of those countries that generated hyperinflation. Recognizing that the pattern of unemployment we experience will be about the same at any constant rate of inflation as at any other, I believe we should choose a zero average inflation rate for the long run.

20

Quick-Fix Economics: A Look at the Issues

ROGER GUFFEY

Roger Guffey is President of the Federal Reserve Bank of Kansas City. This article appeared in the Economic Review *of the Federal Reserve Bank of Kansas City, May 1982.*

The need for a clear public understanding of economic policy is more critical than ever in the face of continuing debates about the nation's basic strategy for wringing out inflation and bringing about sustainable economic growth. The cornerstones of this strategy, as you know, are reduced taxes, reduced government spending, reduced regulation, and slower growth in money and credit. In my judgment, this program is generally on track. Taxes are being reduced, regulations are being pared, and growth in the supply of money and credit is being reduced by the Federal Reserve.

However, our current economic concerns reflect the fact that a major element of the program—reduced government spending—has not been fully implemented. As a result large budget deficits are now being projected for years to come. These deficits in turn are fueling inflationary expectations, keeping interest rates high, and thereby casting a pall over the economic outlook.

In periods of economic weakness such as we are now experiencing, there are always calls for quick-fix economic solutions and proposals for tinkering with economic policy procedures or market forces.

In evaluating quick-fix solutions for reducing high interest rates we must remember that the Federal Reserve has adopted and is adhering to a policy of reducing the growth of money over time to a rate consistent with sustainable noninflationary economic growth. It is well accepted that moderate growth in money and credit translates into a reduced pace of inflation. And, in my judgment, the Federal Reserve's long-run targets are absolutely appropriate and consistent with the nation's overall economc strategy. The record is quite clear. The Federal Reserve has established its credibility by achieving slower growth in money over time and, by doing so, has contributed importantly to a welcome reduction in the rate of inflation.

Despite this credible record of Federal Reserve monetary policy, proposals for quick fixes to bring down interest rates continue to be heard. Some of these proposals are indeed very beguiling.

One proposal receiving attention these days is a suggestion that the Federal Reserve be made a part of the U.S. Treasury. Such a change would bring the Federal Reserve under the control of the administration, making it easier, some believe, to "coordinate" the tools of monetary and fiscal policy and therefore to meet our nation's desired economic goals.

There is no question that the Federal Reserve is a public institution and that it must be responsive to political input in the broad sense. We in the Federal Reserve recognize that the central bank must take into account both the wishes and the long-run best interests of the American public. Our steady anti-inflation course of recent years is evidence, I believe, of that accountability.

But the proposals to fold the Federal Reserve into the Treasury are not, in my view, consistent with this broader interpretation of political responsiveness. Rather, these proposals would subject the monetary policy process to the short-run influences of political expediency. Moreover, mechanisms are already in place—through the Full Employment and Balanced Growth Act—to require the Federal Reserve to establish periodic monetary targets and then report to Congress on progress toward meeting those targets.

When Congress designed the Federal Reserve System and delegated to it the responsibility for managing the money supply, the central bank's independence was clearly established. Congress has observed an independent Federal Reserve for nearly seventy years and has continued to reaffirm the separation of monetary policy implementation from partisan politics. The reason for doing so is abundantly clear. World economic history is full of lessons of what happens when politicians become involved in managing money. Inevitably too much money is created. This is followed by rampant inflation and a deterioration of the nation's economic and political framework.

Therefore we should be particularly wary of attempts to weaken the independence and the resolve of the central bank to keep monetary policy on a proper course no matter how the winds of political expediency may blow at a given time.

Most rational observers would agree that tampering with Federal Reserve independence is fundamentally unwise. But other ideas are being proposed which appear to be less far-reaching in impact. These proposals make specific suggestions about how the Federal Reserve should *conduct* monetary policy. The most vocal ideas come from some of those whom I view as extreme monetarists, who believe that the growth of money should and can be controlled with absolute precision, with predictable economic growth and stability the natural result.

It's true that because of the link between money and economic activity, the Federal Reserve has adopted procedures and is currently formulating policy within a generalized monetarist framework, such as by using the monetary targeting approach. And the adoption of this targeting approach has helped the Federal Reserve contribute importantly to the declining inflation rate. Nevertheless our monetarist critics continue to be unhappy. If only the Federal Reserve would smooth out short-run money growth, they say, interest rates would then come down. Or, they say, if the Federal Reserve would focus on just one measure of money, erratic money growth behavior would then be avoided. Let's look at these two issues.

First, what about the proposition that the Federal Reserve should closely control the short-run growth of money? If this were done, it is contended, the money growth path would be smooth, uncertainty would vanish, and interest rates would fall.

In my view, however, the Federal Reserve simply cannot control the monetary growth rate precisely on a weekly, monthly, or even a quarterly basis. Most of the nation's money stock consists of deposits at depository institutions, and the public's use of these deposits are not and should not be controlled by the Federal Reserve. We do have the ability to influence the money supply over the longer term by affecting the volume of reserves available, which in turn influences the lending and investing activities of depository institutions.

Furthermore, and more important to the issue, the Federal Reserve has no control over the public's demand for money, which we know to be quite volatile in the short run. This volatility frequently causes wide short-run swings in the growth rate of money. Thus the Federal Reserve can do little about short-run swings in money growth, and no tinkering with monetary control procedures will allow the Federal Reserve to closely control the weekly, monthly, or quarterly growth rate of money. I should also note that those who advocate procedures for greater short-run control completely ignore or discount the greater interest rate volatility that would accompany such procedures.

Next, what about the proposal that erratic short-term money growth could be avoided if the Federal Reserve would simply focus on one definition of money? In my view, such tunnel vision would be risky, primarily because of the rapid financial innovation now taking place.

The recent growth of money-market funds, cash sweep accounts, and other new financial techniques is a troubling issue for monetary policy at the present time. Innovation is having an important impact on the public's demand for money balances, complicating our understanding of what constitutes money and, as a result, the relationship of money to economic activity.

For example, financial innovation has led to some reduction in the public's demand for traditional transaction balances. This shift affected the closely watched M1 measure of money in 1981 and is probably continuing this year. For other, not fully understood reasons, M1 has been surprisingly strong this year, making interpretation of its behavior more difficult. The broader measures of money have also been difficult to interpret, because of financial innovation. For example, M2 has been affected by the public's shifts to money-market funds and other funds included in this broad measure. In view of these problems of interpretation, it seems clear to me that it would be a mistake for the Federal Reserve to focus on only one of the current measures of the money supply.

Thus the Federal Reserve must retain its flexibility in the face of financial innovation. If the monetary aggregates are made less reliable guides by innovation, then the risk of errant policy can only be compounded by limiting the Federal Reserve's flexibility to watch various aggregates.

Some of our monetarist friends have put forward other proposals of a technical nature. For example, they suggest that imposing a system of contemporaneous reserve requirements on depository institutions would improve our short-run monetary control. A companion proposal calls for the Federal Reserve to adopt a penalty discount rate. Our research indicates that a penalty rate would help monetary control *only* if contemporaneous reserve accounting were implemented. And if we did implement CRA, such procedures would be costly for financial institutions to implement and, our research shows, would produce little meaningful benefit in achieving firmer monetary control. More important, these two changes would likely increase interest rate volatility substantially, and lead to undesirable disruptions in the financial and real sectors of the economy.

Aside from these proposals by monetarists, others who are concerned about high interest rates have suggested that the Federal Reserve simply take action to increase the money supply now. After all, their argument goes, an increased supply surely will bring down the price. While the appeal of this view is understandable, I believe that an attempt to increase the money supply beyond the current targets would be dangerous and ill-advised given the current environment.

To understand why such a simple proposal would be ill-advised, it is useful to examine why interest rates are so high in the current environment. We all know,

for example, that interest rates should fall as economic activity declines. Unfortunately, downward pressure on rates because of economic weakness is being largely offset by other factors—primarily the public's perception of the effects of very large federal budget deficits. These large deficits remain the most important factor, in my judgment, in explaining the persistence of high interest rates. Because budget deficits must be financed by borrowing in the nation's capital markets, this heavy demand is helping keep rates high. Many investors also apparently believe that the large projected deficits will lead to a renewal of strong inflationary pressures and sharply higher interest rates as soon as the economy recovers from the recession. It is obvious to me that because of these uncertainties, investors are reluctant to make long-term commitments. By avoiding the bond markets and staying short, investor psychology is contributing to the high levels of interest rates.

However, assume for a moment that the Federal Reserve did take action to increase the supply of money and credit. What would be likely to happen? First, there might indeed be some temporary reductions in short-term interest rates. But as concerns about a rekindling of inflation spread, lenders would seek to protect themselves against inflation by incorporating a higher inflation premium into their rates. Because of these inflationary fears, long-term rates would not move down, but would likely move even higher. As a result, users of long-term credit, such as housing and the corporate business sector, would be left high and dry. And corporations would continue to find it difficult to restructure their balance sheets.

Thus, in my judgment, interest rates can only be brought down by a resolution of the federal budget stalemate. So long as that impasse persists, any Federal Reserve action to add monetary fuel to the economy will have a perverse effect. Furthermore, lower interest rates will not result from the application of monetary gimmickry or by taking away the independence of the Federal Reserve. In fact such proposals do a disservice because they divert the attention of policy-makers and the public through claims that simplistic solutions are at hand for complex problems.

While there are no easy solutions to our near-term economic problems, I think it is a mistake to be a gloomy pessimist. Despite our problems, I reject the notion that a 1930s-style economic depression is in the wings. Rather, I see economic recovery beginning about midyear, spurred by increases in consumer spending. With continued progress on the inflation front, consumers will be in a more confident mood when the midyear tax cut takes effect. Their spending will encourage business to build inventories, and the process of recovery should be under way.

Whether the recovery is robust or modest in 1982 will depend largely upon the course of interest rates. Continued high rates will dampen recovery, while lower rates will have a more positive effect. As I have noted, the key to lower rates and the trigger for renewed economic growth is to resolve the stalemate over fiscal policy by making significant reductions in the projected budget deficits. Reduced deficit projections will restore investor and consumer confidence that the nation is willing to deal with its problems. In addition, less deficit financing will tend to relieve pressure in financial markets and reinforce downward influences on interest rates coming from moderating inflation.

Looking beyond the economic problems of 1982, I am optimistic. The nation's broad economic strategy, which incorporates deregulation and incentives for savings, investment, and productivity, shows real potential as a path to a bright economic future. From my perspective, the Federal Reserve's commitment to a monetary policy which seeks to foster noninflationary economic growth fits perfectly with these other objectives.

There is a strong economic future ahead of us. I am confident that the recovery will occur and that an extended period of economic growth is out there waiting to begin. There is no reason we cannot achieve this potential if we have patience, if we act firmly now to achieve an accord over the deficit issue, and if we resist the tempting sirens of economic quick-fix solutions.

21

Open-Market Operations: A Case Study

FEDERAL RESERVE BANK OF NEW YORK

This article is taken from Open Market Operations, *published by the Federal Reserve Bank of New York in 1973. It is by Paul Meek, Monetary Adviser of the Bank.*

The Manager of the Federal Reserve System Open Market Account has made his decision. He will buy about $250 million in United States Treasury bills, which mature within the next twelve months. The time is just before noon on the Tuesday before Thanksgiving Day. In a room on the eighth floor of the Federal Reserve Bank of New York, eight securities traders gather around an officer of the securities department to receive instructions.

Each of the eight returns to his seat around a U-shaped trading desk. Each presses a button on a telephone console with wires linked to the nation's 20 or so primary dealers in United States Government securities. The trader's ring sounds a buzzer in the trading room of one of the two to four Government securities dealers he has been assigned to call.

"Jack," says the Reserve Bank's trader, "what can you offer in bills for cash delivery?"

Taking a quick look at the list of Treasury bills which the dealer firm owns, Jack replies, "Bill, I can offer you for cash $5 million of January 4 bills to yield 5.45 percent, $10 million of January 25 bills at

5.50—$10 million of March 22 bills at 5.50—and $8 million of May 17 bills at 6.12."

Bill says, "Can I have those offerings firm for a few minutes?"

"Sure."

Within a few minutes the "go-around" of the Government securities market is completed. Each of the eight Reserve Bank traders has recorded the results of his calls on special forms. The officer-in-charge attaches each to a board until the full array of individual dealer offerings is before him. Addition quickly shows that dealers have offered $753 million in Treasury bills for sale for cash—that is, with delivery and payment that very day.

A glance at a list of the Federal Reserve System's current holdings enables the experienced Reserve Bank officer to choose the issues likely to be most useful for future System operations. Seeking the best—that is the highest—yield on each issue, the officer checks a large quotation board across the open end of the U-shaped trading desk. This shows yields to maturity as they were in the market just before the "go-around" began. After selecting the specific offers he will accept, the officer informs the traders and they return to their telephone consoles to tell the dealers.

"Jack, we'll take the $5 million of January 4 bills at 5.45 and the $10 million of January 25 bills at 5.50 both for cash; no, thanks, on the others."

Within thirty minutes from the time the initial decision was made, all the calls have been completed. The Manager has selected and purchased $242 million in Treasury bills for cash. The paper work remains. On the same day, the clearing bank that handles each dealer's paper work will instruct the Federal Reserve Bank of New York, usually by wire, to deliver the specific Treasury bills purchased to the System's account. The Federal Reserve will credit its payments for the securities to the reserve account of the bank concerned. The bank, in turn, will credit the dealer's account with the proceeds of the sale. The transfer of these bills takes place through the Government Securities Clearing Arrangement in which changes in the Treasury securities holdings of the System and of the dealers are reflected as bookkeeping entries. This arrangement considerably reduces the physical transfer of such securities.

The day's open market purchases will not retain their separate identities in the Federal Reserve System's weekly report on the monetary system. They will be merged with all other operations conducted during the week that ends on Wednesday, the next day. The figures, normally released to the press at 4 P.M. on Thursday in New York and Washington, will be released this week on Friday afternoon because of the holiday.

The next morning many officers of banks, financial corporations and business concerns will turn automatically to the weekly Federal Reserve statement appearing in leading newspapers to see if there have been any significant shifts in the reserve positions of the nation's banks. All who are charged with raising money or investing funds for their firms know that changes in bank reserves normally have a major impact on the cost and availability of borrowed money in the national market for credit. They will spot the Federal Reserve's large open market purchases in the pre-Thanksgiving week and ask themselves: "Is the Federal Reserve only moving to make it possible for the banks to meet the public's seasonal demands for cash and credit, or is it moving to increase, or reduce (after allowance for seasonal factors), the ability of banks to extend credit?" Such questions can rarely be answered on the basis of a single week's figures. Only over a peri-od of several weeks will financial men be able to sort out any gradual shift in Federal Reserve policy from transitory fluctuations in bank reserves.

All Part of a Day's Work

Each day presents a new challenge to the Manager of the Open Market Account. Yet each day has much in common with every other day. Let us consider that Tuesday before Thanksgiving Day and follow the developments which led to the purchase of $242 million in Government securities. On such a day, as on all days, the Manager must bear in mind the current directive and the consensus of the last FOMC [Federal Open Market Committee] meeting. Let us suppose that the directive calls for fostering growth in the money and credit aggregates conducive to sustainable economic expansion and that these broad objectives are to be pursued by keeping reserves generally in line with the paths developed by the FOMC's staff.

The main outlines of the task which lies ahead are at least roughly visible to the Manager early on Tuesday morning. He has before him the preceding day's projections of the behavior expected of nonborrowed reserves over the coming three weeks. Tuesday's projections will be available a bit later at about 10:45 A.M. The projections are based upon the behavior of reserve factors over the same calendar period during the past several years. They also take into account any special factors such as a Treasury financing.

Yesterday's projections indicated that the Manager will have to supply reserves in substantial amounts to offset reserve drains and provide for the seasonal rise in required reserves. Indeed the day before, Monday, the Manager provided $280 million in reserves by making $65 million in repurchase agreements with dealers early in the afternoon, after buying $215 million in Treasury bills outright for cash in the morning.

Useful as they are as a rough yardstick, the projections cannot be used as a precise guide to operations. Each year, for all its similarities to the past, produces a pattern of financial flows that is all its own. The Manager and his experienced officers must look to the Federal funds market itself for signals of the timing and magnitude of the reserve pressures actually at work on this particular day.

The new business day begins a few minutes after 9 A.M. in the trading room of the Federal Reserve Bank of New York, The news tickers are pounding out the financial news that has accumulated since it closed down the night before. The securities traders scan the closing quotations recorded on the board across the open end of the U-shaped trading desk to reorient themselves before the new day begins. The traders concerned with the routine flow of Treasury, member bank and foreign transactions begin to check on the day's orders.

Dealer Conference

By 9:15 A.M., two officers of the securities department hurry to a tenth-floor conference room to meet with one or two representatives of a Government securities dealer firm. Dealers confer every business day on a rotating schedule with the Reserve Bank officers directly responsible for the conduct of open market operations. At these conferences, the dealers comment on market developments and on any matter of interest to the firm. The Reserve Bank officers listen and ask questions.

This morning, representatives of three dealers are scheduled to appear, one after the other. At the first conference, a senior partner of a dealer firm observes that the market has been rather quiet during the last few days, and that he has been rather disappointed by the lack of corporate demand for Treasury bills. He finds that insurance companies and pension funds are holding off on bond purchases until the $100-million bond issue of the XYZ Corporation due to be offered on Wednesday hits the market. The dealer gives his views on whether the Treasury should issue short-term or long-term securities, or both, in meeting its cash needs, and indicates the kind of reception he thinks the market would give the new issues. After answering questions asked by one of the Reserve Bank officers, the dealer departs at 9:30 A.M.

Two representatives of a second dealer firm enter the conference room. Among other things, they indicate that while the market as a whole has been quiet, their firm has handled some sizable transactions in the last few days. They feel that many investors have large cash positions and are merely waiting for more attractive yields. One also feels that conditions in the money market were a little tight yesterday afternoon even after the System's intervention; his firm had to pay a relatively high interest rate to obtain financing for its position through loans and repurchase agreements negotiated with banks and others. The second firm's representatives leave at 9:45 A.M., and the vice president in charge of the dealer operations of a New York

City bank enters. The third conference covers much the same ground. The last dealer departs at 10 A.M., and the Reserve Bank officers return to their offices to prepare for the daily call from the U.S. Treasury.

The Treasury Call

Each morning shortly after 10 A.M., the Fiscal Assistant Secretary of the Treasury uses a direct telephone line to compare notes with the Manager or his deputy on the outlook for the Treasury's cash balance at the Reserve Banks. Their objective is to coordinate changes in the Treasury's balance at the Reserve Banks with the System's management of bank reserves. They estimate the amount of funds that need to be transferred from the Treasury's Tax and Loan accounts at commercial banks to the Reserve Banks in order to maintain a working balance in the face of checks they expect to be presented for payment at the Reserve Banks. (The Treasury channels a large part of its receipts from taxes and from sales of its securities through Tax and Loan accounts to reduce the sudden impact of these large flows on bank reserves.)

Today, the Assistant Secretary tells the Reserve Bank officer that his projections of daily Government receipts and expenditures indicate that the Treasury will need to transfer $500 million from Treasury Tax and Loan accounts at about 275 large commercial banks across the country (the Class C banks) to its account at the Federal Reserve Banks. This will be in addition to calls previously scheduled on Tax and Loan accounts at other commercial banks. The Reserve Bank official notes that projections of the New York Bank's staff point to a need to call about $300 million to maintain the Treasury balance at about the desired level. However, since bank reserve positions are expected to be under pressure from seasonal factors, the Reserve Bank officer and Assistant Secretary agree that the call be limited to 30 percent of the previous night's Treasury balances at the "C" banks—about $350 million.

The conversation over, the Reserve officer dials another officer in the Bank to inform him that the Treasury has decided to make a special call today on the "C" banks. By 11 P.M., the large banks will have been informed that they must transfer 30 percent of the Treasury's deposits with them at Monday's close to their district Reserve Banks. These transfers out of their reserve accounts are intended only to offset the bulk of the increase in member bank reserves expected to flow from the deposit of Treasury checks drawn on the Treasury's accounts at the Federal Reserve Banks. In practice, these checks are likely to be deposited widely over the country so that the big-city banks may find that the transfer of Treasury deposits from them to the Reserve Banks exceeds the amount of Treasury checks deposited with them. Typically, these banks will need to step up their overnight borrowing in the Federal funds market.

Getting the "Feel" of the Market

In the meantime, the Government securities market has become active. At the trading desk, opening quotations are beginning to come in. Several of the traders around the desk are talking to dealers to learn if any trend is developing. Other traders have a pretty good fix on orders to be executed for foreign accounts or for Treasury trust accounts. Reports have arrived from the research and statistics departments on dealer positions and on the previous day's reserve positions and Federal funds transactions of eight major banks in New York City and 38 banks in other cities. On hand also is a complete nationwide picture of the reserve positions of member banks as of Monday's close, including information on the distribution of reserves among money market banks and other reserve city and country banks.

Shortly after 10 A.M., two clerks bring the quotation board up to date with "runs" of price and yield quotations obtained from telephone calls to securities dealers. The Federal Reserve's traders already know from their conversations with dealers what the board shows—that the market is steady with few changes either up or down. They also know that there has been little trading except for the professional activity of the dealers who are testing each other's markets by occasionally "hitting a bid"—selling securities at the price bid by another dealer. About 10:45 A.M., the desk receives the first tentative quotation on Federal funds. The quote is 6 percent, a shade higher than yesterday's rate of 5³/₄ percent, which exceeded the 5¹/₂-percent discount rate at which member banks can borrow from their Reserve Banks.

One member of the staff calls each of the nonbank dealers to find out the volume of funds needed to replace loans maturing today or to finance securities for which payment must be made today. A few minutes before 11 A.M., his tabulation shows that the dealers

need loans of about $950 million to finance their present securities holdings. Money was available at yesterday's close at 6 percent, but the dealers are not too sure about today. Several think money may be harder to get and more expensive.

The officer in charge of the desk, who has just been joined by the Account Manager and another officer, summarizes for them the early morning market developments. Together they review the newest projection of the factors affecting bank reserves over the next three weeks—a report received only moments before from the research department. A last-minute check with the traders reveals that banks and others are beginning to sell Treasury bills to the dealers in greater volume than buyers are coming to the dealers for bills. Treasury bill yields are beginning to rise—that is, prices are beginning to decline.

Meanwhile, a preliminary call is made to the Board of Governors in Washington and to the office of one of the Reserve Bank presidents currently on the FOMC. Information is provided on the full range of data available on bank reserves and the money and Government securities markets. Thus, the Reserve Bank president will have before him the data on which the desk's plan of action is based. The officers hurry to an adjoining office to participate in a very important telephone conversation—the conference call, which takes place at about 11:10 A.M.

The Conference Call

"Washington and Minneapolis are standing by" announces the telephone operator, completing the three-way telephone hookup that each morning enables the Account Manager to review developments with the staff of the Board of Governors in Washington and one of the Reserve Bank presidents currently serving on the FOMC. Sitting in on the conversation in New York today are the President of the Bank, the Manager of the System Account, and the officers of the securities department. One of the officers seated directly behind a telephone microphone speaks:

"Conditions have changed somewhat since we spoke yesterday. The Government securities market opened steady this morning with very few changes in prices and rates, and with little activity. But Treasury bills now seem to be in increasing supply so that yields are rising. There are some indications that long-term investors are holding off to see how the market will take the $100-million bond issue of the XYZ Corporation tomorrow. Our first tentative information on Federal funds showed a bid of 6 percent, $1/4$ percentage point above yesterday's closing rate, and word just received from the trading room indicates that funds have now begun to trade at $6^1/4$ percent. Dealer financing needs this morning are about $950 million. The banks have raised their call loan rates on dealer loans from $6^1/4$ percent to $6^1/2$ percent.

"Yesterday, nonborrowed reserves dipped slightly despite our action to supply reserves. The outlook is for a sharp decline in reserves today and tomorrow. New York City and Chicago banks are under pressure and have been heavy buyers of Federal funds on each of the last three business days. Banks in several other major cities show reserve deficiencies. Today's call on the 'C' banks will withdraw $350 million and will probably add to pressure on the money market banks."

The officer then reads the Manager's proposed plan for the day:

"In view of the expected stringency in reserves, the Account plans to purchase securities for cash. If the market continues to tighten, we may buy as much as $300 million of Treasury bills. Repurchase agreements with the dealers can be used to supply additional reserves if needed."

The conversation is, of course, more detailed than the above colloquy, and conclusions are supported by a marshalling of facts. Prospective developments in the next couple of days and weeks are discussed. Participants in Washington and Minneapolis may report additional information. They express views as to appropriateness of the proposed action.

By 11:30 A.M., the call is usually completed. A member of the Board's staff who participated promptly summarizes the call in a memorandum sent to each member of the Board of Governors. A telegram from the Board provides each Reserve Bank president with a summary of the telephone discussion, within an hour or two after the call is concluded.

The Decision

Shortly before noon conditions in the market begin to jell rapidly, indicating a sharp increase in reserve pressures. Federal funds are heavily bid for at $6^1/4$ per-

cent and dealers, New York City banks, and other participants in the funds market report that funds are hard to find. Dealers report they have not been able to make any progress in meeting their financing needs by borrowing from their out-of-town contacts even though they have been offering to pay $6^1/8$ percent for money.

The Manager reviews the evidence: "The market has really started tightening up. We had better move in right away in size to prevent this from getting out of hand. Let's go in and buy about $250 million in treasury bills for cash today."

The Manager of the System Open Market Account has made his decision. Eight securities traders gather around an officer of the securities department to receive instruction. As we have seen, within thirty minutes the Reserve Bank's traders purchase $242 million in Treasury bills for cash in a "go-around" of the market. A summary report from the New York Reserve Bank of the day's developments and System action will be on the desks of the Board members and all Reserve bank presidents on the following morning.

The officers continue to watch the situation after the "go-around" is completed at around 12:20 P.M. The Federal funds rate eases back to 6-percent bid for a time, but then the brokers report that the bid appears to be building while the supply available remains limited. Given the persistence of tightness, the Manager approves the recommendation of the desk officers that the System purchase about $300 million of Treasury and Federal agency securities under overnight repurchase agreements. By 1 P.M. the additional injection of reserves has been made—bringing the day's total to $542 million. A better balance returns to the Federal funds market.

The market may debate whether the day's action was designed simply to head off the developing strain in the market or whether it had broad policy significance. The market may not be able to be sure on that score until it can look back on several weeks of action and see if a cumulative easing of bank reserves overlays the weekly fluctuations not ironed out by System operations. But for today it is sufficient that the reserve strains which threatened to become acute have disappeared.

Tomorrow is another day . . .

22

Rational Expectations—Fresh Ideas That Challenge Some Established Views of Policy Making

CLARENCE NELSON

This is an excerpt from the 1977 Annual Report *of the Federal Reserve Bank of Minneapolis.*

"Monetary policy cannot systematically stimulate the economy to lower unemployment rates."

That startling claim is one of the consequences of a new view of economic policy that has been termed, "rational expectations." This new view attacks widely held beliefs about how the economy works and challenges many prevailing theories about what economic policy can achieve.

These new ideas are so fundamentally important to the current predicament facing our nation's economy and to the future course of national economic policy that policy makers—and the general public affected by policy makers' choice—need to understand the logic and evidence that support the rational expectations view.

But most recent work in the theory and in the analysis of past economic experience—including major contributions made by the Research Department of this Bank—has been too technical to be understood by a more general audience. Hopefully this article will explain the essential ideas of the rational expectations challenge in fairly simple lan-

guage. By doing that, we hope to encourage discussion of rational expectations among elected officials, policy makers, and a wider public.

We'll begin by briefly defining what we mean by "rational expectations" and by identifying the kind of policy to which it applies. Our discussion will then address the following points:

1. why traditional views about how economic policy works are wrong,
2. why rational expectations is a valid view of the world,
3. what happens when current methods of policy making are used in a rational expectations world, and
4. in the light of rational expectations ideas, what can macroeconomic policy really hope to achieve.

"Rational Expectations": What It Means.

When the term "rational expectations" first appeared in an economic journal article in 1961, it was given a specific technical meaning connected with economic models. In an everyday, practical sense rational expectations is simply an assumption about people's behavior. The assumption claims that people make economic decisions in a way that tends to take into account all available information bearing significantly on the future consequences of their decisions. And they tend to use that information in a way so as not to repeat their past mistakes. The information we're talking about can include, among other things, knowledge about government policy actions already taken and about strategies or approaches government policy makers regularly take when economic signals begin to change. So, rational expectations attributes to people a reasonably thorough, broad-view approach to appraising the future on matters that are going to make a big dollars-and-cents difference to them.

Put that way, there's certainly nothing startling about the rational expectations idea: Most of us have believed all along that rationality in that sense is a reasonable thing to attribute to economic decision makers—business people, labor leaders, workers, investors, or consumers. What is startling is that the ideas underlying current policy views deny such rationality. Current views about how policy achieves its effects depend on people *failing* to act in their own best interests. When we recast the decision-making process to allow people to act with "rational expectations," policy no longer has the same effects. And that's the heart of the problem we're examining in this article.

The Importance of Expectations in Decision Making.

All economists agree that people's beliefs about the future affect their decisions today. Employers and employees negotiate wage contracts with some picture in mind about what will happen to the cost of living or to other related wage rates over the life of a contract. Consumers deciding whether to purchase a car have expectations about future income, job prospects, future cash outlays, and perhaps sources of credit in an emergency—if only to judge whether the automobile installment payments can be met. Similarly, a business firm deciding whether to invest in new factories must form expectations about such things as future sales, future labor and other input costs, and future tax rates.

According to the rational expectations view, people

use in the best way possible whatever information they have; and they do not tend to repeat previous errors. People are forward looking, and prospective government actions play an important part in their picture of the future. The myriad of commercially available newsletters, analytical reports, and forecasting services reminds us that forecasting government actions has become big business. And even though people must make plans in an environment of considerable uncertainty (and, therefore, are likely to make some mistakes), they do learn to avoid repeatedly misusing information that will bear on their future. That's because the economic process rewards those who make good forecasts and penalizes those who don't.

Types of Policies under Question.

We should emphasize that the kind of policy making we're looking at embraces attempts to manage, or influence, demand for goods and services in order to smooth out the business cycle. Sometimes these kinds of policies are called *demand management* policies, *aggregate demand* policies, or simply *countercyclical* policies. (We'll use these terms interchangeably.)

Virtually everyone who reads the newspapers is aware of the continuing public discussion of these policies. Government choices regarding how much it will spend in relation to how much it will tax, when used as deliberate countercyclical measures, are called *fiscal* policies. Decisions by the Federal Reserve to increase or decrease bank reserves, directed similarly, are called *monetary* policies. When the federal government deliberately takes action to spend more than it taxes away from businesses and individuals, fiscal policy is said to be *expansionary*. When the Federal Reserve acts to increase bank reserves—a kind of starter kit for expanded money and credit growth in the private economy—monetary policy is said to be *expansionary* and is viewed to be either a complement to expansionary fiscal policy or a stimulus in its own right. Both of these types of economic policy are commonly thought to be potent ways to help get a weak economy moving again.

I. What's Wrong with Traditional Views of the Policy Process?

Since rational expectations ideas have developed as criticism of some prevailing ways of viewing the economy and the role of policy, the case for rational expectations is, to a large extent, the case against these current views. The traditional views we're talking about are those claiming that routinely applied fiscal and monetary stimulus in times of recession, and restraint in times of boom, will improve the general performance of the economy over the longer term and make people, on the whole, better off. What we want to show in the next few sections is that people's expectations, when formed "rationally," will generally frustrate government's attempts to successfully pursue activist demand management policies.

We'll do this by outlining the process through which activist policies are widely believed to get results and show how they depend on people behaving in ways inconsistent with their own best interests. Next we'll offer a rational expectations version of the policy process as a more realistic representation of people's decision making and indicate how that representation seems consistent with some evidence from recent experience. We think the rational expectations view is persuasive.

Two stories of how activist countercyclical fiscal and monetary policies are believed to work will be traced out. In the first story policy has its effect through the labor market and hinges on the way labor reacts to changes in wages and prices. The other story has policy working via financial markets and hinges on the way changes in interest rates induce (or discourage) new investment. These two perceptions of the channels connecting policy with the economic outcome aren't mutually exclusive; they could easily be combined into a single, more general story. The stories, though, are often told separately, and since some of our readers will be more familiar with one or the other it will be useful to consider each of them in turn. The two perceived policy channels we are about to consider probably contain the essence of what most legislators' and policy makers' views depend on in order for activist policies to get results.

Story One: Policy That Takes Effect Through Wage Decisions.

Central to some widely held views of the policy process are wage-setting decisions in the labor market. This story, a rather standard Keynesian one, depends very much on labor *not* rationally forming expectations about future conditions at the time wage contracts are set.

We start with an economy in recession. Govern-

ment policy makers want to stimulate hiring and producing by private business firms. They know the way to get business firms to expand *more* than already planned is to take policy actions that will cause business to see additional profit opportunities. So government increases the amount of money it spends for goods and services relative to the amount of money it draws in from the private economy in the form of taxes. And it creates money to pay for the difference. Prices move up as business experiences the effects of added spending for its products. All this time labor is not supposed to look ahead to the end of the story with its promise of rising prices, and so it continues to work at very nearly the same old wage. That's what creates new profit opportunities for business—prices for business output go up, but its major input cost, wage rates for labor, does not. The outcome: business expands, and as it does it hires more labor.

In this scenario, workers go along with unchanged wage rates in the face of prospectively higher prices. They find themselves in the peculiar situation of offering more labor at lower "real-wage rates," that is, wage rates measured in terms of the amount of goods they'll buy. That shortsightedness on the part of labor is crucial if this channel for policy action is to work as claimed. For if workers bargained for their wages in full anticipation that prices would rise, or if wages were "indexed" to automatically follow general price level increases, then that perceived policy channel would fail to work.

This simplified Keynesian story does no particular violence to the mechanism many policy activists believe enables government to start the economic ball rolling. It requires that workers in the labor market be oblivious to (or largely tolerant of) the prospect that an unchanging wage along with a rising general price level will progessively erode the amount of real goods and services their wages will buy. Since that kind of decision making hardly seems rational, it's easy to guess the forthcoming rational expectations criticism.

First, the process will work only if labor does not, in the course of its wage-bargaining and job-seeking behavior, anticipate the consequent general rise in prices. It's clear that fiscal and monetary policies deliberately attempting to stimulate total dollar spending in the economy would not be able to operate through this price- and wage-setting disparity if those policies were fully predicted or expected. That's because labor wouldn't willingly or knowingly enter into a contract that dooms workers to a shrinking real income when no changes in technology or productivity have occurred that force upon the whole of the economy—owners and managers of business as well—such a real loss in living standards. And in the absence of that kind of self-diminishing agreement, business would have no net expansion in profit opportunities to exploit.

Second, any policy process that operates by fooling people—as this Keynesian mechanism certainly requires—may work the first time, but cannot be expected to go on fooling people repeatedly. That's axiomatic from the rationalists' point of view. Any logical story of the policy process must grant labor in general and workers in particular at least reasonable acumen when it comes to making commitments affecting their personal economic interests. That much is granted to other actors in the story, of course. Our conclusion then is that the activist policy process we've been describing will not bring about any overall real expansion in the private economy—*unless it catches people by surprise.*

Some indications of labor market response to prospective inflation. One of the arguments supporters of activist countercyclical policy make against the rational expectations view starts with the observation that labor frequently locks itself into contracts by fixing the course of wages for as much as three years into the future. That fact, plus perhaps some slowness on the part of workers in recognizing what's happening to prices in general, means there's a built-in delay in wage adjustments. But, so the story goes, product prices can respond quickly to a policy stimulus, and therefore temporary profit opportunities, at least, can be created by policy action. That provides incentive for business to expand, if only temporarily, and thus some potency is retained by activist policy.

That fragile loophole cannot be relied on in the pursuit of any systematic countercyclical policy. Contracts are periodically rewritten and can certainly take into account any earlier misreading of government policy strategy on the practical principle of "once burned, twice cautious." One possible response by labor to being caught short in midcontract because of unpredictable policy moves by government is simply to shorten the contract period the next time. That course was pointed out in 1971 by United Auto Workers President Leonard Woodcock when he said, ". . . if labor contracts can be torn up based upon the stroke of a pen [a reference to the Wage-Price Freeze on August 15, 1971], then obviously we can no longer in the future negotiate contracts for any longer than one year."

An alternative response by labor is to stay with longer-term contracts but base them on a better forecast of inflation. In fact, the closer labor can come to having wages fully adjusted for changes in cost-of-living indexes, the closer it comes to making a "perfect" forecast. That situation, from labor's point of view, would be the ultimate in rational expectations and would obviously frustrate the Keynesian policy mechanism described earlier.

A telling illustration of the way labor has moved to protect its real earnings in the recent environment of high price inflation is the data on the percentage of workers covered by cost-of-living clauses in their contracts. We've plotted that data in Figure 1. It suggests that labor is in fact responding in a "rational" way to government's continuing failure to deliver on its announced policy goals for containment of inflation.

FIGURE 1. Percent of Workers under Contract Covered by Cost-of-Living Escalation

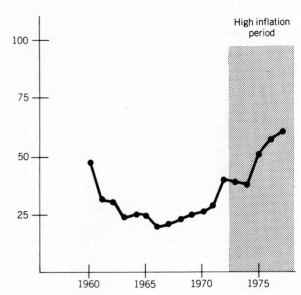

Source: Monthly Labor Review

Story Two: Countercultural Policy that Takes Effect By Way of Interest Rate Channels.

Now let's look at another commonly held notion of how monetary-fiscal stimulus makes things move. This one operates through a different market, the market for investment funds, and seems to depend on a kind of shortsightedness by suppliers of funds regarding their prospective "real" interest earnings. The earnings-versus-inflation discrepancy that policy appears to exploit here parallels labor's "illusion" about its wage in the first story. According to this policy story, policy makers' actions to expand the rate of money growth will influence business expansion decisions and consumer spending decisions through interest rates.

The story goes as follows.

Start with the perception that the economy is in, or going into, a recession. Policy authorities act to expand the money supply growth rate. The Federal Reserve does this by stepping up its buying of securities from the public (through a network of dealers in New York). By that deliberate action the public ends up with a flow of new cash, and banks end up with a flow of new reserves that enable them to expand loans to businesses, if they can find customers, by several times the amount of the new reserves.

Other things being equal, the buying action of the Fed drives securities prices up, and that means interest rates are driven down on those securities. The subsequent action by banks seeking to make loans at a faster pace than they would have done otherwise, or to buy bonds in greater volumes than they would have done otherwise, helps move still other interest rates down.

In the next step, business firms expand investment in new production facilities. One way to imagine why they would do so is to consider interest on borrowed business funds as simply another cost of doing business, just as wages for labor inputs are a cost of doing business. As expectations adjust to the prospect of lower interest costs, some investment possibilities not previously viewed as profitable will suddenly appear profitable—expected revenues don't change, but expected costs go down because the interest cost component has gone down. Thus, plant and equipment investments are undertaken, new workers are hired, and new output is produced.

The last step in the story simply recognizes that the added new workers start some new spending of their own, which further raises demand, causing additional businesses to expand their output, and so on. Thus, national product expands by some multiple of the initial investment stimulus, and we've succeeded in bringing about large real effects on the economy through small changes in monetary policy.

Once this process gets underway (plant expansion, new hiring, and all that), the increased private spending would, just as in the first story, likely bring forth some mixture of price increases and real quantity increases in the flow of goods and services. This story seems even to allow wage rates to be bid up approximately in line with prices as expansion moves along. The prospect of wage rate increases can be a part of business firms' expectations—as long as the necessary capital funds have been or can be acquired through borrowing at bargain interest rates.

Interest rate responses to monetary-fiscal actions appear to be the crucial link in the story we've just told. Interest rate responses also seem to provide the main channel through which monetary policy actions affect employment and output in the large macroeconometric models of the United States economy currently used by government to assist in determining policies and by business to assist in determining its strategies. The large multi-equation "MPS" model developed by the Federal Reserve, Massachusetts Institute of Technology, University of Pennsylvania, and the Social Sciences Research Council has five directly defined channels that depend on interest rate movements. Some dozen different interest rates appear in the equations to help generate quarter-by-quarter predictions of total spending for such categories as consumer durables, automobiles, producers' durable equipment, and residential construction. The interest rate linkage seems also to be a key part of the looser and more generalized anecdotal story that you might get if you asked some policy makers how their decisions affect the economy.

In the rational expectations view, however, those stories are wrong. The interest-rate-link story doesn't take a broad enough perspective and doesn't adequately accommodate the way people rationally form their expectations. While it's undeniable that Federal Reserve action to buy securities and expand bank reserves results in bidding interest rates down, that response is temporary and fleeting. The point is that rational lenders and investors, who look ahead to later chapters of the story, see that any Federal Reserve push to expand money growth rates will ultimately raise the growth in the general price level. Foreseeing that outcome, lenders won't want to tie up funds in long-term loans at rates of interest which they had calculated to be acceptable under an outdated view of future inflation. If they were to commit their funds with no upward adjustment of their lending rate, they would be agreeing to accept a lower rate of return in terms of the goods and services they would subsequently be able to buy. And nothing in the outlook has changed that should lead them to want to do that.

Instead, they would add an "inflation premium" to

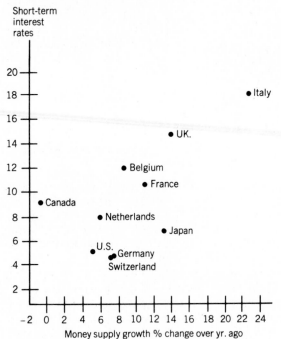

FIGURE 2a. Interest Rate vs. Money Growth for OECD Countries

Nov. 1976 short-term interest rates vs. rate of money growth Nov. 1976 over Nov. 1975.

Source: Federal Reserve Bank of New York

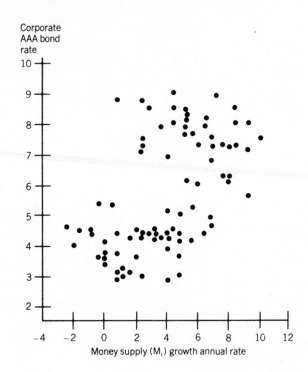

FIGURE 2b. Interest Rate vs. Money Growth

Quarterly average U.S. data 1954 through 1977

the interest rates they are willing to settle for—a little insurance policy against the heightened prospects for inflation. And interest rate levels finally settled on in the financial markets have got to reflect that premium. Finally, if the long-term interest rates relevant for business capital expansion go up by the full amount of expected inflation, as the rationalists argue would occur with any foreseen inflation, all costs—including interest as a cost—will go up proportionately to the expected price rise so that nothing will have changed in terms of exploitable profit opportunities. In short, when policy moves are anticipated or quickly sensed in market signals, this financial market channel to policy results we've been describing won't work either.

So what's the evidence that interest rates don't behave as the conventional policy view would argue they should? Any simple look at the relationship between money growth and interest rate levels in the historical record is bound to ignore a lot of other

factors also influencing how those two things behave. Yet the fact that economic data just don't show high rates of money growth regularly associated with low levels of interest rates must, at the very least, raise doubts about the dependability of that perceived route for policy actions. You can look at experience across countries [Figure 2a] or over a period of time within the United States [Figure 2b] and see that *higher* interest rates, now lower, appear, it anything, to go along with higher rates of money expansion—probably reflecting higher actual and expected inflation rates.

To sum up, the rational expectations view argues that conventionally perceived policy channels— whether operating through wage costs, interest costs, or any other market-responsible variable—are wrong because they depend on having people behave contrary to their own clear best interests, repeatedly neglecting important information they have or can have about any systematically applied policy.

II. How Valid Is Rational Expectations As a Representation of People's Behavior?

Some critics argue that rational expectations demands too much wisdom and perceptiveness of people to be believable. But the validity of rational expectations does not require that *every* consumer or worker or business manager be the "complete seer" of future prices and other economic events. For example, in the case of wage bargaining by organized labor, only the union leadership actually engaged in the bargaining process—not each and every rank-and-file member—need have an informed view about what government policy is and what its consequences for future price levels are likely to be. Today's union leadership, as we pointed out in our review of policy channels in the previous section, does, in fact, acknowledge its concern about prospective "real" earnings. Small agricultural enterprises or commodity dealers need not have specialized resources of their own to forecast supply and demand movements and the effects of government policies. All they need do to learn what the experts are expecting in future market situations is pick up the newspaper, or the phone, and check on quoted futures prices—or subscribe at modest price to one of many private newsletters. In the case of small borrowers and investors, the information possessed by large and sophisticated borrowers and suppliers of funds becomes very quickly and widely reflected in publicized interest rates. Studies have shown that financial markets, including the stock markets, are efficient users of information in the sense that prices quickly adjust to reflect expert information on all the factors—government policy included—bearing on future profitability.

Clearly the major industrial and commercial firms in the economy have a crucial financial stake in correctly forecasting how they will be affected by changes in government policy. Any actions they take, because of changed expectations, in product or resource markets will quickly carry the message of their reappraisal to other participants, large and small, on both sides of the market.

Finally, when wage rates of a particular firm get out of line with other firms competing for the same labor pool, reaction by only a few workers is necessary, in general, in order to cause the firm to adjust its wage rates to the prevailing market. Perhaps none of the workers need take direct action if the firm monitors the market and adjusts its salary structure, as many firms do, using projections based on market surveys. Such surveys will reflect what's happening at the more responsive firms, including the effects of escalator provisions and other union bargaining results. In sum, the rational expectations argument is that information about the likely future is transmitted in the marketplace in the same way as information about the present. A given individual or firm need not be the "complete seer" of the future any more than of the present.

III. What Happens to Activist Macro Policy in a Rational Expectations World?

In earlier sections we reviewed arguments for disbelieving that macro policy actions can work the way conventional perceptions say they do, and we presented reasons for thinking that the kind of world policy makers must deal with is something very close to a rational expectations world.

The serious problem, then, is the following: If people really do behave as rational expectations models their behavior, then many existing beliefs about the results policy can achieve are incorrect. As we've abundantly stressed already, macro policy initiatives that people anticipate will be frustrated by the changes people will then make in their plans. More particularly, any policy move to stimulate aggregate spending will be largely dissipated by price rises.

Econometric models are constructed of mathematical equations, often designed to be solved on computers in a way capable of simulating the future course of an economy. Results can then be cranked out quarter-by-quarter to produce numerical forecasts of employment, prices, or whatever economic variables are contained in the model. It's now a commonplace that models of this sort—some with as many as several hundred equations—have since the mid-1960s become increasingly important information bases for business decision making and for government policy decision making.

Conventional policy transmission channels, such as the wage illusion described in section I, are also built into traditional econometric models often used as a basis for evaluating alternative policy actions. Those models, of course, were not designed to reflect rational expectations, but there generally is a way to impose on them a form of rational expectations. *When that's done, the revised macro model reveals that activist economic policy does not have much of an impact on the economic outcome—apart from what it does to prices.*

Conventional Policy Stimulus in a Slack Economy.

There is a widely held view that says, if the economy is operating with a great deal of slack, or "excess capacity," any policy-spending stimulus will have little effect on prices and will mainly result in an increased real quantity of output. Only when the economy nears "capacity" output, claims that view, will extra stimulus spending fail to bring forth much new physical output and instead be largely dissipated on price increases. Neither economic theory nor empirical evidence supports that view.

There is no compelling theoretical reason to believe that some kind of critical point exists in the economy's overall scale of operation that abruptly distinguishes price-quantity responses taking place above that point from those taking place below. That doesn't mean that physical constraints or bottlenecks might not occur at the individual plant or industry level to temporarily block output increases from occurring in response to stronger demand. But for the economy as a whole, substitution possibilities are enormous, so spending can shift to other lines or services where bottlenecks or constraints will not, in general, be reached at the same time. Thus, the economic concept of aggregate production suggests only gradual transition of cost, price, and profitability relationships over the full range of operating levels for the economy as a whole.

The observed Phillips relationship, which does not in general exhibit a sharp bend, provides a rough, practical verification that such is the case. And that ought to indicate, to those who still believe in an exploitable Phillips curve, that the policy maker gets no "free ride" as the economy expands from its low points in relative operating levels.

There is further empirical evidence to that point: one of our studies, using data for the United States economy, has shown that the reported capacity utilization rate does not help explain inflation rates when the effects of other factors bearing on price changes are analytically separated out. That is, whatever the cause of price level changes, that cause doesn't appear to act any differently when excess capacity is high than when it is low.

It's true that a government monetary or spending stimulus sometimes will be dissipated nearly totally in price increases. At other times it will bring forth greater physical quantities of goods and services but *only* when accompanied by an increase in prices. The determining factor between these two alternatives has nothing to do with "capacity utilization," but instead depends on whether or not the stimulus has been *anticipated* by people who make buy-and-sell decisions in the economy.

In summary, there is no activist policy — at any level of excess capacity — that does not bring forth price increases at the same time it causes output expansion, and nowhere does the relative amount of output vs. price response change greatly as "excess capacity" is used up.

IV. Some Conclusions: Given the New Views—What Can Macroeconomic Policy Really Do?

The policy view built around rational expectations ideas does not argue that monetary actions by the Federal Reserve and fiscal actions by Congress and the Administration can't have an effect on production and employment. They can and do, but only when they surprise people.

As we've repeatedly emphasized, a crucial distinction required by the new view is that between policy actions that are expected and policy actions that are surprises — only the latter cause people to alter their expectations about opportunities for gain and hence to adjust their planned behavior.

In the case of policy actions that are expected, the new view argues there is neither an empirical nor theoretical basis for believing they can be exploited by policy makers for any beneficial real effect. Included in this category are predictable policies such as the Federal Reserve's traditional "leaning against the wind" (which is to say being "extra" restrictive in supplying reserves when the economy approaches high operating rates and being "extra" liberal when the economy has begun to slump), as long as that leaning is done consistently. The only economic effect of expected policy actions, if on the stimulus side, would be to boost general inflation.

Policy actions that come as a surprise to people, on the other hand, will, in general, have some real effects. Policy surprises cause people to change their plans, because the expectations on which they based those plans have been jolted. In the technical literature, much of the defense of activist policy against the rational expectations attack has hinged on preserving ways in which surprise could continue to provide workable leverage for the policy maker, even though decision agents are granted rational expectations. We've already discussed a few of these arguments — for one, the idea that people lock themselves into contracts on prices or wages. This, activists argue, enables policy makers to use surprise when needed, by catching people in midcontract, to foster a particular policy objective. We pointed out in section II why that argument is faulty. Another activist idea is that government policy makers have better information or superior knowledge about how the economy works, and so they can take an action that people won't catch on to, at least for a long enough time to enable some policy results. The premise about superior knowledge in the government sector is clearly faulty, and section II talked a bit about the efficiency of private sector information.

These arguments are at best attempts to patch up questionable policy theory by finding special conditions under which the policy of "surprise" can be routinely used by government to smooth out swings in the business cycle. Rationalists doubt, at one level of questioning, that stabilization efforts based on surprise really give the policy maker much to work with. To the extent surprise policy involves a deliberate strategy of fooling people (in the sense that had the people only known the truth they wouldn't have done what the government's action got them to do) it may easily work the first time, but then fail to be effective the second or third time because people have escalated their awareness of what government is likely to do in any given situation. And unless the "surprise-that-works" is later repeated, under similar conditions and in a consistent and logical way, it is not possible to distinguish government policy making from a random, or even perverse, game.

At a deeper level, rationalists doubt that it would be wise, or fair, for the government to attempt "policy by surprise" even if policy makers were sufficiently resourceful to invent unendingly new surprise ways to boost the money supply and government spending.

One of the most important ideas emerging from the new view, as we pointed out in section III, is that the "business cycle" might at last be adequately explained as a property of a properly working market economy. In such a view, individuals are thought to react to profit incentives and to imperfectly extract information about those incentives from changes in price signals that are in part useful information and in part meaningless "noise." An economic system doing the most efficient possible job of reading the information being reflected in price signals will still experience some irreducible business cycle swings. That's because the economic process contains inherent mechanisms that convert random shocks on prices into a more persistent, short-term misreading of changing profit opportunities. When misread by enough people, that action can stimulate a cumulative swing in output that will continue until the misreading is realized and retrenchment sets in. Random shocks to prices and markets are always with us. Some arise from natural catastrophes or man-made embargos, but Lucas argues that an important source of shocks to prices may have been erratic "surprise" actions by policy makers themselves.

The new view conjectures that some amount of cyclical swing in production and employment is inherent in the *micro* level processes of the economy that no government *macro* policies can, or should attempt to, smooth out. *Expected* additions to money growth certainly won't smooth out cycles, if the arguments in this paper are correct. *Surprise* additions to money growth have the potential to make matters worse. That's because surprise policies, and the prospect of other future surprise policies, lead to greater uncertainty in people's expectations about future prices, wages, and interest rates — and those are prime ingredients in people's ongoing decision making. These new theories say the information value of price signals is *eroded* by erratic and unpredictable government policy action. Given the importance to an efficiently working market economy of information conveyed by prices, the potential of activist general demand policy to do costly mischief must be considered a serious one. Government's potential to systematically exploit surprise shocks is drastically limited in a rational expectations world.

The Road Ahead . . .

If it's true that traditionally perceived activist policy goals are unattainable through macroeconomic policy channels, what goals should guide monetary and fiscal policy? What should monetary policy try to do?

One strategy that seems consistent with the significant, though largely negative, findings of rational expectations would have monetary policy focus its attention on inflation and announce, and stick to, a policy that would bring the rate of increase in the general price level to some specified low figure. To be sure, merely to announce such a policy at this point in time would be a "surprise" — perhaps a rather large one given the past history of policy — and is therefore likely to have, for a period of time, some effects on the planned level of output and employment. But there's no way to avoid some lurching when a trajectory is changed. After a period of adjustment, so we've argued here, a steady and consistent pursuit of some publicly known, modest growth for the money supply would not have detrimental effects on employment levels because the general price level impact of monetary policy would be built into people's expectations.

Given that sort of primary dedication to a lower inflation path, the general objective of monetary policy suggested by rational expectations ought to be elimination or reduction of uncertainty about the future general price level — to make it as predictable and dependable as possible around some low average rate of growth. That course, rationalists argue, would do more than any alternative macro policy posture to contribute to long-term steady economic growth and high employment rates.

While we might have reasonable confidence in the wisdom of that general strategy, the rational expectations view can offer little on the question of how best to implement such a policy operationally. That's one of the unfinished tasks for research. In the meantime, the broader issues we've raised are topics for deep reflection and debate by those responsible for designing and controlling the economic policies of this nation. That's a responsibility that ought also to concern informed citizens who, after all, will reap the benefits of good policies and pay the costs of poor ones.

23

Financial Innovation and Monetary Policy

LYLE E. GRAMLEY

*Lyle Gramley is a member of the Federal Reserve Board.
This article appeared in the* Federal Reserve Bulletin, *July
1982.*

Innovation in financial markets has proceeded at an
impressive pace for a quarter-century. Recently the
pace seems to be accelerating. While the implications
of these developments for central banking are of most
concern to the United States, they nevertheless are
relevant for other countries as well. First, these innovations affect U.S. interest rates and credit conditions, which in turn have profound effects on financial markets around the world. Second, innovations
beginning in one market are likely to spread eventually to others.

Innovations and Their Sources

The key forces giving rise to financial innovation
in the United States are found in the economic, interest rate, and regulatory environment of the past two
decades. During most of the period since World War
II the U.S. economy has suffered from a rising rate of
inflation. As borrowers and lenders came to expect
inflation to continue, or even to accelerate, market
interest rates moved progressively higher (Figure 1).

Higher market rates of interest raised the penalty
associated with holding deposits whose yields were
limited by law or regulation. The yields that depository institutions could pay were limited by prohibitions or ceilings on the payment of explicit interest,

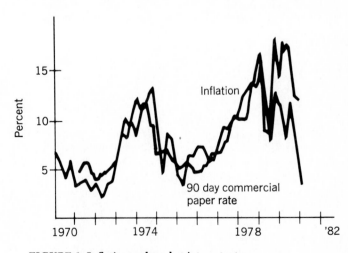

FIGURE 1. Inflation and market interest rates

121

and also by requirements to hold non-interest-bearing reserves, which reduce the rate of return on the investment of deposit proceeds. Moreover, the thrift institutions, which specialize in mortgage lending, were, and still are, severely limited in their capacity to pay prevailing market interest rates for deposits because they hold a substantial volume of longer-term assets acquired earlier, when inflation and interest rates were lower.

As the public has become increasingly sensitive to the earnings lost by holding non-interest-bearing or low-yielding deposits, they have become more adept at economizing on cash balances and more receptive to new kinds of financial investments. The increased financial sophistication of households and businesses, moreover, has been coupled with technological advances in computers and telecommunications that have reduced the cost of information and of transferring funds.

The innovational process stemming from these forces became evident during the 1950s. At that time, depository institutions did not actively seek deposits, but passively accepted the funds placed with them by the public. For individual institutions, deposit levels were determined exogenously, so that imbalances between deposit flows and net loan extensions were met by adjusting holdings of liquid assets, usually securities issued by the U.S. Treasury.

A heightened sensitivity to interest rate differentials developed during the course of the 1950s among larger business firms, and commercial banks found that they could no longer expect an automatic flow of business funds into non-interest-bearing checking accounts. Banks responded to their eroding liquidity position by issuing large-denomination negotiable certificates of deposit and making secondary markets for them. This was the first in a sequence of steps that ultimately led to dependence on liability management as the principal source of bank liquidity. The ability of banks to compete for these funds was at times hampered by deposit rate ceilings, but in the early 1970s the ceilings on large CDs were eliminated.

In the mid-1970s banks began more aggressively to market instruments of very short maturity—such as repurchase agreements on securities and dollar-denominated deposits at their offshore branches. They also began to issue commercial paper through their parent holding companies. Rates paid on these instruments were not limited by regulation, nor was it necessary to hold reserves against them.

During the past decade the financial sophistication of business firms has increased profoundly. Management of cash positions has assumed an important place in the duties of financial managers, along with their traditional role of ensuring the availability of capital for business enterprise. Considerable effort and investment have gone into the development of information systems, cash-forecasting methods, and techniques for transferring funds that enable firms to minimize their holdings of cash and, in the process, to maximize earnings on working capital.

Individuals as a group were slower than businesses to respond to the forces motivating changes in financial practices, in part because they lacked the necessary financial sophistication. In addition, the alternative financial investments available to individuals were, until recently, limited by minimum denominations on market instruments and the relatively high cost of securities transactions in small amounts. Since the mid-1970s, however, new institutions and instruments have emerged to compete for the savings of individuals. The most widely publicized of these are the money-market mutual funds, which have grown explosively in the past several years (Figure 2). These funds offer small savers the opportunity to invest indirectly in diversified pools of large-denomination money-market instruments such as commercial paper and negotiable CDs. Most of them permit the immediate withdrawal of funds by check or other convenient means. While money-market funds are a repository for savings, they also can serve as transaction balances or as a very close substitute for them.

Other high-yielding investments have attracted considerable public interest as substitutes for money.

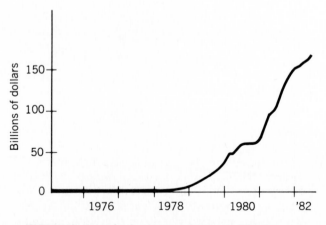

FIGURE 2. Growth of money-market mutual funds

A number of brokerage firms now offer "cash management" accounts, which combine the features of money-market funds and margin accounts. Most of these allow for withdrawal of funds by check in any denomination, and also by debit card. The newest arrangements, "sweep accounts"—some of which are designed primarily for smaller businesses and others for individuals—permit funds to move automatically into or out of conventional transaction balances to investment accounts paying market rates of return.

The increased competition for savings of individuals has forced the financial regulatory authorities to accelerate the liberalization of ceiling rates on their small-denomination time deposits. Also, individuals may now hold checking accounts that bear interest (Figure 3). The Monetary Control Act of 1980 authorized nationwide negotiable order of withdrawal accounts—checkable deposits earning 5¼ percent interest at commercial banks and at thrift institutions—beginning in 1981. These interest-bearing checking deposits now account for almost one-fifth of total transaction balances—that is, of the narrow measure of money, M1.

These innovations have particular relevance for monetary policy. First, transaction balances, as measured by M1, are growing much more slowly than are other financial assets; the income velocity of M1 has approximately doubled in the past twenty years. Second, the differences between money and other financial assets have been narrowing. The new instruments have both transaction and investment characteristics. M1, the conventional measure of transaction balances, now includes interest-bearing checkable deposits that also have a significant savings component. At the same time, money-market funds and cash management accounts, which are not included in M1, are also used partly for transaction purposes. Third, the distinctions among classes of financial institutions, and between financial and nonfinancial firms, have been blurred. To cite just one example, the retail firm of Sears Roebuck has become a financial conglomerate with a nationwide electronic funds-transfer system, a savings and loan association subsidiary, a credit card company with more than 20 million customers, the capability to clear and settle third-party payments, a full-line insurance subsidiary, a nationwide network of more than 1000 offices, and ready access to the commercial paper market. Sears has announced its intention to expand its provision of a wide variety of financial services to the public, including payments services.

The current process of financial innovation is far from complete. Technological advances have spurred changes in the structure of the financial services industry. Automated accounting systems, advanced telecommunications, computer-based cash management systems, and wire transfers of funds underpin some of the innovations already mentioned. Automation of data production and transmission will continue to shape the financial industry. We are, I believe, on the verge of a virtual revolution in electronic payment transfers, which will permit instantaneous flows of funds between financial instruments at very low cost.

Implications for Monetary Policy

Financial innovation in the United States has had important and far-reaching ramifications. It has raised questions about the appropriate definition of money, the precision of the Federal Reserve's control over the money stock, the meaning of changes in money balances, and the mechanism by which monetary policy affects economic activity. It has altered competitive relationships in the market for financial services. It has encouraged individuals and businesses to hold an increasing portion of their financial assets in forms not covered by federal deposit insurance, or at institutions not supervised or regulated by federal authorities. It has added to the risk exposure of many financial institutions. It has fostered the integration of financial markets, and in the process has altered the mechanism of credit allocation among sectors of the economy.

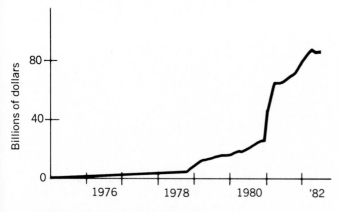

FIGURE 3. Growth of NOW accounts

To deal comprehensively with even one of these issues is beyond the scope of a short paper. But I will try to suggest how financial innovation has affected the conduct of monetary policy in the United States.

The Definition of Money

The difficulties associated with defining money certainly are not new: the existence of money substitutes and "near monies" has always made it hard to decide which assets should be included in a particular measure of money. Traditionally the issue has boiled down to drawing the line somewhere along a spectrum of assets ranked according to degrees of "moneyness," starting with balances serving as a generally accepted means of payment—having only a few investment characteristics—and moving successively to less liquid assets offering higher returns.

Innovation has made the dividing line between money and other financial assets conceptually more arbitrary. Assets with both payment and investment characteristics are more common; moreover, the decline in the cost of shifting from one financial asset to another has widened the spectrum of assets held at any particular time to make payments.

From a purely theoretical standpoint, conceptual arbitrariness in the definition of money need not be a problem for monetary policy. After all, if a central bank can identify and control a monetary variable that is related in a reasonably stable way to economic activity and prices, it can accomplish its broad economic objectives even if the definition of that variable is arbitrary. If the definition of money appears arbitrary, however, it is more difficult for the central bank to maintain credibility with the public. Furthermore, when financial innovation proceeds rapidly, the appropriate concept of money on which to focus attention will almost certainly change, requiring periodic redefinitions of money that create still more credibility problems.

Controlling the Monetary Aggregates

Even more serious problems will arise if the process of innovation undermines the ability of the monetary authority to control money growth. Monetary policy in the United States is implemented by setting targets for several monetary aggregates. The principal target has been the narrow money stock, M1, which comprises currency and checking deposits (Figure 4).

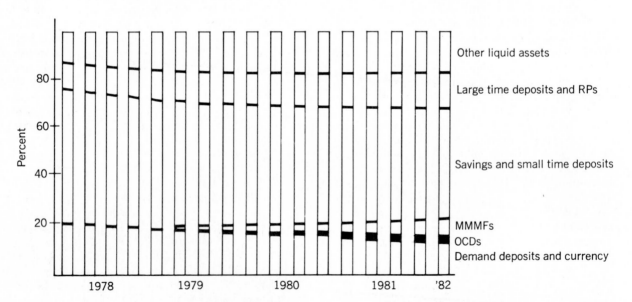

FIGURE 4. Components of liquid asset holdings. M1 is currency held by the public and demand deposits at commercial banks; other checkable deposits; and traveler's checks (included here with OCDs). M2 is M1 plus general-purpose money market mutual funds; savings and small time deposits; and overnight repurchase agreements and overnight Eurodollars (both included here with savings and small time deposits). M3 is M2 plus large time deposits; term RPs; and institution-only MMMFs (included here with large time deposits). L is M3 plus other liquid assets.

Studies at the Federal Reserve indicate that, despite its inadequacies, M1 is more closely related to economic activity and prices than are the more inclusive money aggregates.

Financial innovations have not as yet seriously compromised our ability to control M1. The Monetary Control Act of 1980 extended reserve requirements to all depository institutions, a step that helped to strengthen the link between reserves and M1.

We may, however, be on the threshold of serious problems of monetary control because of innovation. The proportion of money-market funds used for transactions apparently is still quite small, but it may be growing rapidly. Moreover, the spread of sweep accounts may accelerate. Because these sweep arrangements transfer funds out of conventional transaction balances into investment accounts at the end of each business day, they effectively remove transaction balances from the reserve requirements of the Federal Reserve. To deal with this development, the Federal Reserve needs legislation authorizing it to impose reserve requirements on all financial instruments that serve as the functional equivalent of transaction balances, regardless of the issuer.

A second kind of problem for monetary control arises if the money variable the central bank seeks to control, or at least a substantial part of it, pays a market-related rate of interest. For example, actions of the Federal Reserve to restrain the growth of bank reserves appear to have less immediate effect on M2 growth than they used to. The restraint on reserve growth increases market rates of interest, but rates on the nontransaction components of M2 rise as well. There is consequently little incentive to shift out of these elements of M2 into nonmonetary assets. Efforts to keep the growth of such a money variable within narrow limits could foster wider short-run fluctuations in interest rates. Eventually, of course, increases in interest rates may slow income growth and thereby moderate the demand for M2. In effect such a process amounts to slowing the economy to slow money growth, a sequence the reverse of that contemplated in the use of a financial variable for monetary targeting.

Stability of Money Demand

In recent years the principal problem that financial innovation has caused for monetary policy has not concerned the ability of the Federal Reserve to control the money stock. Rather, it has concerned the

relationship among the money stock, economic activity, and interest rates.

Successful use of a monetary variable as an intermediate target of central bank policy requires relative stability in the relationship between money and economic activity. Before 1974 one could predict reasonably well the amount of M1 that the public would want to hold given the size of the economy and the level of interest rates. Since then, however, growth of M1 has been considerably slower, relative to the rise of nominal gross national product, than historical relationships suggested. More important, the period since 1974 has been characterized by greater short-run instability of money demand.

Estimates of shifts in the public's demand for money are imprecise, but studies by Federal Reserve Board staff suggest that they are too large to be ignored in the conduct of monetary policy. For example, over the four quarters of 1975 measured growth of M1 amounted to 5.1 percent. However, the demand for money—at given levels of nominal GNP and interest rates—may have declined about 3¾ percent during 1975. According to this estimate, *effective* money growth (the actual increase *plus* the downward shift in money demand) was nearly 9 percent over the four quarters. By contrast, the decline in money demand in 1977 is estimated to have added less than half a percentage point to effective money growth.

Shifts in money demand make it much more difficult to conduct monetary policy by setting targets for money growth. The Federal Reserve can, and does, try to estimate these shifts and take them into account in the formulation of monetary policy. But the estimates are necessarily imprecise, even for historical periods (Figure 5). Worse still, at the time of change

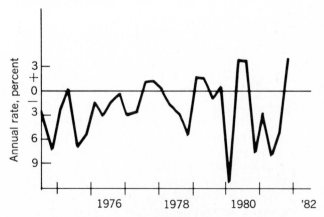

FIGURE 5. Error in money demand, based on FRB quarterly econometric model forecasts

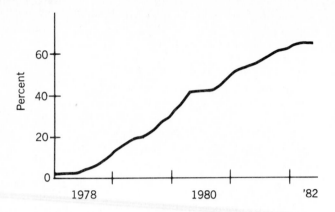

60

Percent

40

20

0

1978   1980   '82

FIGURE 6. Share of nontransaction M2 bearing market-related interest rates

in growth of M1 deposits from a predetermined path an observer can never be sure whether it reflects a shift of money demand or the effects of change in economic activity on needs for transaction balances. The appropriate policy response is, of course, very different in the two circumstances.

Financial innovation has also affected the relationship between the more inclusive monetary aggregates and GNP. In past periods of rising market interest rates, growth of M2 (which includes savings and time deposits of individuals) tended to slow abruptly because funds were diverted from depository institutions to market securities. But the composition of M2 has changed materially since 1978; now more than 60 percent of its nontransaction component consists of assets bearing market-related yields (Figure 6). As noted above, such a composition affects the ability of the Federal Reserve to control the growth of M2 in the short run. Also, it tends to alter the relationship of M2 to GNP. Thus even in the face of substantial variations in interest rates, the velocity of M2 has changed relatively little over each of the last three years, in contrast to the rather wide swings that used to occur.

The problems posed by the instability of money demand cannot be solved by making the monetary base the target. Such a step is unlikely to improve monetary policy. The monetary base is an arbitrary combination of the various components of the monetary aggregates. Its largest component is currency, whose magnitude has always been—and, I believe, always should be—determined by public demand. The remaining portion of the base, bank reserves, is basically a weighted sum of the reservable deposit com-

ponents of the monetary aggregates, with the weights determined by reserve ratios. When the significance of movements in the aggregates is uncertain, so also is the significance of changes in the monetary base. Furthermore, there is little reason to think that stability in the growth of the monetary base will produce economic stability. Over the 1970s yearly growth rates of the monetary base never deviated more than 1½ percentage points from their decade average. Nevertheless the 1970s was a period of considerable economic instability.

Another suggestion is that we replace monetary aggregates by a broad credit aggregate as an intermediate target of monetary policy. This suggestion has some intellectual appeal. Some broad credit aggregates appear to be relatively closely and stably related to nominal GNP. Unfortunately, the suggestion seems impractical. The data on credit flows in the United States become available to the monetary authority with very long lags, and they are subject to large revisions. They could hardly serve, therefore, as a useful target for monetary policy.

Still another suggestion is that the Federal Reserve abandon its attempts to use quantitative targets as intermediate objectives of monetary policy, and instead seek directly to establish the level of real interest rates. From the standpoint of economic theory this approach has some merit. From the standpoint of the practice of central banking, however, it has several deficiencies. First, the level of real interest rates is not directly observable; we observe only nominal interest rates and then infer what real interest rates might be by guessing the price expectations of borrowers. Second, it is extremely difficult to ascertain the real interest rates needed to produce the desired performance of the economy. The economic effects of a given level of real interest rates will change with the sectoral mix of GNP, tax rates, and the period over which monetary restraint is in effect. Third, and perhaps most important, public acceptance of monetary restraint is more readily achieved when the central bank focuses on reducing the growth of money and credit than when it sets interest rates openly and directly.

I believe, therefore, that the use of monetary aggregates as intermediate targets of monetary policy continues to be justified, despite the instability of money demand generated by financial innovation. Inevitably, however, the pursuit of monetary aggregate targets under present circumstances requires both judgment and flexibility. Short-run movements of the money stock have even less meaning as indicators of monetary policy than they once did. Moreover, monetary targets are best expressed in rather wide ranges; the Federal Reserve's present target ranges for money growth of 3 percentage points are certainly not too wide, given the kind of uncertainty that surrounds movements in the monetary aggregates. Also, we need to continue to use multiple targets, rather than to focus on any single measure of money. Indeed, greater weight may need to be given to the broader monetary aggregates in the future as a consequence of the relative instability of the demand for M1. Finally, we must stand ready to accept growth of money outside our target ranges—or to modify those ranges—when changes in the public's asset preferences warrant it.

Transmission of the Effects of Monetary Policy

The mechanism through which changes in monetary policy are transmitted to the nonfinancial sectors of the economy has also been influenced by innovation. Twenty-five years ago monetary restraint worked partly through reductions in the availability of credit to potential borrowers. Financial markets at that time were less integrated, so that when inflows of deposits to depository institutions declined and liquid assets were drawn down, banks and thrift institutions were forced to reduce their lending to homebuyers, small businesses, and other borrowers who depended heavily upon them. The rationing process did not rely exclusively upon higher interest rates; on the contrary, nonprice rationing methods predominated in many sectors of the financial market. Usury laws and legislated ceiling rates on government-insured loans also acted to reduce the availability of mortgage credit and consumer installment lending. And statutory limits on the rates of interest that could be paid by states and municipalities blocked the flows of credit to those political subdivisions.

Innovations and regulatory changes have led to a gradual breakdown in the barriers to credit flows that existed in particular markets. As a result monetary policy now transmits its effects to the economy largely through changes in real interest rates.

This shift in the channels of transmission of monetary policy has both positive and negative effects. It improves the efficiency with which money and capital markets allocate resources among competing uses. It also rewards savers more fully, thus encouraging saving for investment purposes.

But when monetary restraint does not result in curtailment of the availability of credit to potential borrowers, real interest rates may have to rise to much higher levels than they otherwise would to moderate aggregate demand. Such a development will be especially likely if monetary restraint is accompanied by an expansive fiscal policy. Moreover, the real interest rates confronted by different sectors of the economy are not the same, because expected price increases vary substantially from one sector to another. For example, wholesale prices of farm products generally are lower now than a year ago, in contrast to substantial increases in the wholesale prices of nonfarm products. The experience of sharply rising real interest rates, moreover, is one that farmers are unprepared to deal with. Before 1978 agricultural borrowers obtained funds principally from rural banks, whose lending rates were largely insulated from developments in the national money markets.

Higher interest rates in our money markets affect borrowers abroad as well as in our own country. The opening up of capital markets has increased international access to the U.S. financial system, and has made the effects of domestic monetary policy register more heavily and more rapidly abroad. The huge amount of dollar indebtedness of developing countries means that their debt service costs are powerfully affected by changes in U.S. interest rates. For the industrialized countries the primary concern is that relative interest rates have a heavy impact on exchange rates in the short run. A sharp rise in U.S. interest rates therefore may confront them with the dilemma of accepting a depreciation of their currency relative to the dollar or taking steps to raise their own interest rates.

The Stability of the Financial System

Another way in which financial innovation may affect monetary policy is through its effects on the risks of enterprise. I would conjecture that innovation increases the risks of financial intermediation. Because it does so it may limit the ability to use monetary policy aggressively to fight inflation.

In the United States the risks of financial intermediation have increased for a number of reasons. First, some financial intermediaries, such as the thrift institutions, have been less able than others to adjust to rapid change. Second, fluctuating interest rates have tempted financial institutions with a high propensity to gamble to speculate in an effort to increase net interest margins. Moreover, it is difficult for supervisors and examiners to monitor and assess the interest-rate-risk exposure of a financial institution. Third, innovation has sharpened the competition among the suppliers of financial services, thus narrowing profit margins. Fourth, new forms of activity, such as foreign lending, have increased the chances for mistaken judgments. Fifth, and perhaps most important, reliance on liability management as a principal source of liquidity has increased the risk exposure of individual institutions. The problem of maintaining an image of soundness has taken on critical importance because sources of funding can evaporate at a mere hint of difficulty. Reliance on purchased funds has also intensified the interdependence among institutions. For example, if one institution appears to be in trouble, depositors may decide, out of an excess of caution, to remove funds from others.

The risks stemming from financial innovation have spread beyond financial institutions to the nonfinancial sectors of the economy. Interest rates in the U.S. economy have been more volatile in recent years—partly, in my judgment, because innovation has affected the way financial markets function. Interest rate movements have also become less predictable. As a consequence, banks and other lenders are seeking to avoid, or at least to minimize, interest rate risk—risk that they once accepted willingly. In the process they have shifted the risks of fluctuating interest rates to other sectors, which may be less able to bear them. Futures markets for financial assets may help eventually to shift the burden of interest rate risk to those most willing and best able to bear it, but those markets are not as yet well developed.

Problems of this kind have not caused the Federal Reserve to deviate from a monetary policy designed to reduce inflation by gradually slowing the growth of money and credit. The process of financial innovation is not complete, however, and we cannot be sure of what the future will bring. At a minimum, concerns about the way innovation increases the fragility of the financial system will make it increasingly important to support policies of monetary restraint with aggressive use of fiscal policy to fight inflation.

PART FOUR

Inflation and
Anti-Inflation
Policies

During the past fifteen years inflation has been a serious economic problem. In the opening paper, the Congressional Budget Office describes the effects of inflation, as well as its causes. Then it discusses various policy options for reducing inflation, such as deflationary fiscal or monetary policies, incomes policies, wage-price controls, specific market interventions, and tax-based incomes policies. The next article, taken from the 1982 Annual Report of the Council of Economic Advisers, concludes that "The policies of the [Reagan] administration are based on the view that the cost of continuing to endure the high rates of inflation of the 1970s would be greater than the costs of implementing a successful non-inflationary policy."

In the next paper, Robert M. Solow takes up the various price indexes that are used to measure the rate of inflation and discusses the nature of inflation. He is less fearful of inflation than Arthur F. Burns, the author of the following article. According to Burns, "our long-run problem of inflation has its roots in the structure of our economic institutions and the financial policies of our government." He believes that some form of incomes policy might be useful.

In the early 1980s there has been considerable concern over the size of actual and prospective federal deficits. The next item, taken from the 1982 Annual Report of the Council of Economic Advisers, indicates why deficits matter, how deficits can be measured, and the relationship between deficits and inflation. Finally, the article by Brian Horrigan describes one response to inflation—indexation. He concludes that "It would be far better to have no inflation and no indexation than even a little of either or both."

24

Inflation

CONGRESSIONAL BUDGET OFFICE

This article comes from Recovery with Inflation, *published by the Congressional Budget Office in 1977.*

The Meaning of Inflation

Inflation is often taken to mean a continuing rise in the *general* price level. A difficulty with this definition is that it glosses over a fundamental characteristic of inflation: Inflation changes relative prices. That is, if a quart of milk costs twice as much as a loaf of bread before inflation, it is unlikely to cost exactly twice as much during or immediately after inflation. If a week's wages buy a television set before inflation, there is no assurance that they will do so afterwards.

In fact, inflation without changes in relative prices has never occurred; if it did, no one would mind very much. If pensions, wages, salaries, rent, profits, and the prices of all goods and services increased at the same rate, it would be a nuisance, but no one would be badly harmed.

Public concern with inflation is based in large part on its effects on the structure of relative prices and incomes. Some examples are given in Figure 1. The upper left graph compares the annual percent change in the Consumer Price Index (CPI) with the annual percent change in average hourly (nonfarm) labor compensation. Because output per worker grows over time, compensation tends to rise faster than prices. As may be seen in the figure, however, the margin of compensation over prices narrows during accelerating inflation. Indeed, in 1974 under the combined effects of inflation and recession, the CPI rose faster than compensation, and real earnings—the purchasing power of an hour's work—declined.

The behavior of the CPI and the prices of two specific types of goods, agricultural products and fuel, are compared in the upper right graph. Differences between the rate of change in the CPI and the rate of change in farm and fuel prices have tended to increase during periods of accelerating inflation. Moreover, while rising farm and fuel prices in 1972–73 and 1973–74, respectively, received much publicity, farm prices increased less than the overall CPI in 1967–68, 1970–71 and 1974–76. Similarly, fuel was becoming relatively cheaper during most of the period from 1958 through 1970.

The lower left graph depicts variations in the rates of change of crude and intermediate materials and finished goods prices. Price changes among these three

131

broad categories appear most disparate during periods of increasing inflation. All three charts show the tendency for all prices to increase during inflation; but some prices increase much faster than others, with some prices leading the average and others following with a lag.

Why Relative Price Changes Occur During Inflation

The relation between inflation and changes in relative prices is one in which causation seems to run both ways: changes in relative prices are caused by inflation and inflation is caused by increases in the absolute (and relative) prices of individual goods and services.

Inflation causes changes in relative prices because most individual prices are *not* changed either continuously or simultaneously. Over the past five calendar years, the annual rate of inflation in the United States, as measured by the CPI, has been 3.3, 6.2, 11.0, 9.1 and 5.8 percent. For relative prices to have remained unchanged, all prices would have had to rise continuously or in simultaneous steps at the same rate as the average. The facts are otherwise. Prices that change day-to-day or in lockstep with others are the exception; for example, open-market interest rates, prices of equity shares, and some wholesale commodity prices. The lower right hand graph of Figure 1 provides an example of one price that in recent years has responded quickly to changes in the rate of inflation—the three-month Treasury bill (interest) rate—and an example of one that responds more slowly—the maximum interest rate paid on regular savings accounts at federally insured commercial banks. From 1965 to the present, the ceiling rate on savings accounts was changed only twice; over most of this period the rate of inflation exceeded the interest ceiling.

Another infrequently adjusted price is the wage rate. Most wages are adjusted for inflation no more than once a year. Of the 10 million workers covered by major collective bargaining agreements (those covering more than 1,000 employees), fewer than 25 percent receive cost-of-living adjustments more frequently than once a year. In contrast, income tax rates rise automatically with current dollar income because of the progressive rate structure. Worse yet, some pensions and annuities are permanently fixed in dollar amount and thus decline in real value during inflation. In sum, because all prices do not increase at the same

time or at the same rate, inflation changes relative prices and the distribution of real income.

An increase in an individual price also pushes up the general level of prices. The large absolute (and relative) increase in the price of energy is a commonly cited, recent example. Higher prices for petroleum and related increases in prices of electricity, natural gas, and coal contributed to a higher price level directly and indirectly by raising the cost of producing almost everything else. As was observed in late 1973 and 1974, the immediate effect of pervasively higher prices for goods and services accompanied by slowly changing wages and salaries was that consumer spending for some goods was reduced. Reductions in spending lower output and raise unemployment. Monetary and fiscal policies may become more expansionary in response to higher unemployment rates. These policies may reduce unemployment, but they are also apt to perpetuate a high rate of inflation. Thus, individual price increases, through their effects on costs, unemployment, and government policy, can lead to inflation.

The Causes of Inflation

Prices of individual goods and services are jointly determined by buyers and sellers. At each possible price, there is some quantity of the good that suppliers are willing to sell and that purchasers are willing to buy. The market price will tend toward that price at which desired sales are equal to desired purchases. Market prices are raised by developments that reduce the quantity offered for sale at any particular price (a fall in supply) or that increase the quantity buyers offer to purchase at any particular price (an increase in demand). When speaking of the entire economy, therefore, it is convenient to classify the causes of a higher general price level into those that increase aggregate demand and those that decrease aggregate supply.

Aggregate demand may be increased by an expansionary monetary policy, a tax cut, an increase in government spending, a rise in the propensity to consume, an investment boom, or growing foreign demand for U.S. goods. Aggregate supply may be reduced by crop failures; the formation of cartels to restrict supply and raise price; restrictions on imports such as tariffs, quotas, and "orderly marketing agreements"; higher minimum-wage laws; and government regulations and private agreements that interfere with an efficient use of resources.

FIGURE 1: **Inflation, Relative Prices, and Incomes**

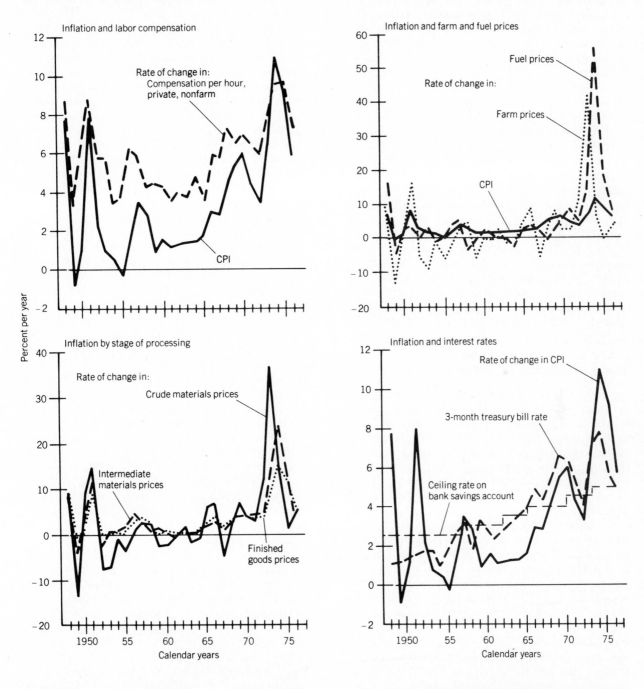

Sources: U.S. Department of Labor, Bureau of Labor Statistics for price and compensation data. Farm prices, fuel prices, and prices by stage of processing are compo- nents of the Wholesale Price Index. U.S. Treasury Department for Treasury bill rate. Federal Reserve Board for ceiling rate on bank savings accounts.

Many of these factors were at work between the mid-1960s and the inflation surge of 1973–74. Monetary growth accelerated; government spending increased sharply during the Vietnam War; the tax incentives and sustained expansion of the early 1960s created a major investment boom. An expanding world economy coupled with U.S. devaluations stimulated exports and raised the price of imports, and crop failures were widespread in the early 1970s. Finally, world oil prices quadrupled in 1974. These factors were the major causes of the subsequent period of rapid inflation.

In assessing the recent high inflation, it is important to recognize a fundamental difference in inflation triggered by a fall in supply as distinct from one caused by an increase in aggregate demand. The difference is that with a fall in aggregate supply, such as might result from a crop failure or a reduced supply of energy, some real output is irretrievably lost. Economic policy cannot offset the direct, real effects of poor growing conditions or reduced supplies of natural resources, although policy can limit output reductions in sectors not directly affected by supply changes. Inflation triggered by increased demand, in contrast, will not initially reduce real output.

The Persistence of Inflation

One basic reason for the persistence of inflation is that policymakers strive to achieve low unemployment as well as low inflation. When aggregate demand weakens and unemployment rises, economic policymakers may respond with more expansive policies. Similarly, efforts by policymakers to offset the unemployment effects associated with a fall in supply provide underpinning for continuing upward price pressures.

The response of economic policy to the unemployment effects of changes in aggregate demand and supply is not the only source of persistence in rising prices. Another very important one is the way consumers, labor, and business adapt to the expectation of inflation. In order to describe these adjustments, it is useful to distinguish cases in which inflation occurs unexpectedly from those cases in which the inflation is anticipated. Consider first an economy with approximate price stability, in which the annual rate of price change varies only between 1 and 3 percent with an average of 2 percent. This was roughly the U.S. experience from the Korean War to the Vietnam War. Given the previous ten years' experience, it was

reasonable to assume in 1965 that the inflation rate in the future would be about 2 percent. Reasonable, but wrong.

Because the inflation of the late 1960s and early 1970s was largely unanticipated, the implicit and explicit contracts of trade, finance, and employment were drawn without provision for inflation. As a result, inflation changed the relative price structure and thus led to large redistributions of income and wealth. Creditors generally suffered losses to debtors when debtors made repayment in dollars with reduced purchasing power. Workers whose wages did not keep pace with the average rate of change in prices saw their real incomes decline. In general, those who had agreed to supply goods and services at specified prices on the assumption of a modest rise in prices were stuck with prices that were "too low" until those prices could be renegotiated.

The magnitude of losses resulting from the failure to foresee the inflation caused people to anticipate future inflation and to change their behavior accordingly. The length of long-term, fixed-price contracts tended to be shortened, More time and effort were diverted from other uses to the attempt to forecast price changes and to profit from those forecasts. Catch-up wage settlements were made. Provisions for automatic cost-of-living adjustments were negotiated into many labor contracts. At the beginning of 1977, about 60 percent of the workers covered by major collective bargaining agreements were entitled to some cost-of-living escalation. In 1965, only 25 percent of these workers were entitled to such wage adjustments. Where permitted to do so by regulation, interest rates rose to include a higher inflation premium. For example, the long-term, AAA-rated corporate bond rate rose from 4.5 percent in 1965 to 8.8 percent in 1975. Household survey data show that changed expectations about the future course of prices were not confined to labor leaders, firms, and large investors. The Survey Research Center at the University of Michigan reported that respondents who expected the next year's inflation rate to exceed 4 percent increased from 27 percent in 1966 to 55 percent in 1975.

These changes in the anticipated rate of inflation and in people's behavior reduced, though they did not eliminate, the redistributional consequences of subsequent inflation. By reordering commercial agreements and financial plans on the expectation of inflation, however, they also provided inflation with a very strong momentum.

Once the expectation of inflation becomes incorporated into contracts, informal agreements, and plans, stopping that inflation becomes a very complex feat. Suppose, for example, that economic policymakers try to stop an anticipated inflation quickly through sharply restrictive monetary and fiscal policies. The first effect of these policies is to reduce total spending. But with many prices already scheduled to rise, the principal impact of the spending cutback will be to increase unemployment and to idle productive capacity. In time, these output effects will cause some downward revisions in actual and expected prices, if the demand weakness is considered to be more than just a temporary aberration. These price revisions, in turn, will tend to restore employment levels. Until inflationary expectations are revised downward, though, the major impact of the anti-inflation policy will be on real economic variables such as employment, production, and income.

An actual rate of inflation *below* the anticipated rate also has redistributional consequences similar in character but opposite in sign to those resulting from an actual rate *above* the anticipated rate. In this case, debtors lose and creditors gain. Buyers who have contracted to purchase goods at prices reflecting inflationary expectations lose and sellers gain.

Although the distinction between anticipated and unanticipated inflation is helpful in assessing inflation's effects and in appreciating how it acquires a momentum, all inflation is to some extent unanticipated. Not everyone will anticipate the actual rate correctly. Given wide variations in the actual inflation rate, such as that of the United States during the last five years, people will anticipate, with varying degrees of likelihood, a range of inflation rates. A large number of possible outcomes amounts to increased uncertainty. Such uncertainty is, in itself, undesirable and many people would pay something to avoid it. But awareness of a whole range of possible inflation rates also means that, as prices change, economic units will not be able to distinguish clearly a relative price change (for example, a change in the real value of what they have to sell) from a general inflation price change. People, therefore, experience greater difficulty in interpreting the meaning of price changes during inflation. As a result, the price mechanism becomes a less efficient communications system.

Policy Options for Reducing Inflation

If policymakers wish to attempt to slow inflation, a wide variety of options is available. Most of these either reduce aggregate demand or increase aggregate supply. Four types of policies are considered here: a deflationary macroeconomic policy; wage-price controls or guidelines; ad hoc price reduction measures aimed at selected markets; and tax incentives designed to encourage price stability. These policies would have different effects on inflation, both with respect to timing and total impact. Most would prove costly in terms of other Congressional goals.

A Deflationary Fiscal or Monetary Policy

There is a sense in which it is correct to say that inflation continues only because economic policy permits it to do so. Monetary and fiscal policies exist that could arrest the rise in the price level. The cost of those policies in terms of unemployment and lost production would be great, however. Given the strength of inflationary expectations, even the goal of a modest reduction in the rate of inflation risks stalling the recovery, though the inflation-arresting effects of such a policy could be pronounced in the more distant future. The trade-off of current employment and output for future price stability could be avoided only if price expectations were to be revised down quickly in response to a deflationary policy and if the prices in contracts and agreements could be adjusted immediately in line with those new expectations.

Econometric analysis carried out by CBO suggests that a fiscal policy change equivalent to a $43 billion cut in federal government expenditures—about two percent of GNP—below a current policy projection starting in fiscal year of 1978 would be required to reduce the inflation rate by 1 percentage point in 1980. As shown in Table 1, such a policy is estimated

Table 1: Estimated Effect of a Cut in Federal Government Spending to Reduce Inflation by 1 Percentage Point, Fiscal Years 1978, 1979, and 1980

	1978	1979	1980
Change in federal purchases (billions of dollars)	−43	−43	−43
Change in the inflation rate* (percentage points)	−0.3	−0.8	−1.0
Change in real GNP (billions of 1972 dollars)	−51	−61	−40
Change in the unemployment rate (percentage points)	+1.2	+1.6	+1.2

Note: In all cases, "change" refers to the difference from a baseline projection without the spending reduction.

*Fourth quarter over fourth quarter change in the CPI.

to reduce real GNP (1972 dollars) by $51 billion in the first year and $61 billion (about 4 percent) in the second year. The negative effect on employment would be at its peak in the second year, when the average annual unemployment rate would be increased by 1.6 percentage points, or about a million and a half unemployed workers.

Incomes Policy or Wage-Price Controls

The importance of inflationary expectations in the perpetuation of inflation and the desire to reduce those expectations without paying a high price in terms of unemployment has often prompted the suggestion that wages and prices ought to be controlled more or less directly through so-called incomes policies.

The United States has had some experience with several forms of these: mandatory controls during the Korean War; guideposts and "jaw-boning" (attempting to affect prices by persuasion) during 1962-66; the New Economic Policy of 1971-74 which included periods of wage-price freeze as well as more flexible mandatory and voluntary controls; and the current activities of the Council on Wage and Price Stability whose principal instruments are persuasion and publicity.

Controls on prices and wages *seem* to be a direct and low-cost cure for inflation. During periods when such controls have been in effect, they appeared to have held down the rate of inflation somewhat. But, while the cost of a general deflationary monetary or fiscal policy is likely to be painfully apparent in the unemployment figures, the substantial costs of incomes policies are mostly hidden. The more restrictive the policy—a complete freeze is an extreme example—the greater the likelihood it will succeed in temporarily holding down the measured rate of inflation, but the greater its costs.

A recent CBO study of incomes policies reviewed U.S. experience and identified some of the difficulties associated with these programs. Fundamental among these has been the difficulty of establishing a ruling "principle behind the policy;" that is, a set of decision standards that are efficient and equitable while also effective and feasible. Such a set of standards may not exist. As a consequence, the policies seem to lead to inefficiencies and inequities and a breakdown of public support. The administrative cost of controls can also be substantial. In addition, these policies are often thought to create a depressing climate for business enterprise and investment.

Specific Market Interventions

There are two distinct, separable aspects of an anti-inflation strategy of intervention in particular markets. For one, it is suggested that the government intervene directly in some markets to hold down prices. For the other, the intent is to reduce and abolish government-mandated minimum prices.

The notion of a selective incomes policy is based on the idea that by directly retarding the rate of increase for those key goods and services that are going up in price most rapidly, inflation can be slowed. Rapid price increases in a particular sector are usually symptomatic of fundamental conditions peculiar to that industry. For example, a recent Council on Wage and Price Stability study of health care cost found ". . . that unique structural characteristics of the health care industry underlie its extraordinary inflationary behavior." Specifically, ". . . the primary supplier of medical services, the physican, usually determines the level of services required by the consumer. . . . Moreover, medical services are largely paid for through a system of third-party payors, insurance companies and government health programs . . ." that weakens the incentives physicians, hospitals, and patients may have to hold down costs. "Any policies aimed at mitigating inflation in this sector must address these structural peculiarities."

Even if some form of intervention—such as the proposed Hospital Cost Containment Act of 1977 which aims to restrict the growth of hospital revenues and capital expenditures—is adopted and proves effective in substantially cutting the rise in medical costs, the direct effect on inflation will be rather small. For example if the 1976 rise in medical care costs had been cut by one-fourth, the CPI would still have risen by 5.6 percent instead of the 5.8 percent actually realized.

A number of government policies, adopted for other reasons, are in force whose effects are to raise prices. Examples include minimum wage laws, agricultural and dairy price supports, restrictions on imports, the regulation of transportation rates, and environmental and health/safety regulations. Reduction or repeal of these measures over a period of time is sometimes suggested as a means of reducing the rate of increase in prices and lowering inflationary expectations. Repeal, of course, would cause some considerable losses to the beneficiaries of these policies and hence would encounter determined opposition.

All of these options for stopping inflation are costly: general deflation risks ending the recovery; wage and price controls can temporarily suppress inflation but at the cost of misallocating resources and creating inequities; selective controls aimed at particular sectors of the economy will eventually have to come to grips with the underlying reasons for rising prices in that sector; and many interests will defend the continuation of government price supports.

Tax-Based Incomes Policies and Related Proposals

In recent years there have been proposals to use tax incentives and other schemes to encourage more moderate price behavior. Like the incomes policies described above, these mechanisms are generally directed at decisions of individuals, with the goal of ensuring that wage rates, on average, do not rise much faster than labor productivity. Rather than overriding market forces, these newer proposals attempt to take advantage of market incentives by making moderate price and wage increases a matter of self-interest for firms and employees.

The best known of these proposals involves tax incentives to reward or penalize wage decisions that deviate from some established standard. A number of such tax proposals exist but only two specific examples are described below.

The first approach, aimed at employers, would tax employers who grant wage increases in excess of the standard. It is assumed that the tax surcharge could not easily be passed on to consumers by way of higher prices because some competitors might not have incurred as large a surcharge. As a result of the tax, employers would become more resistant to wage demands.

A more recent proposal uses tax incentives to restrain employee wage demands. Under this proposal, payroll taxes would be reduced for employees in proportion to the degree of wage restraint exercises. If the average wage for a firm increased 1 percent less than some designated standard, then the payroll tax rate would be cut by, perhaps, a full percentage point for the employees of that firm. The tax cut would last for one year only, unless wage increases in the following year were again held below that year's standard.

Other innovative anti-inflation mechanisms would not employ tax incentives, but would rely instead on the federal distribution of marketable wage increase permits, without which firms could not raise wages. These permits would allow wage increases equal to 3 percent of the annual wage bill (the assumed productivity increase) and would be distributed to firms in accordance with their previous annual wage bill and collected from firms according to current wages paid. Because the permits could be traded, growing firms that need to attract more workers would seek additional permits while others, particularly declining firms, would seek to sell their unused permits. But the overall wage bill for the economy could not legally increase faster than the value of total permits issued.

All of these proposals would encounter numerous administrative problems. How is the "standard" wage increase to be determined? How are catch-up wage increases and long-term contract agreements to be handled? The tax proposals would have to be carefully designed to prevent the establishment of loopholes.

Moreover, these proposals implicitly assume that labor cost pressures are the principal cause of inflation—a conjectural notion at best. Attempts to broaden the proposals to include profits, interest, and rent would, however, greatly increase their administrative complexity.

Nevertheless, the advantage of proposals that provide incentives for more moderate price changes cannot be dismissed. This appears to be an area where further research, and perhaps some experimentation, could be useful. For now, these proposals must be regarded as uncertain because they are untried.

25

The Nature of the Inflation Process

COUNCIL OF ECONOMIC ADVISERS

This item was taken from the 1982 Annual Report of the Council of Economic Advisers.

Inflation is essentially a monetary phenomenon. This is not to deny the importance of other factors, such as changes in the price of petroleum, in causing increases in the general price level. What the statement does deny, however, is that persistent inflation can be explained by nonmonetary factors.

Monetary policy actions affect primarily nominal quantities—exchange rates, the price level, national income, and the quantity of money—as well as the rate of change in nominal quantities. But central bank actions do not have significant long-run effects in achieving *specific* values of real magnitudes—the real rate of interest, the rate of unemployment, the level of real national income, the real quantity of money— or rates of growth of real magnitudes.

Economists recognized long ago that output and employment may be no higher when prices are high than when they are low. A main point of Adam Smith's *Wealth of Nations* is that a country's wealth and income depend on the country's real resources and the way in which production is organized, and not on the level of prices. It was realized that changes in the price level had some short-term effects on out-

put, but these effects were recognized as the result of transitory changes in demand.

The classical gold-standard mechanism embodied these principles. Unanticipated increases in the flow of gold from abroad stimulated domestic production but gradually raised domestic prices relative to foreign prices. The rise in domestic prices then reduced exports and raised imports, thereby lowering domestic production and employment and eventually lowering prices. The continuous ebb and flow of gold was expected, but the timing of the movements could not be predicted accurately. Inability to predict the movements was recognized as a cause of changes in prices and output.

Once people anticipate that prices will rise, they seek higher wages for their labor and higher prices for their products. The increase in employment produced by stimulative policies vanishes, but the inflation remains. Attempts to reduce unemployment by increasing inflation will work only if people are fooled by the changes in policy. Once people learn to expect inflation, the short-run gains in employment disappear.

It is often stated that inflation is an intractable problem, caused by forces beyond our control. But the monetary nature of inflation suggests that this is not so. More important, it suggests that a decrease in money growth is the necessary strategy to end inflation. Frequent use of monetary policy to reduce unemployment at certain times and inflation at others would raise the prospect of generating the same kind of cyclical behavior in economic activity that we have experienced in the past and analyzed in the previous section.

Stop-and-go policies cause uncertainty, hamper the ability of monetary authorities to achieve noninflationary conditions, and ultimately raise the transitional costs of eliminating inflation. The next section discusses in detail the nature of these costs.

The Costs of Inflation

Over the last decade, as inflation worsened, the attention of the general public focused on the detrimental effects that rapidly rising prices have on economic performance. These effects were felt in many ways, but the mechanisms by which inflation generated them were not well understood.

The effects of inflation fall into two general categories: (1) those that occur because no one is able to predict the precise rate of inflation; and (2) those that occur even when the rate of inflation is fully anticipated.

The concept of a "fully anticipated inflation" implies a rate of inflation that people can predict and hence take action to minimize its effects. But it is doubtful that a high rate of inflation that was also predictable could ever exist because the same lack of monetary discipline which leads to unacceptably high inflation is also likely to lead to more variable inflation. Indeed, periods of high inflation rates generally have been associated with periods of higher variability of inflation rates. It would take at least as much monetary discipline to maintain a constant high inflation rate as it takes to maintain price-level stability. Once a positive rate of inflation is accepted it becomes difficult to argue against a slightly higher rate.

One of the most important costs of unanticipated inflation is its arbitrary redistribution of wealth and income. Economic transactions are often formalized in contracts that require one party to pay a fixed dollar amount to the other party at some point in the future. When both parties anticipate inflation during the life of the contract, these future dollar payments will be adjusted upward to compensate for their expected lower real value. This upward adjustment is the so-called inflation premium. If, however, the actual rate of inflation turns out to be different from the anticipated rate, the real terms of the contract will have been altered arbitrarily. If the actual rate is higher than anticipated, the fixed payments in dollars will have a lower than expected real value, and the debtor will gain at the expense of the creditor. The same kind of arbitrary transfer occurs when workers and firms agree to wage contracts that implicitly or explicitly assume rates of inflation which later turn out to be incorrect.

In a market economy, changes in the price of one good relative to another signal changes in demand and supply conditions among various markets. An uncertain rate of inflation obscures these signals and thereby reduces economic efficiency. Since prices are rising more or less together during a general inflationary period, the fact that a price has risen is no guarantee that it has risen relative to other prices. The difficulty of distinguishing between relative and absolute price changes increases as inflation and its variability increase. This leads people to use more time and resources to attempt to decipher relative price changes, as opposed to engaging in more productive activities. Differently stated, inflation tends to make the economic information that people accumulate through experience more rapidly obsolescent than when prices are stable.

Perhaps more important, inability to correctly anticipate inflation creates confusion about relative prices over time and compounds the problem of efficient resource allocation. Economic decision-making especially in the private sector, is inherently forward-looking. Decisions made today determine tomorrow's levels of capital stock, production, and consumption. Decisions based on correct anticipation of future relative prices lead to a more efficient allocation of resources over time. High and variable inflation, on the other hand, leads to divergent inflation expectations, and therefore to a larger proportion of incorrect decisions.

Because inability to anticipate the rate of inflation correctly increases the uncertainty associated with economic decisions, especially those that involve fixed-dollar commitments far into the future, it leads to a shortening of the time horizon over which such commitments are made. In the financial markets, uncertainty about inflation causes a relative decline in the volume of long-term bond financing. Neither borrowers nor lenders are willing to compensate the other adequately for the risk. Consequently the sales volume of fixed-rate long-term debt instruments shrinks and the volume of real investment normally financed in this way decreases. More generally, productive activities yield a relatively lower real return than activities aimed at "beating" inflation. Hence as more and more resources are devoted to coping with the uncertainty that accompanies inflation, fewer resources are available for real productive activities.

Two costs of anticipated inflation have been widely recognized. In the economics literature they have been dubbed "menu" and "shoe leather" costs. Because inflation requires frequent changes in published (that is, "menu") prices, these changes absorb resources that could be used in other activities. "Shoe leather" costs are those incurred by people attempting to minimize their money holdings by more frequent trips to the bank. Since a great deal of money is held as a non-interest-bearing asset, its real value declines with inflation. People therefore make more strenuous efforts to realize the highest return on their assets and hence they economize on non-interest-bearing balances.

The interaction of a nonindexed tax system with inflation would impose costs even if the rate of inflation were correctly anticipated. Imperfect adjustment for inflation in the taxation of both current labor income and income from capital causes changes in inflation to affect real after-tax levels of income. These in turn alter the level and composition of these activities relative to each other and relative to activities on which the return is not distorted. One analyst has estimated the unavoidable costs from this cause alone to be 0.7 percent of gross national product (GNP), and perhaps as high as 2 to 3 percent of GNP. The indexation of tax brackets beginning in 1985, as legislated by the Economic Recovery Tax Act of 1981, will substantially reduce this problem.

The interaction between the tax system and inflation also affects capital formation because of the way in which depreciation allowances are treated. Depreciation allowances for capital assets are based on historical cost rather than current replacement cost. During periods of high inflation the difference between historical cost and replacement cost widens rapidly, leading to allowances smaller than would be considered justifiable. Since deductions for depreciation are determined on the basis of the actual purchase price, smaller real deductions mean higher capital costs. This in turn reduces the pace of investment and hence of economic growth.

The Costs of Reducing Inflation

There is, as noted above, a short-lived trade-off between unemployment and the rate of inflation. This means that policies designed to reduce inflation significantly will temporarily increase unemployment and reduce output growth. The temporary decline in output growth induced by anti-inflation policies forms a rough benchmark against which the subsequent benefits of reduced inflation can be compared. The extent of these costs of reducing inflation depends on four factors: (1) the institutional process of setting wages and prices; (2) the role of expectations in this process; (3) the policy instruments employed to reduce inflation; and (4) the initial rate of inflation.

Flexibility in wages and prices reduces the transitional costs of ending inflation. A policy-induced decline in the growth rate of monetary aggregates will be associated with a decline in the growth of real output, but the more rapidly this decline in output is followed by a moderating of inflation, the more rapidly will output growth return to a rising trend. One important factor affecting the flexibility of wages and prices is the institutional environment in which they are determined. The costs of continuously negotiating and resetting prices and wages, for example, has given rise to the common practice of changing wage and price agreements relatively infrequently. While this practice makes economic sense for individuals and firms, it builds a degree of inertia into the system.

Wage contracts in major industries in the United States typically cover a two- or three-year period. Since these contracts specify basic wage increases over the life of the contract, the current rate of wage inflation was determined in part as long as three years ago. Because major wage contracts are staggered over approximately three years, wage settlements in the first year of each "three-year round" tend to set the pattern for settlements in the following two years. This extends the influence of any year's wage settlements beyond the lives of the contracts. In addition, many contracts include automatic cost-of-living adjustments that preclude downward wage flexibility, even when it might be justified by conditions specific to a particular industry or firm.

Government regulations or standards that dictate prices or wages, reduce competition, or otherwise reduce the flexibility of firms and workers in responding to economic conditions also add to the inflexibility of wages and prices. Programs now under way to bring regulatory relief to industries that have been overregulated in the past should diminish this source of rigidity.

Decisions concerning the determination of prices and wages are dominated by perceptions of future market conditions, such as the expected rate of inflation. Workers will accept nominal wage increases that, given their expectation of inflation, imply an acceptable real wage. If their expectations about inflation are revised downward in light of announced policies to end inflation, wage and price increases will moderate. The pace of this adjustment in expectations is an indication of the degree of public confidence in anti-inflationary policies.

The primary policy tool for ending inflation is a decrease in the rate of growth of money. The question of how rapidly the monetary deceleration should proceed must be answered in the context of public expectations. In view of past experience, when efforts to reduce inflation were abandoned as the short-run costs began to accrue, the public has come to expect that such policies will continue to be short-lived and that inflation will persist. Frequent swings from restrictive to stimulative policy and back have led to a "wait and see" attitude on the part of the public. The mere announcement of new policies is not sufficient to convince people that they will be carried out. Rather, public expectations regarding the future course of policy are adjusted only gradually as policy actions turn out to be consistent with policy pronouncements. The credibility of policy authorities, like the credibility of anyone else, is enhanced when they do what they say they are going to do. For the Federal Reserve this means setting money growth targets consistent with a sustained decrease in the rate of inflation and then adhering to those targets. The more success the Federal Reserve has in meeting those targets, the less time it will take before the public is convinced of the policy's credibility.

In the current environment, even if a successful effort is made to reduce money growth, past experience with high and variable inflation will affect the speed at which financial markets reflect progress toward a long-run noninflationary policy. Having repeatedly suffered sizable capital losses on their holdings of long-term bonds, investors will be unwilling to commit new funds to these markets unless they are compensated for the risk that the current commitment to overcome inflation might be abandoned. Without adequate compensation for this risk, individuals will continue to prefer to invest in short-lived rather than long-lived financial assets. While this preference may prevent investors from maximizing the expected return on their assets, it allows them to minimize the adverse effects of future increases in inflation and interest rates.

Present concern about future monetary growth, inflation, and interest rates is related to the knowledge that the Federal budget will continue to show large deficits for the next several years. Financial investors fear that these deficits will cause either a sharp increase in interest rates—which would slow the recovery from recession—or an increase in monetary growth if the Federal Reserve attempts to hold interest rates down by adding reserves to the banking system through open market purchases of government securities.

Interest rates that are considerably higher than the current rate of inflation can have an adverse effect on investment and real economic growth. The level of long-term interest rates at the end of 1981 did not reflect investor willingness to believe that inflation will decline over the next several years. The presumably large but unmeasurable premiums being demanded by investors constitute a major obstacle to achieving rising output and employment with falling inflation.

Expectations about future rates of money growth, like expectations of future inflation, are likely to be more divergent the greater the variability of past money growth. These expectations should converge more rapidly as the Federal Reserve improves its ability to control money growth. More precise control of money growth around the target path will reduce the difficulty of inferring from actual growth rates whether or not the announced targets are in fact a reliable indicator of future money growth. In such an environment, variations in money growth will reflect only random and short-lived deviations, which would have little effect on either short- or long-run expectations about monetary policy. But failure to achieve more precise monetary control, by impeding a rapid adjustment of expectations, would significantly raise the costs of reducing inflation. Thus the payoffs of greater precision could be quite large.

In summary, high and varying inflation imposes costs on society by reducing future standards of living. These costs, though presumed to be large and pervasive, are not easily calculated. There is a temporary output loss in the initial stage of a transition to price stability. Such loss, however, must be weighed against the future increases in output that would be achieved by ending inflation. The policies of the administration are based on the view that the cost of continuing to endure the high rates of inflation of the 1970s would be greater than the costs of implementing a successful noninflationary policy.

26

The Intelligent Citizen's Guide to Inflation

ROBERT M. SOLOW

Robert M. Solow is Professor of Economics at Massachusetts Institute of Technology. This paper appeared in The Public Interest in 1975.

Two broadly opposite frames of mind seem to dominate the current discussion of inflation. One says that we are beset by some utterly mysterious plague of unknown origin. If it is not stopped soon, it will cause unimaginable, or at least unspecified, disasters. The only hope is that some Pasteur or Jenner or Ehrlich will discover The Cure. The other view is that it is all quite simple. There is some one thing we have failed to do: control the money supply or balance the budget or legislate price controls or abolish the unions. As soon as we do it, the problem will then go away.

This essay is written in the belief that both these currents of opinion are wrong. I do not, however, have an alternative solution to offer. Indeed, I rather doubt that there is a Solution, in the sense of some policy that your average mixed capitalist economy can reasonably be expected to pursue which will drastically reduce the tendency to inflation, without substituting some equally damaging and intractable problem instead.

What I can hope to do is to explain the vocabulary and intellectual framework evolved by economists for discussing and analyzing inflation. By itself, this will

contribute to clarity of thought—much, perhaps most, of current popular discussion is hopelessly confused. I hope to be able to go further than that, however. There are some positive statements one can reasonably make about the behavior of modern mixed economies. We know less than we would like to know, but much more than nothing. Where I verge on speculation, or where there are real differences of opinion within the economics profession, I will try to be honest about it.

What Is Inflation?

Inflation is *a substantial, sustained increase in the general level of prices.* The intrinsic vagueness of "substantial" is harmless. One would not want to use a heavyweight word to describe a trivial rise in the price level; granted, it will never be perfectly clear where to draw the line, but neither can it be important since only a word is at stake. "Sustained" is a little trickier. One would not want to label as inflationary a momentary (six-month? one-year?) upward twitch of the price level, especially if it is soon reversed. There is no point in being forced to describe mere short-term fluctuations in prices as alternating bouts of inflation and deflation. "Sustained" also carries some connotation of "self-perpetuating" and that raises broader questions. It is obviously important to know whether each step in an inflationary process tends to generate further inflation unless some "outside" force intervenes, or whether the inflationary process is eventually self-limiting. The answer need not be the same for all inflations, and it certainly depends on what you mean by "outside." So it is probably best not to incorporate this aspect as a part of the definition.

It is the notion of the "general price level" that will lead us somewhere. Economists make a sharp and important distinction between the system of relative prices and the general price level. Relative prices describe the terms on which different goods and services exchange for *one another;* the general price level describes the terms on which some representative bundle of goods and services exchanges for *money.* Imagine an economy in which the only goods produced are meat and vegetables, and first suppose that all exchange is barter; some people trade meat for vegetables with other people who want to trade vegetables for meat. If one pound of meat exchanges for three pounds of vegetables, then the relative price is established. But since there is no money, there is no such thing as the general price level. Notice that inflation is inconceivable in a barter economy. It would be logically contradictory for "all prices" to rise at the same time. Suppose that, because of a change in tastes or a natural catastrophe, one pound of meat should come to exchange for six pounds of vegetables. One could say that the price of meat (in terms of vegetables!) had doubled. But that is exactly the same thing as saying that the price of vegetables (in terms of meat!) had halved. A carnivorous farmer would find himself worse off; but a vegetarian rancher would be sitting pretty.

So inflation has intrinsically to do with money. Now let us introduce some greenbacks to serve as money in our meat-and-vegetables economy. Suppose meat goes for $1.50 a pound and vegetables for 50 cents a pound—i.e., one pound of meat for three of vegetables, as before. Now suppose that at a later time meat goes to $3.00 a pound and vegetables to $1.00. The relative price is unchanged. From most points of view the meat-and-vegetables economy goes along as if nothing has happened, and from most points of view nothing has. (Not quite nothing: A tradesman or a miser who happened to be sitting on a load of greenbacks at the time will have taken quite a beating.)

We can go a step further. Suppose the average daily diet consists of one pound of meat and one pound of vegetables (though very few individuals may actually consume exactly the average diet). We could agree to measure the general price level by the money cost of the average consumption bundle. In that case, we would say that the price level was 200 in the initial situation, and 400 after the price increases. (It is the custom to choose some year as "base year" and set its price level arbitrarily at 100. If the initial year is the base year, then the later price level would be 200.) In any case, we would certainly want to say that the general price level had doubled, and if it had doubled in exactly 12 months, we would say that the rate of inflation had been 100 per cent a year.

Since the prices of all goods and services had exactly doubled, it is no trick to say that the general price level had doubled. But we now have a routine that will take care of less obvious situations. Suppose meat goes from $1.50 to $2.40 a pound and vegetables from 50 cents to 60 cents. The price of meat has risen by 60 per cent, that of vegetables by 20 per cent. But the cost of the average consumption bundle rises from $2.00 to $3.00 (or the price index from 100 to 150). So we could say that the price level had gone up by 50 per cent. Notice also that this time relative prices have also changed: A pound of meat exchanges for four pounds of vegetables at the new prices. The vegetarian rancher gains at the expense of the carnivorous farmer, but *that is because of the change in relative prices.* In the case of "pure inflation," when *all* prices change *in the same proportion,* nobody loses (except owners of money) and nobody gains (except owers of money).[1]

Perhaps the simplest way to define inflation is as a loss in the purchasing power of money. That has the merit of emphasizing the fact that inflation is essentially a monetary phenomenon. But there is a possible semantic trap here. Some economists believe that the whole inflationary mechanism is primarily or exclusively monetary, in particular that the main or only cause of inflation is too rapid a growth in the supply of money. They may be right or they may be wrong. (I happen to think that doctrine is too simple by half.)

[1]The smart kids in the class will now ask: If meat gets more expensive relative to vegetables, won't consumers buy less meat and more vegetables, and won't that change the makeup of the average consumption bundle, and what will that do to the price index? They can go on to the course in Index-Number Theory, but they will find it dull.

But the mere fact that you can have inflation only in a monetary economy is neither here nor there, just as the fact that you can't have a drowning without water doesn't prove that the way to understand drowning is to study water, I will come back to this analytical question later.

Measuring Inflation

In the real world there are thousands of goods and services, whose relative prices are changing all the time in complicated ways. The measurement of the general price level thus becomes a major statistical enterprise. But it is done, and generally according to the principles just described. In fact, the American reader is confronted with at least three separate indexes of the general price level: the Consumer Price Index (CPI), the Wholesale Price Index (WPI), and the GNP Deflator. Since there are some conceptual differences among them, and since they may occasionally say different things, it is worthwhile to understand exactly what each of them means.

The CPI (what is sometimes called the cost-of-living index) is produced and published monthly; it is closest in principle to the kind of price index described earlier. At intervals of a decade or more, the Bureau of Labor Statistics (BLS) conducts an expensive survey of the spending habits of families of different size, income, and other characteristics. From this survey it calculates the typical budget of a middle-income, urban wage-earner or clerical worker with a family of four. Then each month it actually prices out that budget in a number of cities around the country. If the cost of that bundle goes up or down by 1 per cent, the CPI goes up or down by 1 per cent.

That is certainly a reasonable and meaningful price index, but it does have some drawbacks. (Of course, any method of reducing all those thousands of price changes to a single number will have drawbacks.) It relates only to consumers; the prices of industrial machinery and raw materials could go sky-high, and the CPI would register that fact only later, when cost increases filtered down to retail prices. Moreover, the CPI relates only to some consumers—those middle-income, urban, wage-earning families of four. Old people, or poor people, or oil millionaires, who buy different bundles, may have different experiences. Finally, economists have a technical reservation. The CPI covers, as its concept dictates it should, everything consumers spend money on, including sales

taxes, monthly mortgage payments, used cars, and so on. It reflects changes in state and local taxes, interest rates, used-car prices, etc. For some purposes, economists would prefer a price index confined to currently produced goods and services. Certainly it matters whether a rise in the CPI reflects mainly higher sales taxes and interest rates or higher prices for food and clothing.

The WPI, also available monthly, is based on prices collected at the wholesale level. Its coverage is wide but rather peculiar, for several reasons. For one thing, it omits all services, medical care, house rents, etc. For another, it counts some prices over and over again, and thus gives them more weight than they deserve. For example, a change in the price of raw cotton will appear first as a crude material, then again as it is reflected in the price of cloth, then again as it is reflected in the price of clothing. This pyramiding overemphasizes crude material prices and can cause the WPI to behave quite erratically, especially when the prices of materials are changing. Its main utility is that, just because of its coverage of the early stages of fabrication, it often catches price developments early. The WPI, like the other indexes, is broken down into sub-indexes (in the case of the WPI, farm products, processed foods, industrial materials, various categories of finished manufactures, etc.), and these may be very informative.[2]

The GNP Deflator

The GNP Deflator is by and large the economists' favorite. Unlike the CPI, it covers only currently produced goods and services, and unlike the WPI, it avoids all double-counting. But it is constructed in a more complicated way. The Department of Commerce calculates every quarter the country's Gross National Product. This is essentially the value at current market prices of the current flow of newly produced final goods and services. (The force of "final" is that one omits goods and services which are immediately used up in the production of something else, because their value will be included in the value of the final product.) At the same time, Commerce also calculates the GNP "in constant prices." That is, it takes

[2]For more on the WPI, and for a very informative and interesting article complementary to this one, I recommend "Inflation 1973: The Year of Infamy" by William Nordhaus and John Shoven in the May/June 1974 issue of *Challenge* magazine.

the current flow of final goods and services, but instead of valuing them at this quarter's prices, it values them at the prices of some fixed year, currently 1958. For instance, in 1973 the GNP in current prices was $1,295 billion, but the GNP in 1958 prices was $839 billion, because 1958 prices were lower than 1973 prices.

How much had prices risen between 1958 and 1973? The natural computation is $1,295/$839 = 1.54, for an increase of 54 per cent. If the 1973 flow of output valued in 1973 prices is 54 per cent higher than the *same* flow of output valued in 1958 prices, then the obvious inference is that the general level of prices must have risen by 54 per cent since 1958. So the general formula for the GNP Deflator in year X is: GNP in year X in current prices/GNP in year X in base-year prices. (Exercise: Convince yourself that the GNP Deflator for the base year itself is automatically 1.00 or 100, because in the base year GNP in current prices and GNP in base-year prices are the same quantity.)

Economists like this price index for the analysis of inflation not because it is obscure, but for the reasons I mentioned before: It eliminates double-counting, and it focuses on the pricing of currently produced goods, not existing assets. For that very reason, of course, it may not reflect exactly the experience of consumers. Another disadvantage is that the GNP Deflator is available only at quarterly intervals.[3]

All price indexes suffer from a common difficulty. Commodities change in character and quality. How can the BLS price the same consumer-bundle in 1955 and 1975 when many of the things consumers buy in 1975 did not exist, and so had no prices, in 1955? How can the Commerce statisticians value 1975 GNP in 1958 prices, when there were no 1958 prices for some of the items entering the 1975 GNP? If the price of an ordinary shirt rises 10 per cent in the course of a year, but simultaneously the wrinkle-resisting properties of the shirt are improved, how is one to decide how much of the 10 per cent represents the greater value of an improved product and how much represents pure price increase? The agencies do the best they can, but it is hardly a job that can ever be done perfectly. It used to be thought that there was systematic underallowance for quality improvements to such an

extent that an annual rise of 1 or 2 per cent in the measured price level could be ignored as not being a true price increase; but no one knows for sure. Perhaps the best conclusion is that one ought not to attach great significance to small changes in price indexes.

This discussion of price indexes has given us another concept of absolutely fundamental importance for rational discussion. GNP in constant prices is in an important sense a "physical" concept. It is an attempt to measure the size of the flow of actual production in a way that is independent of inflationary and deflationary aberrations. When GNP in constant prices changes, it is because the production of goods and services has changed, not because prices have changed. In terms of my earlier example, the difference between the 1968 GNP of $707 billion in 1958 prices and the 1973 GNP of $839 billion in 1958 prices permits us to say that "aggregate output" rose by 18.7 per cent between those years. In the jargon, GNP in constant prices is called "real GNP" or "real aggregate output." We will be coming back to it.

The Last One Hundred Years

Figures 1 and 2 show what has happened to the general price level since 1867. The price index used is the GNP Deflator.[4] Figure 1 shows the price index itself on what is called a logarithmic scale, to draw attention to the proportional changes that really matter. The base year is 1929 = 100. The fact that the price level in 1973 (291.5) is almost four times that in 1867 (78.0) is not to be taken as utterly precise, in view of the vast difference between the commodities making up the GNP in 1867 and those actually produced in 1973. But for orders of magnitude, the figures will do. Steep portions of the curve represent periods of more severe inflation; when the curve points downward, the price level was actually falling.

Figure 2 converts the price index into percentage rates of inflation and deflation; prices are rising when this curve is above the zero line, and falling when it is below.

---

[3]There is another minor problem. The basis for putting a price on the output of governments—education, police services, "plumbers'" services, etc.—is pretty tenuous, though these are all part of the GNP. It is possible to produce a price index for privately produced GNP, nearly all of which is actually sold on a market.

[4]I owe the figures to Professor Benjamin Klein of the University of California at Los Angeles, who pieced them together from estimates made by Robert Gallman for 1874–1909 and Simon Kuznets for 1910–1946, and the official Commerce Department figures for 1947–1973. The earlier figures are based on very sketchy data.

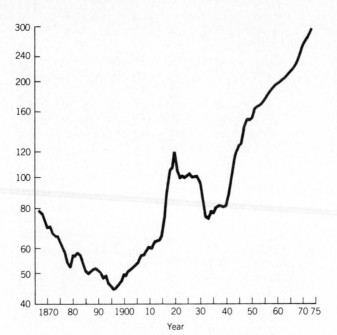

FIGURE 1. **The Price Index, 1867–1973 (1929 Base)**

The broad outlines of the history of the price level are easily read from the charts. From the end of the Civil War to the end of the 19th century, the predominant trend was deflationary. The GNP Deflator fell by more than 40 per cent between 1867 and 1896. Although the curve turned upward about then, by the eve of the First World War the price index had gone back up only to the level of 1873.

Really big inflationary bursts are associated with major wars, and their aftermath. Between 1914 and 1920, prices almost doubled. Between 1940 and 1948, prices almost doubled. The Korean War added only about 10 per cent to the price level. In the case of the Vietnamese War it is hard to know where to start; between 1966 and 1972, the index rose about 30 per cent.

But that is only half of it, and in some ways the less interesting half. There were at least two years of deflation after the First World War; by 1922 the index was back to the 1917–1918 level. The depression of the 1930's, like those of the 1870's and 1890's, pushed the price level down. The index, pegged at 100 in 1929, fell to 73.3 in 1933, rose to 80.3 in 1936, and stayed there until the eve of the Second World War in 1940. But the last minus-sign on Figure 2 appears briefly in

1949 when the first of the mild postwar recessions lowered the price index by a point. (On a quarterly basis one could find a somewhat bigger decline.) From 1950 on we have had a quarter-century without a dip in the general price level. The best one can find is the period beginning with the recession of 1958, running through the milder recession of 1960, and continuing during the slow return to approximate full employment at the end of 1965. During that interval, the Deflator rose at an average annual rate of about 1.5 percent. It is simply not possible to know with any confidence what would have happened if the escalation of the war either had not occurred or had not been allowed to overheat the economy in the last years of the Johnson Administration.

Why Is Pure Inflation a Bad Thing?

There seems to be universal agreement that rising prices are a cause for alarm and perhaps fear. Candidates for office accuse incumbents of having fostered inflation or failed to prevent it, and promise to eliminate it themselves. Incumbents announce that they are working on the problem. And surveys of public opinion show that very many ordinary people regard inflation of the price level as one of the most serious problems they face, or at least as an important background worry. Yet it is fair to say that public discussion offers no insight at all into the precise way in which a rising price level damages the current or prospective welfare of the representative citizen. Occasionally, the implied mechanism in the background makes no sense at all. Such a peculiar situation clearly deserves the most thorough investigation.

For the sake of clarity, let us first make an abstraction and think about a "pure" inflation, during which all prices rise at the same proportional rate—so many per cent per year—so that relative prices are unchanged throughout. Real inflations don't happen that way; but if we are to understand how and why inflation is a burden on society, we had better be able to understand the hypothetical special case of a pure inflation. After all, relative prices can change without any change in the general price level; we ought not to confuse the effects of the one with those of the other.

Well, then, who gets hurt in a pure inflation? If you think back to our meat-and-vegetables economy, it is hard to see how producers, including workers, suffer at all. So long as the prices of meat and vegetables, and wage rates in both industries, go up at the same percentage rate, every participant in the economy continues to have the same purchasing power over all goods and services as before. The inflation appears to have no "real" effects. The general point is that a person's economic welfare depends on the prices of the things he or she buys and sells, including labor and the services of property; if the prices of all those things go up or down in the same proportion, then economic welfare stays the same.

Now there is an optical illusion that clearly plays some role in popular discussions of inflation. Many people see no connection between the prices of the things they buy and the prices of the things they sell. The ordinary person works hard and feels that each year's wage increase is deserved. When it turns out that prices have also increased, so that all or part of the wage increase is illusory, the ordinary person regards that price rise—inflation—as a form of theft, a hand in his or her pocket. But of course, wages could not have increased had prices not increased. I cannot estimate how widespread this illusion may be, but there can hardly be any doubt that such an illusion does exist.[5]

If you want to know how the country as a whole is doing, then the course of the price level will not tell you. In narrowly economic terms, the proper measure of success is the flow of goods and services produced and made available to the society for consumption and other uses. The closest thing we have to look at is the real GNP, which we have already met. GNP in constant prices is the most comprehensive available measure of the performance of the economy in doing what it is supposed to do—the generation of want-satisfying commodities. It is far from perfect for reasons that involve the treatment of depreciation, environmental effects of economic activity, the organization of work, the "quality of life," governmental activity, and other things, but none of them has to do with inflation. So if inflation is a net burden to society, that ought to show up in a reduction of real GNP, or at least a slowing-down of its normal upward trend. But that is not what happens; in fact the opposite is more nearly true. Peri-

[5]No one could make that mistake in the simple meat-and-vegetables economy. But the real world is more complicated. For instance, the timing of price and wage increases is irregular, with some temporary advantage from getting in early, and some loss from getting in late. Moreover, the normal experience is that standards of living rise as productivity improves. Then only part of a wage increase is eroded away by price increases, but even the loss of that part is felt as robbery.

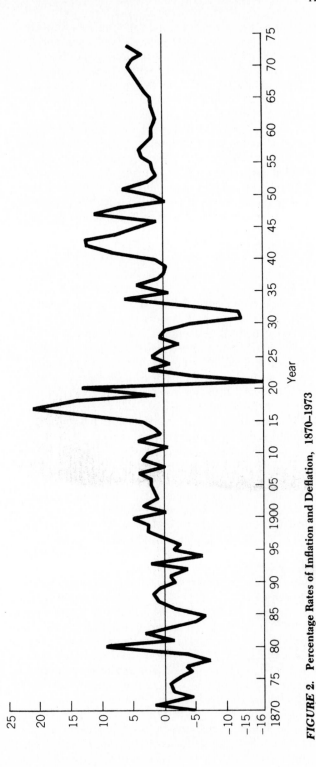

FIGURE 2. Percentage Rates of Inflation and Deflation, 1870–1973

ods of prosperity are somewhat more likely to coincide with periods of inflation and periods of recession are somewhat more likely to coincide with intervals of stable or more slowly rising prices.[6]

Is the social cost of inflation a mirage? There is one earlier hint that needs to be followed up. In a monetary economy—the only kind that can have inflation—holders of cash see their real wealth eroded by a rising price level, even in a pure inflation. So do creditors who hold claims for payment fixed in money terms. Offsetting at least some of these losses are the gains of debtors, who can pay back in dollars of smaller purchasing power what they had borrowed and spent in dollars of higher real value. Perhaps the true social costs of inflation are to be found among the holders of money, or among cash creditors more generally.

Anticipated Inflation

Another distinction—this time between anticipated and unanticipated inflation—is required for this analysis. So let us take the strongest case first: a pure inflation which is confidently and accurately expected by everyone in the economy. Suppose you lend me a dollar today and I agree to pay back $1.05 a year from today. Then we have agreed on an interest rate of 5 per cent annually. (You laugh, somewhat bitterly. But it's just an example.) If we both correctly expect the general price level to be quite steady during the next year, then that is all there is to it. You as lender and I as borrower are both willing to make the transaction at an interest rate of 5 per cent a year. Now imagine instead that we both confidently expect the general level of prices (which means each individual price and wage, since we are talking about a pure inflation) to be 4 per cent higher a year from now. I would be delighted to take your dollar today and pay you $1.05 in a year. Why not? If meat is a dollar a pound today and will be $1.04 a pound in a year, then in effect you would be lending me a pound of meat today, and I would be obliged to pay you only 1.05/1.04 or about 1.01

[6]There is an exception to all this, but it need not concern us. Imagine a country which must import a large fraction of its basic necessities, like food and oil, and pay for them with exports of other commodities. Such a country may experience steady or rising real production, but if world food and oil prices are rising faster than the prices of its exports, its own standard of living could deteriorate. The United States is not in that position because it is so nearly self-sufficient; but of course it is hardly a hypothetical possibility for Japan and some European countries.

pounds of meat next year. In *real* terms, you would be getting interest at 1 per cent a year, not 5 per cent. Of course for the same reasons that I would be pleased at the transaction, you would not be. In fact, if we were both prepared to make the deal at 5 per cent with stable prices, we ought both to be prepared to make the deal at 9 per cent when we both confidently expect the price level to rise at 4 per cent a year; in the real purchasing-power terms that matter, you will then be collecting interest at 5 per cent per year. In the professional jargon, the *real* rate of interest (5 per cent) is the *nominal* or *money* rate of interest (9 per cent) less the expected rate of inflation (4 per cent). Thus the very high interest rates of early 1974 have to be read against the substantial inflation of the same period. Real rates are not as high as nominal rates; in fact, they are lower by about the expected future rate of inflation—about which we can only guess. Of course, anyone who borrows long and is locked in at high interest rates is left holding the bag if the inflation should unexpectedly slow down or stop.

What follows? *If* the inflation is fully anticipated by everyone, *if* everyone has complete access to the capital markets, and *if* all interest rates are free to adjust to expectations about the price level, and do so quickly and smoothly, then borrowers and lenders will be able to protect themselves against inflation. Once again, the inflation would seem to have no real effects.

Well, not quite. Those qualifications are pretty strong. Obviously, we will have to consider the case of unanticipated inflation; but even before we get to that there are some important things to say. First of all, some assets bear no interest at all: the important ones are currency and balances in ordinary checking accounts. They constitute the money supply. It would be mechanically difficult for the Treasury to pay interest on currency. Commercial banks are restrained by law from paying interest on checking accounts. (They do the next best thing by providing financial services free of charge, or at a fee that diminishes with the size of balance; but that is hardly the same thing and cannot in any case serve the same purpose as a nominal interest rate in adjusting to expectations about rising prices.) So, even if the inflation is correctly anticipated, holders of currency and checking accounts will suffer (as they would symmetrically gain if deflation should ever come back into style). These losses to holders of money are not, so to speak, net losses to society, because there are corresponding gains to others. In the case of checking accounts, the gainer is the bank and its stockholders, who earn the higher nominal interest rates on their own assets and pay no interest—except for those free financial services—on deposit liabilities. In the case of currency, the U.S. Government, in the person of the Federal Reserve, is the issuer of the paper, but it is rather special paper, and a special kind of liability, and in any case not very important.

The "Deadweight Loss"

Since anticipated inflation redistributes to others part of the wealth of holders of money, it is natural that businesses and people should try to reduce their holdings of money when they expect prices to be rising. One can hardly do without any cash in the modern world, but nevertheless it is usually possible to substitute effort for liquidity. Corporations can buy relatively liquid short-term securities and try correspondingly harder to synchronize inflows and outflows of cash. Individuals can rely more on savings banks as a repository of funds, making correspondingly more frequent trips downtown to deposit and withdraw cash, and to transfer funds to a checking account just before large payments have to be made. Indeed they can, and the figures suggest that they do. It is true that this minimization of cash holdings costs time, trouble, and shoe leather. Clever comptrollers are thinking about cash management when they could be worrying about higher things. Moreover, and this is the point, these expenditures of time and effort are a real net burden to society, not merely a transfer to others. They are sometimes described as a "deadweight loss" to emphasize this. They are a true cost of inflation in the same sense that the maintenance of expensive police forces is a cost of crime. Some economists seem to regard these losses as the main social cost of pure inflation. But in that case, something very peculiar is afoot, because one finds it hard to believe that they amount to much. For *this* governments tremble and people cry on the pollster's shoulder? Even if you add in the computational difficulties of planning with changing prices, the discomfort that comes from not knowing whether your anticipations about future price levels are approximately right or dangerously wrong, it is hard to get excited.[7]

[7]In very rapid inflations—what are usually called "hyperinflations"—the losses from holding money are so great that one observes a genuine flight from the currency, whence come the stories from Germany in the 1920's of children meeting

There is one other important "real" effect of anticipated pure inflation; it works through the tax system. Think of any progressive tax, a tax that takes a higher fraction of a higher income than of a lower income. Now let all prices, and thus all before-tax incomes, rise in the same proportion. Nobody's purchasing power has changed. But the general rise in nominal incomes will drive everyone into a higher tax bracket. If the general rise in prices amounted to X per cent, incomes after tax will rise by less than X per cent, because of the higher effective tax rate, and the government's revenues will rise by more than X per cent, for the same reason. So taxpayers suffer a loss in purchasing power after taxes, and their loss is the Treasury's gain. Our tax system is not as progressive in action as it is on paper, but nevertheless this effect is quite real. The sharpest case is that of someone whose income is low enough not to be taxable at all; pure inflation can push such a person into the taxable range and thus impose a loss of real income.

In summary, a perfectly anticipated pure inflation imposes a small deadweight loss on society, mostly through a waste of effort directed toward economizing on the holding of money; in addition, it redistributes wealth, from holders of cash and checking accounts to banks, and from everyone to the Treasury. Not good, one is tempted to say, but no worse than a bad cold. Real GNP, for all its faults, is the best measure we have of the current production of valued goods and services; that's the number to watch.

Unanticipated Inflation

Now real-life inflations are not perfectly anticipated. Neither do they come as a complete surprise. But different people have different opinions about the future of the price level; not all of them can be right, and most of them can be wrong. The consequences of this fact are important, but still special. Interest rates cannot adjust to cushion both debtors and creditors from the effects of pure inflation. Some people will be caught with their pants down: those creditors who

their fathers at the factory gate to bicycle madly into town and spend the day's pay before it has had a chance to depreciate further. In such cases there may be a return to barter. This kind of disorganization of the economy and society can be very costly, but it is not what we have to talk about. Even at relatively small rates of inflation, a little ingenuity can sometimes invent substitutes for the non-interest-bearing checking account—e.g., the *NOW account*.

have locked themselves into long-term loans at interest rates that do not fully reflect the particular rate of inflation that happens, and borrowers who have agreed to pay high nominal interest rates in the expectation of faster inflation than actually materializes. Of course, for each of these unlucky lenders and borrowers, there is a lucky borrower or lender. Needless to say, when the losers include the broad class of pensioners whose expectations of a viable old age are dashed, it is not a trivial matter.

These gains and losses are not restricted to loans. *Anyone* who has concluded a long-term contract of any kind, stipulated in money terms, stands to gain or lose, depending on which side of the contract we are talking about and whether the rate of inflation turns out in fact to be higher or lower than had been expected when the terms of the contract were agreed. (If rapid inflation continues, we can expect to see more long-term contracts with renegotiation clauses, or with rates of payment explicitly tied to some index of prices. These are a form of insurance against windfall gains and losses from unexpectedly fast or slow inflation.)

Finally, it should be realized that many people, especially non-rich people, are more or less excluded from the benefits of higher nominal interest rates in an inflationary period. Small savers lack either the knowledge or the minimal stake needed to gain access to the sorts of assets whose yields will provide protection against inflation. The small saver is limited in practice to savings accounts and Series E government bonds. The rate on Series E bonds is not set by a market but is managed by the Treasury, and usually kept low enough to constitute a swindle on the non-rich. (One wonders what would happen if Secretaries of the Treasury were required by law to keep all their private wealth in Series E bonds.) The maximum deposit rate payable by savings banks is also limited by law, and by the peculiar role of those institutions as essentially nothing but mortgage lenders. Heaven does not protect the working girl.

The net result of all this is that imperfectly anticipated inflation—the only kind we have—generates massive redistribution of wealth between some borrowers and some lenders, some buyers and some sellers. From a very lofty point of view, these are still transfers, not a net burden on society as a whole. But that doesn't make them good. Moreover, in the public mind these transfers come to look like a net loss: The gainers attribute their gains to their own perspicacity,

energy, and virtue; the losers attribute their losses to inflation.

"Impure" Inflation

Pure inflation is an abstraction, though a necessary and useful one. If you can't understand the workings of pure inflation, you will never be able to understand what is actually happening. What is actually happening, of course, is a mixture: The general price level is rising, and at the same time relative prices are changing, sometimes drastically. The price indexes I described earlier are supposed to measure the pure inflationary component of the complicated set of price changes we experience. When I tell you that in the 12 months between June 1973 and June 1974 the CPI rose by 11.1 per cent, the WPI by 14.5 per cent, and the GNP Deflator by 9.7 per cent, I am saying something like: It is approximately as if there were a pure inflation of about 10 per cent, accompanied by a "pure" change in relative prices around a stationary level. In fact, I can add such information as this: The price of food went up by 14.7 per cent during the year, while rents went up by 4.7 per cent, so there was clearly a rise in the price of food relative to rental housing.

This is conceptually clear (though not quite as clear as I am pretending). The trouble is that what you observe and feel in the course of the year is the Total Experience, and it is by no means easy to sort out in one's mind the causes and consequences of a rising general level of prices and the causes and consequences of simultaneous changes in relative prices. This difficulty is complicated further by the fact that price movements are not synchronized. Even if, when all is said and done, the price of A and the price of B are both going to rise by X per cent, A may take off first and B only later. You would think that these timing differences would all come out in the wash, but they may actually have important independent consequences of their own.

The important thing to say about an inflation in which some prices and some incomes rise faster than others is that the *redistribution* of income can become both quite drastic and quite haphazard. It may be that real GNP is high and rising, so that the country as a whole is not being deprived of goods and services and the satisfactions they bring. But definable groups in the population may find their own standards of living deteriorating, either because the prices of the things they buy are rising faster than the average, or because the prices of the things they sell—including their labor—are rising slower than the average of all prices. And often enough it will appear to them that the inflation is the cause of their troubles, when in fact the real thief is the accompanying change in relative prices. Some economically and socially pointless or harmful redistributions can happen just because certain prices and incomes are less flexible than others and adapt sluggishly to a generally inflationary climate.

There are fewer valid universal generalizations about these redistributions than one might think. The rhetorical commonplaces are not always true. If is often said that inflation is especially hard on the poor. One careful study by Robinson G. Hollister and John G. Palmer found that this was not the case in the inflationary episodes of the 1950's, and until 1967, if by "the poor" you mean those below the official poverty line (that is, pretty damn poor). Their figures show that a cost-of-living index weighted the way the poor spend their incomes rose no faster than, perhaps slightly less fast than, the official middle-income CPI. The sources of income that matter for the poor—mainly wages and salaries, Social Security benefits, and various forms of social assistance—just about kept pace with other forms of income in purchasing-power terms. And the poor have little wealth exposed to the risk of erosion. Hollister and Palmer conclude: " . . . because the relative position of the poor seems to improve during inflationary periods and overall real income gains per capita occur during such periods, the poor as a whole must be gaining both absolutely and relatively in economic well-being during periods in which inflationary processes operate."

But not all inflations are alike. Between 1947 and 1967, food prices rose a little more slowly than the CPI as a whole. In 1973, I hardly need tell you, food prices went up about three times as fast as the rest of the CPI. Poor people spend a larger fraction of their incomes on food than richer people do. Moreover, as it happens, food costs at home went up faster than restaurant prices in 1973, and hamburger faster than steak. It would not be surprising to find that the inflation of 1973 did contribute to a redistribution of income away from poor people.[8]

Are We in a Whole New Ball Game?

In trying to understand the accelerated inflation of the last few years, it is worth remembering that the same thing has been happening everywhere. Here, for instance, are the percentage rates of increase of the CPI for a number of advanced countries between January/February 1973 and January/February 1974:

Country	Percentage rate of inflation of CPI
Japan	24.1
Denmark	14.6
United Kingdom	13.2
Italy	12.6
France	10.9
Switzerland	10.8
United States	9.7
Canada	9.3
Norway	8.7
Sweden	8.4
Austria	8.3
Netherlands	8.2
Belgium	7.9
West Germany	7.5

You will notice that the United States is somewhere around the middle of this league. A similar table compiled for 1970-71, say, would show rates of inflation centered around 5 per cent rather than 10 per cent.

By itself, the universality of inflation tells us very little. It could come about because all countries are exposed to the same forces, characteristic of modern advanced economies or because the international trading and monetary system works to spread the impact of forces originating anywhere in the system, or because different countries happen to be inflating for different reasons, and find it easier to do so when others are doing the same. Or the explanation could involve elements of all these possibilities. I am going to concentrate on the first line of explanation, but I believe each of the other two has something to say. My main reason for insisting on the importance of these comparative figures is to warn that no entirely parochial account of the causes of inflation will do.

---

[8]Poor people spend a larger fraction of their income on housing than rich people do, and a smaller fraction on transportation, especially automobile transportation. So the run-up in oil prices has more complicated effects: The rise in fuel oil prices hits the poor worse than the rich, but the rise in gasoline prices affects the rich more than the poor. Of course, all this is apart from the fact that any reduction in purchasing power is harder to take when you're poor.

Modern mixed-capitalist economies seem to have an inflationary bias near full employment. That is a description, not an explanation, but it seems to summarize the situation. An economy that is running along moderately prosperously, but hardly straining its capacity to produce, will see its price level drift upward. In the good old days, the demands of war or the stimulus of excessively expansionary policy might bring an economy to flat-out operation and consequent inflation, but a return to more normal levels of demand would stabilize prices, and a touch of recession might bring on actual deflation. The trouble is that nowadays economies begin to inflate while they are showing no signs of excess pressure, and to reverse the price rise would appear to require longer and deeper recessions than seems reasonable or natural. The question is: Why should that be? Why, for instance, do so few prices ever actually fall?

Let me answer a question with a question. Is it possible that the price level was *more* stable on the average in the good old days because the economy was *less* stable on the average? More particularly, until very recently it was reasonable to fear that any momentary weakness in the economy might be the prelude to substantial and prolonged recession. Under those circumstances, businesses might see the wisdom of cutting prices early and often, to protect markets and market shares against competitors in their own and neighboring industries who would also be feeling the pinch of widespread market softness. The same fear might be expected to stiffen the resistance of employers to wage demands; a longish period of reduced sales and lowered prices is no time to bear the burden of higher wage costs, and discontent in the work-place is easier to handle when production has to be cut back anyway. To complete the circle, the danger of prolonged unemployment would induce workers to accept wage reductions, or at least reductions relative to long-term productivity gains. It is not hard to believe that the reality of major recessions and depressions would account for greater flexibility of prices and wages in the downward direction.[9]

If the threat of prolonged recession is absent, the situation is quite otherwise. There is less pressure to reduce prices when markets soften, if it is expected that they will soon improve. Similarly, there is less incentive to resist wage increases if prices are being maintained or even raised themselves; and if production will soon need to be increased, one is less likely to tempt strikes, ill will, and the reputation of being a lousy employer. Finally, when mass unemployment is unlikely workers are able more confidently to keep up the pressure for higher wages.

---

[9] The same argument would work in reverse. Prices and wages would respond more quickly and amply upward when markets tighten. In fact, the knowledge that prices could easily rise or fall later would make it easier to let them fall or rise now. All that I need from this argument is an explanation of the fact that prices used sometimes to fall. If prices never fall, there is no way the price trend can ever be horizontal.

27

The Inflationary Bias in Our Economy

ARTHUR F. BURNS

Arthur F. Burns is a former Chairman of the Board of Governors of the Federal Reserve System. This article is taken from a speech he gave at the University of Georgia in 1975.

Our country is now engaged in a fateful debate. There are many who declare that unemployment is a far more serious problem than inflation, and that monetary and fiscal policies must become more stimulative during the coming year even if inflation quickens in the process. I embrace the goal of full employment, and I shall suggest ways to achieve it. But I totally reject the argument of those who keep urging faster creation of money and still larger governmental deficits. Such policies would only bring us additional trouble; they cannot take us to the desired goal.

The American economy has recently begun to emerge from the deepest decline of business activity in the postwar period. During the course of the recession, which began in late 1973, the physical volume of our total output of goods and services declined by 8 per cent. The production of factories, mines, and power plants fell even more—by 14 per cent. As the overall level of economic activity receded, the demand for labor rapidly diminished and unemployment doubled, reaching an intolerable 9 per cent of the labor force this May.

The basic cause of the recession was our nation's failure to deal effectively with the inflation that got under way in the mid-sixties and soon became a dominant feature of our economic life. As wage and price increases quickened, seeds of trouble were sown across the economy. With abundant credit readily available, the consruction of new homes, condominiums, and office buildings proceeded on a scale that exceeded the underlying demand. Rapidly rising prices eroded the purchasing power of workers' incomes and savings. Managerial practices of business enterprises became lax and productivity languished, while corporate profits—properly reckoned—kept falling. Inventories of raw materials and other supplies piled up as businessmen reacted to fears of shortages and still higher prices. Credit demands, both public and private, soared and interest rates rose to unprecedented heights. The banking system became overextended, the quality of loans tended to deteriorate, and the capital position of many banks was weakened.

During the past year many of these basic maladjustments have been worked out of the economic system by a painful process that could have been avoided if inflation had not gotten out of control. As the demand

153

for goods and services slackened last winter, business managers began to focus more attention on efficiency and cost controls. Prices of industrial materials fell substantially, price increases at later stages of processing became less extensive, and in many instances business firms offered price concessions to clear their shelves. With the rate of inflation moderating, confidence of the general public was bolstered and consumer spending strengthened. Business firms were thus able to liquidate a good part of their excess inventories in a rather brief period. Meanwhile, as the demand for credit diminished, tensions in financial markets were relieved, and the liquidity position of both banks and business firms generally improved.

These self-corrective forces internal to the business cycle were aided by fiscal and monetary policies that sought to cushion the effects of economic adversity and to provide some stimulus to economic recovery. On the fiscal side, public employment programs were expanded, unemployment insurance was liberalized, and both personal and corporate income taxes were reduced. On the monetary side, easier credit conditions were fostered, resulting in lower interest rates and a rebuilding of liquidity across the economy.

With the base for economic recovery thus established, business activity has recently begun to improve. Production of goods and services turned up during the second quarter and is continuing to advance. The demand for labor has also improved. Both the number of individuals at work and the length of the work week are rising again, and unemployment has declined three months in a row. Retails sales have risen further, and of late residential construction has joined the recovery process.

Along with these favorable developments, however, some ominous signs have emerged. Despite an occasional pause, inflation once again may be accelerating. By the second quarter of this year, the annual rate of increase in the general price level was down to 5.5 per cent—about half the rate of inflation registered in the same period a year earlier. But over the summer, prices began to rise more briskly.

This behavior of prices is particularly worrisome in view of the large degree of slack that now exists in most of our nation's industries. Price increases in various depressed industries—aluminum, steel, auto, industrial chemicals, among others—are a clear warning that our long-range problem of inflation is unsolved and, therefore, remains a threat to sustained economic recovery.

History suggests that at this early stage of a business

upturn, confidence in the economic future should be strengthening steadily. A significant revival of confidence is indeed underway, but it is being hampered by widespread concern that a fresh outburst of double-digit inflation may before long bring on another recession. By now, thoughtful Americans are well aware of the profoundly disruptive consequences of inflation for our economy. They also recognize that these consequences are not solely of an economic character. Inflation has capricious effects on the income and wealth of a nation's families, and this inevitably causes disillusionment and discontent. Social and political frictions tend to multiply, and the very foundations of a society may be endangered. This has become evident in other nations around the world, where governments have toppled as a result of the social havoc wrought by inflation.

If we in the United States wish to enjoy the fruits of a prosperous economy and to preserve our democratic institutions, we must come to grips squarely with the inflation that has been troubling our nation throughout much of the postwar period, and most grievously during the past decade.

A first step in this process is to recognize the true character of the problem. Our long-run problem of inflation has its roots in the structure of our economic institutions and in the financial policies of our government. All too frequently, this basic fact is clouded by external events that influence the rate of inflation—such as a crop shortfall that results in higher farm prices, or the action of a foreign cartel that raises oil prices. The truth is that, for many years now, the economies of the United States and many other countries have developed a serious underlying bias toward inflation. This tendency has simply been magnified by the special influences that occasionally arise.

A major cause of this inflationary bias is the relative success that modern industrial nations have had in moderating the swings of the business cycle. Before World War II, cyclical declines of business activity in our country were typically longer and more severe than they have been during the past thirty years. In the environment then prevailing, the price level typically declined in the course of a business recession, and many months or years elapsed before prices returned to their previous peak.

In recent decades, a new pattern of wage and price behavior has emerged. Prices of many individual commodities still demonstrate a tendency to decline when demand weakens. The average level of prices, however, hardly ever declines. Wage rates have become even more inflexible. Wage reductions are nowadays rare even in severely depressed industries and the average level of wage rates continues to rise inexorably in the face of widespread unemployment.

These developments have profoundly altered the economic environment. When prices are pulled up by expanding demand in a time of prosperity, and are also pushed up by rising costs during a slack period, the decisions of the economic community are sure to be influenced, and may in fact be dominated, by expectations of continuing inflation.

Thus, many businessmen have come to believe that the trend of production costs will be inevitably upward, and their resistance to higher prices—whether of labor, or materials, or equipment—has, therefore, diminished. Labor leaders and workers now tend to reason that in order to achieve a gain in real income, they must bargain for wage increases that allow for advances in the price level as well as for such improvements as may occur in productivity. Lenders in their turn expect to be paid back in cheaper dollars and, therefore, tend to hold out for higher interest rates. They are able to do so because the resistance of borrowers to high interest rates is weakened by their anticipation of rising prices.

These patterns of thought are closely linked to the emphasis that governments everywhere have placed on rapid economic growth throughout the postwar period. Western democracies, including our own, have tended to move promptly to check economic recession, but they have moved hesitantly in checking inflation. Western governments have also become more diligent in seeking ways to relieve the burdens of adversity facing their peoples. In the process they have all moved a considerable distance toward the welfare state.

In the United States, for example, the unemployment insurance system has been greatly liberalized. Benefits now run to as many as sixty-five weeks, and in some cases provide individuals with after-tax incomes almost as large as their earnings from prior employment. Social security benefits, too, have been expanded materially, thus facilitating retirement or easing the burden of job loss for older workers. Welfare programs have been established for a large part of the population, and now include food stamps, school lunches, medicare and medicaid, public housing, and many other forms of assistance.

Protection from economic hardship has been extended by our government to business firms as well. The rigors of competitive enterprise are nowadays eased by import quotas, tariffs, price-maintenance laws, and other forms of governmental regulation. Farmers, home builders, small businesses, and other groups are provided special credit facilities and other assistance. And even large firms of national reputation look to the federal government for sustenance when they get into trouble.

Many, perhaps most, of these governmental programs have highly commendable objectives, but they have been pursued without adequte regard for their cost or method of financing. Governmental budgets—at the federal, state, and local level—have mounted and at times, as in the case of New York City, have gotten out of control. In the past ten years, federal expenditures have increased by 175 per cent. Over that interval, the fiscal deficit of the federal government, including government-sponsored enterprises, has totaled over $200 billion. In the current fiscal year alone, we are likely to add another $80 billion or more to that total. In financing these large and continuing deficits, pressure has been placed on our credit mechanisms, and the supply of money has frequently grown at a rate inconsistent wihh general price stability.

Changes in market behavior have contributed to the inflationary bias of our economy. In many businesses, price competition has given way to other forms of rivalry—advertising, changes in product design, and "hard sell" salesmanship. In labor markets, when an excessive wage increase occurs, it is apt to spread faster and more widely than before, partly because workmen have become more sensitive to wage developments elsewhere, partly also because many employers have found that a stable work force can be best maintained by emulating wage settlements in unionized industries. For their part, trade unions at times seem to attach higher priority to wage increases than to the jobs of their members. Moreover, the spread of trade unions to the rapidly expanding public sector has fostered during recent years numerous strikes, some of them clearly illegal, and they have often resulted in acceptance of union demands—however extreme. Needless to say, the apparent helplessness of governments to deal with this problem has encouraged other trade unions to exercise their latent market power more boldly.

The growth of our foreign trade and of capital movements to and from the United States has also increased the susceptibility of the American economy to inflationary trends. National economies around the world are now more closely interrelated, so that inflationary developments in one country are quickly communicated to others and become mutually reinforcing. Moreover, the adoption of a flexible exchange rate system—though beneficial in dealing with large-scale adjustments of international payments, such as those arising from the sharp rise in oil prices—may have made the Western world more prone to inflation by weakening the discipline of the balance of payments. Furthermore, since prices nowadays are more flexible upward than downward, any sizable decline in the foreign exchange value of the dollar is apt to have larger and more lasting effects on our price level than any offsetting appreciation of the dollar.

The long-run upward trend of prices in this country thus stems fundamentally from the financial policies of our government and the changing character of our economic institutions. This trend has been accentuated by new cultural values and standards, as is evidenced by pressures for wage increases every year, more holidays, longer vacations, and more liberal coffee breaks. The upward trend of prices has also been accentuated by the failure of business firms to invest sufficiently in the modernization and improvement of industrial plant. In recent years, the United States has been devoting a smaller part of its economic resources to business capital expenditures than any other major industrial nation in the world. All things considered, we should not be surprised that the rate of improvement in output per manhour has weakened over the past fifteen years, or that rapidly rising money wages have overwhelmed productivity gains and boosted unit labor costs of production.

Whatever may have been true in the past, there is no longer a meaningful trade-off between unemployment and inflation. In the current environment a rapidly rising level of consumer prices will not lead to the creation of new jobs. On the contrary, it will lead to hesitation and sluggish buying, as the increase of the personal savings rate in practically every industrial nation during these recent years of rapid inflation indicates. In general, stimulative financial policies have considerable merit when unemployment is extensive and inflation weak or absent; but such policies do not work well once inflation has come to dominate the thinking of a nation's consumers and businessmen. To be sure, highly expansionary monetary and fiscal policies might, for a short time, provide some additional thrust to economic activity. But inflation would inevitably accelerate—a development that would create even more difficult economic problems than we have encountered over the past year.

Conventional thinking about stabilization policies is inadequate and out of date. We must now seek ways of bringing unemployment down without becoming engulfed by a new wave of inflation. The areas that need to be explored are many and difficult, and we may not find quickly the answers we seek. But if we are to have any chance of ridding our economy of its inflationary bias, we must at least be willing to reopen our economic minds. I shall briefly sketch several broad lines of attack on the dual problem of unemployment and inflation that seem promising to me.

First, governmental efforts are long overdue to encourage improvements in productivity through larger investment in modern plant and equipment. This objective would be promoted by overhauling the structure of federal taxation so as to increase incentives for business capital spending and for equity investments in American enterprises.

Second, we must face up to the fact that environmental and safety regulations have in recent years played a troublesome role in escalating costs and prices and in holding up industrial construction across our land. I am concerned, as are all thoughtful citizens, with the need to protect the environment and to improve in other ways the quality of life. I am also concerned, however, about the dampening effect of excessive governmental regulations on business activity. Progress toward full employment and price stability would be measurably improved, I believe, by stretching out the timetables for achieving our environmental and safety goals.

Third, a vigorous search should be made for ways to enhance price competition among our nation's business enterprises. We need to gather the courage to reassess laws directed against restraint of trade by business firms and to improve the enforcement of these laws. We also need to reassess the highly complex governmental regulations affecting transportation, the effects on consumer prices of remaining fair trade laws, the monopoly of first-class mail by the Postal Service, and the many other laws and practices that impede the competitive process.

Fourth, in any serious search for noninflationary measures to reduce unemployment, governmental policies that affect labor markets have to be reviewed. For example, the federal minimum wage law is still pricing many teenagers out of the job market. The Davis-Bacon Act continues to escalate construction costs and damage the depressed construction industry. Programs for unemployment compensation now provide benefits on such a generous scale that they may be blunting incentives to work. Even in today's environment, with about 8 per cent of the labor force unemployed, there are numerous job vacancies—perhaps because job seekers are unaware of the opportunities, or because the skills of the unemployed are not suitable, or for other reasons. Surely, better results could be achieved with more effective job banks, more realistic training programs, and other labor market policies.

I believe that the ultimate objective of labor market policies should be to eliminate all involuntary unemployment. This is not a radical or impractical goal. It rests on the simple but often neglected fact that work is far better than the dole, both for the jobless individual and for the nation. A wise government will always strive to create an environment that is conducive to high employment in the private sector. Nevertheless, there may be no way to reach the goal of full employment short of making the government an employer of last resort. This could be done by offering public employment—for example, in hospitals, schools, public parks, or the like—to anyone who is willing to work at a rate of pay somewhat below the federal minimum wage.

With proper administration, these public service workers would be engaged in productive labor, not leaf-raking or other make-work. To be sure, such a program would not reach those who are voluntarily unemployed, but there is also no compelling reason why it should do so. What it would do is to make jobs available for those who need to earn some money.

It is highly important, of course, that such a program should not become a vehicle for expanding public jobs at the expense of private industry. Those employed at the special public jobs will need to be encouraged to seek more remunerative and more attractive work. This could be accomplished by building into the program certain safeguards—perhaps through a constitutional amendment—that would limit upward adjustment in the rate of pay for these special public jobs. With such safeguards, the budgetary cost of eliminating unemployment need not be burdensome. I say this, first, because the number of individu-

als accepting the public service jobs would be much smaller than the number now counted as unemployed; second, because the availability of public jobs would permit sharp reduction in the scope of unemployment insurance and other governmental programs to alleviate income loss. To permit active searching for a regular job, however, unemployment insurance for a brief period—perhaps 13 weeks or so—would still serve a useful function.

Finally, we also need to rethink the appropriate role of an incomes policy in the present environment. Lasting benefits cannot be expected from a mandatory wage and price control program, as recent experience indicates. It might actually be helpful if the Congress renounced any intention to return to mandatory controls, so that businesses and trade unions could look forward with confidence to the continuance of free markets. I still believe, however, that a modest form of incomes policy, in some cases relying on quiet governmental intervention, in others on public hearings and the mobilization of public opinion, may yet be of significant benefit in reducing abuses of private economic power and moving our nation toward the goal of full employment and a stable price level.

Structural reforms of our economy, along some such lines as I have sketched, deserve more attention this critical year from members of the Congress and from academic students of public policy than they are receiving. Economists in particular have tended to concentrate excessively on overall fiscal and monetary policies of economic stimulation. These traditional tools remain useful and even essential; but once inflationary expectations have become widespread, they must be used with great care and moderation.

Our nation cannot now achieve the goal of full employment by pursuing fiscal and monetary policies that rekindle inflationary expectations. Inflation has weakened our economy; it is also endangering our economic and political system based on freedom. America has become enmeshed in an inflationary web, and we need to gather our moral strength and intellectual courage to extricate ourselves from it.

28

Federal Deficits in Perspective

COUNCIL OF ECONOMIC ADVISERS

This item was taken from the 1982 Annual Report of the Council of Economic Advisers.

The president and the Congress together determine the annual level of government spending and tax rates. These decisions, when carried out in the context of prevailing economic conditions, determine the size of the federal budget deficit. The deficit cannot be known in advance; it can only be projected using assumptions about the future course of the economy.

Why Deficits Matter

The administration is strongly committed to reducing the projected deficits in the years ahead. A variety of economic reasons, as well as considerations of practical policy-making, make deficits a cause for continuing concern. In particular, the magnitude of the projected deficits demands attention to their current and prospective economic impacts.

Financing a budget deficit may draw on private saving and foreign capital inflows that otherwise would be available to the private sector. The federal government's demand for funds is insensitive to changes in interest rates—that is, the Treasury will raise the funds that it requires regardless of interest rates. Weak and marginal borrowers may be "rationed" out of the market by higher interest rates unless saving flows are adequate.

The impact of a specific deficit will vary, however, depending on the conditions that lead to it. For example, during a recession—as now exists—the borrowing requirements of business and consumers tend to be relatively small. At such a time a given deficit can be financed with less pressure on interest rates than during a period of growth, when business and consumer demands for credit are increasing. This is why it is important for the government to reduce the budget deficit in fiscal 1983 and beyond, a period of anticipated rapid economic growth when private investment demands are expected to rise substantially.

The impact of a deficit of a given size will also depend on the extent of private saving in the economy. An economy with a higher saving rate can absorb the demands of public sector borrowing more easily than one with lower saving and still accommodate the needs of private borrowers. Much of the administration's tax program is designed to increase the private saving of

158

the nation. As a consequence, both public and private borrowing will be accommodated more easily.

A higher volume of federal borrowing to finance deficits makes the task of the Federal Reserve System more difficult when it is following a policy of monetary restraint. However, maintenance of monetary restraint is a key part of the administration's program and hence the potentially inflationary effects of monetizing the federal deficit will not be realized.

Continued budget deficits may generate uncertainty about the ability of government to control spending. Any increases in interest rates which reflect this uncertainty in turn will tend to increase further the size of the deficit. In contrast, the maintenance of a long-term policy to reduce the size of budget deficits—the policy of the administration—will tend to counterbalance the pressures for further increases in government spending.

Measuring the Deficit

It is important to recognize that there are several measures of the deficit. The unified deficit, the figure generally cited as "the deficit," includes only the deficit arising from on-budget expenditures. But the federal government borrows to finance off-budget activities as well.

Of course, the federal government constitutes only one part of the public sector; state and local budgets affect the economy in a fashion similar to the federal budget. Given the large transfers of federally raised funds to state and local budgets, federal, state, and local deficits should be considered jointly. Because the other levels of government have been accumulating funds to meet employee pension obligations, their budgets tend to be in current surplus (although some states and localities are generating unfunded liabilities for future retirement payments). In calendar year 1981, when the federal government reported a total deficit of $62 billion (on the national income and product accounts basis), the state and local sector showed a surplus of $37 billion.

Regardless of how inclusive the definition of the deficit, it is not only the annual deficit that affects the economy but also the trend in deficits over the business cycle and beyond. Because of the structure of certain spending and tax programs, deficits tend to vary inversely with the economy. To some extent, deficits that are generated when the economy is weak can be made up when the economy is strong. It is the trend of deficits that serves as an indicator of fiscal discipline.

The relative size of the deficit is far more important than the dollar magnitude. To the extent that deficits affect the economy, the effects of a given deficit will be relatively small in a large economy and large in a small economy. From a historical perspective, the projected budget deficits for fiscal years 1982–1984 are clearly substantial, yet they are not unprecedented when measured against the size of the economy. In recent years only the fiscal 1976 deficit was larger, as a share of GNP, than the projected deficit for fiscal 1982, as Table 1 indicates. However, the ratio is projected to decline fairly rapidly so that by 1985 the deficit, relative to GNP, will be below the average for the decade of the 1970s.

In view of concern over the current projections of a large deficit during economic recovery in 1982, it is worth noting that the 1976 deficit also occurred during a period of economic recovery. In the four quarters ending in June 1976, nominal GNP rose 12 percent, real output gained 6 percent, and interest rates were essentially unchanged.

An Analysis of Deficits and Debt Financing

A given deficit is consistent with different levels of spending and taxes. Even if economic conditions do not change, a deficit may increase because spending is increased and tax rates are not increased to yield the necessary added revenues, or because spending is unchanged but tax rates are reduced, or because spending is reduced but lower tax rates reduce revenues by a greater amount.

These three circumstances may yield the same deficit but have quite different effects. The effects will depend on the timing, level, and composition of government spending as well as the means used to pay for that spending. The spending imposes a cost on the economy by taking resources away from private use. As discussed earlier, government spending may augment or it may substitute for private spending. It will therefore alter decisions about private spending. Each of the methods of financing spending imposes costs in addition to the simple transfer of resources from the private sector to the public sector. The manner of financing, like the type of government spending, will alter the incentives which determine private resource allocation and hence may reduce economic efficiency.

Table 1. Total Federal Budget and Off-Budget Surplus or Deficit and Gross National Product, Fiscal Years 1958–87
(Amounts in billion of dollars)

Fiscal year	Total federal budget and off-budget surplus or deficit (−)	
	Amount	As percent of GNP
1958	−2.9	−0.7
1959	−12.9	−2.7
1960	.3	.1
1961	−3.4	−.7
1962	−7.1	−1.3
1963	−4.8	−.8
1964	−5.9	−1.0
1965	−1.6	−.2
1966	−3.8	−.5
1967	−8.7	−1.1
1968	−25.2	−3.0
1969	3.2	.4
1970	−2.8	−.3
1971	−23.0	−2.2
1972	−23.4	−2.1
1973	−14.9	−1.2
1974	−6.1	−.4
1975	−53.2	−3.6
1976	−73.7	−4.5
1977	−53.6	−2.9
1978	−59.2	−2.8
1979	−40.2	−1.7
1980	−73.8	−2.9
1981	−78.9	−2.8
1982[a]	−118.3	−3.8
1983[a]	−107.2	−3.1
1984[a]	−97.2	−2.6
1985[a]	−82.8	−2.0
1986[a]	−77.0	−1.7
1987[a]	−62.5	−1.3

[a] Estimates.

Sources: Department of Commerce (Bureau of Economic Analysis), Department of the Treasury, Office of Management and Budget, and Council of Economic Advisers.

If the government wants to pay for its spending on a current basis, it can set tax rates so that revenues equal outlays. However, the distorting effects of the tax system will reduce total output, now and in the future. At recent marginal tax rates the associated cost may be quite high.

If the government issues bonds instead of raising taxes, it must pay interest on the added debt. Furthermore, government debt creation can impose added costs by absorbing private saving and hence reducing growth. Economic growth will not be reduced to the extent that an increase in private saving offsets the decline in government saving measured by growing federal indebtedness. Private saving may increase, for example, if households anticipate that their future taxes will increase and they respond by setting aside additional saving to pay for the expected increase in tax liabilities. Since individuals' saving also tends to be affected by what services they perceive they are getting from the government, the composition of government spending associated with the deficit will play a key role in determining the response of saving.

Distortions may also occur in the allocation of resources if the government chooses to finance deficits by adding excessively to the monetary base.

Whichever approach, or combination of approaches, the government chooses to pay for its spending, it cannot avoid the reality that government spending, while it may confer benefits on the economy, also imposes costs. The choice among financing mechanisms depends on which is the least-cost approach, or on what approach imposes the most appropriate patterns of costs on the economy over time.

Evaluating these costs is not a simple matter. Since deficits affect expectations about the future course of economic policies, only part of the effect of a deficit is an immediate consequence of what the increases in debt do to markets. Deficits also work indirectly through the changes they produce in individual expectations and the resultant changes in their behavior. Neither the direct effect nor the effect on expectations is readily observable. In addition, analysts differ in their views about the relative effects of different conditions on inflation, investment, and economic growth. Unless these differences in opinion are recognized, debates that ostensibly focus on the deficit often mask broader, underlying debates on how the economy works.

Deficits and Inflation

It is now generally agreed that continued excessive growth in the money supply will cause sustained inflation. Thus deficits financed by money creation will have persistent inflationary consequences.

Additional government debt might also raise the price level through its impact on desired money balances. If the increased supply of government bonds raises interest rates, households and firms will respond by reducing their money balances and increasing total nominal spending. This implies an increase in velocity. Unless the monetary authorities offset the higher velocity by reducing the monetary base, both the price level and output will rise in the short run, although the mix of increases in the price level and in output is indeterminate. To the extent workers and firms believe that deficits are inflationary, however, and bargain accordingly, the relative effects on the price level will be correspondingly larger.

The magnitude of the increase in aggregate demand that results from added government debt will depend both on the responsiveness of money demand to interest rates and on the size of the increase in interest rates. For the former, empirical studies consistently show the demand for money to be only weakly responsive to interest rates, so that any given increase in interest rates will result in a relatively small increase in nominal spending.

As to the size of the increase in interest rates resulting from the added debt, the evidence is less clear-cut. There are two forces moderating any increase. First, market interest rates equate the demand for financial assets with their supply. In any given year, added debt represents only a small increment to the total stock of government debt, and is also small by comparison with the market value of other assets in the economy. Second, a higher interest rate today means that saving is more attractive and current consumption relatively less attractive. Thus the effect of additional government debt on interest rates will tend to be moderated by an increase in the flow of private saving attracted by the higher rates.

On the other hand, two factors may add to the increase in interest rates. If participants in financial markets believe that deficits are inflationary, long-term bond rates may include an additional inflation premium in response to larger deficits. The incremental uncertainty caused by deficits may also increase real interest rates. This results in large measure from the past history of discretionary, countercyclical policies. The prospect of large deficits contributed to uncertainty in the financial markets in 1981 and may have raised market interest rates to a higher level than they otherwise would have been.

If added debt does raise the price level through its effect on desired money balances, this is not equivalent to continued inflation. For the price level to increase in a sustained fashion, the annual increments to government debt would have to grow continually at a rate faster than the growth of the economy. Thus deficits will be inflationary only if the monetary authorities monetize the debt or if the added debt continually grows as a share of GNP. This is precisely why the administration is determined to reduce the budget deficit in fiscal 1983 and beyond. The maintenance of monetary restraint will ensure that deficits will not be monetized and that the potentially inflationary effects that might otherwise result from government borrowing will not be realized.

Debt Financing, Crowding Out, and Growth

It has been argued that net government borrowing may preempt credit that otherwise would have been used to finance private investment. Unless the supply of private saving expands to provide completely for the increased government borrowing, thereby preventing a rise in real interest rates, the additional government debt will tend to deter some private investment. Some saving could also come from abroad. If international credit flows respond sufficiently to only slightly higher interest rates, significant crowding out of U.S. private investment may be prevented.

When private saving rates are relatively high (perhaps because of a tax system that fosters saving rather than consumption), a larger deficit can be accommodated more easily than if saving rates are low. In recent years, for example, Japan and a number of Western European nations have experienced larger budget deficits (measured as a percent of their gross domestic product) than has the United States. As a result of higher rates of saving, however, their ratios of private investment to GNP have also been higher.

Any current increase in government debt leaves future generations facing either a higher tax bill or lower government services, or a combination of the two, than would otherwise have prevailed. This reduces their economic well-being in two ways. First, if current generations do not provide their successors with the resources to pay for the accumulated debt, current deficits make future generations worse off. But even if later generations inherit the additional resources to meet the tax bill, the tax revenues are likely to be collected in ways that distort their economic choices and impair the efficient operation of their economy. There is, then a trade-off between these later distortions and the distortions from taxing now. Again, a choice of the less costly alternative must be made. In the case of government spending in wartime, for example, it has long been recognized that the cost of taxing all at once may be significantly larger than the cost of issuing debt and paying the debt with taxes spread over many years.

The Deficit and Politics of the Budget

Perhaps the most damaging effects of deficits are not directly economic but result from the political process. There are many advocates for government spending because the beneficiaries of spending have an interest in promoting it. At the same time, those who pay for additional government spending through taxes have an interest in holding taxes down. But the interests of future taxpayers are not well represented in our political process. Deficit spending allows government to be financed in a way that is almost invisible to the taxpayer, and the pull and tug of the political process may result in more government spending than is generally desired. To counteract this tendency, many have argued that policy-makers ought to follow a rule—such as balancing the budget each year (that is, financing it only through taxes) or limiting federal revenues to a fixed percent of GNP—to restrain the tendency toward excessive government spending.

Perhaps the most useful and practical of these rules is the simplest rule: balance the budget. Even this needs to be seen as a long-run rule, however, since the business cycle does cause variations that are difficult to calculate and offset. Furthermore, a strategy of reducing taxes in advance of spending cuts implies that it will take some time to achieve the desired level of deficits. Enforcing a trend toward a balanced budget would impose the fiscal discipline necessary to restrain the growth of government and send a message of governmental restraint to private individuals who can incorporate this essential information into their planning.

In sum, government spending can never be costless. Although the government can use direct taxes, debt finance, or money creation to pay its bills, each imposes costs on the economy. The goal of fiscal policy is to achieve the mix of financing that minimizes these costs. Given the high cost of further direct taxes on capital and labor income, and the high costs imposed on society by excessive expansion of the monetary base, the administration has chosen what it views at this time as the least costly means of financing government spending. But its current actions are an essential part of a long-term strategy of reducing the scope of the federal government. To achieve this end, the administration will continue to enforce a trend toward a balanced budget.

29

Indexation: A Reasonable Response to Inflation

BRIAN HORRIGAN

Brian Horrigan is an economist at the Federal Reserve Bank in Philadelphia. This article appeared in the Business Review *of the Federal Reserve Bank of Philadelphia, October 1981.*

Until I was eight, I got a five dollar bill every year for my birthday from Grandpa. Then, because of inflation, the amount rose to ten dollars. On my next birthday, I expect it to rise to twenty dollars.
—*Ben, nine years old, quoted in* Forbes

Indexation on the Rise

Indexation has become quite common in the United States. About 9 million workers—some 10 percent of nonagricultural civilian employment—are covered by cost-of-living-adjustment (COLA) clauses. Over 35 million people who receive social security or government pensions, and over 16 million food stamp recipients, have their benefits linked to a price index.

Indexation is extensive in the rest of the world too. In the Scandinavian countries, as well as in Britain, Belgium, and Italy, and even in stable Switzerland, virtually all wages, welfare payments, and taxes are indexed. Indexation rarely is total, though; usually, wages are adjusted only by some fraction of the increase in the cost of living.

The Brazilian experiment in monetary correction (as indexation sometimes is called) has attracted a lot of attention as an example of how it is possible to reduce inflation rapidly with minimal economic disruption. In 1964 Brazilian inflation was running at about 90 percent per year while the real economy stagnated under controls. At that point the Brazilian government reduced the growth rate of money, eliminated many controls, reduced the size of the government deficit, and instituted partial indexation. The inflation rate dropped to about 30 percent in three years and fell further to about 15 percent in 1973, while real income per capita grew at about 7 percent per year from 1968 to 1973.

The inflation situation in the U.S. is not as severe as Brazil's was, but many economists are convinced that the U.S. should pursue a similar policy: reduce the deficit and money growth, eliminate price controls, and index wages, taxes, and transfer payments. They contend that indexation can minimize the economic slowdown that usually accompanies a reduction in the inflation rate.

163

How Inflation Hurts

In a decentralized market economy, prices provide both information and incentives to producers and consumers for rational economic planning. Inflation—a rise in the average of all prices—distorts the relations among the prices of various goods and services, and in the process it makes those relations less stable. When people get confused about the state of the economy, they make mistakes about investment, purchases, and employment: resources are misallocated and society is less well off in the face of increased uncertainty.

The degree of misallocation of resources depends largely on how much inflation is anticipated by the public. The cost of *unanticipated inflation*—an increase in the price level that catches the public by surprise—is far greater than that of *anticipated inflation*—an increase that the public expects and can prepare for. If everyone could forecast the inflation rate perfectly—and people do spend a lot of time and effort trying—much of the misallocation of resources caused by inflation and much of the hostility toward inflation would end. A foreseen inflation rate would be built into all contracts and agreements.

What if the actual inflation rate is different from what people expect? If a labor contract embodies one inflation rate and the actual inflation rate turns out to be higher than anticipated, laborers get stuck with lower real wages (the purchasing power of their wages is reduced). If the inflation rate is lower than expected, laborers get unexpectedly higher real wages— at the expense of their employers. To protect themselves from these redistributional swings in income, labor negotiators have sought to build more and more inflation insurance into their contracts in the form of indexation. And it's not hard to see why many employers have been willing to go along.

Why Labor Calls for Indexation

Indexation has an unmistakable appeal when the outlook for prices is highly uncertain. It gives the impression of slicing through inflation's Gordian knot in a single stroke. For all its promised benefits, however, indexation has to be used with a measure of delicacy if it's to produce the desired result.

An Example

Suppose the American Widget Corporation (AWC) signs a three-year contract with the Widget Workers Union (WWU) specifying that wages will rise 5 percent a year for each year of the contract. Both management and the union expect consumer prices—including AWC's prices—to rise 3 percent a year. If worker productivity rises at about 2 percent a year and prices rise as expected, AWC should have no trouble meeting its payroll.

But what if, contrary to expectations, consumer prices rise at 7 percent a year, not 3 percent? Then *real* wages will drop at the rate of 2 percent a year (5 percent less 7 percent leaves a minus 2 percent), even though *nominal* wages rise. Meanwhile AWC finds its revenues increasing faster than its payroll as unanticipated inflation transfers real income from workers to the managers and stockholders of the company. Because the workers' real wages are dropping, AWC finds it profitable to step up production and increase the number of employees and the number of hours worked. AWC has a boom, and if most of the companies in the economy are in the same position as AWC, the entire economy has a boom. Unanticipated inflation fools workers into working more hours than they would have if they had anticipated the lower real wage.

Suppose that when the contract expires after three years the WWU negotiates a large initial raise plus an agreement to increase wages at 9 percent a year for three years. The wage settlement in this example is not inflationary; it is only a response to high inflation. The large initial raise simply restores real wages to where they would have been had unanticipated inflation not cheated workers of some of their real wages. And the high annual increase in future wages is designed to give the workers raises to match their increased productivity, after allowing for the expected 7 percent inflation rate.

Suppose now that policy-makers decide to end inflation by taking restrictive monetary and fiscal measures. Aggregate demand rises more slowly and inflation tapers off at the same time that AWC must give a 9 percent annual wage hike to its employees. Since the new inflation rate is lower than anticipated, the *real* wages of the workers are *higher* than expected. With revenues rising more slowly than anticipated and real wages rising faster, AWC must cut back production and lay off workers. If many companies are in the same position as AWC, the entire economy slides into a recession, even though inflation still rages. When the contract expires, workers will have to accept a reduction in their real wages to be reeemployed.

The Benefits of Indexation

These dislocations need not occur if labor contracts with a fixed wage increase are replaced by contracts containing a COLA clause. Unanticipated variations in the inflation rate produce far less economic disruption when wages are indexed to consumer prices than when they are changed contractually without an explicit link to the inflation rate. With COLA, for example, an initial contract is negotiated for a small fixed-percentage wage increase—reflecting productivity increases—plus a cost-of-living adjustment. If the fixed portion of the increase were, say, 2 percent and the inflation rate were 7 percent, indexed wages would rise by 9 percent. If inflation is 3 percent, wages rise 5 percent. With full indexing the real wage rate is not affected significantly by the inflation rate. Therefore if all the labor contracts in the economy were indexed, the temporary boom that accompanies an unanticipated increase in inflation would not occur. And the recession that accompanies an unanticipated decrease in inflation wouldn't occur either. Thus if the main reason government won't implement the monetary and fiscal policies necessary to end inflation is that it is afraid to cause a recession (as some have suggested), then indexation facilitates an anti-inflationary program by reducing its costs.

If wage indexation promises to reduce both the undesirable effects of inflation and policy-makers' incentives for letting inflation continue, it would seem appropriate to index to the hilt, adjusting wages with each upward (or downward) tick of the chosen price index. But as with most policy actions, wage indexing can produce certain unwanted results alongside the desired ones.

Supply Shocks Complicate the Issue

The prices of goods and services reflect both supply conditions and demand conditions. Expansionary monetary and fiscal policies increase prices by increasing demand. Changes in supply-side factors, such as the cost of raw materials or labor productivity, also change prices. Over the last decade the U.S. has undergone several sharp supply shocks which boosted the price level, and indexation gives unfortunate results when used in an environment of supply-induced inflation.

In particular, while indexation moderates fluctuations in employment induced by demand-caused in-flation, it *aggravates* fluctuations in employment occasioned by inflation brought on from the supply side. The reason is that though a demand shock increases the price level, it does not change worker productivity. Hence employment need not change when wages are indexed. But a supply shock does reduce worker productivity, so real wages must fall if employment is to stay the same. Since real wages cannot readily adjust downward with productivity when wages are indexed, supply shocks produce a drop in employment.

Suppose that a supply shock (such as a sudden, dramatic increase in the price of oil) causes worker productivity to drop. AWC finds that its labor costs per widget have risen. The company will continue to employ the same number of workers only if real wages decline. If the workers are not covered by a COLA clause, their real wages will drop, so fewer of them (or none) will have to be laid off. If workers are protected against inflation by a COLA clause, though, their real wages can't drop, so AWC will have to lay some of them off. Thus the effect of indexing on employment depends crucially on whether inflation is demand-induced or supply-induced.

Looking at it another way: If an increase in the scarcity of some commodity such as oil, steel, or wheat requires a reduction in real incomes throughout the economy, inflation will help to spread the shock by reducing real incomes everywhere. With perfect indexation, everyone tries to keep the same size slice of the pie even though the whole pie is smaller. The only way to trim workers' income down to size after a supply shock in an indexed world is simply to lay off workers—or else break the contract and renegotiate.

Thus supply shocks make the chances of success for indexation somewhat more tenuous. But even with a demand-induced inflation it's still a good trick to find the level and technique of indexing that will capture most of the achievable benefit while incurring the least possible cost.

Optimal Indexation

One way to get a fix on how much to index is to see how workers protect themselves against inflation under a system of nonindexed labor contracts.

Shortening the duration of contracts is one method they use to reduce the costs of misestimating the inflation rate. If inflation is fluctuating, frequent renegotiation of labor contracts will keep the real wage rate more nearly constant than long-term contracts can. Indeed, during hyperinflations (those exceeding 100 percent per week), contracts longer than a week vanish from the economy. But shortening the labor contract is an expensive way to cope with inflation because negotiation costs can be formidable. Also, the more frequently contracts are renegotiated, the higher union militancy and worker discontent appear to be. The inflation rate in the United States, for instance, is correlated positively with strike activity. Internationally, high worker militancy in Britain and Italy (both with chronically high inflation rates) and lower worker militancy in Switzerland and West Germany (both with relatively low inflation rates) are consistent with the view that inflation causes strikes.

Shortening and indexing contracts both are imperfect and costly ways of coping with inflation uncertainties. But despite their costs, they are attractive to both labor and management, though in different mixes under different conditions. When inflation is induced primarily by pumped-up demand, indexation will get the most emphasis in labor contracts. When supply interruptions are chiefly responsible for a round of inflation, negotiators will rely more heavily on shortening labor contracts. There is no one formula that's best for dealing with all cases of uncertainty about inflation: the best combination of index and contract length will vary from country to country, from industry to industry, and from time to time. With their relative incomes at stake, though, both management and labor will try hard to find the formula that meets their needs best.

Should government get involved in this process? Given the complexities of labor negotiations, which are occasioned by wide variations in shocks to various industries, mandating a single economy-wide indexing scheme or prohibiting indexation would not be socially beneficial. An unfettered market seems best able to consider the large amount of information required to decide what kind of labor agreement works best in a given instance.

As wage indexing in the private sector becomes more common, however, it raises questions of both efficiency and equity for government, since government must compete for workers in the private labor market. Should wages in government be linked to those in the private sector? And if wages are indexed, how about transfer payments and taxes? These are issues that government can't avoid addressing.

Conclusion

Indexation is, at best, a necessary evil. Indexation is costly to administer and it makes the economy more sensitive to supply shocks. It would be far better to have no inflation and no indexation than even a little of either or both. But given the prospect that inflation will continue, indexation is a lesser evil than no indexation.

When inflation disappears, indexation will vanish with it from the private economy. But until it does, Americans and others will look on indexation as one of the few tools they have to protect their economic well-being.

PART FIVE

Economic Growth, Productivity, and Energy Problems

During much of the 1960s most countries, including the United States, regarded economic growth as a major social goal. At the start of the decade, John F. Kennedy ran for president on a platform emphasizing the importance of economic growth. But during the 1970s and 1980s many politicians and not a few economists have questioned the desirability of further economic growth. In the opening article, E. J. Mishan argues that "continued economic growth by Western societies is more likely on balance to reduce rather than increase social welfare." Indeed, he characterizes the American economy "as a spectacle of growing resources pressing against limited wants."

Another group, composed partially of engineers, is concerned about the desirability of further economic growth because they feel that we will run out of raw materials. In particular, the Club of Rome's study of "The Limits to Growth," carried out by Dennis Meadows and his colleagues, concludes that continued economic growth is impossible because of the drain on our raw materials and the increases in pollution and population. Most economists disagree with this conclusion. As Robert Solow points out in the next paper, there are many inadequacies in the Meadows model, the most notable defect being the absence of any recognition of the workings of the price system. Also, Solow points out some of the factors leading a great many economists to oppose Mishan's position.

Population growth can have an important impact on the rate of economic growth; and the next article, taken from Thomas Malthus's famous *Essay on the Principle of Population*, presents his ideas concerning the tendency of population to increase beyond the available food supplies. Economic growth is due in considerable measure to productivity growth and technological change. In the next paper, the editor summarizes what is known about the relationship between research and development (R & D) on the one hand, and the rate of economic growth and productivity increase on the other. Because R & D can result in external economies, it is often argued that a market economy will tend to underinvest in R & D. The evidence bearing on this issue, as well as the relevant theory, is discussed in this paper.

The President's Commission for a National Agenda for the Eighties discusses a variety of policies that might be adopted to increase the rate of economic growth in the United States. The commission recommends, among other things, that the government encourage innovation, reduce inflation, improve the utilization of human resources, and stimulate saving and investment. As Laurence Seidman points out in the next article, one way to stimulate saving is to transform the income tax into a personal consumption tax. He discusses the pros and cons of making such a transformation.

Energy is intimately related to economic growth. To help solve our energy problems, there have been proposals for a huge subsidy program for synthetic fuels. In the next paper, Robert Pindyck argues against such a program. Robert Stobaugh and Daniel Yergin, in the following article, emphasize the importance of conservation in dealing with our nation's dependence on foreign oil.

30

The Case against Economic Growth

E. J. MISHAN

E. J. Mishan is Professor of Economics at the London School of Economics and Political Science. This selection is taken from his book The Costs of Economic Growth, *published in 1967.*

The notion of economic expansion as a process on balance beneficial to society goes back at least a couple of centuries, about which time, however, the case in favor was much stronger than it is today when we are not only incomparably wealthier but also suffering from many disagreeable by-products of rapid technological change. Yet so entrenched are the interests involved, commercial, institutional, and scientific, and so pervasive the influence of modern communications, that economic growth has embedded itself in the ethos of our civilization. Despite the manifest disamenities caused by the postwar economic expansion, no one today seeking to advance his position in the hierarchy of government or business fails to pay homage to this sovereign concept.

[My own] general conclusion is that the continued pursuit of economic growth by Western societies is more likely on balance to reduce rather than increase social welfare. And some additional light on the pattern of arguments employed is shed by enumerating the set of conditions that, if met, would ensure a positive relation between economic growth and welfare.

First, that the economy be highly competitive in structure in all its branches, or else so organized that in all sectors the outputs of goods are such that their prices tend to equal their corresponding marginal costs.

Second, that all the measurable effects on other people or firms arising in the production and use of any good—other than those effects which already register on the market mechanism in the form of alterations in product and factor prices—be brought into the cost calculus.

Third, that in increasing *per capita* output over time the process of economic growth does not bring about a less equitable distribution of income.

Fourth, that the consuming public be fully conversant with the comparative qualities and performances of all new goods coming on to the market.

Fifth, that the public, regarded as producers, become no worse off in adapting themselves to new techniques of production.

Sixth, that the so-called relative income hypothesis does not hold; or, less stringently, that an overall

169

increase in real income *per capita* will have more than negligible effects in making some people feel better off without making others feel worse off.

Seventh, that the welfare experienced by men from sources other than goods produced by the economic system is small enough to be neglected.

Though it goes without saying that none of these conditions is likely to be met in today's wealthy societies, some of the conditions are more important than others. Observations, both slight and significant on each of the first six conditions, may be found in the professional literature. Since it lends itself to elegant formulation, the first condition is the one treated in most detail. Indeed, owing to the traditional presumption in favor of competition and free trade, measures of the degree of monopoly in the economy and, occasionally, of allocative waste associated therewith, are of continued interest to economists. Yet the scope for improvements in welfare by policies designed to increase competition is, I should think, very slight in comparison with the losses of welfare from neglect of the other conditions. The concern with external effects, relevant to the second condition, is hardly less pronounced. A good deal of the interest in these external effects, however, may be imputed to the intellectual fascination with optimality problems—not alas, to universal alarm at what is happening to our environment. I have suggested that the potential contribution to social welfare of adopting a policy of correcting outstanding external diseconomies is vastly underrated, and this for several reasons: (1) because of the present difficulties of measurement; (2) because of the mistaken view that the disamenities inflicted are limited, since there appear to be incentives to voluntary agreement for their control; and (3) because of a sense of resignation induced by the slippery problems connected with hypothetical and actual compensation. To these professional reasons we may add the popular impression—which in consequence of the above reasons also appeals to many economists— that economic growth provides a more direct and certain means of advancing welfare.

In illustrating some of the chief sources of external diseconomies no attempt was made to disguise the author's conviction that the invention of the private automobile is one of the great disasters to have befallen the human race. Given the absence of controls, the growth of population and its increased wealth and urbanization would, in any case, have produced overgrown cities. Commercial and munici-

pal greed, coupled with architectural apathy, share the responsibility for a litter of shabby buildings. But it needed the motor-car to consummate these developments, to fill our days with clamor and fumes, to suburbanize the countryside and to subutopianize suburbia, and to ensure that any resort which became accessible should simultaneously become unattractive. The motor industry has come to dominate the economy as brazenly as its products dominate our physical environment, and our psychology. The common sight today, of street after street strewn thick with layabout cars, no longer dismays us.

The other two rapidly growing sources of disamenity used in illustrating the external diseconomies thesis were air travel and tourism. No effective legislation putting the onus on airlines has been contemplated. The noise created is limited only by what the authorities believe people can be made to put up with. And the public may be conditioned over time to bear with increasing disturbance simply (1) because of the difficulties and cost of organizing protests; (2) because of the apparent hopelessness of prevailing upon the authorities to put the claims of the residents before the claims of "progress," that is, the airlines; and (3) because of the timidity felt in pressing one's claims against so effective a retort as "the national interest." If there is a national interest, however, our discussion reveals the case for the Government's bearing the cost of its safeguard; not the unfortunate victims of aerial disturbance. The least that should be done to promote social welfare is to extend to the public some choice in the matter by legislating for wholly noise-free zones— zones that are, however, desirable in other respects and easily accessible.

As for the rapid destruction by mass tourism of the world's dwindling resources of natural beauty, a small contribution towards preservation could be made by the prohibition of motorized vehicles within selected areas and by the discontinuing of air services to such areas. Once the public becomes aware of the spread of devastation, international agreement on more radical measures may be forthcoming—if by then there is anything left worth preserving.

In sum, [my] thesis is that if men are concerned primarily with human welfare, and not primarily with productivity conceived as a good in itself, they should reject economic growth as a prior aim of policy in favor of a policy of seeking to apply more selective criteria of welfare. Such a policy would involve (1) legislation recognizing the individual's right to amenity, which legislation would spearhead the attack on much of our postwar blight; and (2) a substantial diversion of investible resources from industry to the task of replanning our towns and cities—in general, to direct our national resources and our ingenuity to recreating an environment that will gratify and inspire men. Finally, if public opinion cannot, for the present, be swung overwhelmingly towards this alternative view of the primary ends of policy, any regard at all to the declared doctrine of increasing the range of choices available to men warrants an extension to existing minorities of separate facilities in matters both large and small— though especially in respect of viable areas wherein a man of moderate means may choose to dwell unmolested by those particular features of modern technology that most disturb his equanimity.

If the moving spirit behind economic growth were to speak, its motto would be "Enough does not suffice." The classical description of an economic system makes sense in today's advanced economy only when stood on its head. Certainly the American economy presents us with a spectacle of growing resources pressing against limited wants. Moreover, the pace of change in the patterns of people's wants destroys the base on which the economist's comparison of social welfare is raised: if all seven conditions mentioned were met, the mere fact of continually changing tastes alone would prevent the economist from inferring that economic growth *per capita* increased welfare. Moreover, the vagaries of fashion can become burdensome and the multiplication of goods disconcerting.

Once we move away from the economist's frame of reference, other factors bearing on social welfare loom large. Expanding markets in conditions of material abundance depend upon men's dissatisfaction with their lot being perpetually renewed. Whether individual campaigns are successful or not, the institution of commercial advertising accentuates the materialistic tendencies in society and promotes the view that the things that matter most are the things money will buy—a view to which the young, who have plenty of

need of the wherewithal, if they are to avail themselves of the widely advertised opportunities for fast living and cool extravagance, are peculiarly vulnerable, and which explains much of their vociferous inpatience and increasing violence.

These and other informal considerations lead to pessimistic conclusions. Technological innovations may offer to add to men's material opportunities. But by increasing the risks of their obsolescence it adds also to their anxiety. Swifter means of communications have the paradoxical effect of isolating people; increased mobility has led to more hours commuting; increased automobilization to increased separation; more television to less communication. In consequence, people know less of their neighbors than ever before in history.

The pursuit of efficiency, itself regarded as the lifeblood of progress, is directed towards reducing the dependence of people on each other, and increasing their dependence on the machine. Indeed, by a gradual displacement of human effort from every aspect of living, technology will eventually enable us to slip swiftly through our allotted years with scarce enough sense of physical friction to be certain we are still alive.

Considerations such as these, which do not lend themselves to formal treatment, are crucial to the issue of human welfare. And the apparent inevitability of technological advance does not thereby render them irrelevant. Death too is inevitable. But one does not feel compelled to hurry towards it on that account. Once we descry the sort of world towards which technological growth is bearing us, it is well worth discussing whether humanity will find it more congenial or not. If, on reflection, we view the prospects with misgivings, we are, at least, freed from the obligation to join in the frequent incantations of our patriotic growthmen. More positively, we have an additional incentive to support the policy of reducing industrial investment in favor of large-scale replanning of our cities, and of restoring and enhancing the beauty of many of our villages, towns and resorts.

31

The Limits to Growth

DONELLA MEADOWS, DENNIS MEADOWS, J. RANDERS, and WILLIAM BEHRENS

Donella Meadows, Dennis Meadows, J. Randers, and William Behrens carried out the well-known study of the limits of economic growth for the Club of Rome. The following article is from their book The Limits to Growth, *published in 1972.*

I do not wish to seem overdramatic, but I can only conclude from the information that is available to me as Secretary-General, that the Members of the United Nations have perhaps ten years left in which to subordinate their ancient quarrels and launch a global partnership to curb the arms race, to improve the human environment, to defuse the population explosion, and to supply the required momentum to development efforts. If such a global partnership is not forged within the next decade, then I very much fear that the problems I have mentioned will have reached such staggering proportions that they will be beyond our capacity to control.

U THANT, 1969

The problems U Thant mentions—the arms race, environmental deterioration, the population explosion, and economic stagnation—are often cited as the central, long-term problems of modern man. Many people believe that the future course of human society, perhaps even the survival of human society, depends on the speed and effectiveness with which the world responds to these issues. And yet only a small

fraction of the world's population is actively concerned with understanding these problems or seeking their solutions.

Human Perspectives

Every person in the world faces a series of pressures and problems that require his attention and action. These problems affect him at many different levels. He may spend much of his time trying to find tomorrow's food for himself and his family. He may be concerned about personal power or the power of the nation in which he lives. He may worry about a world war during his lifetime, or a war next week with a rival clan in his neighborhood.

These very different levels of human concern can be represented on a graph like that in Figure 1. The graph has two dimensions, space and time. Every human concern can be located at some point on the graph, depending on how much geographical space it includes and how far it extends in time. Most people's worries are concentrated in the lower left-hand corner of the graph. Life for these people is difficult, and they must devote nearly all of their efforts to providing for themselves and their families, day by day. Other people think about and act on problems farther out on the space or time axes. The pressures they perceive involve not only themselves, but the community with which they identify. The actions they take extend not only days, but weeks or years into the future.

A person's time and space perspectives depend on his culture, his past experience, and the immediacy of the problems confronting him on each level. Most people must have successfully solved the problems in a smaller area before they move their concerns to a larger one. In general the larger the space and the longer the time associated with a problem, the smaller the number of people who are actually concerned with its solution.

There can be disappointments and dangers in limiting one's view to an area that is too small. There are many examples of a person striving with all his might to solve some immediate, local problem, only to

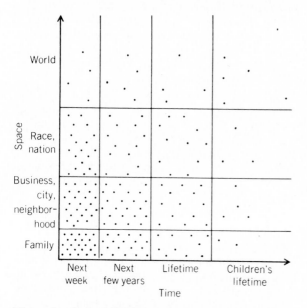

Figure 1. Human Perspectives

Although the perspectives of the world's people vary in space and in time, every human concern falls somewhere on the space-time graph. The majority of the world's people are concerned with matters that affect only family or friends over a short period of time. Others look farther ahead in time or over a larger area—a city or a nation. Only a very few people have a global perspective that extends far into the future.

find his efforts defeated by events occurring in a larger context. A farmer's carefully maintained fields can be destroyed by an international war. Local officials' plans can be overturned by a national policy. A country's economic development can be thwarted by a lack of world demand for its products. Indeed there is increasing concern today that most personal and national objectives may ultimately be frustrated by long-term, global trends such as those mentioned by U Thant.

Are the implications of these global trends actually so threatening that their resolution should take precedence over local, short-term concerns?

Is it true, as U Thant suggested, that there remains less than a decade to bring these trends under control?

If they are not brought under control, what will the consequences be?

What methods does mankind have for solving global problems, and what will be the results and the costs of employing each of them?

These are the questions that we have been investigating in the first phase of The Club of Rome's Project on the Predicament of Mankind. Our concerns thus fall in the upper right-hand corner of the space-time graph.

Problems and Models

Every person approaches his problems, wherever they occur on the space-time graph, with the help of models. A model is simply an ordered set of assumptions about a complex system. It is an attempt to understand some aspect of the infinitely varied world by selecting from perceptions and past experience a set of general observations applicable to the problem at hand. A farmer uses a mental model of his land, his assets, market prospects, and past weather conditions to decide which crops to plant each year. A surveyor constructs a physical model—a map—to help in planning a road. An economist uses mathematical models to understand and predict the flow of international trade.

Decision-makers at every level unconsciously use mental models to choose among policies that will shape our future world. These mental models are, of necessity, very simple when compared with the reality from which they are abstracted. The human brain, remarkable as it is, can only keep track of a limited number of the complicated, simultaneous interactions that determine the nature of the real world.

We, too, have used a model. Ours is a formal, written model of the world.[1] It constitutes a preliminary attempt to improve our mental models of long-term, global problems by combining the large amount of information that is already in human minds and in written records with the new information-processing tools that mankind's increasing knowledge has produced—the scientific method, systems analysis, and the modern computer.

Our world model was built specifically to investigate five major trends of global concern—accelerating industrialization, rapid population growth, widespread malnutrition, depletion of nonrenewable resources, and a deteriorating environment. These trends are all interconnected in many ways, and their development is measured in decades or centuries, rather than in months or years. With the model we are seeking to understand the causes of these trends, their interrelationships, and their implications as much as one hundred years in the future.

The model we have constructed is, like every other model, imperfect, oversimplified, and unfinished. We are well aware of its shortcomings, but we believe that it is the most useful model now available for dealing with problems far out on the space-time graph. To our knowledge it is the only formal model in existence that is truly global in scope, that has a time horizon longer than thirty years, and that includes important variables such as population, food production, and pollution, not as independent entities, but as dynamically interacting elements, as they are in the real world.

Since ours is a formal, or mathematical, model it also has two important advantages over mental models. First, every assumption we make is written in a precise form so that it is open to inspection and criticism by all. Second, after the assumptions have been scrutinized, discussed, and revised to agree with our best current knowledge, their implications for the future behavior of the world system can be traced without error by a computer, no matter how complicated they become.

We feel that the advantages listed above make this model unique among all mathematical and mental world models available to us today. But there is no reason to be satisfied with it in its present form. We intend to alter, expand, and improve it as our own knowledge and the world data base gradually improve.

In spite of the preliminary state of our work, we believe it is important to publish the model and our findings now. Decisions are being made every day, in every part of the world, that will affect the physical, economic, and social conditions of the world system for decades to come. These decisions cannot wait for perfect models and total understanding. They will be made on the basis of some model, mental or written, in any case. We feel that the model described here is already sufficiently developed to be of some use to decision-makers. Furthermore, the basic behavior modes we have already observed in this model appear to be so fundamental and general that we do not expect our broad conclusions to be substantially altered by further revisions.

We have used a computer as a tool to aid our own understanding of the causes and consequences of the accelerating trends that characterize the modern world, but familiarity with computers is by no means necessary to comprehend or to discuss our conclusions. The implications of those accelerating trends raise issues that go far beyond the proper domain of a purely scientific document. They must be debated by a wider community than that of scientists alone. Our purpose here is to open that debate.

The following conclusions have emerged from our work so far. We are by no means the first group to have stated them. For the past several decades, people who have looked at the world with a global, long-term perspective have reached similar conclusions. Nevertheless, the vast majority of policy-makers seems to be actively pursuing goals that are inconsistent with these results.

Our conclusions are:

1. If the present growth trends in world population, industrialization, pollution, food production, and resource depletion continue unchanged, the limits to growth on this planet will be reached sometime within the next one hundred years. The most probable result will be a rather sudden and uncontrollable decline in both population and industrial capacity.

2. It is possible to alter these growth trends and to establish a condition of ecological and economic stability that is sustainable far into the future. The state of global equilibrium could be designed so that the basic material needs of each person on earth are satisfied and each person has an equal opportunity to realize his individual human potential.

---

[1] The prototype model on which we have based our work was designed by Professor Jay W. Forrester of the Massachusetts Institute of Technology. A description of that model has been published in his book *World Dynamics* (Cambridge, Mass.: Wright-Allen Press, 1971).

3. If the world's people decide to strive for this second outcome rather than the first, the sooner they begin working to attain it, the greater will be their chances of success.

These conclusions are so far-reaching and raise so many questions for further study that we are quite frankly overwhelmed by the enormity of the job that must be done. We hope that people in many fields of study and in many countries of the world, will raise the space and time horizons of their concerns and join us in understanding and preparing for a period of great transition—the transition from growth to global equilibrium.

32

Is the End of the World at Hand?

ROBERT M. SOLOW

Robert M. Solow is Professor of Economics at Massachusetts Institute of Technology. This article was published in Challenge in 1973.

I was having a hard time figuring out how to begin when I came across an excerpt from an interview with my MIT colleague Professor Jay Forrester, who is either the Christopher Columbus or the Dr. Strangelove of this business, depending on how you look at it. Forrester said he would like to see about 100 individuals, the most gifted and best qualified in the world, brought together in a team to make a psychosocial analysis of the problem of world equilibrium. He thought it would take about ten years. When he was asked to define the composition of his problem-solving group, Forrester said: "Above all it shouldn't be mostly made up of professors. One would include people who had been successful in their personal careers, whether in politics, business, or anywhere else. We should also need radical philosophers, but we should take care to keep out representatives of the social sciences. Such people always want to go to the bottom of a particular problem. What we want to look at are the problems caused by interactions."

I don't know what you call people who believe they can be wrong about everything in particular, but

expect to be lucky enough somehow to get it right on the interactions. They may be descendants of the famous merchant Lapidus, who said he lost money on every item he sold, but made it up on the volume. Well, I suppose that as an economist I am a representative of the social sciences; and I'm prepared to play out the role by talking about first principles and trying to say what the Growth vs. No-Growth business is really about. This is going to involve me in the old academic ploy of saying over and over again what I'm not talking about before I ever actually say what I think I am talking about. But I'm afraid that some of those boring distinctions are part of the price you have to pay for getting it right.

First of all, there are (at least) two separate questions you can ask about the prospects for economic growth. You can ask: Is growth desirable? Or you can ask: Is growth possible? I suppose that if continued economic growth is not possible, it hardly matters whether or not it's desirable. But if it is possible, it's presumably not inevitable, so we can discuss whether we should want it. But they are separate questions, and an answer to one of them is

176

not necessarily an answer to the other. My main business is with the question about the possibility of continued growth; I want to discuss the validity of the negative answer given by the "Doomsday Models" associated with the names of Forrester and Meadows (and MIT!) and, to a lesser extent, with the group of English scientists who published a manifesto called "Blueprint for Survival." The main concern of Dr. E.J. Mishan, on the other hand, was with the desirability of continued economic growth (and, at least by implication, with the desirability of past economic growth). If I spend a few minutes poaching on his territory, it is mainly because that seems like a good way to get some concepts straight, but also just to keep a discussion going.

Sorting Out the Issues

Arguments about the desirability of economic growth often turn quickly into arguments about the "quality" of modern life. One gets the notion that you favor growth if you are the sort of person whose idea of heaven is to drive at ninety miles an hour down a six-lane highway reading billboards, in order to pollute the air over some crowded lake with the exhaust from twin 100-horsepower outboards, and whose idea of food is Cocoa Krispies. On the other hand, to be against economic growth is to be a granola-eating, backpacking, transcendental-meditating canoe freak. That may even be a true statistical association, but I will argue that there is no necessary or logical connection between your answer to the growth question and your answer to the quality-of-life question. Suppose there were no issue about econom-ic growth; suppose it were impossible; suppose each man or each woman were equipped to have only two children (one bomb under each wing); suppose we were stuck with the technology we have now and had no concept of invention, or even of increased mechanization through capital investment. We could still argue about the relative merits of cutting timber for building houses or leaving it stand to be enjoyed as forest. Some people would still be willing to breathe carbon monoxide in big cities in return for the excitement of urban life, while others would prefer cleaner air and fewer TV channels. Macy's would still not tell Gimbel's. Admen would still try to tell you that all those beautiful women are actually just looking for somebody who smokes Winchesters, thus managing to insult both men and women at once. Some people

would still bring transistor radios to the beach. All or nearly all of the arguments about the quality of life would be just as valid if the question of growth never arose.

I won't go so far as to say there is no connection. In particular, one can argue that if population density were low enough, people would interfere much less with each other, and everyone could find a part of the world and style of civilization that suited him. Then differences of opinion about the quality of life wouldn't matter so much. Even if I grant the truth of that observation, it is still the case that, from here on out, questions about the quality of life are separable from questions about the desirability of growth. If growth stopped, there would be just about as much to complain about; and, as I shall argue later on, one can imagine continued growth that is directed against pollution, against congestion, against sliced white bread.

I suppose it is only fair to admit that if you get very enthusiastic about economic growth you are likely to be attracted to easily quantifiable and measurable things as objects of study, to point at with pride or to view with alarm. You are likely to pay less attention to important, intangible aspects of the standard of living. Although you can't know whether people are happier than they used to be, you can at least determine that they drink more orange juice or take more aspirin. But that's mere weakness of imagination and has nothing to do in principle with the desirability of economic growth, let alone with its possibility.

There is another practical argument that is often made; and although it is important, it sometimes serves as a way of avoiding coming to grips with the real issues. This argument says that economic growth, increasing output per person, is the only way we are likely to achieve a more equitable distribution of income in society. There is a lot of home truth in that. It is inevitably less likely that a middle-class electorate will vote to redistribute part of its own income to the poor than that it will be willing to allocate a slightly larger share of a growing total. Even more pessimisti-cally, I might suggest that even a given relative distribution of income, supposing it cannot be made more nearly equal, for political or other reasons, is less unattractive if the absolute standard of living at the bottom is fairly high than it is if the absolute standard at the bottom is very low. From this point of view, even if economic growth doesn't lead to more equity in distribution, it makes the inequity we've got more tolerable. I think it is one of the lessons of history as recent as the McGovern campaign that this is a realistic statement of the prospects.

It is even clearer if one looks, not at the distribution of income within a rich country like the U.S., but at the distribution of income between the developed countries of the world and the underveloped ones. The rich Western nations have never been able to agree on the principle of allocating as much as one percent of their GNP to aid underveloped countries. They are unlikely to be willing to share their wealth on any substantial scale with the poor countries. Even if they were, there are so many more poor people in the world that an equally shared income would be quite low. The *only* prospect of a decent life for Asia, Africa, and Latin America is in more total output.

But I point this out only to warn you that it is not the heart of the question. I think that those who oppose continued growth should in honesty face up to the implications of their position for distributional equity and the prospects of the world's poor. I think those who favor continued growth on the grounds that only thus can we achieve some real equality ought to be serious about that. If economic growth with equality is a good thing, it doesn't follow that economic growth with a lot of pious talk about equality is a good thing. In principle, we can have growth with or without equity; and we can have stagnation with or without equity. An argument about first principles should keep those things separate.

What Has Posterity Done for Us?

Well, then, what *is* the problem of economic growth all about? (I'm giving a definition now, not stating a fact, so all I can say is that I think this way of looking at it contributes to clarity of thought.) Whenever there is a question about what to *do*, the desirability of economic growth turns on the claims of the future against the claims of the present. The pro-growth man is someone who is prepared to sacrifice something useful and desirable right now so that people should be better off in the future; the anti-growth man is someone who thinks that is unnecessary or undesirable. The nature of the sacrifice of present enjoyment for future enjoyment can be almost anything. The classic example is investment: We can use our labor and our resources to build very durable things like roads or subways or factories or blast furnaces or dams that will be used for a long time by people who were not even born when those things were created, and so

will certainly have contributed nothing to their construction. That labor and those resources can just as well be used to produce shorter-run pleasures for us now.

Such a sacrifice of current consumption on behalf of the future may not strike you as much of a sacrifice. But that's because you live in a country that is already rich; if you had lived in Stalin's Russia, that need to sacrifice would be one of the reasons you would have been given to explain why you had to live without comfort and pleasures while the Ministry of Heavy Industry got all the play. If you lived in an underdeveloped country now you would face the same problem: What shall you do with the foreign currency earned by sales of cocoa or copper or crude oil—spend it on imports of consumer goods for those alive and working now, or spend it on imports of machinery to start building an industry that may help to raise the standard of living in thirty years' time?

There are other ways in which the same choice can be made, including, for instance, the direction of intellectual resources to the invention of things (like the generation of electricity from nuclear fusion) that will benefit future generations. Paradoxically, one of the ways in which the present can do something for the future is to conserve natural resources. If we get along with less lumber now so that there will be more forests standing for our grandchildren, or if we limit the present consumption of oil or zinc so that there will be some left for the twenty-first century, or if we worry about siltation behind dams that would other-wise be fun for fishermen and water-skiers, in all those cases we are promoting economic growth. I call that paradoxical because I think most people identify the conservation freak with the antigrowth party whereas, in this view of the matter, the conservationist is trading present satisfaction for future satisfaction, that is, he is promoting economic growth. I think the confusion comes from mixing up the quality-of-life problem with the growth problem. But it is nonethe-less a confusion.

Why should we be concerned with the welfare of posterity, given the indubitable fact that posterity has never done a thing for us? I am not anthropologist enough to know how rare or common it is that our culture should teach us to care not only about our children but about their children, and their children. I suppose there are good Darwinian reasons why cultures without any future-orientation should fail to survive very long in the course of history. (But remember that they had a merry time of it while they lasted!) Moreover, we now enjoy the investments made by our ancestors, so there is a kind of equity in passing it on. Also, unless something terrible happens, there will be a lot more future than there has been past; and, for better or worse—probably worse—there will be more people at each future instant than there are now or have been. So all in all, the future will involve many more man-years of life than the present or the past, and a kind of intergenerational democracy suggests that all those man-years-to-be deserve some consideration out of sheer numbers.

On the other hand, *if* continued economic growth is possible—which is the question I'm coming to—then it is very likely that posterity will be richer than we are even if we make no special efforts on its behalf. If history offers any guide, then, in the developed part of the world at least, the accumulation of technological knowledge will probably make our great-grandchildren better off than we are, even if we make no great effort in that direction. Leaving aside the possibility of greater equality—I have already discussed that—there is hardly a crying need for posterity to be on average very much richer than we are. Why should we poor folk make any sacrifices for those who will in any case live in luxury in the future? Of course, if the end of the world is at hand, if continued economic growth is *not* possible, then we ought to care more about posterity, because they won't be so well off. Paradoxically, if continued growth is not possible, or less possible, then we probably ought to do more to promote it. Actually, there's no paradox in that, as every student of economics will realize, because it is a way of saying that the marginal return on investment is high.

Overshoot, Collapse, Doom

There is, as you know, a school of thought that claims that continued economic growth is in fact not possible anymore, or at least not for very long. This judgment has been expressed more or less casually by several observers in recent years. What distinguishes the "Doomsday Models" from their predecessors is that they claim to much more than a casual judgment: they deduce their beliefs about future prospects from mathematical models or systems analysis. They don't merely say that the end of the world is at hand—they can show you computer output that says the same thing.

Characteristically, the Doomsday Models do more than just say that continued economic growth is impossible. They tell us why: in brief, because (a) the earth's natural resources will soon be used up; (b) increased industrial production will soon strangle us in pollution; and (c) increasing population will eventually outrun the world's capacity to grow food, so that famine must eventually result. And, finally, the models tell us one more thing: the world will end with a bang, not a whimper. The natural evolution of the world economy is not at all toward some kind of smooth approach to its natural limits, wherever they are. Instead, it is inevitable—unless we make drastic changes in the way we live and organize ourselves—that the world will overshoot any level of population and production it can possibly sustain and will then collapse, probably by the middle of the next century.

I would like to say why I think that the Doomsday Models are bad science and therefore bad guides to public policy.

The first thing to realize is that the characteristic conclusion of the Doomsday Models is very near the surface. It is, in fact, more nearly an assumption than a conclusion, in the sense that the chain of logic from the assumptions to the conclusion is very short and rather obvious.

The basic assumption is that stocks of things like the world's natural resources and the waste-disposal capacity of the environment are finite, that the world economy tends to consume the stock at an increasing rate (through the mining of minerals and the production of goods), and that there are no built-in mechanisms by which approaching exhaustion tends to turn off consumption gradually and in advance. You hardly need a giant computer to tell you that a system with those behavior rules is going to bounce off its ceiling and collapse to a low level. Then, in case anyone is inclined to relax into the optimistic belief that maybe things aren't that bad, we are told: Imagine that the stock of natural resources were actually twice as big as the best current evidence suggests, or imagine that the annual amount of pollution could be halved all at once and then set to growing again. All that would happen is that the date of collapse would be postponed by T years, where T is not a large number. But once you grasp the quite simple essence of the models, this should come as no surprise. It is important to realize where these powerful conclusions come from, because, if you ask yourself "Why didn't I realize earlier that the end of the world was at hand?" the answer is not that you weren't clever enough to figure it out for yourself. The answer is that the imminent end of the world is an immediate deduction from certain assumptions, and one must really ask if the assumptions are any good.

It is a commonplace that if you calculate the annual output of any production process, large or small, and divide it by the annual employment of labor, you get a ratio that is called the productivity of labor. At the most aggregative level, for example, we can say that the GNP in 1971 was $1,050 billion and that about 82 million people were employed in producing it, so that GNP per worker or the productivity of a year of labor was about $12,800. Symmetrically, though the usage is less common, one could just as well calculate the GNP per unit of some particular natural resource and call that the productivity of coal, or GNP per pound of vanadium. We usually think of the productivity of labor as rising more or less exponentially, say at 2 or 3 percent a year, because that is the way it has in fact behaved over the past century or so since the statistics began to be collected. The rate of increase in the productivity of labor is not a constant of nature. Sometimes it is faster, sometimes slower. For example, we know that labor productivity must have increased more slowly a long time ago, because if we extrapolate backward at 2 percent a year, we come to a much lower labor productivity in 1492 than can possibly have been the case. And the productivity of labor has risen faster in the past twenty-five years than in the fifty years before that. It also varies from place to place, being faster in Japan and Germany and slower in Great Britain, for reasons that are not at all certain. But it rises, and we expect it to keep rising.

Now, how about the productivity of natural resources? All the Doomsday Models will allow is a one-time hypothetical increase in the world supply of natural resources, which is the equivalent of a one-time increase in the productivity of natural resources. Why shouldn't the productivity of most natural resources rise more or less steadily through time, like the productivity of labor?

Of course it does for some resources, but not for others. Real GNP roughly doubled between 1950 and 1970. But the consumption of primary and scrap iron increased by about 20 percent, so the productivity of iron, GNP per ton of iron, increased by about 2.5 percent a year on the average during those twenty years. The U.S. consumption of manganese rose by 30 percent in the same period, so the productivity of manganese went up by some 70 percent in twenty

years, a bit under 2.25 percent a year. Aggregate consumption of nickel just about doubled, like GNP, so the productivity of nickel didn't change. U.S. consumption of copper, both primary and secondary, went up by a third between 1951 and 1970, so GNP per pound of copper rose at 2 percent a year on the average. The story on lead and zinc is very similar, so their productivity increased at some 2 percent a year. The productivity of bituminous coal rose at 3 percent a year.

Naturally, there are important exceptions, and unimportant exceptions. GNP per barrel of oil was about the same in 1970 as in 1951: no productivity increase there. The consumption of natural gas tripled in the same period, so GNP per cubic foot of natural gas fell at about 2.5 percent a year. Our industrial demand for aluminum quadrupled in two decades, so the productivity of aluminum fell at a good 3.5 percent a year. And industrial demand for columbium was multiplied by a factor of twenty-five: in 1951 we managed $2.25 million of GNP (in 1967 prices) per pound of columbium, whereas in 1970 we were down to $170 thousand of GNP per pound of columbium. On the other hand, it is a little hard to imagine civilization toppling because of a shortage of columbium.

Obviously many factors combine to govern the course of the productivity of any given mineral over time. When a rare natural resource is first available, it acquires new uses with a rush; and consumption goes up much faster than GNP. That's the columbium story, no doubt, and, to a lesser extent, the vanadium story. But once the novelty has worn off, the productivity of a resource tends to rise as better or worse substitutes for it appear, as new commodities replace old ones, and as manufacturing processes improve. One of the reasons the productivity of copper rises is because that of aluminum falls, as aluminum replaces copper in many uses. The same is true of coal and oil. A resource, like petroleum, which is versatile because of its role as a source of energy, is an interesting special case. It is hardly any wonder that the productivity of petroleum has stagnated, because the consumption of energy—both as electricity for domestic and industrial use and in the automobile —has recently increased even faster than GNP. But no one can doubt that we will run out of oil, that coal and nuclear fission will replace oil as the major sources of energy. It is already becoming probable that the high-value use of oil will soon be as feed stock for the petrochemical industries, rather than as a source of energy. Sooner or later, the productivity of oil will rise out of sight, because the production and consumption of oil will eventually dwindle toward zero, but real GNP will not.

So there really is no reason why we should not think of the productivity of natural resources as increasing more or less exponentially over time. But then overshoot and collapse are no longer the inevitable trajectory of the world system, and the typical assumption-conclusion of the Doomsday Models falls by the wayside. We are in a different sort of ball game. The system might still burn itself out and collapse in finite time, but one cannot say with any honesty that it must. It all depends on the particular, detailed facts of modern economic life as well as on the economic policies we and the rest of the world pursue. I don't want to argue for any particular counterstory; all I want to say now is that the overshoot-collapse pattern is built into the models very near the surface, by assumption, and by implausible assumption at that.

Scarcity—and High Prices

There is at least one reason for believing that the Doomsday story is almost certainly wrong. The most glaring defect of the Forrester-Meadows models is the absence of any sort of functioning price system. I am no believer that the market is always right, and I am certainly no advocate of laissez-faire where the environment is concerned. But the price system is, after all, the main social institution evolved by capitalist economies (and, to an increasing extent, socialist economies too) for registering and reacting to relative scarcity. There are several ways that the working of the price system will push our society into faster and more systematic increases in the productivity of natural resources.

First of all, let me go back to the analogy between natural resources and labor. We are not surprised to learn that industry quite consciously tries to make inventions that save labor, i.e., permit the same product to be made with fewer man-hours of work. After all, on the average, labor costs amount to almost three-fourths of all costs in our economy. An invention that reduces labor requirements per unit of GNP by 1 percent reduces all costs by about 0.75 percent. Natural resource costs are a much smaller

proportion of total GNP, something nearer 5 percent. So industry and engineering have a much stronger motive to reduce labor requirements by 1 percent than to reduce resource requirements by 1 percent, assuming—which may or not be true—that it is about as hard to do one as to do the other. But then, as the earth's supply of particular natural resources nears exhaustion, and as natural resources become more and more valuable, the motive to economize those natural resources should become as strong as the motive to economize labor. The productivity of resources should rise faster than now—it is hard to imagine otherwise.

There are other ways in which the market mechanism can be expected to push us all to economize on natural resources as they become scarcer. Higher and rising prices of exhaustible resources lead competing producers to substitute other materials that are more plentiful and therefore cheaper. To the extent that it is impossible to design around or find substitutes for expensive natural resources, the prices of commodities that contain a lot of them will rise relative to the prices of other goods and services that don't use up a lot of resources. Consumers will be driven to buy fewer resource-intensive goods and more of other things. All these effects work automatically to increase the productivity of natural resources, i.e., to reduce resource requirements per unit of GNP.

This is not an argument for laissez-faire. We may feel that the private decisions of buyers and sellers give inadequate representation to future generations. Or we may feel that private interests are in conflict with a distinct public interest—strip-mining of coal is an obvious case in point, and there are many others as soon as we begin to think about environmental effects. Private market responses may be too uncoordinated, too slow, based on insufficient and faulty information. In every case there will be actions that public agencies can take and should take; and it will be a major political struggle to see that they are taken. But I don't see how one can have the slightest confidence in the predictions of models that seem to make no room for the operation of everyday market forces. If the forecasts are wrong, then so are the policy implications, to the extent that there are any realistic policy implications.

Every analysis of resource scarcity has to come to terms with the fact that the prices of natural resources and resource products have not shown any tendency to rise over the past half-century, relative to the prices of other things. This must mean that there have so far been adequate offsets to any progressive impoverishment of deposits—like improvements in the technology of extraction, savings in end uses, or the availability of cheaper substitutes. The situation could, of course, change; and very likely some day it will. If the experienced and expert participants in the market now believed that resource prices would be sharply higher at some foreseeable time, prices would *already* be rising, as I will try to explain in a moment. The historical steadiness of resource prices suggests that buyers and sellers in the market have not been acting as if they foresaw exhaustion in the absence of substitutes, and therefore sharply higher future prices. They may turn out to be wrong; but the Doomsday Models give us absolutely no reason to expect that—in fact, they claim to get whatever meager empirical basis they have from such experts.

Why is it true that if the market saw higher prices in the future, prices would already be rising? It is a rather technical point, but I want to explain it because, in a way, it summarizes the important thing about natural resources: conserving a mineral deposit is just as much of an investment as building a factory, and it has to be analyzed that way. Any owner of a mineral deposit owns a valuable asset, whether the owner is a private capitalist or the government of an underdeveloped country. The asset is worth keeping only if at the margin it earns a return equal to that earned on other kinds of assets. A factory produces things each year of its life, but a mineral deposit just lies there: its owner can realize a return only if he either mines the deposit or if it *increases in value*. So if you are sitting on your little pile of X and confidently expect to be able to sell it for a very high price in the year 2000 because it will be very scarce by then, you must be earning your 5 percent a year, or 10 percent a year, or whatever the going rate of return is, each year between now and 2000. The only way this can happen is for the value of X to go up by 5 percent a year or 10 percent a year. And that means that anyone who wants to use any X any time between now and 2000 will have to pay a price for it that is rising at that same 5 percent or 10 percent a year. Well, it's not happening. Of course, we are exploiting our hoard of exhaustible resources; we have no choice about that. We are certainly exploiting it wastefully, in the sense that we allow each other to dump waste products into the environment without full accounting for costs. But there is very little evidence that we are exploiting it too fast.

Crowding on Planet Earth

I have less to say about the question of population growth, because it doesn't seem to involve any difficult conceptual problems. At any time, in any place, there is presumably an optimal size of population—with the property that the average person would be somewhat worse off if the population were a bit larger, and also worse off if the population were a bit smaller. In any real case it must be very difficult to know what the optimum population is, especially because it will change over time as technology changes, and also because it is probably more like a band or zone than a sharply defined number. I mean that if you could somehow plot a graph of economic welfare per person against population size, there would be a very gentle dome or plateau at the top, rather than a sharp peak. . . .

At the present moment, at least for the United States, the danger of rapid population growth seems to be the wrong thing to worry about. The main object of public policy in this field ought to be to ensure that the choice of family size is truly a voluntary choice, that access to the best birth-control methods be made universal. That seems to be all that is needed. Of course, we know very little about what governs voluntary fertility, about why the typical notion of a good family size changes from generation to generation. So it is certainly possible that these recent developments will reverse themselves and that population control will again appear on the agenda of public policy. This remains to be seen.

In all this I have said nothing about the Doomsday Models because there is practically nothing that needs to be said. So far as we can tell, they make one very bad mistake: in the face of reason, common sense, and systematic evidence, they seem to assume that at high standards of living, people want more children as they become more affluent (though over most of the observed range, a higher standard of living goes along with smaller families). That error is certainly a serious one in terms of the recent American data—but perhaps it explains why some friends of mine were able to report that they had run a version of the Forrester World Dynamics Model starting with a population of two people and discovered that it blew up in 500 years. Apart from placing the date of the Garden of Eden in the fifteenth century, what else is new?

There is another analytical error in the models, as Fred Singer has pointed out. Suppose resource exhaustion or increased pollution conspires to bring a reduction in industrial production. The model then says that birth rates will rise because, in the past, low industrial output has been associated with high birth rates. But there is nothing in historical evidence to suggest that a once-rich country will go *back* to high birth rates if (as I doubt will happen) its standard of living falls from an accustomed high level. Common sense suggests that a society in such a position would fight to preserve its standard of living by reducing the desired family size. In any case, this is another example of a poorly founded—or unfounded—assumption introduced to support the likelihood of overshoot-and-collapse.

Paying for Pollution

Resource exhaustion and overpopulation: that leaves pollution as the last of the Doomsday Devils. I think that what one gets from the Doomsday literature is the notion that air and water and noise pollution are an inescapable accompaniment of economic growth, especially industrial growth. If that is true, then to be against pollution is to be against growth. I realize that in putting the matter so crudely I have been unjust; nevertheless, that is the message that comes across. I think that way of looking at the pollution problem is wrong.

A correct analysis goes something like this. Excessive pollution and degradation of the environment certainly accompany industrial growth and the increasing population density that goes with it. But they are by no means an inescapable by-product. Excessive pollution happens because of an important flaw in the price system. Factories, power plants, municipal sewers, drivers of cars, strip-miners of coal and deep-miners of coal, and all sorts of generators of waste are allowed to dump that waste into the environment, into the atmosphere and into running water and the oceans, without paying the full cost of what they do. No wonder they do too much. So would you, and so would I. In fact, we actually do—directly as drivers of cars, indirectly as we buy some products at a price which is lower than it ought to be because the producer is not required to pay for using the environment to carry away his wastes, and even more indirectly as we buy things that are made with things that pollute the environment.

This flaw in the price system exists because a scarce resource (the waste-disposal capacity of the environment) goes unpriced; and that happens because it is owned by all of us, as it should be. The flaw can be corrected, either by the simple expedient of regulating the discharge of wastes to the environment by direct control or by the slightly more complicated device of charging special prices—user taxes—to those who dispose of wastes in air or water. These effluent charges do three things: they make pollution-intensive goods expensive, and so reduce the consumption of them; they make pollution-intensive methods of production costly, and so promote abatement of pollution by producers; they generate revenue that can, if desired, be used for the further purification of air or water or for other environmental improvements. Most economists prefer this device of effluent charges to regulation by direct order. This is more than an occupational peculiarity. Use of the price system has certain advantages in efficiency and decentralization. Imposing a physical limit on, say, sulfur dioxide emission is, after all, a little peculiar. It says that you may do so much of a bad thing and pay nothing for the privilege, but after that, the price is infinite. Not surprisingly, one can find a more efficient schedule of pollution abatement through a more sensitive tax schedule.

But this difference of opinion is minor compared with the larger point that needs to be made. The annual cost that would be necessary to meet decent pollution-abatement standards by the end of the century is large, but not staggering. One estimate says that in 1970 we spent about $8.5 billion (in 1967 prices), or 1 percent of GNP, for pollution abatement. An active pollution abatement policy would cost perhaps $50 billion a year by 2000, which would be about 2 percent of GNP by then. That is a small investment of resources: you can see how small it is when you consider that GNP grows by 4 percent or so every year, on the average. Cleaning up air and water would entail a cost that would be a bit like losing one-half of one year's growth, between now and the year 2000. What stands between us and a decent environment is not the curse of industrialization, not an unbearable burden of cost, but just the need to organize ourselves consciously to do some simple and knowable things. Compared with the possibility of an active abatement policy, the policy of stopping economic growth in order to stop pollution would be incredibly inefficient. It would not actually accomplish much, because one really wants to reduce the amount of, say, hydrocarbon emission to a third or a half of *what it is now*. And what no-growth would accomplish, it would do by cutting off your face to spite your nose.

33

The Principle of Population

THOMAS MALTHUS

Thomas Malthus was one of the great figures of economics. This article comes from his famous Essay on the Principle of Population, *published in 1798.*

In an inquiry concerning the improvement of society, the mode of conducting the subject which naturally presents itself is:

1. To investigate the causes that have hitherto impeded the progress of mankind towards happiness; and,

2. To examine the probability of the total or partial removal of these causes in the future.

To enter fully into this question, and to enumerate all the causes that have hitherto influenced human inprovement, would be much beyond the power of an individual. The principal object of the present essay is to examine the effects of one great cause intimately united with the very nature of man; which, though it has been constantly and powerfully operating since the commencement of society, has been little noticed by the writers who have treated this subject. The facts which establish the existence of this cause have, indeed, been repeatedly stated and acknowledged; but its natural and necessary effects have been almost totally overlooked; though probably among these effects may be reckoned a very considerable portion of

that vice and misery, and of that unequal distribution of the bounties of nature, which it has been the unceasing object of the enlightened philanthropist in all ages to correct.

The cause to which I allude, is the constant tendency in all animated life to increase beyond the nourishment prepared for it.

It is observed by Dr. Franklin, that there is no bound to the prolific nature of plants or animals but what is made by the crowding and interfering with each other's means of subsistence. Were the face of the earth, he says, vacant of other plants, it might be gradually sowed and overspread with one kind only, as, for instance, with fennel: and were it empty of other inhabitants, it might in a few ages be replenished from one nation only, as, for instance, with Englishmen.

This is incontrovertibly true. Throughout the animal and vegetable kingdoms Nature has scattered the seeds of life abroad with the most profuse and liberal hand; but has been comparatively sparing in the room and the nourishment necessary to rear them. The germs of existence contained in this earth, if they could freely develop themselves, would fill millions of worlds in the course of a few thousand years. Necessity, that imperious, all-pervading law of nature, restrains them within the prescribed bounds. The race of plants and the race of animals shrink under this great restrictive law; and man cannot by any efforts of reason escape from it.

In plants and irrational animals, the view of the subject is simple. They are all impelled by a powerful instinct to the increase of their species, and this instinct is interrupted by no doubts about providing for their offspring. Wherever, therefore, there is liberty, the power of increase is exerted, and the superabundant effects are repressed afterwards by want of room and nourishment.

The effects of this check on man are more complicated. Impelled to the increase of his species by an equally powerful instinct, reason interrupts his career, and asks him whether he may not bring beings into the world for whom he cannot provide the means of support. If he attend to this natural suggestion, the restriction too frequently produces vice. If he hear it not, the human race will be constantly endeavouring to increase beyond the means of subsistence. But as, by that law of our nature which makes food necessary to the life of man, population can never actually increase beyond the lowest nourishment capable of supporting it, a strong check on population; from the difficulty of acquiring food, must be constantly in operation. This difficulty must fall somewhere, and must necessarily be severely felt in some or other of the various forms of misery, or the fear of misery, by a large portion of mankind.

That population has this constant tendency to increase beyond the means of subsistence, and that it is kept to its necessary level by these causes, will sufficiently appear from a review of the different states of society in which man has existed. But, before we proceed to this review, the subject will perhaps be seen in a clearer light, if we endeavor to ascertain what would be the natural increase of population, if left to exert itself with perfect freedom; and what might be expected to be the rate of increase in the productions of the earth, under the most favourable circumstances of human industry.

It will be allowed that no country has hitherto been known, where the manners were so pure and simple, and the means of subsistence so abundant, that no check whatever has existed to early marriages from the difficulty of providing for a family, and that no waste of the human species has been occasioned by vicious customs, by towns, by unhealthy occupations, or too severe labour. Consequently in no state that we have yet known, has the power of population been left to exert itself with perfect freedom.

Whether the law of marriage be instituted or not, the dictate of nature and virtue seems to be an early attachment to one woman; and where there were no impediments of any kind in the way of a union to which such an attachment would lead, and no causes of depopulation afterwards, the increase of the human species would be evidently much greater than any increase which has been hitherto known.

In the northern states of America, where the means of subsistence have been more ample, the manners of the people more pure, and the checks to early marriages fewer, than in any of the modern states of Europe, the population has been found to double itself, for above a century and a half successively, in less than twenty-five years. Yet, even during these periods, in some of the towns, the deaths exceeded the births, a circumstance which clearly proves that, in those parts of the country which supplied this deficiency, the increase must have been much more rapid than the general average.

In the back settlements, where the sole employment is agriculture, and vicious customs and unwholesome occupations are little known, the population has been found to double itself in fifteen years. Even this extraordinary rate of increase is probably short of the utmost power of population. Very severe labour is requisite to clear a fresh country; such situations are not in general considered as particularly healthy; and the inhabitants, probably, are occasionally subject to the incursions of the Indians, which may destroy some lives, or at any rate diminish the fruits of industry.

According to a table of Euler, calculated on a mortality of one in thirty-six, if the births be to the deaths in the proportion of three to one, the period of doubling will be only twelve years and four-fifths. And this proportion is not only a possible supposition, but has actually occurred for short periods in more countries than one.

Sir William Petty supposes a doubling possible in so short a time as ten years.

But, to be perfectly sure that we are far within the truth, we will take the slowest of these rates of increase, a rate in which all concurring testimonies agree, and which has been repeatedly ascertained to be from procreation only.

It may safely be pronounced, therefore, that population, when unchecked, goes on doubling itself every twenty-five years, or increases in a geometrical ratio.

The rate according to which the productions of the earth may be supposed to increase, will not be so easy to determine. Of this, however, we may be perfectly certain, that the ratio of their increase in a limited territory must be of a totally different nature from the ratio of the increase of population. A thousand millions are just as easily doubled every twenty-five years by the power of population as a thousand. But the food to support the increase from the greater number will by no means be obtained with the same facility. Man is necessarily confined in room. When acre has been added to acre till all the fertile land is occupied, the yearly increase of food must depend upon the melioration of the land already in possession. This is a fund, which, from the nature of all soils, instead of increasing, must be gradually diminishing. But population, could it be supplied with food, would go on with unexhausted vigour; and the increase of one period would furnish the power of a greater increase the next, and this without any limit.

From the accounts we have of China and Japan, it may be fairly doubted whether the best directed efforts of human industry could double the produce of these countries even once in any number of years. There are many parts of the globe, indeed, hitherto uncultivated and almost unoccupied; but the right of exterminating, or driving into a corner where they must starve, even the inhabitants of these thinly peopled regions, will be questioned in a moral view. The process of improving their minds and directing their industry would necessarily be slow; and during this time, as population would regularly keep pace with the increasing produce, it would rarely happen that a great degree of knowledge and industry would have to operate at once upon rich unappropriated soil. Even where this might take place, as it does sometimes in new colonies, a geometrical ratio increases with such extraordinary rapidity, that the advantage could not last long. If the United States of America continue increasing, which they certainly will do, though not with the same rapidity as formerly, the Indians will be driven farther and farther back into the country, till the whole race is ultimately exterminated, and the territory is incapable of further extension.

These observations are, in a degree, applicable to all the parts of the earth where the soil is imperfectly cultivated. To exterminate the inhabitants of the greatest part of Asia and Africa, is a thought that could not be admitted for a moment. To civilise and direct the industry of the various tribes of Tartars and Negroes, would certainly be a work of considerable time, and of variable and uncertain success.

Europe is by no means so fully peopled as it might be. In Europe there is the fairest chance that human industry may receive its best direction. The science of agriculture has been much studied in England and Scotland; and there is still a great portion of uncultivated land in these countries. Let us consider at what rate the produce of this island (Great Britain) might be supposed to increase under circumstances the most favourable to improvement.

If it be allowed that by the best possible policy, and great encouragements to agriculture, the average produce of the island could be doubled in the first twenty-five years, it will be allowing, probably, a greater increase than could with reason be expected.

In the next twenty-five years, it is impossible to suppose that the produce could be quadrupled. It would be contrary to all our knowledge of the properties of land. The improvement of the barren parts would be a work of time and labour; and it must be evident to those who have the slightest acquaintance with agricultural subjects, that in proportion as cultivation extended, the additions that could yearly be made to the former average produce must be gradually and regularly diminishing. That we may be the better able to compare the increase of population and food, let us make a supposition, which, without pretending to accuracy, is clearly more favourable to the power of production in the earth than any experience we have had of its qualities will warrant.

Let us suppose that the yearly additions which might be made to the former average produce, instead of decreasing, which they certainly would do, were to remain the same; and that the produce of this island might be increased every twenty-five years, by a quantity equal to what it at present produces. The most enthusiastic speculator cannot suppose a greater increase than this. In a few centuries it would make every acre of land in the island like a garden.

If this supposition be applied to the whole earth, and if it be allowed that the subsistence for man which the earth affords might be increased every twenty-five years by a quantity equal to what it at present produces, this will be supposing a rate of increase much greater than we can imagine that any possible exertions of mankind could make it.

It may be fairly pronounced, therefore, that considering the present average state of the earth, the means of subsistence, under circumstances the most favourable to human industry, could not possibly be made to increase faster than in an arithmetical ratio.

The necessary effects of these two different rates of increase, when brought together, will be very striking. Let us call the population of this island eleven millions, and suppose the present produce equal to the easy support of such a number. In the first twenty-five years the population would be twenty-two millions, and the food being also doubled, the means of subsistence would be equal to this increase. In the next twenty-five years, the population would be forty-four millions, and the means of subsistence only equal to the support of thirty-three millions. In the next period the population would be eighty-eight millions, and the means of subsistence just equal to the support of half that number. And, at the conclusion of the first century, the population would be a hundred and seventy-six millions, and the means of subsistence only equal to the support of fifty-five millions, leaving a population of a hundred and twenty-one millions totally unprovided for.

Taking the whole earth, instead of this island, emigration would of course be excluded; and, supposing the present population equal to a thousand millions, the human species would increase as the numbers, 1, 2, 4, 8, 16, 32, 64, 128, 256; and subsistence as, 1, 2, 3, 4, 5, 6, 7, 8, 9. In two centuries the population would be to the means of subsistence as 256 to 9: in three centuries as 4096 to 13, and in two thousand years the difference would be almost incalculable.

In this supposition no limits whatever are placed to the produce of the earth. It may increase for ever, and be greater than any assignable quantity; yet still the power of population being in every period so much superior, the increase of the human species can only be kept down to the level of the means of subsistence by the constant operation of the strong law of necessity acting as a check upon the greater power.

34

Contribution of
Research and Development to
Economic Growth in the United States

EDWIN MANSFIELD

Edwin Mansfield is Professor of Economics at the University of Pennsylvania. This excerpt comes from a paper commissioned by the National Science Foundation and published in Science in 1972.

Technological change is clearly an important factor in economic growth, both in the United States and in other countries, both now and in the past. In recent years—after neglecting the study of technological change for a long time—economists have shown a considerable interest in examining the relationship between research and development (R and D), on the one hand, and the rate of economic growth and productivity increase, on the other. In addition, there have been a number of discussions of whether we, as a nation, are underinvesting in certain kinds of R and D.

At the outset, two important points should be noted. First, by focusing attention on the economic effects of R and D, I am not implying that only these effects of R and D are important. On the contrary, increased knowledge is clearly of great importance above and beyond its strictly economic benefits. Second, by looking at our nation's rate of economic growth and productivity increase, I am not assuming explicitly or implicitly that economic growth is, in some simple sense, what public policy should attempt to maximize. Clearly, the desirability of a particular growth rate depends on the way it is achieved, how the

extra production is distributed, how growth is measured, and many other things.

R and D and Economic Growth

The pioneering studies of the relationship between technological change and economic growth occurred in the mid-1950s. Assuming that there were constant returns to scale, that capital and labor were paid their marginal products, and that technological change was neutral, Robert Solow attempted to estimate the rate of technological change for the nonfarm American economy during the period from 1909 to 1949. His findings suggested that, for the period as a whole, the average rate of technological change was about 1.5 percent per year. More precisely, the output that could be derived from a fixed amount of inputs increased at about 1.5 percent per year.

Based on these findings, he concluded that about 90 percent of the increase in output per capita during this period was attributable to technological change, whereas only a minor proportion of the increase was due to increases in the amount of capital employed

188

per worker. This conclusion received a great deal of attention—and caused some consternation among economists who had focused much more attention on the factors underlying the amount of capital employed per worker than on those underlying the rate of technological change. A flurry of papers followed Solow's, each modifying his techniques slightly or using a somewhat different data base.

After the first wave of papers in the mid-1950s, investigators began to feel increasingly uneasy about the basic methodology used in these studies. In essence, this methodology was the following. Economists, who view the total output of the economy as being due to various inputs of productive services into the productive process, began by specifying these inputs as labor and capital and by attempting to estimate the contribution of these inputs to the measured growth of output. Then, whatever portion of the measured growth of output that could not be explained by these inputs was attributed to technological change. The crudeness of this procedure is obvious. Since the effect of technological change is equated with whatever increase in output is unexplained by other inputs, the resulting measure of the effect of technological change does not isolate the effects of technological change alone. It also contains the effects of whatever inputs are excluded—which, depending on the study, may be economies of scale, improved allocation of resources, changes in product mix, increases in education, or improved health and nutrition of workers.

To remedy some of these limitations, a number of additional studies were carried out in the early 1960s, the most comprehensive and influential one being by Edward Denison. Denison attempted to include many inputs—particularly changes in labor quality associated with increases in schooling—that had been omitted, largely or completely, in earlier studies. Since it was relatively comprehensive, his study resulted in a relatively low residual increase in output unexplained by the inputs included. Specifically, Denison concluded that the "advance of knowledge"—his term for the residual—was responsible for about 40 percent of the total increase in national income per person employed during 1929–1957.

Of course, technological change can stem from sources other than organized R and D, as evidenced by the findings of Jewkes et al. concerning the importance of independent investors as a source of major inventions, and the findings by Hollander and others concerning the importance of technological changes that depend in no significant way on formal R and D. Denison estimates that about one-fifth of the

contribution to economic growth of "advance of knowledge" in 1929–1957 can be attributed to organized R and D. But this is the roughest kind of guess, and Denison himself would be the first to admit that this estimate is based largely on conjecture.

Fundamental Problems of Measurement

How firmly based is the current state of the art in this area? In others words, how reliable are the estimates of the contribution of R and D to economic growth in the United States? I have already indicated some of the difficulties present in these estimates. Unfortunately, there are a number of additional problems of a fundamental nature that must be understood as well. First, the measured rates of growth of output on which these estimates are based suffer from a very important defect because, to a large extent, they fail to give proper credit and weight to improvements in the quality of goods and services produced, and these improvements are an important result of R and D. For example, the growth rate would have been the same whether antibiotics were developed or not, or whether we devoted the resources used to reach the moon to public works. In general, only those changes in technology that reduce the costs of end products already in existence have an effect on measured economic growth. Unfortunately, the measured growth of national income fails to register or indicate the effects on consumer welfare of the increased spectrum of choice arising from the introduction of new products.

Second, the models on which these estimates are based may not take into account the full complexity of the relationships among the various inputs. In particular, if the returns to some input are dependent on the rate of technological change, and if this is not recognized explicitly, some of technology's contribution to economic growth will be attributed incorrectly to other inputs. This may be the case with education, since the returns to education would probably have been less if technological change had occurred at a slower pace. It may also be the case with "the reallocation of resources," a factor sometimes used to explain part of the residual increase in output.

Third, it is not clear how one can get from an estimate of the contribution to economic growth of technological change (or advance of knowledge, in Denison's terms) to an estimate of the contribution to economic growth of R and D. Clearly, there is no reason that these two estimates should be the same; on the contrary, one would expect the latter estimate to be smaller than the former. But the estimate that results from the models discussed above is the former estimate, not the latter—which is the one we want. As pointed out, Denison does make an attempt to derive the latter estimate from the former, and to do so, he is forced to make extremely rough assumptions. To a certain extent, numbers must simply be pulled out of the air.

Fourth, there are difficulties in measuring inputs, the measurement of aggregate capital being a particularly nettlesome problem. Since errors in the measurement of inputs will result in errors in the estimated contribution of these inputs to economic growth, these errors will also be transmitted to, and will affect, the residual unexplained increase in output, which is used to measure the contribution of technological change to economic growth. Also, it is difficult to adjust for quality changes in inputs, and there are problems in constructing proper price deflators.

Fifth, difficulties are caused by the fact that much of the nation's R and D is devoted to defense and space purposes. For example, some observers note the tremendous increase in expenditures on R and D in the postwar period and conclude that, because productivity has not risen much faster in this period than it did before the war, the effect of R and D on economic growth must be very small. What these observers forget is that the bulk of the nation's expenditures on R and D has been devoted to defense and space objectives and that the contribution of such expenditures to economic growth may have been limited. Moreover, they fail to realize that improvements in defense and space capability per dollar spent will not show up in measures of output because government output is valued at cost. (Also, they fail to recognize the fact that product improvements and new products often fail to register in output measures and that the effects of R and D often occur with a considerable lag.)

Based on this catalog of problems and limitations, it is clear that the current state of the art in this area is not strong enough to permit very accurate estimates of the contribution of R and D to the economic growth of the United States. At best, the available estimates are rough guidelines. In no sense is this a criticism of the economics profession or of the people working in this area. On the contrary, a great deal of progress has been made since the pioneering ventures into this area a little over a decade ago. Given the small number of people working in this area and the inherent difficulty of the problem, it is hard to see how much more could have been achieved.

R and D and Productivity Increase in Individual Industries

During the late 1950s, important work concerning the rate of productivity increase in various industries was going on at the National Bureau of Economic Research. As part of this work, Terleckyj carried out a study of the relationship between an industry's rate of increase of total factor productivity during the period from 1919 to 1953 and various industry characteristics. According to his results, an industry's rate of growth of total factor productivity was related in a statistically significant way to its ratio of R and D expenditures to sales, its rate of change of output level, and the amplitude of its cyclical fluctuations. Specifically, the rate of growth of total factor productivity increased by about 0.5 percent for each tenfold increase in the ratio of R and D expenditures to sales and by about 1 percent for every 3 percent increase in the industry's growth rate.

Subsequently, two other papers appeared on this topic, one pertaining to agriculture, one pertaining to manufacturing. The agricultural study by Zvi Griliches investigated the relationship in various years between output per farm in a given state and the amounts of land, labor, fertilizer, and machinery per farm, as well as average education and expenditures on research and extension in a given state. The results indicate that, holding other inputs constant, output was related in a statistically significant way to the amount spent on research and extension. Moreover, the regression coefficient of this variable remains remarkably stable when cross sections are deleted or added and when the specification of the model is changed somewhat.

The manufacturing study by Edwin Mansfield was based on data regarding ten large chemical and petroleum firms and ten manufacturing industries in the postwar period. Both for firms and for industries, the measured rate of productivity change was related in a statistically significant way to the rate of growth of cumulated R and D expenditures made by the firm or industry. The specific form of the relationship depends somewhat on whether technological change is assumed to be disembodied (better methods and organization that improve the efficiency of both old capital and new) or capital embodied (innovations that must be embodied in new equipment if they are to be utilized). When technological change was disembodied, the average effect of a 1 percent increase in the rate of growth of cumulated R and D expenditures was a 0.1 percent increase in the rate of productivity increase. When technological change was capital embodied, it was a 0.7 percent increase in the rate of productivity increase.

Evaluation of Productivity Studies

How reliable are these estimates of the relationship between R and D and productivity increase in individual industries? Clearly, one advantage of these studies is that the effect of R and D is not derived indirectly as a residual. Instead, an industry's—or a firm's or area's—R and D expenditures are introduced as an explicit input in the productive process. Thus, it is possible to obtain explicit relationships between R and D and productivity increase; it is no longer necessary to attribute to technology or R and D whatever cannot be explained by other factors. This is a real advantage.

But a number of important problems remain. First, too little is known about the characteristics of the activities that firms call "research and development."

Second, even if one were sure that R and D figures were reliable, there would still be the possibility of spurious correlation. Firms and industries that spend relatively large amounts on R and D may tend to have managements that are relatively progressive and forward looking. To what extent is the observed relationship between R and D and productivity increase due to this factor rather than to R and D?

Third, a large percentage of the R and D carried out by many industries is directed at productivity increase in *other* industries. Consequently, relationships between R and D in an industry or firm and productivity increase in the *same* industry or firm catch only part of the effects of R and D.

Fourth, there is a host of technical problems. To what extent is technological change disembodied, and to what extent is it capital embodied? If R and D is treated as investment in new knowledge—as it is in most of these studies—what depreciation rate should be used? Also, there is the perennial problem of how R and D expenditures should be deflated, as well as the problem of the form of the production function that should be used in particular cases.

Fifth, studies of the relationship between R and D and productivity increase in individual industries suffer, of course, from a number of the same problems that beset studies of the contribution of R and D to economic growth. Some of these problems are inadequacies of the output measures used, poor specification of the relationship among inputs, and difficulties in measuring inputs.

Externalities, Riskiness, and Investment in R and D

At this point, I turn to the question of whether or not, from a purely economic point of view, the United States is underinvesting in R and D. Certain propositions bearing on this question are widely accepted by economists and should be set forth at the beginning of this discussion. The first proposition is that, because the results of research are often of little direct value to the sponsoring firm but of great value to other firms, there is good reason to believe that, left to its own devices, the market would allocate too few resources to R and D—and that the shortfall would be particularly great at the more basic end of the R and D spectrum. The reason for this is fairly obvious: the market operates on the principle that the benefits go to the person bearing the costs, and vice versa. If a firm or individual takes an action that contributes to society's welfare, but it cannot appropriate the full gain, then it obviously is less likely to take this action than would be socially desirable.

The second proposition is that, because R and D is risky for the individual form, there is good reason to believe that the market, left to its own devices, would allocate too few resources to R and D. Of course, the risk to the individual investor in R and D is greater than the risk to society, since the results of the R and D may be useful to someone else, not to himself, and he may be unable to obtain from the user the full value of the information. Because the economic system has limited and imperfect ways of shifting risks, there would be an underinvestment in R and D. For this reason, too, one would expect the underinvestment to be greatest at the more basic end of the R and D spectrum.

These defects of the market mechanism in allocating resources to R and D have long been recognized. Moreover, they have been recognized in the realm of practical affairs and of social organization, as well as in the realm of social science. Our society, taking account of these defects of the market mechanism, does not depend exclusively on the market for an investment in R and D. On the contrary, a very large proportion of the nation's expenditures on R and D stems from government agencies, private foundations, and universities, all of which supplement the R and D supported through the market mechanism. Thus, the relevant question is not whether the market mechanism requires supplementing, but whether the type and extent of supplementary support provided at present is too large or too small, and whether it is allocated properly.

Salient Characteristics of the
Nation's Investment in R and D

Before discussing the above question, several important characteristics of the nation's investment in R and D must be noted. First, as is well known, the nation's investment in R and D is focused very strongly on defense and space technology. During the early 1960s, over 55 percent of the nation's R and D expenditures were for these purposes. With the passage of time, this percentage has decreased, but even in 1970, about 43 percent of the nation's investment in R and D was for these purposes. The relevance to economic growth of much of this huge investment in defense and space R and D has been questioned by many economists.

Numerous groups within the government have been interested in the extent of the benefits to civilian technology—the "spillover" or "fallout"—from military and space R and D. Obviously, the extent of this spillover has implications regarding the extent to which the investment in defense and space R and D has relevance for economic growth. It is perfectly clear that the value of the spillover that has occurred in the past has been substantial—the computer, numerical control, integrated circuits, atomic energy, and many other significant advances having stemmed at least partly from military R and D. However, it is also clear that the contribution of a dollar of military and space R and D to economic growth is considerably less than the contribution of a dollar of civilian R and D. Moreover, in the opinion of some observers, the spillover per dollar of military-space R and D is unlikely to be as great as it was in the past, because the capabilities that are being developed and the environment that is being explored are less closely connected with civilian pursuits than they were in the past.

Second, just as the government's expenditures on R and D are concentrated largely in a few agencies (the Department of Defense, the National Aeronautics and Space Administration, and the Atomic Energy Commission) with defense and space missions, so industry's expenditures on R and D are concentrated in a few industries. In 1969, 82 percent of all industrial R and D expenditures took place in only five industries—aerospace, electrical equipment and communication, chemicals (including drugs), machinery, and motor vehicles. Of course, this concentration is due in part to the fact that these industries perform a great deal of R and D for the federal government. But if one looks only at company-financed R and D, the concentration is nearly the same, with these five industries accounting in 1969 for 75 percent of all company-financed R and D expenditures. Moreover, this concentration seems to be increasing.

Industry's R and D expenditures are also concentrated largely on products, not processes. For example, according to a survey of business firms carried out in the early 1960s, about 47 percent of the firms reported that their main purpose was to develop new products, and about 40 percent reported that it was to improve existing products: only 13 percent reported that it was to develop new processess. However, lest there be any misunderstanding, it should be recognized that one industry's products may be part of another industry's processes. Thus, when a machinery producer improves its products or when a chemical producer improves its products, the result may be an improvement in the processes of industries that buy and use the machinery or chemicals.

Third, this nation's investment in R and D is focused very strongly on development, not research. The distinction between research and development, although hazy and indistinct in some cases, is important. Research is aimed primarily at the search for new knowledge, whereas development is aimed at the reduction of research findings to practice. In 1970, according to estimates made by the National Science Foundation, about two-thirds of the nation's investment in R and D went for development, only about one-third for research. Much of the development work carried out by industry and government is aimed at very specific objectives and involves large expenditures on prototypes and pilot plants. It is important to avoid the (unfortunately common) mistake of confusing this activity with research.

Moreover, it is important to recognize that much of the R and D carried out by industry is aimed at fairly modest advances in the state of the art. Studies seem to indicate that the really major inventions seldom stem from industrial laboratories of major firms, which are primarily contributors of minor "improvement" inventions. Also, surveys indicate that firms exphasize relatively short payout periods for R and D, this emphasis being another indication that most R and D carried out by the responding firms is aimed at improvements or minor changes in existing products. In addition, detailed studies of the characteristics of the R and D portfolio of a number of industrial laboratories provide direct evidence that the bulk of the work involves rather small technical risks.

Nature of the Evidence

A number of economists have been concerned with the question of whether or not the R and D support that society presently gives to supplement the market mechanism is adequate in total and allocated properly. They generally seem to be of the opinion that the nation's investment in R and D may be too small, but this opinion is often characterized as little more than a hunch. They are much more confident that, whether or not the total investment in R and D is too small, the investment is not properly allocated, there being too little R and D devoted to (1) more ambitious attempts to place the technology of various industries on a stronger scientific base; (2) urban transportation, pollution control, and housing; and (3) more competitive and fragmented industries.

What sorts of evidence are these conclusions based on? First, some of these studies rely largely on judgment combined with economic theory.

Second, these studies rely on the results of several econometric investigations which indicate that, for the industries and fields under investigation, the marginal rate of return from an investment in R and D has been very high.

Finally, based on computations for the economy as a whole, Edward Denison concluded that the rate of return from R and D was about the same as the rate of return from investment in capital goods. His estimate of the returns from R and D was lower than the estimates of other investigators, perhaps because he assumed no lag between R and D expenditures and their contribution to economic growth. The calculated rate of return on R and D could be much higher if R and D's contribution occurred only with a lag. In his 1969 presidential address to the American Economic Association, William Fellner estimated the

average social rate of return from technological-progress activities and concluded that it is "substantially in excess" of 13 or 18 percent, depending on the cost base, and that this is much higher than the marginal rate of return from physical investment at a more or less given level of knowledge.

Evaluation of the Evidence

How conclusive is the evidence described above? First, consider the judgmental approach. Clearly, this approach, although sensible and frequently used in all fields, is limited by the large subjective component that inevitably must enter the calculations. It is very difficult to estimate the extent of the external economies arising from particular types of R and D, or to determine whether incentive modifications are small relative to the gap between private and social returns, or to tell whether supplementary R and D provided by government and nonprofit institutions is small relative to the scope of socially desirable work. The weight one places on this evidence must depend on the confidence one puts in the judgment and objectivity of the investigators.

Second, consider the econometric approach. This approach is more objective in many respects. Certainly the assumptions underlying the estimates are specified clearly, and one can see how sensitive the results are to changes in these assumptions. But this does not mean that the results can be accepted uncritically. On the contrary, since most of these estimates depend on, and are derived from, the studies of R and D and productivity growth in individual industries, they are subject to many of the limitations of these studies.

Yet, having taken pains to point out the limitations of the individual bits of evidence that have been amassed, we must not lose sight of an impressive fact: no matter which of the available studies one looks at (other than Denison's), the conclusions seem to point in the same direction. In the case of those using the judgmental approach, there is considerable agreement that we may be underinvesting in particular types of R and D in the civilian sector of the economy. In the case of the econometric studies, every study of which I am aware indicates that the rate of return from additional R and D in the civilian sector is very high.

35

Policies to Promote Economic Growth

PRESIDENT'S COMMISSION FOR A NATIONAL AGENDA FOR THE EIGHTIES

This is an excerpt from the Report of the Panel on the American Economy of the President's Commission for a National Agenda for the Eighties, published in 1980.

Introduction

The 1970s were a decade of economic frustration and disappointment for Americans. If the 1980s are to be different, the highest economic priority for the United States must be to restore substantial economic growth, especially growth of output per person. The panel advocates growth not as an end in itself, but as a requirement for achieving fundamental national goals. Growth will permit continued increases in the standard of living and quality of life for working Americans and their families, and it should both reduce the political obstacles to improved benefits for those dependent on transfer programs and increase their opportunities to become self-sufficient. It will provide increased job opportunities, experience, and seniority for minority and unskilled workers. It will ease the adjustments by workers, firms, and communities that are necessitated by new technologies and changing patterns of international competition. It will make it possible for this country to meet its humanitarian, security, and leadership responsibilities as a world power.

At the same time, the panel does not advocate "growth at all costs." The recent gains in health, safety, and environmental quality need not be sacrificed in order to achieve maximum growth. The panel recognizes that gross national product (GNP) is not a perfect measure of even the economic aspects of national well-being. Growth policies must take into account the "quality" of growth, the distribution of the benefits of growth within the population, and the social consequences of the policies used to achieve growth. Further, substantial economic growth does not necessarily mean a full return to the historically unprecedented growth rates of the 1950s and 1960s. Realism in goal setting is essential to avoid an unwarranted sense of failure.

Achieving a higher real growth rate will not be easy or automatic, but neither should it be impossible. During the decade just ended the United States was buffeted by a series of severe economic shocks, above all the dizzying climb in the relative price of petroleum in a society accustomed to inexpensive and seemingly limitless energy. These developments were bound to have disruptive effects on the U.S. econ-

194

omy, and they did. Although rapid adjustment to major economic change is efficient, the process is painful both to individuals and to society. Thus there is a tendency to cushion the difficulty by spreading the adjustment process over time, even if it means a temporary reduction in the overall growth rate. As the United States enters the 1980s it is clear that adjustments are being made; these adjustments should enhance the opportunities for economic growth in this decade.

Improve the Conduct and Coordination of Government Policies

Perhaps the most important role for government is to provide a more stable and predictable economic environment. Macroeconomic policies should focus more on the long term and should deemphasize attempts at short-term fine-tuning, which proved disappointing in the 1970s, despite the continuing importance of its goals. Both households and firms need greater stability in order to plan for the future with some confidence. Managers can then concentrate more on the long run and on increasing the real output of their firms and less on short-run financial results.

Because some of the critical issues before the country are both interrelated and long-range, a majority of the panel recommends . . . that a new government body be established to analyze long-run trends, attempt to reach agreement on national goals and objectives, and examine alternative ways of achieving them. A minority, including the chairperson, while agreeing on many of these points, believe that such a body would be more effectively placed outside the government.

Encourage Innovation

The largest source of sustained growth in output per worker is improved multifactor productivity. This is, however, neither thoroughly understood nor amenable to close control by government policies. Advances in science and technology play an important part, and these at least can be influenced by tax incentives for research and development in the private sector and by direct government support for basic research.

Also important are improvements in the management and organization of economic activity that oc-cur throughout the economic system and result in new products and services, as well as in new ways of producing and distributing existing ones. Indirect policies to stimulate such innovations include a stable economic environment and the provision of adequate rewards for risk-taking. The government can also encourage cooperative efforts by labor and management to increase productivity and improve the quality of work life at every level within the firm.

Reduce Inflation and Improve the Utilization of Human Resources

Price stability is an important part of a stable economic environment and suggests policies that might achieve greater price stability. Reducing inflation would also remove substantial disincentives to savings and investment, especially under present tax laws. Growth would be facilitated by improved utilization of the labor force.

Stimulate Savings and Investment

Higher savings and investment are vitally important for achieving economic growth, and the share of GNP going into capital investment should be increased. There are a number of general approaches that could be used to stimulate savings and investment.

One broad approach is to induce additional investment by increasing the after-tax return on investment. Some panel members believe that general tax incentives for investment are most effective; among the possibilities, some of which have been used in the past, are an expansion of the investment tax credit, a further acceleration of depreciation schedules, an elimination of the double taxation of dividends, and a partial or complete integration of personal and corporate income taxes. Other panel members feel that narrower, more targeted investment incentives are preferable (e.g., limiting tax benefits to areas of high unemployment or to investments that are thought to have high social productivity) and believe that any tax change should maintain or increase the progressivity of the tax structure.

A second approach is to induce additional savings. A very broad incentive to save would be created by the proposal that savings be deductible from taxable income when they are made, with taxes being assessed only when the savings are spent on consumption. Tax rates and brackets could be adjusted to preserve essentially the same degree of progressivity that is present in the current income schedule. The removal of ceilings on interest rates for small savers, which is to occur in the 1980s under recently enacted legislation, will also encourage savings.

A third broad approach is to reduce federal competition for available savings by reducing the federal budget deficit, leading to lower real interest rates and greater private investment. To finance a deficit, either the government must compete with private investment for available savings, or the Federal Reserve must purchase the additional debt by creating money, leading to higher inflation that also discourages investment.

Increased tax incentives for savings and investment imply either that future federal budget deficits must be larger than otherwise, at least in the short run, or that federal expenditures must grow more slowly than otherwise. Thus there are clear trade-offs among the three broad approaches above, and between all of them combined and the growth of federal expenditures. Any desire to reduce the average budget deficit over the business cycle to facilitate the reduction of inflation further complicates the trade-offs. There is, however, some room for maneuver because the investment decision is a forward-looking act; it can be influenced not just by current taxes but also by future taxes. For this reason it is frequently suggested that tax incentives for investment be enacted soon, but be phased in over a period of years so that the major impact on tax revenues is postponed until a time when, it is hoped, inflation will have been reduced.

Pursue Liberal Trade Policies

International trade is another area in which improved policies would contribute to higher economic growth. Industries affected by increased import competition will naturally want tariffs or other protection, but in most cases this would simply be an attempt—increasingly costly as time passes—to delay adjustment to the natural shifts in comparative advantage that occur as the United States and other countries develop. Protective measures raise the cost of goods and services to U.S. consumers and producers, making growth more difficult. In addition, the adoption of protective measures might provoke retaliation that would harm the industries in which the U.S. export position is strong.

What is needed are carefully designed transition policies that ease the difficulties of adjustment that workers, firms, and communities affected by import competition face, without removing the incentives to adjust. Such policies should facilitate the natural flow of capital and labor away from industries that are losing comparative advantage and toward rapidly growing industries. There are certain basic industries in which national security requires the maintenance of a certain capacity for domestic production. In these cases, adjustment policies should aim at restoring international competitiveness through increased investment, innovation, and cost reduction.

At the same time, trade policy should give greater attention to exports, attempting to reduce the tariff and nontariff barriers of other countries that restrict exports of products in which the United States has a comparative advantage. With greater awareness of, and adequate access to, foreign markets, increased exports could be an important source of overall growth in the U.S. economy.

Stimulate Small Business

Small business is an important source of growth, employment, and technological innovation. Revisions in tax laws to facilitate continuity of family ownership and to provide incentives for investment are needed to stimulate the growth of small business. Also important is increased access to capital, especially venture capital. Government programs to assist small business in improving management techniques should be made more effective. Finally, enhanced efforts to promote the ownership of small businesses by minorities and women would contribute both to growth and to greater equity.

Reduce Vulnerability to Import Interruptions

To provide a margin of insurance against the potentially severe effects of interruptions in the supply of oil and other imported raw materials, both short- and long-term policies are required. In the near term, the Strategic Petroleum Reserve should be filled, and the development of oil supplies outside the Middle East should be encouraged. For the longer term, the government should encourage both conservation and the development of diverse alternative sources of energy and other raw materials.

36

A Personal Consumption Tax: Can It Break the Capital Formation Deadlock?

LAURENCE S. SEIDMAN

Laurence S. Seidman is a faculty member at Swarthmore College. This article appeared in the Business Review *of the Federal Reserve Bank of Philadelphia, February 1981.*

Over a period of many decades the United States' standard of living was the envy of the world. U.S. industry throve, churning out immense quantities of products ranging from the heaviest of heavy equipment to the most delicate of consumer goods. Other nations looked to America for the pattern of a productive economy.

In recent years, however, some of the glamour of the U.S. economy has worn off as the relative productivity growth of American business has taken a nosedive. The causes of the fall in U.S. productivity growth have proved elusive to researchers, but many believe that tax policy is a major contributor. If tax policy could be made to favor saving over present consumption, they say, the United States would have the dollars to reinvest and rebuild its aging industrial plant and to become the world's model for productivity once again.

One way to tilt the balance in favor of saving and against consumption is to modify the income tax so that the income from saving—whether interest, dividends, or capital gains—would be wholly or partially exempt from taxation. But while this approach clearly would encourage saving, it also would tend to give a tax break to those who enjoy high consumption financed by capital income and thus might be objected to on equity grounds. Another approach is to transform the income tax into a direct tax on personal consumption. A personal consumption tax with graduated rates might well turn the trick of encouraging capital investment without running afoul of equity objections.

Why Tax at All?

It would be nice to live in a world without taxes. But as Ben Franklin noted, taxes are as inevitable as death. The reason is that although a strong case can be made for relying on the private sector for much of our economic activity, certain tasks can be performed only by government. Public goods, such as national defense, and social insurance programs, such as social security, can be financed only by compulsory taxation.

Any tax, however, directly imposes a burden on

197

people. Further, it indirectly reduces the efficiency of resource allocation in the private sector and alters the distribution of income. Thus in deciding how to go about taxing, policy-makers have to add the indirect burden from the inefficiency of a tax to its direct burden in order to determine whether the total cost of a government program is less than its benefits. And they must attempt to determine as well what the incidence of the tax will be—on whom it will fall, and how heavily.

Altering the mix of taxes generally will affect both economic efficiency and the distribution of income. Thus both the level and the mix of taxation are important. Some economists believe that changing the tax mix to encourage saving and investment could improve both economic efficiency and the equity of income distribution. Such questions of efficiency and equity seem especially pressing after a decade in which Americans have seen little advance in the standard of living of the average household.

Saving and the Standard of Living

The standard of living of an American worker in 1970 was much higher than that of his counterpart in 1920. Further, he was much better off than a worker in a developing country in 1970. The single most important cause of these differences was that the productivity—output per man-hour—of the American worker had grown tremendously in the half century preceding 1970. And this growth in productivity was induced primarily by investment in more and better machinery (physical capital) and more and better education and training (human capital) per worker. The accumulation of capital per worker has been the key to a rising standard of living and gradual reduction of poverty.

Capital formation comes only from investment, however, and investment comes mainly from private saving. When individuals and business firms reduce their current consumption, more resources are released to produce machinery, factories, education, and training, and to develop new technology. A nation must sacrifice consumption today to enjoy higher output and consumption tomorrow.

The decade of the 1970s witnessed a significant slowdown in the growth rate of labor productivity in the United States—from 3 percent in the early 1960s to perhaps 1 percent at the close of the 1970s. Although the causes are hard to pinpoint, one important source of this deterioration almost surely was in-

adequate investment. Since 1973 the capital-labor ratio has grown less than 2 percent per year in contrast to the 3 percent average growth rate from 1948 to 1973. This slow growth in the capital-labor ratio has been associated with declining U.S. saving rates, which in fact were significantly below those in most other advanced economies even prior to the recent slowdown.

One obstacle to raising the rate of saving and capital formation is the income tax. The income tax discourages saving, and the degree of discouragement increases with the rate of inflation. In the year when saving occurs, the saver is taxed as much as the nonsaver with equal income; and in the future, the saver is taxed on the return he earns. With inflation nibbling away at whatever is left of interest income, saving loses much of its attractiveness.

Thus advocates of capital formation often have recommended the exemption of capital income from personal taxation under the income tax along with the reduction of business taxation. They have argued that if interest, dividends, and capital gains were exempt from tax, individuals would be more encouraged to save; and if business taxes (such as the corporate income tax) were cut, business would find it more profitable to increase spending on new plant and equipment.

But the exemption of capital income has run into significant opposition on grounds of equity. In effect this approach would convert the income tax into a tax on labor income alone. Exemption of capital income would make it possible for wealthy people who enjoy a high level of consumption to pay little or no tax if the consumption were financed primarily by capital income. While defenders of the exemption reply that the past saving and investment of the wealthy helped raise productivity and thus the standard of living of the average worker, these arguments to date have won only a partial exemption of capital income. A wholesale exemption appears to fail the test of political feasibility.

Because attempts to adjust the income tax in favor of saving so far have run into so much resistance, some tax theorists have proposed moving away from the income tax altogether. Their proposal is to tax people on the basis of how much they *consume* rather than on how much they earn. Such a consumption tax approach, they believe, could break this capital formation deadlock by overcoming equity objections.

Taxable consumption would be computed by a process of subtraction that is quite similar to the current procedure under the income tax. Each year, in preparing his return, the taxpayer would add all cash receipts (including wages, salaries, interest, dividends, and receipts from the sale of assets such as stocks and bonds) and subtract the purchase of investment assets along with the net increase in his savings account balance and actual tax payments. The difference—consumption—would be subject to the tax rates given in the tax tables (after any adjustments that Congress decided were appropriate). And these tax rates could be scaled to make sure that the tax fell equitably on all taxpayers.

Thus the basic mechanics of a consumption tax are not hard to envisage. But what impact would such a tax actually have?

What a Consumption Tax Would Do

Any shift in tax policy represents a step from the known to the unknown. Policy changes of almost any sort affect the economy in ways that sometimes are unintended and unforeseen. In the case of a consumption tax, however, it seems fairly clear that certain effects can be predicted.

It Would Raise the Reward to Savers

Savings represent forgone consumption; and since many people find it hard to delay gratification, they find it hard to save. The benefit to saving, however, is that it can allow a larger volume of consumption in the future. It hardly seems farfetched to argue that the more future consumption people can obtain by postponing consumption today, the more they are likely to save.

One way to calculate the benefit from saving is to consider the amount of future consumption it permits relative to the amount of consumption an individual forgoes when he makes a savings decision. If a person saved $1000 at an interest rate of 6 percent, for example, then the ratio of consumption one year ahead to consumption forgone in the present would be $1060/$1000 or 1.06, *provided that interest is not taxed and that there is no inflation.* If interest were taxed this ratio would of course be lower, since part of the reward for saving would not be available for future consumption. But a tax which exempts capital income or a consumption tax would not affect this ratio.

Consider what would happen with an income tax of 33⅓ percent. A person who earned $1500 last year would have had to pay $500 in tax and would have $1000 left over to spend or save. If he saved it, interest on the $1000 still would be $60, but it would be taxed

$20, so after-tax interest would be only $40. The future-consumption factor now would be $1040/$1000, or 1.04. Thus an income tax reduces the future consumption that can be obtained for a given sacrifice of present consumption. Under a tax that exempts all capital income, the factor would stay at 1.06.

Suppose instead that there is a consumption tax—for example, of 50 percent (any rate will do). Out of $1500 of income, the person can consume $1000 on which a tax of $500 would be owed or he can save the $1500 and earn $90 of interest. Out of $1590 in the next year he can consume $1060, on which a tax of $530 would be owed. The ratio of future consumption to presently forgone consumption facing the person would be $1060/$1000, or 1.06.

Thus even with no inflation the reward to saving would be greater under a consumption tax than under an income tax. In the real world, with inflation, this gap in reward widens as the inflation rate rises; the real return to savers becomes smaller and can even become negative under an income tax. In contrast, a consumption tax preserves a positive return for savers.

It seems likely that the higher the return people expect, the more they will choose to save. Although empirical studies have yielded mixed results, one recent study suggested that saving would be increased sharply by a higher return. Stronger confirmation, however, must await further empirical research.

It Would Put More Money in the Hands of Those More Inclined To Save

Just as consequential as the size of the reward to savers is the shifting of after-tax income from heavy consumers to those with more of a saving bent.

People who earn the same incomes may differ greatly in their attitudes toward consumption and thrift. But under an income tax, regardless of their spending and saving behavior, they would pay the same tax, all other things being equal, and would be left with the same after-tax income. The high spender would have as much to spend on consumption as the high saver would have to put away.

The consumption tax would alter this situation by leaving more after-tax dollars with the saver than with the spender of the same income level. And so the saver would have more money available to put into saving. Even if people were not much influenced by an increase in the reward to saving that a consumption tax would bring, the shifting of after-tax dollars to those who are more inclined to save would raise the volume of saving and make more funds available to finance spending on construction and business equipment.

It Would Raise the Real Wage of Labor

A higher saving rate also would enable industry to provide workers with more and better facilities, and the more capital per worker, the higher would be labor productivity and the buying power of wages. Thus converting the income tax to a consumption tax eventually should result in a higher standard of living for workers.

Conversion of the income tax to a consumption tax therefore can be regarded as a longer run antipoverty policy. While social insurance and transfers to those unable to work have an important income-stabilizing role to play, reducing poverty for everyone able to work must depend on a rising growth path for the real wage of labor. Those who give important weight to this goal might find conversion to a progressive consumption tax attractive.

But Some See Difficulties

Although the consumption tax appears to have much to recommend it, some economists and policymakers believe that it could pose certain dangers. These range all the way from recession to inequity to excessive administrative costs.

Some income tax supporters caution, for example, that a switch to a consumption tax could be detrimental to the economy's performance, at least in the short or medium run. If a consumption tax reduces consumption demand, the slack must be taken up by an increase in the demand for capital goods by firms, or total demand will fall and recession will follow (Keynes called this the paradox of thrift). To the extent that increased saving reduces interest rates, business demand for investment goods should be stimulated. But a long time lag, it's feared, could intervene before investment responded, so that a period of weak overall economic activity might follow should a consumption tax be instituted.

The likelihood of this prospect is quite difficult to predict, since a consumption tax never has been tried in the United States. Indeed, if one could anticipate reasonably closely how the macroeconomy would respond to a consumption tax, it might be possible to offset any undesirable consequences with monetary or fiscal policies. But it has been doubted that policy-

makers possess such knowledge. From this point of view the uncertainty surrounding the short-term effects of a consumption tax on total economic activity must be regarded as one of the costs of such a policy to be balanced against expected gains. Not all economists, however, share these fears. They point to the German and Japanese experiences, in which higher saving rates have proved consistent with strong economic performance.

It's possible, also, that changing the rules in the middle of the game—moving from an income tax to a consumption tax—would produce inequities. It would be unfair to tax the consumption of retirees, for example, who had accumulated assets only after paying the income tax all their lives, unless some offsetting adjustment were made. But this inequity could be avoided if, when the consumption tax first was introduced, people above a certain age were given the option of choosing the income tax instead—an option that would be phased out over time. Thus inequities caused by the conversion might be avoided by designing the tax package with care.

Finally, it may seem that a consumption tax would be more difficult to compute for the taxpayer and the IRS. How would saving and investment be distinguished from consumption in practice, and how would consumer durables such as housing and autos be treated? Consumption tax advocates have tried to address these practical questions. One approach suggested for housing, for example, would be to treat annual mortgage payments as a measure of housing consumption in the year they are paid. Further, the consumption tax would eliminate some administrative costs imposed by the income tax, such as the requirement to measure depreciation.

There would be difficulties in switching from an income tax to a consumption tax. On balance, however, many believe that they can be dealt with at an acceptable cost or that they fall short of offsetting the anticipated benefits of a consumption tax.

Conclusion

Converting the income tax into a personal consumption tax could end a prevailing stalemate concerning tax policies to stimulate investment. Advocates of capital formation usually have sought the exemption of capital income under the income tax. Although eliminating the taxation of capital income almost certainly would stimulate saving and investment, opponents have argued that it would be inequitable because it would allow some of the wealthy whose consumption is financed by capital income to pay little or no tax.

A progressive personal consumption tax would ensure that any wealthy person who enjoyed high consumption would pay a correspondingly high tax. At the same time, by excluding saving from taxation in the year it occurred, the consumption tax would encourage saving. Conversion to a consumption tax therefore should promote capital formation and productivity and eventually should raise the real wage of labor. Given current concern about weakness in these areas and about the deadlock that has prevailed over exempting capital income, the proposal to convert the income tax to a consumption tax deserves serious consideration.

37

Should the Federal Government Subsidize Synthetic Fuels?

ROBERT S. PINDYCK

Robert Pindyck is Professor of Applied Economics at Massachusetts Institute of Technology. This is his testimony before the Senate Committee on Banking, Housing, and Urban Affairs on July 25, 1979.

I appreciate having the opportunity to speak here today, although I should mention at the outset that my message may be one that you would rather not hear. Even before the President's address to the nation on July 15, a vast bandwagon had been developing to launch an enormous government synthetic fuels program as a means of "solving" our energy problems. You have already been considering a number of bills that would one way or another provide subsidies for synthetic fuels and other non-conventional energy supplies, and now you must consider the Administration's own proposed program to spend $88 billion on a government corporation to fund the commercialization of synthetic fuels—a program which you will undoubtedly be under considerable pressure to support. The bad news that I must give to you today is that it would be a serious mistake to approve the kind of subsidy program that the Administration has proposed. *By any rational economic criteria, subsidy programs such as that proposed by the Administration are wasteful to the utmost, detrimental to the economic health of the country, and perhaps most important, unlikely to contribute significantly to solving our energy problems, even by 1990.*

It is indeed the case that the U.S. has become unacceptably dependent on imported energy from sources that are increasingly insecure, and as a result, energy markets in this country have become increasingly vulnerable to shortages and disruption. It is indeed the case that we must act quickly to change this situation, and to reverse our growing dependence on foreign energy supplies. But a program that would provide massive subsidies for the commercial development of synthetic fuels is an inefficient and wasteful way to solve our energy problems. Such a program is particularly undesirable today when the rate of inflation is growing even faster than our dependence on foreign oil, and when the need to limit government expenditures overall will impose severe restrictions on other important areas such as health, education, and the environment.

Let me emphasize at the outset that the problem is not that there is no future for synthetic fuels and other non-conventional energy supplies. It is true that most of these new energy sources are more expensive than conventional supplies, even today following OPEC's recent increases in the world price of oil. However, as energy prices continue to rise in the future, some of

202

these new sources of energy will eventually become commercially viable and will someday displace conventional oil and natural gas as major fuels. *But as they become economical they will be produced by private firms with or without a program of government subsidies.*

There are six basic reasons why a synthetic fuels subsidization program is undesirable:

1. Probably the most fundamental reason is that there is simply *no need* for these subsidies. Contrary to what you have been hearing both inside and outside the government, private companies will be quite able to develop these new energy supplies without any government assistance, and government involvement will only raise the cost of these supplies.
2. By converting direct energy purchases into purchases paid for through taxes, *a subsidy program will artificially inflate energy consumption in this country.*
3. Many of the present programs, and in particular the Administration's program, would have the government choose the particular technologies to be developed, and we will thereby run the risk of being locked-in to technologies that may later prove to be less promising than had originally been thought.
4. Vast cost overruns are much more likely in a government-subsidized and -managed program, so that the final cost of synthetic fuels could easily be two, three, or even four times more expensive than current estimates would have us believe.
5. The vast sums of money proposed for these programs will crowd out other much-needed investment, and thereby reduce economic growth in this country, adding to future unemployment.
6. There are other areas where subsidies could be much more cost-effective as a means of reducing our dependence on foreign oil.

Let me now discuss briefly each of these points.

I. There Is No Need for a Subsidy Program

The arguments raised in favor of a government subsidy program usually boil down to the claim that these energy sources have special characteristics—advanced technology, large capital requirements, long lead times, and various uncertainties—that make it difficult or impossible for them to be undertaken by the private sector without government assistance. My colleague Paul Joskow and I have examined these arguments in considerable detail through a project that we have undertaken at the Center for Energy Policy Research of the M.I.T. Energy Laboratory. (I am including a copy of our research report, "Should the Government Subsidize Non-Conventional Energy Supplies?" to be included as part of the record.) We have found all of these arguments to be fallacious, and highly misleading.

First of all, I hope you realize that the production of synthetic fuels does not require or represent fundamental new scientific or technological advances. Shale oil, for example, was first produced in Britain in the 1850s, and gaseous and liquid hydrocarbons were produced from coal in Germany during World War II, and are being produced today in South Africa. Thus, these technologies are well understood, and although there are uncertainties about the ultimate costs of various commercial production facilities, the uncertainties are no larger than those in other commercial ventures that are regularly undertaken by the private sector. As a result, such government involvement as the funding of demonstration plants, which would provide very limited cost data, is simply not needed.

It is true that large capital expenditures are required to produce some of these energy sources on a commercial scale, but this has been true for many other projects undertaken by the private sector. The capital required for the Alaskan oil pipeline, for example, dwarfs the cost of any shale oil or coal gasification project. The magnitudes of the required capital expenditures have not been the impediment to private development of these energy sources, and they will not be in the future.

It is true that the construction and licensing of operating plants for several of these energy sources would require lead times of five to ten years, but they are no longer than those involved in many other private ventures. The lead time is longer, for example, in designing and producing a new commercial aircraft. Furthermore, even the Administration's program makes no claim to reduce this lead time, and it is for this reason that synthetic fuel supplies are not to be expected before 1990.

It is also true that there are significant uncertainties involved in the commercialization of these new energy sources. As I mentioned earlier, there are uncertainties about ultimate production costs, and there are also uncertainties over the future world market prices of conventional fuels. But these uncertainties are no greater than those involved in many other ventures regularly pursued by private companies and financed by the capital market (offshore drilling is an example). Furthermore, the risks associated with these uncertainties can be reduced by the formation of joint ventures (a method widely used for offshore drilling projects).

There are really only two major impediments to the commercialization of new energy technologies—the uncertainties associated with possible future price regulation or taxation, and uncertainties about environmental restrictions. Both of these uncertainties could be removed at virtually no cost.

Firms considering shale oil projects, for example, rightly fear that should the world price of conventional oil rise considerably over the next decade so that the shale oil facility does turn out to be an economic success, the government would probably regulate the price of the shale oil they produce, reducing the profits that could be earned. Private firms usually have no problem with risky projects as long as there is a commensurate potential for profit. The problem with development of new energy technologies today is that firms are unwilling to take a downside risk when they perceive a probable government ceiling on their upside potential. What is needed is the removal of controls on the current *and future* prices of energy supplies. This, together with a revision of those environmental regulations that are unnecessary and unreasonable, and the clarification of environmental standards and regulations that would apply in the future, would permit private firms to develop economical synthetic fuels technologies efficiently and without any need for government subsidies.

II. A Subsidy Program Will Artificially Inflate Energy Consumption

Economists have found that there is one mechanism that works best to limit consumption, and that is the price mechanism. In the case of energy demand, recent econometric and statistical evidence show that the elasticity, or price responsiveness of demand is much larger than many people had originally assumed. There is considerable evidence that major price increases have a significant effect in reducing energy demand, particularly after several years have passed after the price increase.

A massive government subsidy program removes this price incentive, and will thereby contribute to the growth of energy consumption—exactly the opposite result of what we would like our "war on energy" to achieve.

The expenditures required for the subsidy program proposed by President Carter would certainly require general tax revenues above and beyond the Windfall Profits Tax. As a result, the government in effect would be asking taxpayers to finance the difference between the high cost of producing synthetic fuel supplies and the much lower price that consumers would be asked to pay for energy. In fact, Americans would be much worse off with higher taxes than they would be with higher energy prices. Individuals can choose to avoid paying higher energy prices by limiting their energy consumption, but turning down the thermostat does nothing to reduce the taxes that they must pay. As a result, the incentive to conserve energy would be greatly reduced under a subsidy program, and energy consumption will grow.

At the same time, however, production from conventional energy sources will fall because producers will not want to spend their own money looking for oil and natural gas—it will be much easier and less risky to take government handouts for synthetic fuels production. A growing tax burden will then be required to finance a growing share of subsidized energy production.

III. We Will Be Locked-In to Particular Technologies

It is particularly disturbing to see that we are now moving towards the most inefficient and wasteful of several possible means of subsidizing synthetic fuels. If we must have a synthetic fuels program, if indeed this is a political reality, then we should at least try to get as much as we can for the money spent on the program. To do this, we should structure any subsidy program so that it gives the private sector the incentive to develop those new energy technologies which have the greatest economic potential, as well as the ability to respond quickly and efficiently to technological and economic developments. It is for this reason that *the government should stay out of the process of choosing the specific technologies that are to be developed*.

It is private industry, and not the Department of Energy, that is in the best position to determine which new energy technologies are most economical and most promising, and to manage their commercial development most effectively. Private industry is much better able than any government bureaucracy to stop the development of a particular project if it later turns out that it is not as promising as it once appeared. By letting the government commit us to one or more particular technologies, we create a set of political forces which make the termination of an undesirable project difficult, and which make increased subsidies to make the project "successful" very likely.

I hope that a subsidy program is not the inevitable path that we are on, but if it is, the government should at least take a passive role in the subsidy process. A decision should be made as to how much we are willing to spend and how much synthetic fuel supply we expect this expenditure to yield, but it should be left to private industry to decide how to produce those synthetic fuels. To provide an additional incentive, the government could simply announce that it will pay a premium of some number of dollars per barrel over and above the market price for every barrel of synthetic fuel produced—no matter how that fuel happens to be produced. That kind of program would specify clearly how much the government anticipates spending and how much additional energy supply the country will get for the money, while it leaves it to the private sector to determine the most efficient means of responding to these incentives.

IV. A Large Government Program is Likely to Lead to Vast Cost Overruns

It is ironic that President Carter, after having been so critical about cost overruns in government agencies and in government procurement, has now chosen a program that provides almost every incentive for cost overruns. Since the size and form of the subsidy will be linked to the particular costs of synthetic fuels production and the differences between those costs and the world prices of conventional energy supplies, companies contemplating these projects will now have every incentive to inflate their cost estimates.

Private firms have the best incentive to contain costs when their own profits are on the line. This is the simple reason why private firms are better able than a government bureaucracy to terminate projects that no longer seem promising. By creating a massive government subsidy program we remove much of the

incentive that firms normally have to reduce costs. In fact, we have every reason to expect *that the ultimate cost of producing synthetic fuels will be much higher with a subsidy program than it would be without such a program.*

This issue of cost overruns has in fact recently been addressed in a report from the RAND Corporation. That report stresses that the acceleration of synthetic fuel production through a massive government program is likely to make cost overruns even larger. That report argues that a massive subsidy program could lead to cost overruns as high as 200 percent.

V. A Massive Subsidy Program Will Be Detrimental to the Economy

Near the beginning of his television address to the nation on July 15, President Carter said that Americans do not save enough, and that the average savings rate in this country is lower than in almost any other industrialized country. The President is quite correct in his belief that aggregate savings in this country is lower than it should be, that this is severely limiting capital accumulation and the growth of future productive capacity, and is thereby contributing to future unemployment.

What the President did not mention, but I am sure that you are aware of, is that large government deficits are in fact a form of negative savings (they are simply borrowings from the public), and that they are a major reason for our low overall savings rate. It seems to me completely unrealistic to expect the excess profits tax on the oil companies to be sufficient to fund the President's program, so that increases in the Federal deficit are inevitable. A large government subsidy program for synthetic fuel development will further reduce aggregate savings in this country, will "crowd out" investment throughout the economy, and in so doing may severely exacerbate our problem of low growth in productive capacity, thereby contributing to future unemployment.

It is unusual for *a single government program* to have a significant impact on our entire economy. Most government programs are relatively small, so that it is only aggregate government spending and aggregate revenues that have a major effect on investment, inflation, and employment. But the program proposed by the Administration is of almost unprecedented size ($135 billion in total, and $88 billion for synthetic fuels alone, over the next eight to ten years). However this program is financed—whether through the excess profits tax on the oil companies (revenues that could better be used to reduce the burden of social security taxes), through the use of general tax revenues or as part of a larger government deficit, or, through the issuance of "energy bonds" to the public—this program will drain badly needed capital from throughout the economy. This will limit the productive capacity of the economy during the next decade, just at a time when a large number of new job openings will be so badly needed. It will indeed be unfortunate if we win the war on energy through the use of weapons that lead us to lose the war on inflation and unemployment.

VI. There Are Other Areas Where Subsidies Can Be More Cost-Effective

As I said at the beginning, I feel that it is indeed important that we act quickly to solve our energy problems and reduce our dependence on foreign energy supplies. What is upsetting to me is that it appears that we are about to choose programs that are so wasteful and so unlikely to provide an effective solution to our problems. This is particularly disturbing when there are other areas where government involvement could be so much more productive, and where even government subsidies could be much more cost-effective.

If we are going to use government funds to increase domestic energy supplies or to reduce domestic energy consumption, we should do so in ways that give us the most "bang for the buck." There are a number of areas where this could be done, although admittedly they may not sound as glamorous as a large synthetic fuels program. An example would be the subsidization—through tax credits or through outright grants—for home insulation and storm windows. This is an area where we have much better knowledge of what the effective fuel savings would be. The rate of return is high, and it is more or less certain. Furthermore, once the expenditures have been made (e.g., the storm windows have been installed), little further expenditure is needed for maintenance. Also, homeowners—particularly lower income homeowners—may not have the incentive or the ability to make these expenditures without government assistance. The fuel saved from a program such as this would cost far less than the additional fuel produced through a subsidy program for synthetics.

I would like to close by reminding you of something President Carter said in his televised address to the nation on July 15. He told us that "the people are looking for *honest* answers, not *easy* answers." We desperately need to reduce our dependence on imported energy, but President Carter's proposed massive government subsidy program is likely to create more problems than it solves. We must face the fact that a program to develop synthetic fuels is the *wrong* answer. Such a program is an easy answer, but it is certainly not an honest one.

38

Energy Future

ROBERT STOBAUGH AND DANIEL YERGIN

Robert Stobaugh is Professor of Business Administration at Harvard University. Daniel Yergin is a member of the Energy Project at the Harvard Business School. This article is taken from their testimony before the Senate Subcommittee on Energy Conservation and Supply on July 27, 1979.

Robert Stobaugh

I am very concerned by what I observe in our energy problem. I am concerned by the unstable, increasingly unreliable character of America's energy supply system. The current energy supply system poses a basic threat to economic growth, employment, and the dollar—in short, to our economic well-being. I am as concerned about the difficulties America has had in dealing with the energy problem since 1973, and about how little progress has been made. The problem and possible solutions have been misconstrued. We need a balanced energy program. We don't have one. American oil imports have grown rapidly in the 1970s, in spite of our announced policy of limiting such imports.

But the events of the last half year or so—Iran, the interruption of supplies, the huge OPEC price hikes, and of course the gasoline lines—have done wonders in focusing attention on the problem. They have brought home the dangers of our current level of imports and the even greater danger of further depen-

dence. Yet, whatever the announced policies, the United States is still embarked on a course today that leads to more—not less—imports.

We agree with President Carter's recent focus on oil imports—and on the desirability of limiting them. The question staring us in the face, however, is what to do about those imports. It is on that question that we part company with what seems to be the main thrust of the recently enunciated program. It seems to me that current proposals do not match the Administration's goals of holding imports steady and then reducing them. Of course, one sure way that we can meet the goal of limiting imports is through a series of recessions broken only by periods of slow economic growth. The only other way to reach the goal of controlling oil imports is by changing the current emphasis between conservation and synthetic fuels. Instead of a target for 1990 of 2½ million barrels a day for synthetic fuels and ½ million barrels a day for conservation (which includes an undisclosed amount of fuel switching), we should turn the targets upside down. In fact, we believe that a realistic target for conservation savings is

207

even higher than 2½ million—perhaps 5 million barrels a day; in contrast, a target of ½ million barrels a day for synthetic fuels is quite optimistic.

And in terms of expenditures, instead of spending $88 billion on synthetic fuels and $2 billion on conservation, we believe that perhaps $50 billion of federal funds could be spent cost-effectively for conservation, and some solar. In contrast, I seriously question whether over a 10-year period even $20 billion could be spent effectively for synthetic fuels. But I must stress that this is just a good guess; for with the nation's current level of experience, it is not possible to make an accurate estimate.

We agree strongly that the United States should develop a synthetic fuels capability. In our report, *Energy Future*, my colleague Mel Horwitch writes: "liquefaction . . . is one weapon against increased dependence on foreign oil. . . . The Iranian crisis in 1979 again highlighted the danger of U.S. dependence on foreign oil. In my view the need for a synthetic fuels capability is more a matter of national security. . . . The United States needs a credible capability to derive oil from coal. . . . National interest considerations demand that research and development momentum be maintained in this area. . . . A calm and reasonable approach in the short term, and an over-all long-term focus that would include a serious program to utilize coal more cleanly either in direct combustion or as a liquid or gas, will permit more freedom in meeting U.S. energy needs, including choices involving coal."

But the current proposals go about promoting synthetic fuels in the wrong way, in ways that may harm our syn-fuel hopes.

Let me cite five concerns:

1. This synthetic program can only begin to produce sizable quantities in the 1990s at the earliest; yet the problem before us is how to get through the 1980s.
2. The scale is much too large. There is little basis to justify so rapid and so expensive a scale-up. As a professor from a school of business administration, I don't see how a program of this scale in such a short time can be properly administered.
3. The economic and environmental aspects are far more uncertain than has been portrayed.
4. This program will mislead people into thinking yet another miracle cure is about to come to our rescue, promoting another bout of time-wasting complacency.
5. The net result is that an $88 billion program

could seriously damage rather than enhance the long-term prospects for synthetic fuels. Exaggerated expectation could be followed by disappointment, disillusionment, cynicism, and recriminations.

The President spoke strongly about conservation, but the proposals are not strong enough—especially when measured against the problem of imports and the opportunities offered by conservation.

According to the President's own program, the investment cost of saving a "barrel" by conservation[1] costs only one-ninth of what a barrel of synthetic fuels will cost—and the operating costs of many conservation investments are zero compared with the high operating costs expected in synthetic fuel plants. Moreover, conservation goes to work immediately to reduce dependence on imported oil.

We are strongly in favor of synthetic fuels, but a dash of realism needs to be added to the current frenzy over synthetic fuels.

We think some realism needs to be added right down the line. For we see little reason to believe that conventional energy sources can do much to reduce our imports of foreign oil. The failure to acknowledge this reality has helped block progress on solving the problem.

What about domestic oil and gas? We will be lucky if we can prevent production of domestic oil and gas from falling further. The United States has been pretty thoroughly explored and drilled. The oil and gas industries will have to work very hard merely to keep production at current levels. . . . Substantially higher prices for oil and gas have increased drilling; yet the amounts of proven oil and gas reserves have steadily declined. The nation will be fortunate if in 1990, production levels are as high as current levels—10 million barrels of oil (and natural gas liquids) per day and the oil equivalent of 9 million barrels per day of natural gas.

What about coal? America has a lot of coal. We expect an expansion in its use, but less than officially forecast. For coal is caught up in a tangle of interlocking problems—weak demand, transportation bottlenecks, employment strife, environmental concerns. We think that coal's contribution might grow from a current level of 7 million barrels daily of oil equivalent to perhaps 11 million by 1990. But this growth is by no means assured.

What about nuclear power? Today it only provides

[1]including some fuel switching

about three percent of U.S. energy demand. As we all know, it is caught up in a stalemate, primarily over the waste and safety questions. Projections of nuclear capacity have declined dramatically. We will soon see a major debate about what to do about the 90 nuclear power plants now under construction—with an estimated $50 billion already invested. It is most difficult to see nuclear power responding to the problem of oil imports in the 1980s. Nuclear power now provides a little over 1 million barrels daily of oil equivalent. Although our projections suggest that perhaps 2 million barrels daily of oil equivalent might be forthcoming by 1990, in fact, unless issues of safety and waste disposal are resolved, output could actually decrease. A convenient equivalency is that at historical operating rates, it takes about 50 normal-sized nuclear power plants to save 1 million barrels per day of oil in electricity generation.

In other words, America's conventional energy alternatives add up to a bleak outlook for controlling oil imports. This conclusion, of course, is at odds with the more optimistic outlooks shown by many other analysts, especially those who omit political and institutional factors. But in the past econometric and engineering estimates have been very misleading—much too optimistic. So it is unwise to plan on large increases in conventional domestic sources.

Without more flexibility and imagination, we will find ourselves continuing on our present course—towards higher and higher imports, perhaps 14 million barrels a day ten years from now, or towards a series of recessions interspersed with periods of slow economic growth. We believe that there is a better alternative. My colleague, Dr. Daniel Yergin, will tell you about this.

Daniel Yergin

Professor Stobaugh has presented the bad news. It is my happier obligation to present some good news.

The good news is that we do have a reliable energy source—conservation energy—which is probably the cheapest, easiest, most accessible, and largest alternative to imported oil in the decade of the 1980s. That was also the case in the 1970s, but we did not do a great deal to tap the conservation potential in the decade now ending. Beyond the 1980s, we see an increasingly important role for renewable energy sources.

When I talk about conservation, I mean not deprivation, but rather energy efficiency. Unfortunately, most people think of conservation as a threat—scarcity, rationing, cutting-back—a reduction in our standard of living. As I see it, the real threat to our standard of living is not conservation—but *not to conserve*. For *not to conserve* means low economic growth, supply disruptions, higher prices, increased political vulnerability, and domestic instability.

Let me put the matter this way. It does not represent a cut in your standard of living to drive a car that gets thirty miles to the gallon. It does mean a decline in your standard of living to sit in a gas line for three hours—even if you value your time at only a dollar an hour. A winter home heating bill of a thousand dollars takes more out of your standard of living than does a home heating bill of $600.

In other words, given the circumstances that exist today, the best way to protect our standard of living is through energy conservation. Every dollar invested in energy conservation helps our GNP to go up, inflation to go down, and the dollar to become stronger. For it is often not recognized—although it should be—that productive energy conservation spurs investment—and investment spurs the economy.

It is difficult to be precise about the conservation potential, becaues the worlds of energy end-use in the United States are so many and varied.

In our *Energy Future* study, we illustrate a very modest goal—an extra five million barrels a day of conservation energy on top of the three million barrels a day envisioned by the Department of Energy in recent forecasts. We regard that as a modest goal. Yet note that it is twice the goal set for synthetic fuels for 1990. We think that the energy efficiency potential is actually much greater—that, at the very least, the United States could with satisfaction, even pleasure, enjoy very, very, very low growth rates for energy consumption in the years ahead.

What is the evidence? What are the indicators?

1. First, we have learned that the relationship between growth in energy consumption and economic growth is very flexible. This is evident looking at the historical record and at cross-national comparisons. Indeed, we may be approaching a point where the relationship is inverse—growing energy consumption reduces economic growth because of the constraints described by Professor Stobaugh, while greater energy efficiency (lower growth rates in energy consumption) mean higher economic growth.

2. A surprisingly large amount of energy saving can be achieved with relatively easy housekeeping

measures. There are a number of important examples:

— Over a ten-year period, Dow Chemical reduced its energy use per pound of product by 40 percent.
— In 1973, IBM set out to reduce its energy consumption by 10 percent in 34 major locations around the country. It actually cut energy consumption—to its own surprise—by 39 percent.
— 50 to 75 percent reductions in home heating requirements are possible with an accumulation of small fixes.
— Many hospitals have reduced energy consumption by 25 to 40 percent with minimal capital investment.
— A Papermate pen is made in 1979 with 40 percent less energy than in 1973.

The good news is that the conservation potential—the potential for non-disruptive energy conservation—is quite large.

Certainly, we have seen some improvements in energy efficiency in the United States, as the examples above indicate. Yet, what is striking is how little has been achieved in the United States since 1973, at least when measured against the potential, the relative ease—and the stakes involved in *not* getting a handle on our energy consumption. For we must keep in mind that the United States is the world's largest consumer—the Saudi Arabia of consumption if you will.

The barriers to conservation are many and varied. For instance, in the industrial sector a host of obstacles stand in the way:

— payback considerations
— energy costs can be passed along
— energy-saving can have low status in an organization
— energy costs may be a small share of over-all costs
— confusion abounds over such matters as whether there actually is an energy crisis and over whether a firm should switch from oil to coal or gas—or conserve

In the building sector, conservation is faced with:

— a highly decentralized sector where the decision-makers number among the millions
— knowledge is poorly diffused
— financing is difficult and paybacks unfamiliar
— skepticism high

And conservation is a tough subject for people who have to make policies, as well. It is very hard to get into focus. You can all pretty much see a two-billion dollar syn-crude plant in your mind's eye, at least to some degree. What does conservation look like? It is 50 million different things, big and small. There is not much of a constituency lobbying you all for conservation, and when they do, it can, I hate to admit it, sound like sermons and apple pie. It's the nature of the beast. Finally, conservation does not have a whole lot of glamor attached to it. I recall with a smile the comment of a Senate aide. I asked him why his boss, a hard-headed Senate expert on energy issues, had never given a speech on conservation. The aide replied: "It would either be filled with platitudes or be so specific that everybody's nose would fall into his Rice Krispies."

What is necessary, and what we haven't had, is a systematic effort to create a political and economic environment that will encourge energy conservation—that will get beyond rhetoric to reality. Conservation and renewables do not have a fair chance now. Conventional energy sources may have received up to $130 billion dollars in production subsidies from the federal government. There have been the tens of billions of dollars of consumption subsidies through price controls. There are all the institutional habits and impediments. The President may call for conservation and solar, but the streetlights are mostly red in that direction.

How do we get that political and economic environment in which conservation will have a fair chance? We have to get our signals straight. We have to make sure that the traffic lights are all green. That means an adroit mixture of incentives, price, regulations, and information.

May I quote on this point the former director of the French Energy Conservation Agency, who put together probably the most effective energy conservation program of any western country. He observed: "You have to put things together. You have to do regulations, incentives, financial incentives—not only price—and publicity all at the same time. These . . . means of action must be coordinated. . . . It is indispensable to be helped strongly by policy, by the government, especially by the government . . . . If the government's actions are not positive, then they are negative, harmful. If government does not show interest, then all sectors of society imagine that it is not important." The U.S. government has not shown a great deal of practical interest since 1973.

In our *Energy Future* study, we put a lot of emphasis

on incentives. In America, the carrot works pretty well. Our major proposal is to use the proceeds of the inevitable windfall tax on old oil to finance conservation and solar energy, primarily through tax credits, but also through grants, especially for lower income groups and for demonstration projects. We think that those revenues, used in that manner, could buy us a lot more BTUs than if invested primarily in synthetic fuels.

I hate to say this, but we do think that rational pricing makes sense. In the long run, it does not do consumers—or conservation or solar—much good to keep prices below market levels. At the beginning of 1979, the real price of gasoline, corrected for inflation, was the same as in 1960, the year OPEC was formed because oil prices were too low. That price at the beginning of 1979 conveyed the wrong information. It told you that oil was no more highly valued in 1979 than in 1960. It told you not to worry about gasoline mileage when you bought a new car. If people had received the correct information through the price system, the mix of our auto fleet would have been different—and we might well not have sat in gas lines. I think the gas lines were more costly to individuals and American society than would have been the few cents more per gallon that would have resulted from realistic pricing.

Regulation is clearly important, but these regulations should be constructed so that they allow flexibility and do not impede innovation.

Finally—information. This tends to be regarded as the step-child of conservation policy, just as conservation tends to be the step-child of over-all energy policy. Yet conservation depends upon information and communication.

I said "finally." But there is another final point to an effective energy conservation policy. We need to remember equity. We need to remember that lower-income families are hit harder by energy prices than higher-income people. In general, everybody in our society will be better off if we use less rather than more imported oil. But the lower income, those least able to mobilize capital for energy-saving investments, need special help.

PART SIX

International Trade, Finance, and the Less Developed Countries

In recent years, the headlines have trumpeted that the major trading nations of the world have been experiencing difficulties in keeping international trade and financial relationships in effective working order. In the opening article Walter Salant describes how the world economy has changed since 1929. He surveys some major changes in the importance of international transactions relative to total economic activity and in international finance. In the next selection, Hendrik S. Houthakker discusses the competitive position of the United States in world trade; he points out that contrary to some popular opinion, we have not been flooded with imports, and we can compete with low-wage foreign labor. Richard Cooper, in the next article, discusses the relationship between technology and world trade. He stresses that technological innovation, and the international diffusion of innovations, have an important impact on a country's competitive position, and that differences among nations in technological capability are responsible for a substantial amount of international trade.

An important feature of the postwar world economy has been the growth of multinational corporations. Marxist Paul A. Baran argues that "the principal impact of foreign enterprise on the development of the underdeveloped countries lies in hardening and strengthening the sway of merchant capitalism, in slowing down and indeed preventing its transformation into industrial capitalism." In the next paper, the editor discusses various important topics relating to the international transfer of technology, a subject that is receiving increasing attention from policy makers in this area.

In recent years, there has been a rise in protectionist sentiments in the United States. Walter Adams, in the next selection, argues against protectionist measures. And Irving Kravis argues in the following article that "the interests of the U.S.

213

lie in the direction of freer trade. The arguments for a contrary policy . . . are based on incorrect assessments of the facts. . . ."

In the area of international finance, no issue has received more attention, and generated more controversy, than the question of whether exchange rates should be fixed or flexible. Milton Friedman, in the next article, presents the case for flexible exchange rates. He argues that flexible exchange rates can allow international adjustments to take place with fewer undesirable internal adjustments, and that they would allow us to "become masters in our own house." Henry C. Wallich, in the following selection, presents the case for fixed exchange rates. He says that flexible exchange rates would lead to a worldwide acceleration of inflation, and that "their successful functioning would require more self-discipline and mutual forbearance that countries today are likely to muster."

The less-developed countries contain the bulk of the world's population. In the following article, Barbara Ward describes the characteristics of these countries and some of the changes that have been going on in them. She stresses the difficulties involved in raising their economic growth rate, and chides the rich nations for being relatively unconcerned about the fate of the poor nations. Simon Kuznets, in the next selection (which is taken from his Nobel Memorial Lecture), goes further in describing the characteristics of the less-developed countries, and concludes that "substantial economic advance in the less-developed countries may require modification in the available stock of material technology, and probably even greater innovations in political and social structure."

39

How Has the World Economy Changed Since 1929?

WALTER S. SALANT

Walter Salant is Senior Fellow Emeritus at the Brookings Institution. This article is part of a compendium of papers submitted to the Joint Economic Committee of Congress, November 28, 1980.

Changes in World Population and Organization

An observer from outer space, comparing the present world with that of 1929, would be bound to notice several things that few of us looking through one window on earth ordinarily think of. The first is that the population of the world has more than doubled, increasing from some 2 billion to about 4.3 billion. A disproportionate part of this increase has occurred in Africa, Asia, and Latin America, which now contain 76 percent of the world's population, as contrasted with only 66 percent fifty years ago. (See Table 1.)

This vastly larger number of people has been drawing at an increasing rate on resources that do not renew themselves, so that the ratio of population to the storehouse of depletable resources has risen even more than the population.

He would also notice that in 1929 only about 9 percent of the world's population lived in centrally planned economies and that this proportion increased to about 35 percent in the last fifty years, with the population in market economies having shrunk correspondingly from 91 percent to 65 percent.

Besides having increased in number, the people of the world are now organized into a much larger number of self-governing national units. In 1929 there were only 68 independent sovereign states and countries; the number that were politically independent in 1979 had risen to 200.

Increase in the Role of Developing Countries

The reason for the increase in the number of countries is almost entirely that the colonies or protectorates of fifty years ago have become politically independent states. Nearly all are countries of low income, most of them in Africa and Asia. The less economically developed countries that were independent then were, with a few exceptions, confined to Latin America. The increase in the number of politically independent low-income countries, combined with the postwar tension between the Soviet Union and the liberal democracies and the efforts of both sides to win the support or at least maintain the neutrality of the new countries, reinforced by a genuine concern for the poverty of their populations, have given the low-

215

Table 1. Estimated World Population, 1930 and 1978

	1930 (midyear)		1978 (midyear)		Increase	
	Millions	Percentage of total	Millions	Percentage of total	Millions	Percent
World total	2,013	100.0	4,327	100.0	2,314	115
Africa	155	7.7	441	10.2	286	185
United States and Canada	135	6.7	247	5.7	112	83
Central and South America[a]	109	5.4	340	7.9	231	212
Asia (excluding U.S.S.R.)	1,072	53.3	2,492	57.6	1,420	132
Europe (excluding U.S.S.R.)	356	17.7	524	12.1	168	47
Oceania (including Australia)	10	.5	22	.5	12	120
U.S.S.R.	176	8.7	261	6.0	85	48
Non-Communist	1,837	91.3	2,836	65.5	999	54
Communist	176	8.7	1,491	34.5	1,315	747

[a] Central America includes Mexico and Caribbean Islands.

Source: 1930 data from U.N. "Demographic Yearbook, 1960," table 2, p. 118. 1978 data from Department of State, "The Planetary Product," special report No. 58, prepared by Herbert Block, tables 6 and 10.

income countries a much greater voice in the world than they had fifty years ago.

One economic result of the increased concern for these countries is the emergence of intergovernmental aid, both bilateral and multilateral, in the forms both of outright gifts and of loans on more generous terms than those available in financial markets. This is an entirely new phenomenon. Before World War II intergovernmental aid, even to wartime allies, took the form of bilateral lending on commerical terms; there was then no precedent for the provision of public funds to independent states on less-than-commercial terms or of aid on the postwar scale.

The increase in the number of countries also has the potentiality for *reducing* world economic integration. The reason is that it has greatly increased the number of centers of independent policy-making. As a result it has increased the transactions subject to the imposition of barriers to trade and the flow of capital. It has also greatly increased the potentiality and probably the actuality of interferences with adjustments to market changes.

The increase in the number of countries has also widened the possible area of international conflict and the actual proportion of productive effort in the world that is devoted to military expenditure, thereby reducing the proportion available for civilian production, both for consumption and for investment to expand the capacity for such production.

International Economic Interdependence

One of the most common perceptions about long-period changes in the world economy is that economic interdependence among countries has greatly increased. There appears to be little doubt that this perception is correct if we compare the present world economy with that of the 1930s, when protectionism and the world depression cut international trade more than output and when international capital movements dried up almost completely. But if we compare the present world with that of the late 1920s, the correctness of that perception is harder to appraise, mainly, although not entirely, because we lack information about the relation between flows of international and domestic investment and between stocks of internationally mobile and immobile financial assets.

International Trade in Goods and Services

Perhaps the most frequently noted evidence of the increase in interdependence since before World War II is the growth of international trade in goods and services relative to that of total production. In most of the developed countries the value of such trade has risen more rapidly than the value of total output since

1938, owing in part to reductions in the barriers to the international movements of goods. (See Table 2.) It should be recognized, however, that between 1929 and 1938 there was a shrinkage in this relationship, so it is less clear that international trade has increased in relation to output since 1929 than that it has increased since 1938. The reason it is difficult to be sure about this point for most countries is that data comparable over time on the value of total national output in current prices for 1929 consistent with those for later years are available for only a few countries. Estimates for the major industrial countries over a longer period indicate that trade was growing faster than output in

Table 2. Foreign Trade in Goods and Services as a Percentage of GNP, 19 OECD Countries, 1929, 1938, and 1976–78[a]

Country	1929	1938	Average 1976–78
Australia[b]	19.3	18.3	17.1
Austria	NA	17.6[c]	35.6
Belgium	NA	28.2	56.3
Canada	29.0	24.3	26.4
Denmark	NA	26.2	33.5
France	NA	13.1	21.9
Germany	NA	16.5[d]	26.3
Greece	NA	17.8	21.2
Iceland	NA	46.8	42.1
Ireland	NA	25.5	57.7
Italy	NA	7.6	26.8
Japan	19.4	19.7	12.3
Netherlands	NA	28.1	49.0
Norway	33.6	29.2[e]	48.6
Portugal	NA	13.0	26.6
Sweden	NA	20.1[f]	30.2
Switzerland	NA	17.9	35.9
United Kingdom	NA	16.9	32.2
United States	6.3	4.3	10.1
All countries[g]	NA	20.6	32.1

[a] Percentages are based on data in current prices. Trade is defined as one-half of the sum of exports and imports of goods and services, including merchandise, nonmonetary gold, freight, other transportation, travel, investment income in gross amounts received and paid, and other current public and private services.
[b] Fiscal years ending June 30.
[c] 1937.
[d] 1936.
[d] 1939.
[e] Based on GNP for fiscal year.
[f] Unweighted averages of percentages for all countries.

NA = Not available.

many of them until World War I and the growth that has occurred since World War II is a resumption of a pre-1914 trend after an interruption of many years. (As we shall see later, the fact that estimates of national output in 1929 exist for so few countries but are available for all of them now is one of the important ways in which the world of 1929 differed from that of 1979.)

For the OECD countries shown in Table 2, the ratios of foreign trade in goods and services to total national output in 1929 are shown for only five. For three of them these ratios were actually higher than in 1976–1978. The lack of data makes it difficult to say with any great assurance that the relation of international transaction in goods and services to world output has increased since 1929.

It will come as a surprise to most people that Japan was one of the countries whose foreign trade was smaller, in relation to total output, in 1976–1978 than in 1929, the recent ratio being only slightly higher than that of the United States. Most people think of the Japanese economy as much more dependent than the U.S. economy on foreign trade, especially in the light of its dependence on imports for almost all of its supplies of oil. This dependence points to a deficiency in trade-output ratios as indicators of international economic interdependence. That ratio may be high for a country that imports goods that it could produce at home at only slightly higher cost. If the foreign supply were cut off and it had to satisfy its demand from domestic production, it would suffer a possibly painful transitory adjustment and some continuing economic loss because of the higher cost, but the continuing loss would not be great. Contrast that country with one whose imports are much smaller in relation to its total output but consist mostly of essential raw materials that it cannot produce domestically at all, as in the case of oil imports by Japan. Loss of imports would be far more serious in the long run for the second country than for the first one, despite its lower trade-output ratio. Concentration on such ratios diverts attention from the lesson of the old saw that tells us that for want of a nail a kingdom may be lost.

The channels as well as the magnitudes of both trade and direct investment have also changed. Some of these changes have been the result of technological and market developments. Trade in manufactured goods is a larger portion of world trade than it was in the late 1920s. This may be partly the result of faster growth in Europe than in the United States, where trade in manufactured goods is a smaller part of total trade than in Europe, but it is also in part the result of the fact that manufactured goods are now exported in substantial quantities by countries that formerly had little or no capacity to produce them, such as Taiwan, South Korea, Mexico, Brazil, and others.

Similarly, the increase in trade between Middle Eastern countries and others compared to 1929 reflects partly market-induced and technological changes, and not only a rise in the price of oil relative to other goods since then. In fact the price of oil relative to other industrial products has not risen spectacularly since 1929, although it has risen. But the quantity of oil imports and of oil consumption is much greater, relative to total output, throughout the world than it was fifty years ago because oil and its products have become much more deeply embedded in the structure of world production, both as final goods and as inputs into them, so any increase in its price is now much more important than it would have been in 1929.

Other changes in the structure of trade and direct investment have been the result of political and institutional changes. Fifty years ago there were very few politically independent countries in Asia and Africa; most of the now-independent countries in these two continents were colonies or protectorates. Along with some self-governing countries (e.g., Australia, Canada, the Union of South Africa), they were part of a system under which the mother country and its colonies received preferences over outsiders, both in trade with one another and in direct investment. For example, a firm resident in a country outside the British Empire, or that of France, was discriminated against in selling to or investing in a country or colony inside it. Such discrimination has now largely disappeared. Although remnants of it persist because of relationships established in the past, international trade and direct investment are now freer of those political barriers than they were fifty years ago.

International Mobility of Labor and Capital

If we do not confine our attention to trade but consider also the mobility of labor and capital, the conclusion that economic integration has increased in the past fifty years is probably a safe one. Improvements in communication of knowledge about markets, in transportation, and in travel have increased the mobility (i.e., the *potentiality* of movement) not only of goods and services but of labor and of capital among countries. Reductions in the cost of communication have increased the spread of information in every country about economic conditions in other countries and have facilitated business and other international negotiations. Improved and increased knowledge of English in non-English-speaking countries, which have made it a widely used common language, have furthered this spread. At the same time air travel has revolutionized international transportation and this also must have contributed to an increase in the degree of economic integration.

Mobility of goods, capital, and people limits the degree to which prices and wages, when expressed in a common currency, and interest rates can differ in different countries, and it also limits the degree to which their changes may diverge. Insofar as both trade and international migration of labor are concerned, this mobility certainly appears to have increased in the case of the Western European countries that are members of the European Economic Community. It also appears to be true of international direct investment.

The volume of financial capital—stocks not involving control of enterprises, bonds, short-term securities, and bank deposits—that is internationally mobile has probably also increased, although data are lacking to support any confident statement about the relation of current flows of financial assets in the late 1920s to other relevant economic variables.

As to the stock of international mobile assets, as distinguished from their current flows, it may be recalled that relatively large amounts of funds owned in some countries were held in other countries in the late 1920s; the repatriation of those funds contributed to the financial collapse and the deepening of the depression in the early 1930s. Nevertheless it can be said that in the postwar period international financial investment has continued at a high level for a longer period than it had in the late 1920s. The cumulative effect of postwar international investment over time must have been to expand enormously the proportion of the total stock of financial capital that consists of internationally mobile financial assets, including but not confined to Euro-currency bank deposits estimated to amount to some $900 billion at the end of 1978. Despite the lack of data, it appears to be widely accepted that the stock of internationally mobile financial assets has increased greatly since fifty years ago, not only in dollar or other currency values but in relation to such other aggregates as the value of total output, of international trade, of total wealth, or of total financial assets.

The effects of these changes in increasing the integration of the market economies has been offset to some degree, however, by decreased economic relationships between the market economies and the now-far-more-numerous centrally planned economies of the Communist countries.

The international mobility of financial assets has a number of important implications for the operation of the international financial system. First, for a given state of expectations about the stability or movement of exchange rates, the higher the proportion of financial assets that are internationally mobile, the greater the tendency for a deficit or surplus in a country's current account (implying a decrease or increase in its net wealth) to induce an offsetting flow of assets at any given change in the relation between its own and foreign interest rates. To put it the other way around, the larger the proportion of such assets, the less the change in relative interest rates needed to induce the movement of financial assets that offsets a given current-account deficit or surplus. Consequently if financial assets are mobile the burden of adjustment falls less on the current account than if they are not, and the changes in income and price levels needed to restore equilibrium in the total balance of payments (the current and capital accounts combined) are less than they would otherwise be.

International mobility of financial assets, by tending to equalize interest rates among countries, also makes it difficult if not impossible for individual countries, especially small countries, to pursue independent aggregate demand policies. For example, an expansionary monetary policy raises the prices of financial assets (reduces interest rates) when such assets are not internationally mobile, but it raises them less when the volume of internationally mobile financial assets is large; instead, its effect then is to induce the sale of domestic and the purchase of foreign financial assets (an outflow of capital). The resulting outflow of money prevents or restrains the intended reduction of interest rates and the intended increase in the stock of privately held domestic money.

It is less clear whether this conclusion applies when exchange rates are flexible. The answer appears to depend largely on how much a change in exchange rates affects domestic prices and costs at given levels of domestic output and how much it affects output. Consider first the case of expansionary fiscal policy. The greater the international mobility of capital, the more a given degree of fiscal expansion raises the price of domestic currency and reduces demand for exports and domestic goods that compete with imports, thereby offsetting the expansionary fiscal effect. But it is less certain how capital mobility under flexible exchange rates affects the power of monetary policy to influence aggregate demand. When exchange rates are flexible the monetary authority can control the stock of domestic *nominal* money in the hands of the public, but it has less control over the *real* value of that money stock, especially in a small open economy. A given expansion in the stock of domestic money will have a greater effect in depressing the foreign-exchange value of the country's currency the greater is the international mobility of capital. This means that it will have a greater effect both in stimulating output of exports and domestic goods that compete with imports than it would if capital were less mobile, and to that extent it increases the effectiveness of monetary policy. But it will also have a greater effect in raising the prices of tradable goods and thereby the general level of domestic prices, and thus less effect in raising the *real* value of the domestic money stock. That influence reduces the effectiveness of monetary policy. We have no basis, either in theory or experience, for judging which of these opposing effects of international capital mobility is the greater, nor indeed for assuming that the answer would be the same for all countries.

In short, while the financial integration of the world economy increases the possibility of offsetting a disequilibrium in the current account of a country's balance of payments, it probably reduces the ability of any one country to pursue an aggregate demand policy independently of that of the rest of the world, except perhaps in the uncertain case of monetary policy under flexible exchange rates.

International capital flows can also seriously aggravate disequilibria in balances of payments. When, under fixed exchange rates, a deficit in a country's balance of payments develops and the financial markets doubt that it will be eliminated before that country's international reserves are seriously depleted, doubts may arise that the value of its currency will be maintained or that capital will be left free to move out. If such doubts develop, asset-holders, fearing depreciation of assets denominated in that currency, try to convert them into assets denominated in other currencies. Such actions tend to induce the very depreciation that is feared. Fears of political instability can also give rise to such movements. Similarly, under flexible exchange rates initial deficits or fears of political instability can also give rise to efforts to export capital. Under that system an initial disturbance affects the exchange rate immediately and can greatly aggravate its movement. Since the exchange rate is the most important single price in all economies (unless "the" wage rate is regarded as a single price), its volatility resulting from the international mobility of capital can be a potent cause of economic disturbance.

The recognition of increased international interdependence has led to a revival of attention to international effects in the determination of monetary and credit policy. It appears to be widely believed that such policies were formerly based solely on the perceived needs of the domestic economy and that the attention now being given to international factors is something new. This belief is completely incorrect. Indeed it would be more nearly correct to say that under the operation of the international monetary system of fifty or more years ago, international considerations were dominant. Monetary policy was dominated by movements of international reserves. This practice was regarded as essential to balance-of-payments adjustment and the operation of the fixed-exchange-rate system. When, during the 1920s, the Federal Reserve System offset inflows of funds for domestic reasons, it was accused of violating the rules of the game. Then in the late 1920s the Federal Reserve System eased its monetary policy in order to facilitate European efforts to restore monetary stability after World War I, even though the domestic economic situation in the United States was not regarded as calling for that policy. Indeed, many economists attributed the wild stock market speculation of 1927–1929 and the subsequent crash to what they regarded as the Federal Reserve's excessive concern in 1924 and 1927 for the international aspects of policy at the expense of domestic considerations. Again, when the pound sterling cut its tie to gold in September 1931 the Federal Reserve raised discount rates sharply in the belief that a tighter policy was necessary to prevent a flight of capital from the United States, although the domestic economy of the United States was deeply depressed and domestic considerations alone would have called for monetary ease. Other episodes could also be cited to show that the present recognition of international factors is only a return to the past, and a partial one at that.

Interdependence through External Effects

International interdependence has also increased in another way. Many activities of one nation yield benefits to others for which the nation engaged in the activity receives no remuneration or impose costs on them for which it does not reimburse them. These "external effects" have always existed, of course. The damming by one country of a river that flows through another country is an old example. The change during the past fifty years is that the number of such activities has increased, owing in part to new technologies, and the magnitude of the external effects of some old activities has increased. That this is true appears evident if we recall some of the problems that have been forced on our attention in recent years that did not arise fifty years ago: oil spills and other pollution of the oceans, overfishing, air pollution, the spreading of communicable diseases as international travel has multiplied, and as A. P. Lerner has said, inflation itself. Externalized benefits are illustrated by such "public goods" as the control of communicable diseases and the better communication of basic research and technological improvements that cross national boundaries without charge.

These externalities generate pressure for collective action by nations acting jointly. At the same time they undermine the autonomy of national governments with respect to the activities that give rise to them.

The Multiplication of Intergovernmental Organizations

The perception of increased interdependence of national economies, the great increase in the number of politically independent countries, and a growth in awareness of and genuine concern for the poverty of the low-income countries have combined to lead to a multiplication of intergovernmental economic organizations and more informal intergovernmental contacts, both routine and occasional. One need only mention a few of the major new world and regional organizations that did not exist and whose present functions were not being performed fifty years ago: the International Bank for Reconstruction and Development (the World Bank) and its allied institutions, the International Monetary Fund, the General Agreement on Tariffs and Trade, the various regional development banks, the Economic and Social Council of the United Nations and the various regional Economic Commissions, the Organization for Economic Cooperation and Development, the European Economic Community, and the Council for Mutual Economic Assistance (COMECON).

The International Monetary System

Another important difference between the international economy of fifty years ago and the present one is the shift from a system in which exchange rates among currencies were fixed to one in which many currencies, especially those of the major countries, are free to fluctuate, although subject to stabilizing intervention at the discretion of the monetary authorities. This change has resulted from the effects of the increased international mobility of financial assets and the decrease in the flexibility of the national market economies, which will be discussed later in this paper. In combination, these changes increased the extent of balance-of-payments disequilibria and increased the resistance to eliminating them.

Growing balance-of-payments disequilibria and this increased resistance finally led to the breakdown of the system of fixed exchange rates in the early 1970s. No longer do the major countries attempt to maintain the exchange rates of their currencies with those of all other major countries in a very narrow range around fixed parities. We now have a set of "mixed arrangements" rather than a system because, in contrast to the late 1920s when fixed rates were adhered to by practically all countries, there is now a great diversity of exchange-rate arrangements. Among 138 member countries of the International Monetary Fund (IMF) at the end of 1979, for which information about such arrangements was available, 42 peg their currencies to the U.S. dollar and 18 to the French franc, the pound sterling, or some other national currency; 34 members peg their currencies to the composite known as the SDR (Special Drawing Rights) or to some other composite of currencies; 8 are members of the European Monetary System, a cooperative exchange arrangement; 3 adjust their exchange rates to a set of indicators; and 33 members determine their exchange rates in other ways, most of them by letting their currencies float without reference to any par value. A good measure of the importance of flexible exchange rates is the IMF's estimate that about three-quarters of the world's international merchandise trade moves across floating rates.

Disequilibria in the balances of payments of market economies are harder to eliminate under fixed rates than they were a half century ago. The basic reason

is that economies have become less flexible. When exchange rates are fixed, adjustment requires a deficit country to reduce its aggregate income and prices relative to those of surplus countries and, if the general level of world prices is to be stable, that requires absolute contraction on the part of deficit countries and expansion on the part of surplus countries. Such adjustment has become increasingly painful for deficit countries as their price structures have become more resistant to decreases because such contractions now reduce output and employment more and prices less than they formerly did. The system of presumptively fixed exchange rates, which prevailed fifty years ago and until the early 1970s, called for adjustment of prices expressed in national currencies. Under flexible exchange rates which are now so prevalent, a given degree of adjustment is easier for a deficit country because its price and cost level, measured in the currencies of other countries, can be reduced by a decrease in the foreign-exchange value of its currency rather than through the more painful process of widespread decreases in its domestic prices and costs.

It is insufficiently recognized, however, that under flexible rates the difficulties that a deficit country had under fixed rates are to a considerable extent merely transferred to surplus countries. The reason is that a surplus causes a currency to appreciate, which tends to reduce the demand for the surplus country's exports below what it would be in the absence of the appreciation, and by reducing the domestic price of its imports, also to reduce the demand for its domestic products that compete with imports, putting downward pressure on prices, output, and employment in these sectors. One would expect that this effect would increase the resistance in surplus countries to appreciation of their currencies, and the more so the larger are the export- and import-competing sectors of their economies. There is some evidence that there has been resistance to appreciation for this reason and some reason to believe that it would be greater in a noninflationary world, where the downward pressure of currency appreciation on the demand for domestic output would be less welcome.

40

America's Competitive Position in World Trade

HENDRIK S. HOUTHAKKER

Hendrik S. Houthakker is Professor of Economics at Harvard University. During the early years of the Nixon administration, he was a member of the Council of Economic Advisers. The following selection is taken from his testimony before the Senate Subcommittee on Foreign Trade in 1971.

The notion of competitiveness is a somewhat elusive one and the question of whether we are competitive does not admit of a precise answer, although some indications can be given. As a first approximation we may say that a nation is competitive if it is able, through its exports and other activities, to earn the foreign exchange it needs for imports and other purposes. In fact, if we can abstract from capital movements for the moment, a nation may be called competitive if its current account balance—covering goods, services, transportation, and unilateral transfers—is zero at full employment and in the absence of quantitative restrictions. Thus, if this abstraction from capital movements were legitimate, the United States would be competitive at the present time, for our current account balance has generally had a small surplus. We do not yet have any figures for the first quarter of 1971, but for 1970 as a whole the current account surplus was $638 million. It is true that there are restrictions on imports from the United States in certain foreign countries, and that we also have restrictions on certain classes of imports. The severity of these restrictions is hard to measure, but in the aggregate they probably come close to canceling each other out as far as the current account balance is concerned. Consequently, if we could consider only the current account, our export prices would not be too high, despite the fact that wages in the United States are much higher than wages elsewhere. These higher wages are generally offset by our much higher productivity, which is itself the main cause of the much higher wages prevailing in the United States.

This preliminary assessment of our overall position does not mean that we are competitive in all industries. If we were, we would not need any imports, and foreigners would not have the dollars with which to buy our exports. A country that engages in foreign trade usually has a cost advantage in those commodities that it exports and a disadvantage in those that it imports, though sometimes these advantages are distorted by tariffs, subsidies, and other interferences with trade. We have a cost advantage in agricultural staples such as grains and cotton, where our costs are kept low by our relatively abundant supply of land and by the skill of our farmers, but if we tried to grow all of the coffee or bananas consumed here we would find that our costs would be far higher than those in certain tropical countries.

While in the case of agricultural and other primary products the relative cost advantages are strongly influenced by geographical and climatic factors, this is less true for manufactured products, where technology and the availability of capital, skilled labor, and management are likely to be more important. This implies that in manufactured products the pattern of relative advantages is more likely to change over time under the influence of trends in technology, transport costs, consumer demand, and other factors. For many years, for instance, the United States had a cost advantage in steel production, which made us net exporters. We apparently lost this advantage sometime in the late 1950s, when our trade balance in steel turned negative. On the other hand, our aircraft industry appears to have increased its cost advantage over the years.

These changes in the relative position of different industries sometimes cause difficult problems of adjustment. In the case of an industry that is losing its international competitiveness an increase in imports will be the first manifestation of what may be a much more deep-seated problem. Our steel industry, for instance, appears to be handicapped, among other things, by a lack of price competition among domestic producers. Since the demand for steel is subject to change over time, output has to vary excessively if prices are not allowed to help maintain equilibrium. This means that the industry must have excess capacity to be able to cope with demand at its peak. Most of the time, consequently, the industry is unable to use its capacity to full advantage and this keeps down its productivity and raises its costs. There are no doubt other important factors involved in the relative decline of our steel industry, and I mention this particular factor only as an example. The point I want to make is that imports not infrequently are blamed for developments of purely domestic origin.

In fact, there are relatively few important sectors of the economy where imports constitute a large enough percentage of supply to affect employment and profits to a serious extent. The notion that we are being flooded with imports will not bear examination. In 1967, there were only 25 four-digit manufacturing industries—out of a total of about 400—where imports accounted for 20 percent or more of total shipments; these 25 industries represented only 2.5 percent of the value of domestic shipments in all manufacturing.

There is no reason to think that these figures will be very different for more recent years.

Even though the impact of imports is frequently exaggerated, it remains true that the burden of adjustment may be too heavy for any particular industry to bear. This is why adjustment assistance may be necessary. In the last two years several groups of firms and workers have become eligible for such assistance, but more could be done if the law were changed. The President's trade bill of 1969 carried provisions for liberalizing it further. The great advantage of adjustment assistance is that, while sometimes costly in the short run, it promotes the adaptability to changing circumstances, both domestic and worldwide, that has long been one of the main strengths of our economy.

The argument is sometimes made that we cannot expose our workers to foreign competition because wages are much higher in this country than abroad. Protection, according to this argument, would be necessary to maintain the real income of workers. Apart from the difficulties of redeployment, which can be taken care of by adjustment assistance; this argument is without merit and indeed, the reverse of the truth. Our workers get high real income not because they are protected from foreign competition, but because they are highly productive, at least in certain industries. As a nation we have a high per capita real income because our output per capita is high. And our per capita output is high, among other things, because we use our labor force to good advantage. The fact that our wages are high does not prevent us from being net exporters in a number of industries, because productivity is high there, too. If we were to keep a larger proportion of our labor force in low-productivity industries, our per capita output would be reduced, and this would have an adverse effect on the real income of workers generally and of everybody else. Imports are also a significant factor in keeping domestic prices under control by stimulating competition and cost-saving innovations, and thus benefit us as consumers.

There are, of course, cases, especially those involving national security, where we may deliberately want to preserve domestic industries in the face of a cost disadvantage. Even in those national security cases, however, it should not be taken for granted that protection through quotas or otherwise is necessarily the best solution.

So far I have abstracted from capital movements

and talked only about the current account. Much of what I have said also applies to the more realistic situation where capital movements are present. The principal difference is that when there are capital movements the current account balance no longer has to be zero for a country to be competitive. Depending on whether there is an inflow or an outflow of capital, the current account balance will have to be negative or positive to achieve overall equilibrium in the balance of payments.

On the capital account it is useful to distinguish between short-term and long-term capital, and the latter can be further distinguished into direct investment and portfolio investment. We have had a large and growing outflow of capital on direct investment account for many years, while portfolio investment has been more erratic, with surpluses prevailing in recent years. For the sake of simplicity I shall ignore portfolio investment from here on, and leave short-term capital for later discussion. The outflow of funds for direct investment purposes would then have to be offset by a surplus on current account, but this has not happened in recent years. In fact, it is sometimes argued that the net outflow of direct investment funds by itself reflects a lack of competitiveness on our part, though it may also have something to do with the relative abundance of capital in different countries. The net outflow of direct investment means that more American businessmen find it profitable to invest abroad than foreign businessmen find it profitable to invest in the United States. However, direct investment is not always a reflection of relative cost differentials only; it may also be the result of import restrictions, differences in management skills, and technological advantages. Because of these several reasons more and more of our larger corporations have become multinational. While multinational corporations may raise certain problems for Government policy, there is no reason to believe that their existence invalidates the proposition that the best interest of all countries, including the United States, is normally served by unimpeded movement of goods and capital. What these corporations do, in fact, is to make within one firm the same cost comparisons that are also made by the free market, and in so doing they promote greater efficiency in the use of labor and capital everywhere.

I shall only say a few words about short-term capital, which is primarily a monetary phenomenon. The willingness of individuals and firms in different countries to give each other credit depends primarily on relative interest rates and expectations of future changes in exchange rates. Since the United States has a strong economy and a well-organized capital market, the dollar has become the principal reserve currency in the world. Many foreigners, both private and official, have been willing to hold substantial amounts of dollars at prevailing rates of interest in recent years, although occasionally this willingness is impaired by changes in international interest rate patterns or by fears of changes in parities.

Taking all these things—the current account, the long-term capital account, and the normal increase in short-term liabilities to be expected in a growing world economy—together it appears that the United States has often had some difficulty in attaining balance, though the shortfall has generally not been large. The large official settlements deficits that we have had in 1970 and in 1971 are attributable almost entirely to short-term capital movements of a transitory nature, but underlying this there may be a more fundamental problem of limited magnitude. Our imports increased more than our exports from 1964 to 1969, but the adverse effect on the current account was offset to some extent by an improvement in earnings on U.S. investment abroad, and more recently the growth in our exports has overtaken the growth in our imports. Once the expected revival of the domestic economy is realized, the current account may again become less favorable, but the long-term capital account may improve. I cannot definitely say, therefore, that at prevailing prices and exchange rates the United States is not competitive, but I would go so far as to say that it is more likely that we are less than competitive than that we are more than competitive.

In order to maintain and strengthen our competitive position in the future it is of the highest importance that we keep our domestic price level under control by appropriate fiscal and monetary policy. A continuation of present trends in prices and wages would almost certainly aggravate our international problems, even though our rates of increase do not necessarily compare unfavorably with those in other major countries. In addition, maintenance of a normal rate of productivity increase will obviously help our competitive position.

Finally, exchange rates are a significant determinant of competitiveness. Under the international monetary system as it has been operated until now there appears to be a bias toward devaluation of other currencies; moreover there is some evidence that foreign demand for our exports does not rise as rapidly as our own demand for imports, other factors remaining the same. Even though there is no firm evidence of an overall disequilibrium at the moment, it is, therefore necessary that the exchange rate mechanism possess sufficient flexibility to cope with whatever trends may emerge in the future. Greater U.S. competitiveness leading to a stronger export performance by our industries is probably the best defense against the understandable but shortsighted preoccupation with the transitory effects of imports that is now so widespread.

41

Technology and World Trade

RICHARD COOPER

Richard Cooper is Professor of Economics at Harvard University. The following article first appeared in Technology and World Trade, *published by the National Bureau of Standards in 1967.*

Most theoretical discussions of international trade involve what may be called traditional trade, the exchange of food for raw materials or for simple manufactures. David Ricardo, the English inventor of our theory of comparative advantage to explain trade flows, drew his example in terms of wine and cloth.

The United States imports coffee and exports wheat, both as a result of climatic and soil differences. Europe is often characterized as an importer of food, fuels and other raw materials, and an exporter of manufactures.

The composition and direction of trade depends, in the theory, largely on natural endowment, although occasionally special skills are also involved.

It is difficult to reconcile this theoretical picture of trade patterns to the patterns which have actually developed.

Manufactured products now account for nearly 60 percent of the value of world trade, up from 25 percent in the 1920s, and the proportion is still growing. Trade among major industrial countries now accounts for nearly half of world trade and the share of this trade which is manufactures has grown even more rapidly than is true for the world as a whole.

The growth in trade of manufactures does not reflect a need to pay more in manufactures for the food and raw materials needed by the industrial countries. It represents increasingly an exchange of manufactures for manufactures. The growth of this type of trade is due to a variety of factors, including the reduction in trade barriers over the last fifteen years, and the rising importance of brand name products in consumer purchases. But a key factor may also have been the rapid pace of technological innovation which has taken place. An innovation adds to the list of export products, at least temporarily, and trade is stimulated.

Quantifying the Effect of Technology on Trade

We have little quantitative information on the influence of technical change on trade. Nearly ten years ago, the Danish economist, Erik Hoffmeyer, studied the pattern of U.S. trade and found that the United States tended to specialize in what he called

226

research-intensive goods. He found that U.S. exports of these research-intensive goods increased twenty times between the period just before World War I and the mid-fifties, while exports of traditional goods merely trebled.

More recently, several studies have shown that there is a striking relationship between U.S. export performance and several measurements we might think are related to technical change.

Donald Keesing has found, for example, a very high correlation, industry by industry, between research and development expenditures in relation to sales and the U.S. share of exports of manufactures by all the OECD countries. The relationship between U.S. export performance and share of industry employment occupied by scientists and engineers is similarly high. The weight of the evidence leaves little question that there is some relationship, at least for the United States, between export performance and industrial research and development.

This relationship deserves closer scrutiny. First, it should not blind us to the impact of technical change on more traditional forms of trade and, second, we should not take for granted the direction of causality in the relationship just noted.

As to the first point, the impact of technology is clearly not limited to the generation of new products which enter international trade. Our attention is usually focused on these—the visible products, the jet aircraft, the new computer, synthetic fibers, the new drugs. But the influence of technology is far more pervasive than that.

In addition to these product innovations, there are also important process innovations, improvements which lower the cost of producing and moving a wide variety of goods, including goods of the traditional type. Examples of such cost-reducing improvements come to mind in concentrating metal ores, producing steel, weaving cloth, harvesting grain, raising chickens.

Some innovations have a double role. They involve the new product and they lower costs in producing traditional products. The sewing machine and the mechanical reaper are now classic examples; the machinery industry is replete with current examples.

Sometimes the so-called traditional products are themselves improved through advances in technical knowledge. Selective breeding has increased both the yield and the quality of many agricultural products and has produced chickens and turkeys which far surpass their scrawny ancestors in edibility. Purity of refined metals has been increased. New alloys have greatly increased the performance of these metals, and so on through most products.

Furthermore, trade has been greatly encouraged by the impact of technological change on the transportation industry. The big change came in the nineteenth century with the railroad and the steamship, but these changes have not ceased. Ocean freight rates continue to decline relative to the value of goods shipped and large bulk carriers with specialized port facilities will make profitable the movement of large amounts of low value goods, many being the traditional products.

Air transport will come into range of an increasing number of goods as air cargo methods improve. International air freight rates have fallen 20 percent in the last decade while other prices were generally rising, and the trend will probably continue downward.

It is worth recalling, however, that not all technological advances stimulate trade. Some of the major developments have the opposite effect, as when nylon largely replaced silk, or when the Haber process permitted fixation of nitrogen from the air and reduced dependence on natural deposits.

Such developments reduce dependence on geography and substitute, as it were, technology for geography and climate, tending to lower imports.

For all these reasons, it is not possible to identify the impact of technology on trade by focusing on a short list of technologically visible goods. The impact is much more general, operating on production costs and transport costs as well as producing new products; and some improvements may inhibit rather than stimulate trade.

In view of this it may be asked, however, why on such measures as we have there is in fact such a close relationship, at least for the United States, between exports of certain goods and technological inputs into those industries. This close relationship has already been noted. I would suggest, however, that it requires an interpretation somewhat different from the one usually cited or implied. This latter interpretation treats R and D expenditures as largely autonomous, determined primarily, say, by government concern for national defense. But much R and D is itself responsive to commercial demands for new products as incomes grow and for new labor-saving techniques of production as wages increase and labor becomes more expensive. Technical improvements tend to respond to the demands primarily of the domestic market. Many of the resulting improvements also stimulate exports, either by creating new products or by lowering the cost of existing ones.

There is some evidence, at least within the electronics industry—I assume the same is true for other industries—that those firms whose research and development programs are geared toward commercial application, rather than government contract work, do much better, both in the home market and in foreign markets, than is true of firms whose research effort is oriented heavily toward special requirements of government contracts. These often involve very exacting requirements which dominate cost considerations. For commercial applications, cost considerations are important.

A Few Countries Are the Primary Technical Innovators

Domestic demand attracts private research, and research success satisfies new market demands, both at home and abroad. It is not surprising in view of the relationship between the domestic market and directed research, that the great majority of the innovations take place in half-a-dozen to a dozen countries, and that among these the United States plays a leading role.

Quite apart from the effect of size—the proportion of Nobel Laureates in the last fifteen years who have been American corresponds roughly to the U.S. share in free world industrial production, for instance—there are two reasons for supposing that the United States might generate a disproportionate share of commercial innovations. The U.S. economy is on the frontier of experience, as it were, in two respects: first, per capita incomes are higher in the U.S. than elsewhere and have continued so for a number of years; second, closely related to that, wage rates are substantially higher than elsewhere and are continuing to rise, so that American businessmen face before others the need to find new labor-saving techniques of production.

The first of these effects can be seen in a wide range of consumer products which were first produced on a massive scale in the United States—automobiles, household appliances, telephones, hi-fi sets, small boats, small aircraft. The potential demand for such products not only generates improvements in the products themselves, but also induces improvements in productive techniques to service the volume of demand and to bring the product within the reach of the mass consumer a bit sooner.

High Labor Cost as a Stimulus to Innovation

The second effect can be seen in the long history of U.S. innovations directed at the conservation of labor, which has always been high cost relative to other productive factors and which on some occasions has simply not been available in the quantity or quality required to satisfy domestic demand with old techniques of production.

The sewing machine, the linotype machine, the typewriter, shoe machinery, and down to data sorting machinery and the computer are only the best known of these labor-saving innovations.

Labor-saving innovations were often U.S. inventions. The need drew creative attention to possible solutions. Very often the inventions were made elsewhere but first widely used in the United States, where there was a wide receptivity to improvements in techniques.

A typical illustration of the importance of receptivity as distinguished from just the generation of new products is offered by the sewing machine, which in a primitive but effective form was invented by a Frenchman, Thimonnier, sixteen years before Elias Howe constructed his machine in the United States. It was actually used to mass produce uniforms for the French Army (an earlier example of government support for innovation), but the Parisian tailors formed mobs, smashed the machines, and forced Thimonnier to flee to Paris. The labor-short U.S. economy could not afford the luxury of forgoing an important labor-saving device.

Resistance to technological improvement is not absent today on either side of the Atlantic, but presumably it is not carried to the lengths of the Parisian tailors. So long as labor costs are highest in the United States, however, and are expected to rise further, the incentive to devise new labor saving techniques will be strongest there. As wages rise in Europe and elsewhere around the world, businessmen there will be passing through a range of experience already passed in the United States, and the possibility of borrowing labor-saving techniques rather than having to generate them will be much greater.

On both counts, high per capita incomes and high

and growing wage rates, innovation is therefore likely to be somewhat stronger in the United States until incomes elsewhere and labor costs rise to the U.S. level, a day that, at least for Europe, is still some distance off, but is at least within sight.

The choice of technology available to less developed countries will be even wider and it is at present a matter of considerable debate whether they should in general adopt techniques now obsolete in the major industrial nations but which are appropriate to the availability and cost of labor in those countries, or whether they should adopt the latest, most up-to-date techniques even though they are labor-saving.

The Stream of Innovations

Technological innovation can undoubtedly strengthen the competitive position of a country in which the innovation takes place, whether it be one which enlarges exports or displaces imports. However, technological advantage in any one product is transitory. Once a breakthrough has been made, the new information is typically spread widely. Underlying cost considerations will untimately govern where it will be produced and where it will be used.

For the impact on trade, we must look not to the individual product (because of obsolescence it may not even be marketable long enough for basic cost considerations to come into play) but to the stream of new products and processes, each one often replacing previous ones.

The advantage which accrues to a country's trading position depends both on the intensity of the stream of innovations and on the rate at which new knowledge is put into use elsewhere, where the basic cost advantages lie.

Intensity of the stream is partly accidental, the product of individual and uncoordinated inventive effort, but it is increasingly the product of systematic and coordinated application of talent and resources to discovery.

What we may call the research and development industry, programmed expenditures for the development of new techniques and new products, absorbed in the United States only two-tenths of 1 percent of GNP in the early 1920s, but has grown to 2.8 percent of GNP in 1960 and must be 3 percent today. Even excluding government financed research and development, the expenditure grew sharply from the 20s to over 1 percent of GNP for commercially financed R and D today.

Business incentive to develop new products is strong as the public with steadily increasing incomes gets sated with the traditional necessities of life. Other countries have experienced a similarly rapid growth of programmed R and D expenditures over the same period.

Is Spill-Over a Significant Source of Innovation?

Not all of these expenditures contribute to the stream of commercially relevant innovations. Much R and D expenditure, especially in France, Britain, and the United States, is financed by the central government in pursuit of national defense. There is a lively debate about how important is the so-called spill-over from this military research. There are a few examples where military R and D has had clear commercial application, such as the jet engine. In other cases, military R and D has pioneered a field and led to further development work aimed at the civilian market. This was to some extent true of computers which started on government contract.

But students of these spill-overs in the United States find them to be surprisingly small. They are difficult to quantify but it is noteworthy that in the mid-fifties only 4 percent of all patent applications arose from defense contracts, even though the Defense Department financed roughly half of the total U.S. R and D. Furthermore, commercial utilization of private patents arising from government-financed R and D is only 13 percent, compared with around 60 percent for patents arising from private development work. One aerospace firm reported that out of 400 patent applications accumulated by the end of the 1950s, only three had commercial application.

Indeed, there is some concern in this country that very large government R and D programs may actually reduce the stream of commercial innovations by drawing away critical scientific and engineering talent into military and now space work to a greater extent than the pool of such skills is augmented by the attractions of these programs. Fewer men are available for commercial research and development.

Finally, even when there are spill-overs, much commercial R and D is often required to adapt them to the commercial requirements. It has often been firms other than those doing the military work which have made the products commercially successful. As noted above, export success, at least within some industries, seems much more closely related to privately financed research and development expenditures than to total research and development expenditures.

International Diffusion of Technology

The intensity of the stream of innovation is only one factor governing the trade advantage a country gains from technological change. The second important factor is the rate at which new knowledge is diffused abroad. Unless the innovating country enjoys a basic cost advantage in producing the new product, its trade position is enhanced only to the extent that there is a lag in time between its production of the product and new production in other, lower cost locations.

While the evidence we have is only fragmentary, it does not seem as though the international diffusion of new techniques of production or of new products is much more rapid today than it has ever been in the past.

The point is illustrated by the quip of a few years ago which went, "In January, an American invents a new product; in February, Tass announces that a Russian had invented this product thirty years ago; and by March, Japan is exporting the product to the United States."

In times past, great efforts were taken to prevent the diffusion of technological knowledge to preserve monopoly for those with the specialized knowledge. The secret of Tyrian purple was so tightly kept by the Phoenicians that it was lost in the course of time. England, seat of the industrial revolution, was much aware of the advantage it gained by the new machinery and took stringent measures in the eighteenth and early nineteenth centuries to prevent the export of machinery, especially of textile machinery. The export prohibitions on capital goods were not finally removed until 1843.

France has similar restrictions. Many Germans were worried about the export of capital goods right up to the eve of World War I out of fear that it would undercut their markets.

Knowledge can be transmitted through emigration as well as through the export of capital goods. The first spinning mill in the United States was set up by an Englishman, William Slater, in 1790, who had to memorize the machine design before he emigrated. Britain was very much aware of this possibility and imposed heavy fines on skilled English workmen who went abroad. Those who were abroad for more than six months, despite notification from the British Embassy to return, lost their British citizenship and all their property was confiscated.

This kind of impediment to the movement of knowledge was largely swept away by the free trade sentiment of the nineteenth century, and today such restrictions are generally limited to goods of military application. Even without such deliberate impediments to diffusion of technical improvements, diffusion has been slow, but it has been accelerating. The evidence we have is largely anecdotal, but as an illustration consider the typewriter, which was invented in the United States in 1868 and by the mid-eighties had quite a large market in this country. It first appears as a separate entry in U.S. export statistics in 1897 with exports amounting to $1.4 million. A report of 1908, eleven years later, indicates that American typewriting machines had only German competitors in Europe. Actually by that time there were also two British firms with exports of $90,000, a negligible amount compared with U.S. exports of $6-1/2 million. Broadly speaking, it took twenty years from the time of heavy marketing in the U.S. to the time of modest exports by the few leading competitors, Britain and Germany.

Compare this with more recent developments. Within a year of the introduction of stainless steel razor blades by Wilkinson Sword, a British firm, several American firms had competing blades on the market. This was a defensive response and it was rapid. The inauguration of new techniques has only been slightly less spectacular in other areas. Float glass was produced in the United States only four years after the pioneering production began in England. Many computers have been produced in Europe within a relatively few years after they were first marketed in the United States.

Even where international trade is not directly involved, new technology moves quickly. For instance, U.S. firms introduced much more efficient methods for generating electricity from coal in 1949. By 1956, seven years later, all new French generating capacity incorporated the new technology and a substantial part of new British capacity did.

We have other indications of the rapid diffusion of technical knowledge. One is the so-called international patent crisis, where the number of cross-filings has increased to such an extent that most national patent offices are in heavy arrears in their work. A second is the great expansion of patent licensing across national frontiers. The United States alone earned more than $1 billion from foreigners last year in royalties, license fees, and management fees—exports of knowledge, disembodied from exports of goods and even, in many cases, from exports of capital.

Finally, there has been a large and growing amount of direct foreign investment abroad—the creation of the multinational firm. Such investment tends to diffuse technical knowledge and management skills as well as, or even perhaps more than, capital.

Leads or Lags?

I will close by venturing some speculation on these trends. In the first place, they offer some partial explanation for the baffling conjunction of two arguments, one on the eastern side of the Atlantic, that the so-called technological lead of the United States is increasing, and the other on this side of the Atlantic, and with some vigor only a few years ago, that the U.S. competitive position in world markets is being weakened because of a diminution in technological lead. In fact, both arguments probably represent unwarranted generalizations from particular examples and, of course, both tendencies can be observed simultaneously by looking at different industries.

A more sophisticated reconciliation would refer to the two basic dimensions that I have just been discussing. The intensity of the stream of innovations from the United States may have increased—we still await evidence on whether that is acutally so—but at the same time, the rate of diffusion of this knowledge to other countries has also increased. From the viewpoint of competitiveness in international trade, it is the product of these two factors which is important, neither one alone.

Speculating on the Future Basis of Trade

The very rapid diffusion of new technological knowledge along with the great accumulation of capital which is taking place in most countries suggests a deeper irony. It is that most large countries will become more alike over the course of time in their structure of production and levels of income, and they can become economically more self-sufficient. The basis for trade among them will be undercut. There is already some evidence that most Western countries do look more alike in the structure of their production, particularly in manufacturing production, than they did in the past.

Trade has certainly not diminished among these countries, even relative to output, but even while technological change throws up new products for trade, rapid diffusion of this knowledge reduces the underlying basis for trade.

One can even speculate—idly, for most of us—that in the course of time there will be a swingback in relative importance to the traditional trade with which we started out—trade in food and raw materials, whose production costs are rooted in climate and natural endowments—while advances in technology and rapid dissemination of new knowledge permit many countries or small groups of countries to produce their own requirements of the other commodities or services.

Perhaps this is one of those historical reversals to which Professor McLuhan has referred, like the complete cycle from a tailor-made service economy through mass production and back again.

42

The Multinational Firm and Imperialism

PAUL A. BARAN

Paul A. Baran was Professor of Economics at Stanford University. This article comes from his book, The Political Economy of Growth, *published in 1957.*

The principal impact of foreign enterprise on the development of the underdeveloped countries lies in hardening and strengthening the sway of merchant capitalism, in slowing down and indeed preventing its transformation into industrial capitalism.

This is the really important "indirect influence" of foreign enterprise on the evolution of the underdeveloped countries. It flows through a multitude of channels, permeates all of their economic, social, political, and cultural life, and decisively determines its entire course. There is first of all the emergence of a group of merchants expanding and thriving within the orbit of foreign capital. Whether they act as wholesalers—assembling, sorting, and standardizing commodities that they purchase from small producers and sell to representatives of foreign concerns—or as suppliers of local materials to foreign enterprises, or as caterers to various other needs of foreign firms and their staffs, many of them manage to assemble vast fortunes and to move up to the very top of the underdeveloped countries' capitalist class. Deriving their profits from the operations of foreign business, vitally interested in its expansion and prosperity, this comprador element of the native bourgeoisie uses its considerable influence to fortify and to perpetuate the *status quo.*

There are secondly the native industrial monopolists, in most cases interlocked and interwoven with domestic merchant capital and with foreign enterprise, who entirely depend on the maintenance of the existing economic structure, and whose monopolistic status would be swept away by the rise of industrial capitalism. Concerned with preventing the emergence of competitors in their markets, they look with favor upon absorption of capital in the sphere of circulation, and have nothing to fear from foreign export-oriented enterprise. They too are stalwart defenders of the established order.

The interests of these two groups run entirely parallel with those of the feudal landowners powerfully entrenched in the societies of the backward areas. Indeed, these have no reason for complaints about the activities of foreign enterprise in their countries. In fact, these activities yield them considerable profits. Frequently they provide outlets for the produce of landed estates, in many places they raise the value of

232

land, often they offer lucrative employment opportunities to members of the landed gentry.

What results is a political and social coalition of wealthy compradors, powerful monopolists, and large landowners dedicated to the defense of the existing feudal-mercantile order. Ruling the realm by no matter what political means—as a monarchy, as a military-fascist dictatorship, or as a republic of the Kuomintang variety—this coalition has nothing to hope for from the rise of industrial capitalism which would dislodge it from its positions of privilege and power. Blocking all economic and social progress in its country, this regime has no real political basis in city or village, lives in continual fear of the starving and restive popular masses, and relies for its stability on Praetorian guards of relatively well kept mercenaries.

In most underdeveloped countries social and political developments of the last few decades would have toppled regimes of that sort. That they have been able to stay in business—for business is, indeed their sole concern—in most of Latin America and in the Near East, in several "free" countries of Southeast Asia and in some similarly "free" countries of Europe, is due mainly if not exclusively to the aid and support that was given to them "freely" by Western Capital and by Western governments acting on its behalf. For the maintenance of these regimes and the operations of foreign enterprise in the underdeveloped countries have become mutually interdependent. It is the economic strangulation of the colonial and dependent countries by the imperialist powers that stymied the development of indigenous industrial capitalism, thus preventing the overthrow of the feudal-mercantile order and assuring the rule of the comprador administrations. It is the preservation of these subservient governments, stifling economic and social development and suppressing all popular movements for social and national liberation, that makes possible at the present time the continued foreign exploitation of underdeveloped countries and their domination by the imperialist powers.

Foreign capital and the governments by which it is represented have steadily kept their part of the bargain to this very day. Although official opinion at the present time, while admitting that "colonial powers added the weight of government proscription and discouragement to the economic forces handicapping industrial expansion in raw materials producing areas," feels strongly that "those days . . . are gone forever," unhappily nothing could be a more egregious misreading of current history. Whether we look at the British proceedings in Kenya, in Malaya, or in the West Indies, at French operations in Indo-China and North Africa, at the United States' activities in Guatemala and the Philippines, or whether we consider the somewhat "subtler" United States transactions in Latin America and the Far East and the still more complex Anglo-American machinations in the Near East, very little of the *essence* of the imperialism "of those days" can be said to have "gone forever."

To be sure, neither imperialism itself nor its *modus operandi* and ideological trimmings are today what they were fifty or a hundred years ago. Just as outright looting of the outside world has yielded to organized trade with the underdeveloped countries, in which plunder has been rationalized and routinized by a mechanism of impeccably "correct" contractual relations, so has the rationality of smoothly functioning commerce grown into the modern, still more advanced, still more rational system of imperialist exploitation. Like all other historically changing phenomena, the contemporary form of imperialism contains and preserves all its earlier modalities, but raises them to a new level. Its central feature is that it is now directed not solely towards the rapid extraction of large sporadic gains from the objects of its domination, it is no longer content with merely assuring a more or less steady flow of those gains over a somewhat extended period. Propelled by well-organized, rationally conducted monopolistic enterprise, it seeks today to rationalize the flow of these receipts so as to be able to count on it in perpetuity. And this points to the main task of imperialism in our time: to prevent, or, if that is impossible, to slow down and to control the economic development of underdeveloped countries.

That such development is profoundly inimical to the interests of foreign corporations producing raw materials for export can be readily seen. There is of course the mortal threat of nationalization of raw materials producing enterprises that is associated with the ascent to power of governments in backward countries that are determined to move their nations off dead center; but, even in the absence of nationalization, economic development in the source countries bodes nothing but evil to Western capital. For whichever aspect of economic development we may consider, it is manifestly detrimental to the prosperity of the raw materials producing corporations. As under conditions of economic growth employment opportunities and productivity expand in other parts of the economy, and the class consciousness and bargaining power of labor increase, wages tend to rise in the raw materials producing sector. While in some lines of output—on plantations primarily—those increased costs can be offset by the adoption of improved techniques, such mechanization involves capital outlays that are obviously repugnant to the corporations involved. And in mining and petroleum operations even this solution is hardly possible. These in general employ the same methods of production that are in use in the advanced countries, so that the technological gap that could be filled is accordingly very small. With the prices of their products in the world markets representing a fixed datum to the individual companies—at least in the short run—increased labor costs combined with various fringe benefits resulting from growing unionization, as well as rising costs of other local supplies, must lead necessarily to a reduction of profits. If thus the longer-run effects of economic development cannot but be damaging to the raw materials exporting corporations, the immediate concomitants of economic development are apt to be even more disturbing. They will be, as a rule, higher taxes and royalties imposed on the foreign enterprises by the local government seeking revenue to finance its developmental ventures, foreign exchange controls designed to curtail the removal of profits abroad,

tariffs rendering the importation of foreign-made equipment more expensive or raising the prices of imported wage goods, and others—all inevitably interfering with the freedom of action of foreign enterprise and encroaching upon its profitability.

Small wonder that under such circumstances Western big business heavily engaged in raw materials exploitation leaves no stone unturned to obstruct the evolution of social and political conditions in underdeveloped countries that might be conducive to their economic development. It uses its tremendous power to prop up the backward areas, comprador administrations, to disrupt and corrupt the social and political movements that oppose them, and to overthrow whatever progressive governments may rise to power and refuse to do the bidding of their imperialist overlords. Where and when its own impressive resources do not suffice to keep matters under control, or where and when the costs of the operations involved can be shifted to their home countries' national governments—or nowadays to international agencies such as the International Bank for Reconstruction and Development—the diplomatic, financial and, if need be, military facilities of the imperialist power are rapidly and efficiently mobilized to help private enterprise in distress to do the required job.

43

International Technology Transfer

EDWIN MANSFIELD

Edwin Mansfield is Professor of Economics at the University of Pennsylvania. This article is taken from his testimony before the Senate Subcommittee on International Finance in 1978.

In recent years, there has been a very considerable increase in the amount of attention devoted by international trade theorists to technology and technological change. Technology is coming to play a much more significant role in explanations of the pattern of world trade, as evidenced by the work of Johnson, Vernon, Hufbauer, and others. Unfortunately, however, economists have only recently begun to study international technology transfer in a serious way, and far more research is needed.

According to a recent state-of-the-art summary prepared by Piekarz, "we know that U.S. industries spending relatively high amounts on R and D are the leading industries in manufactured exports, foreign direct investment, and licensing. The limited extant research at the level of the firm has not established a relationship between research intensiveness and the share of exports in domestic sales, the ratio of foreign to domestic production, or the share of earnings from foreign licensing. We lack information about the impact of the type or recency of innovations on exports foreign direct investment, and licensing. Also, we do not know the influence of exports, foreign direct investment, and licensing on the rate or direction of R and D and technological innovation by U.S. firms . . . We know that U.S. foreign direct investment and licensing are channels by which foreign countries obtain technological knowledge. We do not know the mechanics, magnitude, or rate at which this technology diffuses abroad. Also, there is no information about the complementarity and substitutability among exports, foreign direct investment, and licensing as channels for technology transfer."

One of the most important gaps in existing knowledge in this area relates to the effects of foreign trade on domestic innovation. In a recent paper, Stobaugh makes this point in the following terms: "Although research on this general subject of the effect of technological innovation on trade, investment, and licensing is in its infancy and deserves support, a more important relationship is the opposite causal flow: what effects do trade, foreign direct investment, and licensing have on technological innovation? A plausible hypothesis is that the possibility of a firm's exporting, making foreign investments, or selling licenses would induce it to engage in certain R and D

235

programs that would not be economical if the U.S. market were the only one considered; thus, U.S. technological innovation would be increased and in turn U.S. economic growth would increase. In spite of the importance of this question, there seems to be a complete void in our knowledge, for I know of no empirical data either to support or deny this hypothesis."

Another important gap in existing knowledge relates to the extent to which U.S. firms use various channels to transfer their technology abroad. There are several ways that a firm can transfer and exploit its technology abroad. First, it can utilize the new technology in *foreign subsidiaries*. For example, if the new technology relates to a new product or product improvement, this new product or product improvement may be made and sold by the firm's foreign subsidiaries. Second, the firm can *export* goods and services that are based on the new technology. For example, if the new technology relates to a new product or product improvement, this new or improved product may be exported. Third, the firm can *license* the new technology to other firms, government agencies, or other organizations that utilize it abroad. Fourth, the firm can engage in *joint ventures* with other organizations, which have as an objective the utilization of the new technology abroad. As Caves, Hufbauer, Stobaugh, and others have stressed, we know little about the relative importance of each of these channels for various types of technology and for various types of firms.

Still another important gap in existing knowledge relates to the overseas R and D activities of U.S.-based firms. When our present studies were begun, the only reasonably comprehensive data concerning the size of overseas R and D expenditures were the Commerce Department's data for 1966. Since then, the Conference Board has published statistics concerning the size of such expenditures in 1971–72. However, little or no information exists concerning more recent years or concerning expected changes in the near future. Also, we know relatively little concerning the reasons why firms carry out R and D overseas, the nature of the work carried out, and the value of this work to firms' domestic operations. Further, we know practically nothing about the minimum efficient scale for an overseas R and D laboratory in various industries, and we have relatively little comprehensive or systematic data concerning changes over time in the relative costs of performing R and D of various sorts in the United States, compared with performing them overseas.

These topics have a bearing both on policy issues and on economic analysis in this area; yet they have been the subject of little or no economic research.

Returns from New Technology Exploited Abroad

As emphasized in the previous section, very little is known concerning the percentage of the total returns from U.S. firms' R and D projects that are expected to stem from foreign sales or foreign utilization. To help fill this gap, we obtained 1974 data on this score from a sample of 30 firms. This sample was composed of two parts, the first containing 20 firms in the fabricated metal products, machinery, instruments, chemical, textile, paper, and tire industries, the second containing 10 major chemical firms. The first subsample was chosen more or less at random from major manufacturing firms in southern New England and the Middle Atlantic states. The second subsample was chosen more or less at random from major chemical firms located in the East. The firms in both subsamples tended to be rather large, and are quite representative of all large firms in their industries with regard to the percent of sales devoted to research and development. In general, the data were obtained from senior R and D executives and from officials involved with the firms' international operations.

If all kinds of R and D projects in all firms are lumped together, how important, on the average, do foreign markets or foreign utilization bulk in the expected returns from these firms' R and D projects in 1974? Although the two subsamples are entirely independent, they provide very similar answers to this question. In the chemical subsample, about 29 percent of an R and D project's returns, on the average, were expected to come from foreign sales or utilization. In the 20-firm subsample, about 34 percent of an R and D project's returns, on the average, were expected to come from these sources. Of course, averages of this sort must be viewed with caution, because they conceal a great deal of variation and are influenced by the industrial (and other) characteristics of the sample. But they provide a reasonable starting point for the analysis.

In recent years, considerable controversy has raged over the effects of direct investment abroad (and other channels of international technology transfer) on America's technological position. According to some observers, such investment may result in a reduction in our technological lead, since U.S. technology may be transferred from our foreign subsidiaries to our foreign competitors. However, a point that is often ignored is that, if U.S. firms could not utilize foreign subsidiaries (or transfer technology abroad in other ways), they might not carry out as much research and development, with the result that our technological position might be weakened. Some economists, like Caves and Stobaugh, have recognized this point, but have cited the unfortunate fact that nothing is really known about the amount by which U.S. R and D expenditures would decline if U.S. firms could not transfer their technology to their foreign subsidiaries, or use other channels of international technology transfer. As a modest first step toward closing this gap, we asked the 30 firms in our sample to estimate how much their R and D expenditures would have changed in 1974 under two sets of circumstances: (1) that they could not utilize any new technology abroad in foreign subsidiaries, (2) that they could not utilize any new technology abroad in foreign subsidiaries, or by licensing the technology abroad, or by exporting new products or processes based on the technology, or by any other means. Although answers to hypothetical questions of this sort must be treated with a great deal of caution, the results should be of interest. Moreover, as we shall see, a comparison of these results with some earlier econometric findings suggests that, if anything, these results may be on the conservative side.

According to the firms' estimates, their R and D expenditures would have fallen significantly under each of the above sets of circumstances. Specifically, for the 20-firm subsample, the estimated reduction would have been about 15 percent if they could not utilize any new technology in foreign subsidiaries, and about 26 percent if they could not transfer any new technology abroad by any means. For the 10-firm chemical subsample, the estimated reduction in 1974 would have been about 12 percent if they could not utilize any new technology in foreign subsidiaries and about 16 percent if they could not transfer any new technology abroad by any means. Thus, the results obtained from the two (quite independent) subsamples are reasonably close. Further, one can compare these results with what would be expected from an econometric model published a number of years ago. This model, which was based on data for chemical and petroleum firms, indicates that a 30 percent reduction in the expected returns from these firms' R and D projects would result in a larger percentage reduction

in their R and D expenditures than indicated above. Thus, since the firms in our sample estimate that about 30 percent of the expected returns from their R and D projects stem from some form of international technology transfer, it appears that, if anything, the above estimates may be on the conservative side.

Channels of International Technology Transfer

While the previous section of this paper indicated that many industrial R and D projects are carried out with the expectation that a considerable portion of their returns will come from abroad, no attention has been focused as yet on the channels (foreign subsidiaries, exports, licensing, joint ventures) by which these firms intend to effect these international transfers of technology. As many researchers have pointed out, very little is known about the extent to which firms of various sorts use each of these channels. For our sample of 30 firms, the percent of all R and D projects (for which foreign returns were estimated to be of substantial importance) where the principal channel (in the first five years after the commercialization of the new technology) was anticipated to be of each type was as follows: foreign subsidiaries, 73 percent; exports, 15 percent; licensing, 9 percent; joint ventures, 3 percent. Thus, the results, which are much the same in the two subsamples, indicate that foreign subsidiaries are expected to be the most frequently-used channel, exports and licensing coming next, followed by joint ventures.

The great preponderance of cases where foreign subsidiaries are regarded as the principal channel during the first five years after commercialization is noteworthy, because, according to the traditional view, the first channel of international technology transfer often is exports. Only after the overseas market has been supplied for some time by exports would the new technology be transferred overseas via foreign subsidiaries, according to this view. To some extent, our results may reflect an increased tendency for new technology to be transferred directly to overseas subsidiaries, or a tendency for it to be transmitted more quickly to them (in part because more such subsidiaries already exist). Such tendencies have been observed in the pharmaceutical industry, where many new drugs developed by U.S. firms have been introduced first by their subsidiaries in the United Kingdom and elsewhere. Also, Baranson's study concludes that

American firms in a variety of industries are more willing than in the past to send their most recently developed technology overseas.

Changes over time would be expected in the principal channel by which a new technology is transferred abroad. In particular, as the technology grows older, there may be a tendency for exports to become a less important channel, since, as noted above, the innovator may supply foreign markets to a greater extent through foreign subsidiaries. Also, licensing may become more important because, as the technology becomes more widely known, foreign countries can take advantage of competition among technologically capable firms to obtain licenses, rather than accept wholly-owned subsidiaries. To see whether such tendencies exist in our sample, we obtained data of the sort described earlier in this section concerning the second, rather than the first, five years after commercialization of the new technology. In accord with these hypotheses. the results suggest that licensing is more important, and exports are less important, in the second five years than in the first.

Overseas R and D: Extent and Nature of Expenditures

It is well known that the overseas research and development activities of U.S.-based firms have become the focus of controversy. Some observers view such activities with suspicion, since they regard them as a device to "export" R and D jobs, or as a channel through which American technology may seep out of actual or potential competitors. Others, particularly the governments of many developing (and some developed) countries, view them as highly desirable activities that will help to stimulate indigenous R and D in these countries. Indeed, the United Nations Group of Eminent Persons recommended that host countries require multinational corporations to contribute toward innovation of appropriate kinds, and to encourage them to do such R and D in their overseas affiliates. Although the amount of controversy in this area might lead one to believe that the overseas R and D activities of U.S.-based firms have been studied quite thoroughly, this is far from the case. As pointed out above, the unfortunate truth is that economists have devoted little or no attention to even the most basic questions concerning these activities.

As a first step toward studying these questions, we constructed a sample of 55 major manufacturing firms, this sample being divided into two parts. The first subsample, composed of 35 firms, was chosen from Fortune's 500. The second subsample composed of 20 firms, was chosen from among major manufacturing firms in the southern New England and the Middle Atlantic states. Strictly speaking, neither subsample was randomly chosen, since some firms that were asked to cooperate refused to do so. Moreover, each of the subsamples concentrated heavily on a relatively few industries—chemicals, petroleum, electrical equipment, and metals and machinery in the first subsample; chemicals, fabricated metal products, and instruments in the second subsample. However, a comparison of the sample with the benchmark figures provided by the Commerce Department for 1966 and by the Conference Board for 1971–72 indicates that the sample is reasonably representative of all U.S. manufacturing with regard to the average percent of R and D expenditures carried out overseas.

Based on data obtained from each of these firms, it appears that about 10 percent of their total company-financed R and D expenditures were carried out overseas in 1974. During the 1960s and early 1970s, this percentage grew substantially; and they estimate that this growth will continue, but at a reduced rate, during the rest of the 1970s. By 1980, they estimate that about 12 percent of their R and D expenditures will be made overseas. Because of the importance in the innovation process of close cooperation and communication among R and D, marketing, production, and top management, location theorists like Vernon have argued that a firm's R and D activities will tend to be centralized near its headquarters. Why then do these U.S.-based firms spend over 10 percent of their R and D dollars overseas? There are a variety of possible reasons, such as the presence of environmental conditions abroad that cannot easily be matched at home, the desirability of doing R and D aimed at the special design needs of overseas markets, the availability and lower cost of skills and talents that are less readily available or more expensive at home, and the greater opportunity to monitor what is going on in relevant scientific and technical fields abroad. In our sample, practically all of the firms that do any R and D overseas said that the principal reason is to respond to the special design needs of overseas markets. In their view, there are great advantages in doing R and D of this sort in close contact with the relevant overseas markets and manufacturing units of the firm.

Based on information obtained from the firms in our

sample, the R and D they do overseas tends to be predominantly development rather than research, and aimed at product and process improvements rather than at new products or processes. Further, this emphasis on development projects aimed at rather minor changes seems to be more pronounced in their overseas than in their domestic R and D, which in part reflects the fact that much overseas R and D has as its primary purpose the modification of U.S. products and processes to suit foreign markets and conditions. Firms seem to differ considerably in the extent to which they have integrated their overseas R and D with their domestic R and D. Some firms, such as IBM, seem to have integrated their R and D activities on a world-wide basis. (Thus, IBM, when it developed the 360 series, gave each laboratory, whether at home or abroad, a specific mission. For example, the smaller machine came from Germany and the medium-sized machine was designed in England.) Such world-wide integration exists in about 45 percent of the firms in our sample that do any overseas R and D, according to the firms. On the other hand, 16 percent say that they attempt no such integration, and the rest say some limited integration is attempted.

Of how much value are overseas R and D to a firm's U.S. operations? Policy makers should be interested in this question because it must be considered in any full evaluation of the effects of overseas R and D (and foreign direct investment) on America's technological position vis-a-vis other countries. As Caves has put it, "To what extent have subsidiaries generated or acquired technologies for transmission back to their American parents . . . ?" Unfortunately, practically no evidence exists on this score. To shed a modest amount of light on this question, we obtained estimates from the firms in our sample concerning the percent of their 1975 overseas R and D expenditures with no commercial applicability to their U.S. operations. Their estimates indicate that, on the average, about one-third of these firms' overseas R and D expenditures have no such applicability. Also, we asked each firm to estimate the amount that it would have to spend on R and D in the United States to get results of equivalent value to its U.S. operations as a dollar spent on R and D overseas. The results indicate that, on the average, a dollar's worth of overseas R and D seems to result in benefits to these firms' domestic operations that are equivalent to about 50 cents of R and D carried out in the United States. Needless to say, these estimates are not precise, and should be viewed only as rough guidelines.

Conclusions

This paper has summarized a variety of empirical findings, many of which have implications for public and/or private policy. In the remaining space, I can indicate only a few of these implications. First, our results do not support the suggestion of some economists that firms base their R and D decisions solely on the basis of expected domestic returns. On the contrary, according to the firms in our sample, about 30 percent of the anticipated returns from their R and D projects, on the average, was expected to come from foreign sources. Based on expected domestic returns alone, these firms estimate that they would spend about 20 percent less on R and D than at present. Of course, these results do not contradict the hypothesis that firms sometimes pay less attention to foreign markets than to those at home. But they do indicate that, although there may be a tendency to emphasize domestic markets, this tendency is not so strong that public policy can assume that decreased opportunities for international technology transfer would have little or no effect on U.S. R and D expenditures. On the contrary, although such measures would not result in enormous cuts in percentage terms, they apparently would prompt a perceptible and significant reduction in R and D expenditure, which would in turn weaken our own technological position.

Second, our results have implications for the current controversies over the channels of international technology transfer. Even in the first five years after the commercialization of the new technology, foreign subsidiaries, rather than exports, licensing, or joint ventures, are expected to be the principal channel for the majority of these firms' projects. In part, this is due to the fact that the firms in our sample tend to be large, and perhaps to the industrial composition of the sample. Without question, it frequently is possible for a firm to substitute one channel of international technology transfer for another. Thus, if foreign subsidiaries could not be used, licensing or exports or joint ventures might be used instead. However, in many cases, these other channels do not seem to be very good substitutes for foreign subsidiaries, in the eyes of the firms. If they could not use foreign subsidiaries as a channel, they estimate that they would reduce their R and D expenditures by about 12–15 percent, on the average. However, whereas it was possible for us to check the estimates in the previous paragraph against the results of an econometric model, this was not possible for these estimates, since no relevant econometric model exists (to our knowledge).

Third, our results provide evidence concerning the importance of overseas R and D expenditures by U.S.-based firms. When compared with the total R and D expenditures in various host countries, their size is particularly striking. In the early 1970s, about one-half of the industrial R and D performed in Canada and about one-seventh of the industrial R and D performed in the United Kingdom and West Germany was done by U.S.-based firms.

Fourth, the firms in our sample estimate that, on the average, each dollar of overseas R and D is of as much value to their U.S. operations as about 50 cents of domestic R and D. This result, although very crude, is of some relevance to the debate over the effects of direct foreign investment by U.S.-based firms on the U.S. technological position vis-a-vis other countries. As our ecomometric results show, there is a very close relationship between the extent of a firm's foreign subsidiaries and the extent of its overseas R and D. To the extent that some overseas R and D is carried out only because of prior foreign investment, such benefits may represent a positive effect of direct foreign investment on the U.S. technological position.

Fifth, the rate of technological change in various industries and firms depends on the amount and efficiency of their overseas R and D expenditures, as well as their R and D expenditures in the United States. Unfortunately, this fact is not recognized in any of the econometric studies carried out to estimate the effects of R and D on U.S. productivity growth. All of these studies confine their attention to R and D expenditures carried out in the United States, in part because this is all that has been included in the official R and D statistics. For well-known reasons, this may lead to biased results, particularly in more recent years when overseas R and D expenditures have been relatively large.

44

The New Protectionism

WALTER ADAMS

Walter Adams is Distinguished University Professor and former President of Michigan State University. This article first appeared in Challenge *in 1973.*

"The lessons of history," said Franklin D. Roosevelt in 1935, "show conclusively . . . that continued dependence on relief induces a spiritual and moral disintegration fundamentally destructive to the national fiber. To dole out relief . . . is to administer a narcotic, a subtle destroyer of the human spirit." Society, Roosevelt argued, has an obligation to care for its citizens who cannot care for themselves. For others the overriding aim should be to provide an opportunity to work, not an opportunity to avoid it. The goal must be rehabilitation rather than relief.

President Nixon would heartily endorse this view. This is the Protestant work ethic—an indelible part of Americana. It is the criterion we use to judge welfare programs for the poor, the disadvantaged, the underprivileged. Curiously enough, it is *not* the standard employed in evaluating welfare programs for the rich, the powerful, the vested interests of corporate America. Thus we bail out Lockheed. We rescue the Penn-Central. We subsidize the oil moguls. We protect the lethargic, somnolent steel oligopoly from foreign competition. Welfare programs, it would seem, are not instituted evenhandedly.

The Burke-Hartke Bill

The issue of corporate welfarism will once again be joined when the Burke-Hartke bill reaches the floor of Congress.[1] In addition to regulating multinational corporations, the bill would impose mandatory import quotas on a wide range of manufactured products whenever an American industry or its workers could claim to be suffering from "undue" foreign competition. The bill, which some consider the most restrictive trade legislation since the Embargo Act of 1807, represents a high watermark of the new protectionism—what *Barron's* calls "the protection racket." It is aggressively backed, not only by politically influential big business industries but also by George Meany and his AFL-CIO.

What has given the Burke-Hartke initiative additional impetus, of course, is the recent deterioration in the U.S. trade balance and the embattled state of the U.S. dollar. By 1971, merchandise imports exceeded

[1]As of October 1, 1973, the Burke-Hartke bill was pending in the House Ways and Means Committee.

241

exports by $2.7 billion—the first officially reported trade deficit since 1893. This alarming trend, said the Administration, would be counteracted by the Smithsonian accord (hailed by Mr. Nixon as "the greatest monetary agreement in history") and the devaluation of the dollar. Making the dollar cheaper, it was said, would stimulate exports and discourage imports, thus correcting or reversing the trade deficit. But nothing of the sort happened. By the end of 1972, the U.S. trade balance had worsened—running at an annual rate of $7 billion—necessitating yet another devaluation of the dollar in February of this year. Obviously, a quite different kind of economic medicine was called for.

To the proponents of Burke-Hartke, the answer is clear: if only imports can effectively be curtailed, a trade deficit can easily be turned into a surplus. Imports, they say, are not only a drain of dollars from the United States: they also threaten the profitability and the very existence of major domestic industries. They undermine the jobs and incomes of the workers employed in these import-impacted industries. At stake, says George Meany, "are the American standard of living and America's prospects for remaining an industrial nation with a wide range of industries, products, and employment."

I don't happen to view imports in the same light. In some cases, I think, imports are merely the symptom of the declining competitiveness of an American industry so long corrupted by a permissive oligopolistic environment that it has become lazy, lethargic, inefficient, and technologically backward. And when an industry has led the quiet life for prolonged periods, in control of a lucrative continental-sized market and insulated from competition, it eventually tends to fall prey to the erosion of that market by imports and substitutes while pricing itself out of world markets and triggering a decline in its export trade. Shutting off imports, or curtailing them substantially by quotalike restrictions, does nothing to cure the underlying disease. It only makes the disease more virulent and debilitating, requiring ever-mounting doses of protectionism for survival. Moreover, it has indirect effects on other domestic industries, which have to pay higher prices for the protected products and thus find their export potential artificially diminished. This has the effect of further straining our balance of trade. Finally, and be no means least important, protectionism adds unneeded fuel to the cost-push inflation which seems to have become endemic in the American economy.

Let me illustrate these points with reference to two major industries—steel and oil. These case studies demonstrate why voluntary quotas where now in effect should not be made mandatory, and why mandatory quotas should be repealed rather than imposed on additional industries.

Steel

The U.S. steel industry is a classic, textbook oligopoly. Domestic producers do not compete among themselves in terms of price. It is simply not the custom of the industry. Instead of price competition, they follow a regime of strict price leadership and followership—more often than not in a monotonously upward direction.

Since the end of World War II, the industry's notorious policy of constant price escalation has contributed a prime stimulus to successive inflationary movements. Thus, between 1947 and 1951, according to the Council of Economic Advisers, "the average increase in the price of basic steel products was 9 percent per year, twice the average increase of all wholesale prices. The unique behavior of steel prices was most pronounced in the mid-1950s. While the wholesale price index was falling an average of 0.9 percent annually from 1951 to 1955, the price index for steel was rising an average of 4.8 percent per year. From 1955 to 1958, steel prices were increasing 7.1 percent annually, or almost three times as fast as wholesale prices generally. No other major sector shows a similar record." After a quiescent stage during the early 1960s, characterized by the moral suasion and "jawboning" of the Kennedy Administration, steel prices resumed their upward movement in 1964—on a gradual, selective, product-by-product basis at first, and on a general across-the-board basis in 1969. The imposition of "voluntary" import quotas in January 1969 and the Nixon Administration's refusal to engage in government-industry confrontations simply accelerated the trend.

The one factor which dampened the industry's enthusiasm for marching in lockstep toward constantly higher price levels was the burgeoning of import competition. Thus, between January 1960 and December 1968, a period of nine years, the composite steel price index increased 4.1 points—or 0.45 points per year. Starting in January 1969, however, after the U.S. State Department had successfully persuaded the Europeans and Japanese to accept "voluntary" quotas on their sales to the United States (i.e., to enter into an informal international steel cartel), imports were cut back drastically and the domestic steel prices resumed their pre-1960 climb. In the four years between January 1969 and December 1972, the steel price index rose 26.7 points—or 6.67 points per year. Put differently, steel prices increased at an annual rate fourteen times greater after the import quotas went into effect than in the previous nine years. All this in the face of recession, low volume, and the idleness of roughly 25 percent of the nation's steel capacity.

As if the import quotas—supplemented by "Buy American" regulations and assorted trade barriers—were not enough to insulate the steel industry from competition, President Nixon approved (and later withdrew) a temporary 10 percent surcharge on imports, including steel. In doing so, he perverted the "infant industry" argument for the benefit of lusty steel giants whose rambunctious excesses had wreaked havoc with past attempts at inflation control. With his arsenal of import restraints, he neutralized the perhaps most effective lid on steel pricing and, at the same time, built up additional steam in an already overheated pressure cooker. He also penalized such major steel-consuming industries as automobiles, construction equipment, and agricultural implements, which found it increasingly difficult to absorb the higher prices for an essential raw material while trying to maintain their competitiveness in domestic and foreign markets.

The case study of steel yields some incontrovertible conclusions. Giantism in this industry is the result of massive mergers of the past. The dominant firms are neither big because they are efficient nor efficient because they are big. Their technological lethargy, especially during the 1950s, when they lagged in introducing the basic oxygen process, continuous casting, and direct reduction of steel, put them at a comparative disadvantage in world competition. Their insensitive, extortionate, oligopolistic price policy displaced American steel from world markets and opened the U.S. market to erosion by imports and substitutes. And, finally, the mercantilist protectionism of the federal government compounded the problems of the industry and the nation's economy and gave legitimacy and endurance to a cartel which could not survive without government succor and support.

Oil

The pattern of protectionism in the petroleum industry is both older and more pervasive. Under the antitrust laws, it is an offense for private firms to fix prices or allocate markets, yet in the name of conservation the government does for the oil companies what they could not legally do for themselves. The process is familiar. The Bureau of Mines in the Department of the Interior publishes monthly estimates of the market demand for petroleum, at current prices, of course. Under the Interstate Oil Compact, approved by Congress, these estimates are broken down into quotas for each of the oil-producing states, which, in turn, through various prorationing devices, allocate so-called allowable production to individual wells. Oil produced in violation of these prorationing regulations is branded "hot oil," and the federal government prohibits its shipment in interstate commerce. Also, to buttress this government-sanctioned cartel against potential competition, oil imports by sea are limited by a tariff, in effect since 1943, and by a mandatory import quota, in effect since 1963.[2]

Finally, to top off these indirect subsidies with more visible favors, and to provide the proper "incentives" for an industry crucial to the national defense, the government authorizes oil companies to charge off a 22 percent depletion allowance against their gross income. In all, the industry is receiving special favors variously estimated at from $3.5 to $7 billion annually—this in addition to having a government-sanctioned cartel provide the underpinning for its control of markets and prices.

The artificially high price of petroleum in the United States has an injurious effect not only on the ultimate consumer but also on those American industries which use it as a raw material and must then try to sell their finished products in competitive world markets. Not long ago, for example, Japanese manufacturers were able to buy Iranian heavy crude oil at a price of $1.35 per barrel. That same oil could have been transported to the U.S. East Coast at a delivered price of $2.10 per barrel before payment of tariff. U.S. manufacturers, however, were compelled to buy their crude oil at an East Coast-delivered price of $3.42 per barrel—i.e., at a differential of $1.32 per

[2]This paper was written prior to the cessation of the oil import quota in 1973 and to the Arab oil embargo in late 1973 and 1974.

barrel before the tariff and $1.22 after the tariff. Such a differential obviously could not exist except for the penalities imposed on U.S. manufacturers by the import quota program.

Major American chemical companies—du Pont, Union Carbide, Dow Chemical, and others—have estimated that domestic oil prices on the East Coast average $1.25 per barrel more than elsewhere in the world; this amounts to 3 cents a gallon, or 60 percent above the world price. This quota-protected price differential, they point out, can be critical, if not fatal, in petrochemical production, in which, in many cases, raw material costs account for more than 50 percent of the cost of the basic product. "Furthermore," they say, "U.S. petrochemical products have only a shrinking level of tariff protection in the domestic market. Foreign petrochemicals, on the other hand, need no import quotas for their shipments to the U.S. market and are not restricted in their access to the low-cost oil of the Middle East, Africa, and South America."

Clearly, the continued growth of our petrochemical industry—which contributes about $1.0 billion to our balance of trade—is vitally dependent on access to competitively priced feedstocks. Its competitive posture in world markets depends on the transformation or total elimination of oil import restrictions and other government price-support programs for the domestic oil industry.

Professor Wayne Leeman has well summarized this aspect of the problem: "So the oil we keep out of the United States benefits our most important competitors. Manufacturers in Japan and Western Europe buy energy, industrial heat, and petrochemical feedstocks at prices which give them a competitive advantage over U.S. producers. And they have this competitive advantage partly because import quotas give U.S. firms only limited access to cheap foreign oil and partly because oil shut out of the Unites States depresses the prices they pay.

But what about national security? Is it not vital to protect the domestic oil industry from foreign competition in order to assure ourselves uninterrupted access to petroleum and petroleum products in times of war or emergency? Are not the current restrictions on oil imports imperative to safeguard the national security? Quite the opposite is true.

First, the only safe and low-cost storage for oil is underground. If domestic oil reserves are to be conserved for use in an emergency, therefore, they should be kept intact rather than depleted by artificial stimulation of domestic production.

Second, to the extent that domestic oil reserves are in scarce supply, we should resist the temptation to deplete them in peacetime and maximize our peacetime reliance on foreign sources—especially those which might be beyond our reach in the event of military conflict.

Third, it seems to me that national security could be much better served by R and D support for developing the technology to convert our gargantuan deposits of oil shale into a cost-competitive fuel—rather than by subsidizing excess developmental drilling that uses up supply instead of preserving it.

In short, as a general guideline we should import low-cost foreign oil at a time when we have free access to it, and conserve our own reserves for such times as foreign oil may no longer be available to us. In this, as in other cases, the imperatives of national security and the dictates of rational economic policy would seem to coincide.

One final observation. If, as some argue, the United States is in the midst of an energy crisis, can we seriously defend the honeycomb of import restrictions which artificially curtail supplies and thus become the pretext for maintaining and escalating domestic prices? All the available evidence points in the opposite direction.

The Protection Racket Has No Winners

In summary, import quotas are inimical to the public interest. Quotas undermine the competitive discipline of the marketplace. They encourage price escalation and cost-push inflation. They penalize industries using quota-protected products as raw materials, thereby reducing the cost- and price-competitiveness of those industries in domestic and world markets. Finally, like any scheme of protectionism, quotas have a narcotic effect on the patient they are ostensibly designed to help. A sick industry no longer has to face up to its problems—to reform if it is to survive. Under a quota system, it can luxuriate in inefficiency and backwardness without penalty, knowing that a permissive government will support its catatonic refusal to face up to reality.

In the long run, this is not sound public policy. It condemns the protected industries to the fate of our coddled railroads. It exposes labor to job and income losses as export-related industries find themselves incapable of absorbing the constantly rising cost burden and as direct foreign investment therefore becomes progressively more attractive. Finally, protectionism saddles the nation with an inefficient, noncompetitive industrial structure, a declining posture in world markets, mounting trade deficits, and a currency increasingly vulnerable to successive devaluations.

45

The Current Case for Import Limitations

IRVING KRAVIS

Irving Kravis is Professor of Economics at the University of Pennsylvania. This piece comes from United States International Policy in an Interdependent World, *published in 1971.*

A new wave of sentiment in favor of import limitations has brought forward some new arguments for import limitations and revived some old ones. The fundamental fact remains that every restriction of supply, whether it be applied to supply of domestic or foreign origin, helps the producers of the restricted products but only at the expense of everyone else. Every current claim for protection, no matter what its guise, is a claim for special preference at the general expense. Let us take the main current arguments for import limitations one by one.

U.S. Imports Have Risen More Rapidly than Exports in Recent Years; Our Trade Surplus Is Much Reduced, and May Even Be Eliminated or Turned into a Deficit

It is not at all clear that the U.S. balance of payments should in the long run have a trade surplus or that a trade surplus needs to be an objective of U.S. Government policy, but even if these points are granted they do not establish the case for import restrictions. Import restrictions will bring retaliation that will reduce the level of trade without any predictable effect on the trade balance. Furthermore, even if other countries were to permit the U.S. to improve its trade surplus through import limitation, item-by-item restrictions would provide neither an equitable nor efficient method. Discriminatory tariff increases or quotas favor the domestic producers of some goods over the domestic producers of others. They also require that the Government rather than the market place determine which imports will be reduced.

If the objective is really to improve the trade balance, a uniform ad valorem tariff surcharge and an export subsidy of the same amount would be more equitable and efficient. Other measures that would accomplish the same result include a depreciation of the dollar and the restriction of the U.S. price level to lower rates of increase than foreign price levels.

246

The United States Has, over the Years, Given Many One-Sided Trade Concessions That Have Opened Its Markets to Foreigners While U.S. Exporters Find Themselves under Serious Handicaps in Foreign Markets

The pervasiveness of this view in the U.S. is remarkable in view of the almost absolute lack of evidence to support it. The available evidence does not indicate that U.S. tariff levels are now substantially lower than those of other major industrial countries or that they have been so reduced in recent years as to enhance substantially the price competitiveness of foreign goods in the U.S. market place. Certainly the disappearance of the U.S. trade surplus since 1964 cannot be explained on these grounds. Tariff changes have had on the average small effects on the landed dollar prices of foreign goods and have been accompanied by roughly equal advantages for U.S. exporters. Much has been made of non-tariff barriers, but, if anything, U.S. non-tariff barriers have increased since 1964 relative to foreign non-tariff barriers. Furthermore, the only attempt to estimate the overall level of effective protection inclusive of tariff and non-tariff barriers, made for the U.S. and the U.K., does not show any great difference between the two countries. This is not to deny that non-tariff barriers have been growing in importance, both at home and abroad, relative to tariffs, nor is it to claim that the non-tariff barriers of Japan and the EEC are not more restrictive than those of the U.S. It is to say that claims that foreigners have one-sided access to the U.S. market are at the minimum grossly exaggerated.

Imports Have an Unfavorable Impact on Employment, Particularly Since They Tend to Be Concentrated in Labor-Intensive Products

It is true that international trade enables us to export the goods of 1,000 manhours and receive back goods that would require more than 1,000 manhours to produce. This is our gain from trade. Every internal improvement has the same effect; we get more goods per manhour. The optimum way to full employment does not lie in make-work policies such as excluding labor-intensive imports or forbidding new labor-saving machines. Protection of labor-intensive industries is certainly not in the best interests of U.S. labor in any long run sense; it leads to the preservation of low-wage jobs which would disappear in a free market and be replaced by higher wage jobs. In my home state of Pennsylvania, the textile workers of yesterday were injured when the textile industry moved south but their successors today are better off than they would be if there had been government intervention to keep the textile industry in Pennsylvania; they are working at better paying jobs in new or expanded industries that are competitive and can export different products to the rest of the U.S. and to the world.

Foreign Competition Is Unfair Because It Is Based on Low Wages

The wage advantage that foreign industries enjoy is no more unfair in a relevant economic sense than is the advantage of superior capital resources or of sophisticated technology enjoyed by many U.S. industries. No sound policy can be based on the principle of eradicating all the economic advantages possessed by any contestant in order to run a sports-like competition that gives an equal chance to all entrants. It is precisely by capitalizing upon the special advantages enjoyed by workers and producers everywhere that we can maximize output per unit of input.

The Advent of the Multinational Corporation Has So Changed the Nature of Trade Relations That the Case for Freer Trade Has Been Made Irrelevant

There is no evidence that the multinational corporation is immune from the economic forces that determine which goods can be most cheaply produced in which countries. On the contrary, it seems likely that the multinational corporation provides decision-makers with better information about the most advantageous location of production than was previously available. Components, such as the Ford engine for the Pinto, are produced abroad when they can be made cheaper.

The effects of multinational corporations on the U.S. trade balance are very difficult to estimate, but multinational corporations can hardly be held responsible for import problems in textiles and a number of other areas where the domestic industry has been in difficulty and has sought protection. In most of the areas in which multinational corporations are important, the U.S. has a strong export position.

In any case, the injury to U.S. interests of which multinational corporations are accused by those seeking trade restrictions is not different from others independently claimed as a basis for import limitations nnd already discussed—e.g., a reduced U.S. trade surplus and job displacement.

The National Security of the United States Requires That Some Industries Be Protected

The national security argument is sometimes applied to natural resource products such as petroleum and sometimes to fabricated products such as steel.

In the case of a natural resource product, it has never been satisfactorily explained how a program which encourages the use of domestic reserves rather than the use of the foreign product will assure adequate domestic supplies in case of an emergency. If national security is dependent upon the ready domestic availability of large quantities of petroleum, what is really called for is a program of subsidization for the exploration of petroleum reserves in the United States and a program that would restrict domestic production to the levels necessary to keep a domestic petroleum industry operational and capable of sudden and large expansion in the event of necessity.

In the case of a manufacturing industry, such as the steel industry, it is argued that protection is necessary to maintain skills that would be lost were the industries subject to unrestricted import competition. In fact, the wartime experience of the United States, like that of every other country, including England, Germany, and Japan, demonstrates very clearly that human skills and ingenuity manage very quickly to produce whatever is needed in wartime.

The national security argument is also weakened by the diminished likelihood of a large-scale conventional war of long duration. A major nuclear war would be brief and horrible and its outcome would not be affected by the size of particular domestic industries such as oil or steel. Non-nuclear wars restricted to particular regions are unlikely to leave the U.S. cut off from all foreign sources of supply.

Protection for national security purposes is also counterproductive politically and diplomatically. Further action to limit steel imports, for example, would strengthen the divisive forces affecting our relations with friendly countries.

The national interests of the U.S. lie in the direction of freer trade. The arguments for a contrary policy, it has been shown, are based on incorrect assessments of the facts, draw unwarranted conclusions from true statements of fact, or stress benefits that may be real and important but either incapable of achievement or can be attained only at large economic and political cost.

The costs include the reduction to the stimulus to innovation, less consumer choice, higher prices, lower exports owing to higher costs and to the exclusion of the U.S. from the growing volume of intra-industry trade, and the deterioration of our relations with friendly countries.

Import limitations involve the use of government power to promote special interests at the general expense.

46

The Case for Flexible Exchange Rates

MILTON FRIEDMAN

Milton Friedman is at the Hoover Institution of Stanford University. The following article is taken from his testimony before the Joint Economic Committee in 1963.

Discussions of U.S. policy with respect to international payments tend to be dominated by our immediate balance-of-payments difficulties. I should like to approach the question from a different, and I hope more constructive, direction. Let us begin by asking ourselves not merely how we can get out of our present difficulties but instead how we can fashion our international payments system so that it will best serve our needs for the long pull; how we can solve not merely this balance-of-payments problem but the balance-of-payments problem.

A shocking, and indeed, disgraceful feature of the present situation is the extent to which our frantic search for expedients to stave off balance-of-payments pressures has led us, on the one hand, to sacrifice major national objectives; and, on the other, to give enormous power to officials of foreign governments to affect what should be purely domestic matters. Foreign payments amount to only some 5 percent of our total national income. Yet they have become a major factor in nearly every national policy.

I believe that a system of floating exchange rates would solve the balance-of-payments problem for the United States far more effectively than our present arrangements. Such a system would use the flexibility and efficiency of the free market to harmonize our small foreign trade sector with both the rest of our massive economy and the rest of the world; it would reduce problems of foreign payments to their proper dimensions and remove them as a major consideration in governmental policy about domestic matters and as a major preoccupation in international political negotiations; it would foster our national objectives rather than be an obstacle to their attainment.

To indicate the basis for this conclusion, let us consider the national objective with which our payments system is most directly connected: the promotion of a healthy and balanced growth of world trade, carried on, so far as possible, by private individuals and private enterprises with minimum intervention by governments. This has been a major objective of our whole postwar international economic policy, most recently expressed in the Trade Expansion Act of 1962. Success would knit the free world more closely together, and, by fostering the international division of labor, raise standards of living

249

throughout the world, including the United States.

Suppose that we succeed in negotiating far-reaching reciprocal reductions in tariffs and other trade barriers with the Common Market and other countries. To simplify exposition I shall hereafter refer only to tariffs, letting these stand for the whole range of barriers to trade, including even the so-called voluntary limitation of exports. Such reductions will expand trade in general but clearly will have different effects on different industries. The demand for the products of some will expand, for others contract. This is a phenomenon we are familiar with from our internal development. The capacity of our free enterprise system to adapt quickly and efficiently to such shifts, whether produced by changes in technology or tastes, has been a major source of our economic growth. The only additional element introduced by international trade is the fact that different currencies are involved, and this is where the payment mechanism comes in; its function is to keep this fact from being an additional source of disturbance.

An all-around lowering of tariffs would tend to increase both our expenditures and our receipts in foreign currencies. There is no way of knowing in advance which increase would tend to be the greater and hence no way of knowing whether the initial effect would be toward a surplus or deficit in our balance of payments. What is clear is that we cannot hope to succeed in the objective of expanding world trade unless we can readily adjust to either outcome.

Many people concerned with our payments deficits hope that since we are operating further from full capacity than Europe, we could supply a substantial increase in exports whereas they could not. Implicitly, this assumes that European countries are prepared to see their surplus turned into a deficit, thereby contributing to the reduction of the deficits we have recently been experiencing in our balance of payments. Perhaps this would be the initial effect of tariff changes. But if the achievement of such a result is to be *sine qua non* of tariff agreement, we cannot hope for any significant reduction in barriers. We could be confident that exports would expand more than imports only if the tariff changes were one sided indeed, with our trading partners making much greater reductions in tariffs than we make. Our major means of inducing other countries to reduce tariffs is to offer corresponding reductions in our tariff. More generally, there is little hope of continued and sizable liberalization of trade if liberalization is to be viewed simply as a device for correcting balance-of-payments difficulties. That way lies only backing and filling.

Suppose then that the initial effect is to increase our expenditures on imports more than our receipts from exports. How could we adjust to this outcome?

One method of adjustment is to draw on reserves or borrow from abroad to finance the excess increase in imports. The obvious objection to this method is that it is only a temporary device, and hence can be relied on only when the disturbance is temporary. But that is not the major objection. Even if we had very large reserves or could borrow large amounts from abroad, so that we could continue this expedient for many years, it is a most undesirable one. We can see why if we look at physical rather than financial magnitudes.

The physical counterpart to the financial deficit is a reduction of employment in industries competing with imports that is larger than the concurrent expansion of employment in export industries. So long as the financial deficit continues, the assumed tariff reductions create employment problems. But it is no part of the aim of tariff reductions to create unemployment at home or to promote employment abroad. The aim is a balanced expansion of trade, with exports rising along with imports and thereby providing employment opportunities to offset any reduction in employment resulting from increased imports.

Hence, simply drawing on reserves or borrowing abroad is a most unsatisfactory method of adjustment.

Another method of adjustment is to lower U.S. prices relative to foreign prices, since this would stimulate exports and discourage imports. If foreign countries are accommodating enough to engage in inflation, such a change in relative prices might require merely that the United States keep prices stable or even, that it simply keep them from rising as fast as foreign prices. But there is no necessity for foreign countries to be so accommodating, and we could hardly count on their being so accommodating. The use of this technique therefore involves a willingness to produce a decline in U.S. prices by tight monetary policy or tight fiscal policy or both. Given time, this method of adjustment would work. But in the interim, it would exact a heavy toll. It would be difficult or impossible to force down prices appreciably without producing a recession and considerable unemployment. To eliminate in the long run the unemployment resulting from the tariff changes, we should in the short run be creating cyclical unemployment. The cure might for a time be far worse than the disease.

This second method is therefore also most unsatisfactory. Yet these two methods—drawing on reserves and forcing down prices—are the only two methods available to us under our present international payment arrangements, which involve fixed exchange rates between the U.S. dollar and other currencies. Little wonder that we have so far made such disappointing progress toward the reduction of trade barriers, that our practice has differed so much from our preaching.

There is one other way and only one other way to adjust and that is by allowing (or forcing) the price of the U.S. dollar to fall in terms of other currencies. To a foreigner, U.S. goods can become cheaper in either of two ways—either because their prices in the United States fall in terms of dollars or because the foreigner has to give up fewer units of his own currency to acquire a dollar, which is to say, the price of the dollar falls. For example, suppose a particular U.S. car sells for $2,800 when a dollar costs 7 shillings, tuppence in British money (i.e., roughly £1 = $2.80). The price of the car is then £1,000 in British money. It is all the same to an Englishman—or even a Scots-man—whether the price of the car falls to $2,500 while the price of a dollar remains 7 shillings, tuppence, or, alternatively, the price of the car remains $2,800 while the price of a dollar falls to 6 shillings, 5 pence (i.e., roughly £1 = $3.11). In either case, the car costs the Englishman £900 rather than £1,000, which is what matters to him. Similarly, foreign goods can become more expensive to an American in either of two ways—either because the price in terms of foreign currency rises or because he has to give up more dollars to acquire a given amount of foreign currency.

Changes in exchange rates can therefore alter the relative price of U.S. and foreign goods in precisely the same way as can changes in internal prices in the United States and in foreign countries. And they can do so without requiring anything like the same internal adjustments. If the initial effect of the tariff reductions would be to create a deficit at the former exchange rate (or enlarge an existing deficit or reduce an existing surplus) and thereby increase unemployment, this effect can be entirely avoided by a change in exchange rates which will produce a balanced expansion in imports and exports without interfering with domestic employment, domestic prices, or domestic monetary and fiscal policy. The pig can be roasted without burning down the house.

The situation is, of course, entirely symmetrical if the tariff changes should initially happen to expand our exports more than our imports. Under present circumstances, we would welcome such a result, and conceivably, if the matching deficit were experienced by countries currently running a surplus, they might permit it to occur without seeking to offset it. In that case, they and we would be using the first method of adjustment—changes in reserves or borrowing. But again, if we had started off from an even keel, this would be an undesirable method of adjustment. On our side, we should be sending out useful goods and receiving only foreign currencies in return. On the side of our partners, they would be using up reserves and tolerating the creation of unemployment.

The second method of adjusting to a surplus is to permit or force domestic prices to rise—which is of course what we did in part in the early postwar years when we were running large surpluses. Again, we should be forcing maladjustments on the whole economy to solve a problem arising from a small part of it—the 5 percent accounted for by foreign trade.

Again, these two methods are the only ones available under our present international payments arrangements, and neither is satisfactory.

The final method is to permit or force exchange rates to change—in this case, a rise in the price of the dollar in terms of foreign currencies. This solution is again specifically adapted to the specific problem of the balance of payments.

Changes in exchange rates can be produced in either of two general ways. One way is by a change in an official exchange rate—an official devaluation or appreciation from one fixed level which the Government is committed to support to another fixed level. This is the method used by Britain in its postwar devaluation and by Germany in 1961 when the mark was appreciated. This is also the main method contemplated by the IMF which permits member nations to change their exchange rates by 10 percent without approval by the Fund and by a larger amount after approval by the Fund. But this method has serious disadvantages. It makes a change in rates a matter of major moment, and hence there is a tendency to postpone any change as long as possible. Difficulties cumulate and a larger change is finally needed than would have been required if it could have been made promptly. By the time the change is made, everyone is aware that a change is pending and is certain about the direction of change. The result is to encourage flight from a currency, if it is going to be devalued, or to a currency, if it is going to be appreciated.

There is in any event little basis for determining precisely what the new rate should be. Speculative movements increase the difficulty of judging what the new rate should be, and introduce a systematic bias, making the change needed appear larger than it actually is. The result, particularly when devaluation occurs, is generally to lead officials to "play safe" by making an even larger change than the large change needed. The country is then left after the devaluation with a maladjustment precisely the opposite of that with which it started, and is thereby encouraged to follow policies it cannot sustain in the long run.

Even if all these difficulties could be avoided, this method of changing from one fixed rate to another has the disadvantage that it is necessarily discontinuous. Even if the new exchange rates are precisely correct when first established, they will not long remain correct.

A second and much better way in which changes in exchange rates can be produced is by permitting exchange rates to float, by allowing them to be determined from day to day in the market. This is the method which the United States used from 1862 to 1879, and again, in effect, from 1917 or so to about 1925, and again from 1933 to 1934. It is the method which Britain used from 1918 to 1925 and again from 1931 to 1939, and which Canada used for most of the interwar period and again from 1950 to May 1962. Under this method, exchange rates adjust themselves continuously, and market forces determine the magnitude of each change. There is no need for any official to decide by how much the rate should rise or fall. This is the method of the free market, the method that we adopt unquestioningly in a private enterprise economy for the bulk of goods and services. It is no less available for the price of one money in terms of another.

With a floating exchange rate, it is possible for Governments to intervene and try to affect the rate by buying or selling, as the British exchange equalization fund did rather successfully in the 1930s, or by combining buying and selling with public announcements of intentions, as Canada did so disastrously in early 1962. On the whole, it seems to me undersirable to have government intervene, because there is a strong tendency for government agencies to try to peg the rate rather than to stabilize it, because they have no special advantage over private speculators in stabilizing it, because they can make far bigger mistakes than private speculators risking their own money, and because there is a tendency for them to cover up their mistakes by changing the rules—as the Canadian case so strikingly illustrates—rather than by reversing course. But this is an issue on which there is much difference of opinion among economists who agree in favoring floating rates. Clearly, it is possible to have a successful floating rate along with governmental speculation.

The great objective of tearing down trade barriers, of promoting a worldwide expansion of trade, of giving citizens of all countries, and especially the underdeveloped countries, every opportunity to sell their products in open markets under equal terms and thereby every incentive to use their resources efficiently, of giving countries an alternative through free world trade to autarchy and central planning—this great objective can, I believe, be achieved best under a regime of floating rates. All countries, and not just the United States, can proceed to liberalize boldly and confidently only if they can have reasonable assurance that the resulting trade expansion will be balanced and will not interfere with major domestic objectives. Floating exchange rates, and so far as I can see, only floating exchange rates, provide this assurance. They do so because they are an automatic mechanism for protecting the domestic economy from the possibility that liberalization will produce a serious imbalance in international payments.

Despite their advantages, floating exchange rates have a bad press. Why is this so?

One reason is because a consequence of our present system that I have been citing as a serious disadvantage is often regarded as an advantage, namely, the extent to which the small foreign trade sector dominates national policy. Those who regard this as an advantage refer to it as the discipline of the gold standard. I would have much sympathy for this view if we had a real gold standard, so the discipline was imposed by impersonal forces which in turn reflected the realities of resources, tastes, and technology. But in fact we have today only a pseudo gold standard and the so-called discipline is imposed by governmental officials of other countries who are determining their own internal monetary policies and are either being forced to dance to our tune or calling the tune for us, depending primarily on accidental political developments. This is a discipline we can well do without.

A possibly more important reason why floating exchange rates have a bad press, I believe, is a mistaken interpretation of experience with floating rates, arising out of a statistical fallacy that can be seen easily in a standard example. Arizona is clearly the worst place in the United States for a person with tuberculosis to go because the death rate from tuberculosis is higher in Arizona that in any other State. The fallacy in this case is obvious. It is less obvious in connection with exchange rates. Countries that have gotten into severe financial difficulties, for whatever reason, have had ultimately to change their exchange rates or let them change. No amount of exchange control and other restrictions on trade have enabled them to peg an exchange rate that was far out of line with economic realities. In consequence, floating rates have frequently been associated with financial and economic instability. It is easy to conclude, as many have, that floating exchange rates produce such instability.

This misreading of experience is reinforced by the general prejudice against speculation; which has led to the frequent assertion, typically on the basis of no evidence whatsoever, that speculation in exchange can be expected to be destabilizing and thereby to increase the instability in rates. Few who make this assertion even recognize that it is equivalent to asserting that speculators generally lose money.

Floating exchange rates need not be unstable exchange rates—any more than the prices of automobiles or of Government bonds, of coffee or of meals need gyrate wildly just because they are free to change from day to day. The Canadian exchange rate was free to change during more than a decade, yet it varied within narrow limits. The ultimate objective is a world in which exchange rates, while free to vary, are in fact highly stable because basic economic policies and conditions are stable. Instability of exchange rates is a symptom of instability in the underlying economic structure. Elimination of this symptom by administrative pegging of exchange rates cures none of the underlying difficulties and only makes adjustment to them more painful.

The confusion between stable exchange rates and pegged exchange rates helps to explain the frequent comment that floating exchange rates would introduce an additional element of uncertainty into foreign trade and thereby discourage its expansion. They introduce no additional element of uncertainty. If a floating rate would, for example, decline, then a pegged rate would be subject to pressure that the authorities would have to meet by internal deflation or exchange control in some form. The uncertainty about the rate would simply be replaced by uncertainty about internal prices or about the availability of exchange; and the latter uncertainties, being subject to administrative rather than market control, are likely to be the more erratic and unpredictable. Moreover, the trader can far more readily and cheaply protect himself against the danger of changes in exchange rates, through hedging operations in a forward market, than he can against the danger of changes in internal prices or exchange availability. Floating rates are therefore more favorable to private international trade than pegged rates.

Though I have discussed the problem of international payments in the context of trade liberalization, the discussion is directly applicable to the more general problem of adapting to any forces that make for balance-of-payments difficulties. Consider our present problem, of a deficit in the balance of trade plus long-term capital movements. How can we adjust to it? By one of the three methods outlined: first, drawing on reserves or borrowing; second, keeping U.S. prices from rising as rapidly as foreign prices or forcing them down; third, permitting or forcing exchange rates to alter. And, this time, by one more method: by imposing additional trade barriers or their equivalent, whether in the form of higher tariffs, or smaller import quotas, or extracting from other countries tighter "voluntary" quotas on their exports, or "tieing" foreign aid, or buying higher priced domestic goods or services to meet military needs, or imposing taxes on foreign borrowing, or imposing direct controls on investments by U.S. citizens abroad, or any one of the host of other devices for interfering with the private business of private individuals that have become so familiar to us since Hjalmar Schacht perfected the modern techniques of exchange control in 1934 to strengthen the Nazis for war and to despoil a large class of his fellow citizens.

Fortunately or unfortunately, even Congress cannot repeal the laws of arithmetic. Books must balance. We must use one of these four methods. Because we have been unwilling to select the only one that is currently fully consistent with both economic and political needs—namely, floating exchange rates—we have been driven, as if by an invisible hand, to employ all the others, and even then may not escape the need for explicit changes in exchange rates.

We affirm in loud and clear voices that we will not and must not erect trade barriers—yet is there any doubt about how far we have gone down the fourth route? After the host of measures already taken, the Secretary of the Treasury has openly stated to the Senate Finance Committee that if the so-called interest equalization tax—itself a concealed exchange control and concealed devaluation—is not passed, we shall have to resort to direct controls over foreign investment.

We affirm that we cannot drain our reserves further,

yet short-term liabilities mount and our gold stock continues to decline.

We affirm that we cannot let balance-of-payments problems interfere with domestic prosperity, yet for at least some four years now we have followed a less expansive monetary policy than would have been healthy for our economy.

Even all together, these measures may only serve to postpone but not prevent open devaluation—if the experience of other countries is any guide. Whether they do, depends not on us but on others. For our best hope of escaping our present difficulties is that foreign countries will inflate.

In the meantime, we adopt one expedient after another, borrowing here, making swap arrangements there, changing the form of loans to make the figures look good. Entirely aside from the ineffectiveness of most of these measures, they are politically degrading and demeaning. We are a great and wealthy nation. We should be directing our own course, setting an example to the world, living up to our destiny. Instead, we send our officials hat in hand to make the rounds of foreign governments and central banks; we put foreign central banks in a position to determine whether or not we can meet our obligations and thus enable them to exert great influence on our policies; we are driven to niggling negotiations with Hong Kong and with Japan and for all I know, Monaco, to get them to limit voluntarily their exports. Is this posture suitable for the leader of the free world?

It is not the least of the virtues of floating exchange rates that we would again become masters in our own house. We could decide important issues on the proper ground. The military could concentrate on military effectiveness and not on saving foreign exchange; recipients of foreign aid could concentrate on how to get the most out of what we give them and not on how to spend it all in the United States; Congress could decide how much to spend on foreign aid on the basis of what we get for our money and what else we could use it for and not how it will affect the gold stock; the monetary authorities could concentrate on domestic prices and employment, not on how to induce foreigners to hold dollar balances in this country; the Treasury and the tax committees of Congress could devote thier attention to the equity of the tax system and its effects on our efficiency, rather than on how to use tax gimmicks to discourage imports, subsidize exports, and discriminate against outflows of capital.

A system of floating exchange rates would render the problem of making outflows equal inflows unto the market where it belongs and not leave it to the clumsy and heavy hand of Government. It would leave Government free to concentrate on its proper functions.

The price of gold should be determined in the free market, with the U.S. Government committed neither to buying gold nor to selling gold at any fixed price. This is the appropriate counterpart of a policy of floating exchange rates. With respect to our existing stock of gold, we could simply keep it fixed, neither adding to it nor reducing it; alternatively, we could sell it off gradually at the market price or add to it gradually, thereby reducing or increasing our governmental stockpiles of this particular metal. In any event, we should simultaneously remove all present limitations on the ownership of gold and the trading in gold by American citizens. There is no reason why gold, like other commodities, should not be freely traded on a free market.

The Case for Fixed Exchange Rates

HENRY C. WALLICH

Henry C. Wallich is a member of the Federal Reserve Board. The following article is taken from his testimony before the Joint Economic Committee in 1963.

Flexible rates have achieved a high measure of acceptance in academic circles, but very little among public officials. This raises the question whether we have a parallel to the famous case of free trade: almost all economists favor it in principle, but no major country ever has adopted it. Does the logic of economics point equally irrefutably to flexible rates, while the logic of politics points in another direction?

The nature of the case, I believe, is fundamentally different. Most countries do practice free trade within their borders, although they reject it outside. But economists do not propose flexible rates for the states of the Union, among which men, money, and goods can move freely, and which are governed by uniform monetary, fiscal, and other policies. Flexible rates are to apply only to relations among countries that do not permit free factor movements across their borders and that follow, or may follow, substantially different monetary and fiscal policies. It is the imperfections of the world that seem to suggest that flexible rates, which would be harmful if applied to different parts of a single country, would do more good than harm internationally.

It is quite arguable that the Appalachian area would benefit if it could issue a dollar of its own, an Appalachian dollar which in that case would sell, probably, at 60 or 90 cents. Exports from that region would increase, and unemployment would diminish. A great many good things would happen, but we are also aware of what it would do to the economy of the United States—and, therefore, we do not propose that solution. The question is, Do we want to look upon the world as quite different from the United States, as hopelessly divided into self-contained units where cooperation and efforts to coordinate policies are doomed to frustration? In that case, flexible rates may be the best way to avoid a very bad situation. But should we not try to establish within the world something that begins to approximate the conditions that prevail within a country, in the way of coordination of policies, freer flow of capital and of goods and so try to achieve the benefits of one large economic area within the world? This is what we should try for.

The proponents of flexible rates argue, in effect, that flexible rates can help a country get out of almost any of the typical difficulties that economies experience. This is perfectly true. If the United States has a balance-of-payments deficit, a flexible exchange rate allows the dollar to decline until receipts have risen and payments fallen enough to restore balance. If the United States has unemployment, flexible rates can protect it against the balance-of-payments consequences of a policy of expansion. We would then have less unemployment. If the United States has suffered inflation and fears that it will be undersold internationally, flexible rates can remove the danger.

All of these advantages are quite clear.

Other countries have analogous advantages. If Chile experiences a decline in copper prices, flexible rates can ease the inevitable adjustment. If Germany finds that other countries have inflated while German prices have remained more nearly stable, flexible rates could help to avoid importing inflation. If Canada has a large capital inflow, a flexible rate will remove the need for price and income increases that would otherwise be needed to facilitate the transfer of real resources.

There are other adjustments, however, that must be made in all of these cases. If a country allows its exchange rate to go down, some price adjustments still remain to be made. Furthermore, each time a country makes this kind of adjustment, allowing its exchange rate to decline, other countries suffer. If the U.S. dollar depreciates, we undersell the Europeans. It could be argued that if the U.S. price levels go down instead of the exchange rate, we also undersell the Europeans, and if because of a declining price level we have unemployment we would be buying still less from them. Nevertheless, there is a difference. A price adjustment tends to be slow and is likely to be no greater than it need be and tends to be selective for particular commodities. In contrast, an exchange rate movement is unpredictable. It can be large—we could easily have a drop of 10 or 20 percent in an exchange rate. It comes suddenly. And it compels other countries to be on their guard.

Why, given the attractions of flexible rates, should one advise policymakers to stay away from them? Since the dollar problem is the concrete situation in which flexible rates are being urged today, it is in terms of the dollar that they must be discussed. In broadest terms, the reason why flexible rates are inadvisable is that their successful functioning would require more self-discipline and mutual forbearance than countries today are likely to muster. Exchange

rates are two sided—depreciation for the dollar means appreciation for the European currencies. To work successfully, a flexible dollar, for instance, must not depreciate to the point where the Europeans would feel compelled to take counteraction. I believe that the limits of tolerance, before counteraction begins today are narrow and that a flexible dollar would invite retaliation almost immediately.

In the abstract, the European countries perhaps ought to consider that if the United States allows the dollar to go down, it is doing so in the interests of all-round equilibrium. They ought perhaps to consider that with a stable dollar rate the same adjustment might have to take place through a decline in prices here and a rise in prices there. In practice, they are likely to be alive principally to the danger of being undersold by American producers if the dollar goes down, in their own and third markets. The changing competitive pressure would fall unevenly upon particular industries, and those who are hurt would demand protection.

The most likely counteraction might take one of two forms. The Europeans could impose countervailing duties, such as the United States also has employed at times. They could alternately also depreciate European currencies along with the dollar or, what would amount to almost the same thing, prevent the dollar from depreciating. This might involve the European countries in the purchase of large amounts of dollars. If they are to peg the dollar, they could minimize their commitment by imposing a simple form of exchange control that the Swiss practiced during the last war. The Swiss purchased dollars only from their exporters, also requiring their importers to buy these dollars thereby stabilizing the trade dollar, while allowing dollars from capital movements—finance dollars—to find their own level in the market.

The large volume of not very predictable short-term capital movements in the world today makes such reactions under flexible rates particularly likely.

A sudden outflow of funds from the United States, for instance (because of the fear of budget deficits or many other things that could happen), would tend to drive the dollar down. As a result, American exporters could undersell producers everywhere else in the world. It seems unlikely that foreign countries would allow a fortuitous short-term capital movement to have such far-reaching consequences. It would not even be economically appropriate to allow a transitory fluctuation in the capital account of the balance of

THE CASE FOR FIXED EXCHANGE RATES □ 257

payments to have a major influence on the current account. Such a fluctuation should not alter the pattern of trade, because the situation is likely to be reversed. Other countries therefore would probably take defensive action to make sure that no industry is destroyed and after several years may have to be rebuilt because of the ups and downs of short-term capital movements.

It can be argued that under flexible rates the effects of such a movement would be forestalled by stabilizing speculation on a future recovery of the dollar. This is possible. It is possible also, however, that speculation would seek a quick profit from the initial drop in the dollar, instead of a longer run one from its eventual recovery. Then short-run speculation would drive the dollar down farther at first. In any case there is not enough assurance that speculators will not make mistakes to permit basing the world's monetary system upon the stabilizing effects of speculation.

In the case of countries which import much of what they consume, such as England, a temporary decline in the local currency may even be self-validating. If the cost of living rises as the currency declines, wages will rise. Thereafter, the currency may never recover to its original level.

This points up one probable consequence of flexible exchange rates: a worldwide acceleration of inflation. In some countries the indicated ratchet effect of wages will be at work. If exchange rates go down, wages will rise, and exchange rates cannot recover. In the United States the rise in the cost of imports would not be very important. But the removal of balance-of-payments restraints may well lead to policies that could lead to price increases. The American inflation of the 1950s was never defeated until the payments deficit became serious. Elsewhere, the removal of balance-of-payments disciplines might have the same effect. Rapid inflation in turn would probably compel governments to intervene drastically in foreign trade and finance.

I am aware that there is a choice to be made here—more employment or more stable prices. If we pursued more sensible policies and exerted a little more self-restraint, this choice would not be upon us. But if we insist on raising costs and raising prices in the presence of unemployment then this unpleasant choice must be made. As Mr. Friedman has said, it is quite clear that the discipline of the balance of payments has made for a more restrictive policy in this country than would have been followed in the absence of this discipline. It is quite conceivable that the

absence of balance-of-payments disciplines would have strong inflationary effects in some countries. In that case governments would be compelled immediately to intervene drastically in foreign trade and finance; in other words, flexible exchange rates would contribute to their own extinction or to exchange control.

The prospect that flexible rates would greatly increase uncertainty for foreign traders and investors has been cited many times. It should be noted that this uncertainty extends also to domestic investment decisions that might be affected by changing import competition or changing export prospects. It has been argued that uncertainties about future exchange rates can be removed by hedging in the futures market. This, however, involves a cost even where cover is readily available. The history of futures markets does not suggest that it will be possible to get cover for long-term positions. To hedge domestic investment decisions that might be affected by flexible rates is in the nature of things impracticable.

The picture that emerges of the international economy under flexible rates is one of increasing disintegration. Independent national policies and unpredictable changes in each country's competitive position will compel governments to shield their producers and markets. The argument that such shielding would also automatically be accomplished by movements in the affected country's exchange rate underrates the impact of fluctuations upon particular industries, if not upon the entire economy. That international integration and flexible rates are incompatible seems to be the view also of the European Common Market countries, who have left no doubt that they want stable rates within the EEC. The same applies if we visualize the "Kennedy round" under the Trade Expansion Act. I think if we told the Europeans that, after lowering our tariffs, we were going to cast the dollar loose and let it fluctuate, we would get very little tariff reduction. They would want to keep up their guard.

If the disintegrating effects of flexible rates are to be overcome, a great deal of policy coordination, combined with self-discipline and mutual forbearance, would be required. The desired independence of national economic policy would in fact have to be foregone—interest rates, budgets, wage and prices policies would have to be harmonized. If the world were ready for such cooperation, it would be capable also of making a fixed exchange rate system work. In that case, flexible rates would accomplish nothing that could not more cheaply and simply be done with fixed rates. It seems to follow that flexible rates have no unique capacity for good, whereas they possess great capacity to do damage.

A modified version of the flexible rates proposal has been suggested. This version would allow the dollar and other currencies to fluctuate within a given range, say 5 percent up and down. This "widening of the gold points" is believed to reduce the danger of destabilizing speculation. It might perhaps enlist speculation on the side of stabilization, for if the dollar, say, had dropped to its lower limit, and if the public had confidence that that limit would not be broken, the only movement on which to speculate would be a rise. The spectacle of a currency falling below par may induce, according to the proponents, a strong political effort to bring it back.

This proposal likewise strikes me as unworkable. For one thing, I doubt that people would have a great deal of confidence in a limit of 5 percent below par, if par itself has been given up. Political support for holding this second line would probably be less than the support that can be mustered to hold the first. For another, the execution of the plan would still require the maintenance of international reserves, to protect the upper and lower limits. But with fluctuating rates, dollar and sterling would cease to be desriable media for monetary reserves. International liquidity would become seriously impaired. A third objection is that under today's conditions, the complex negotiations and legislation required, in the unlikely event that the plan could be negotiated at all, could not go forward without immediate speculation against the dollar before the plan goes into effect.

It remains only to point out that, even in the absence of a high degree of international cooperativeness, a system of fixed exchange rates can be made to work. It can be made to work mainly because it imposes a discipline upon all participants, and because within this discipline there is nevertheless some room for adjustment. The principal sources of flexibility are productivity gains and the degree to which they are absorbed by wage increases. Wages cannot be expected to decline. But their rise can be slowed in relation to the rate of productivity growth, in which case prices would become more competitive relative to other countries. With annual productivity gains of 2 to 3 percent in the United States and more abroad, it would not take many years to remove a temporary imbalance.

48

The Poor Nations

BARBARA WARD

Barbara Ward was the Albert Schweitzer Professor of International Economic Development at Columbia University. This selection is taken from her book The Rich Nations and the Poor Nations, *published by W. W. Norton in 1962.*

How are we to define the "poor" nations? The phrase 'underdeveloped' is not very satisfactory for it groups together very different types of underdevelopment. India and Pakistan, for instance, are heirs of a great and ancient civilization and have many of the other attributes—in art, literature, and administration—of developed states, even though they are also very poor. Other areas—one thinks of the Congo—are developed in virtually no sense at all. I think, therefore, that perhaps the most satisfactory method of defining poverty at this stage is to discuss the question simply in terms of per capita income—the average income available to citizens in the various countries. If you fix the level of wealth of 'wealthy' communities at a per-capita income of about $500 a year, then 80 percent of mankind lives below it. The mass of mankind live well below the income level of $500 per head a year; and in some countries—one thinks particularly of India—per capita income may be as low as $60. Yet between 400 and 500 million people live in India—something like two-fifths of all the poor people in the uncommitted world. So the gap between rich and poor is tremendous and, as we have already noticed, it is tending to widen further.

What is the cause of this? Why is there this great blanket of poverty stretched across the face of the globe? Before we attempt an answer, we should, I think, remember that ours is the first century in which such a question can even be put. Poverty has been the universal lot of man until our own day. No one asked fundamental questions about a state of affairs which everyone took for granted. The idea that the majority could have access to a little modest affluence is wholly new, the breakthrough of whole communities to national wealth totally unprecedented.

To return to our question: the contrast between the wealth of the West and the poverty of nearly everybody else does have some puzzling features. For centuries, for millennia, the East had been the region of known and admired wealth. It was to the Orient that men looked when they spoke of traditional forms of riches: gold and diamonds, precious ointments, rare spices, extravagant brocades, and silks. In fact, for over a thousand years, one of the great drives in the Western economy was to open trade with the wealthier East. And one of the problems facing that trade—as far in the past as in the days of imperial Rome—was the West's inability to provide very much

259

in return. It is hard to sell bear rugs to merchants at Madras, especially during the monsoon. Nor is the contrast between the East's endowment and the relative poverty of the West simply a matter of history. Today, for instance, Indonesia seems obviously better endowed in a whole range of ways than are some European countries—one might perhaps pick Norway.

In spite of these puzzles, there are some underlying physical causes which explain why some countries have been left behind in the world's present thrust towards greater wealth. Many of the tropical soils have been submitted to millennia of leaching under the downpour of heavy rains and are precarious soils for agriculture. Nor is the climate of tropical regions precisely designed for work. When the temperature rises to ninety degrees and the humidity to 90 percent, you do not feel like rushing out and solving one of the first problems in Euclid. Even less do you want to cut a tree—favourite occupation of Victorian gentlemen—or dig a ditch.

Wherever the monsoon is the rain-bringing force, there is an underlying element of instability in farming. The concentration of rain in a few months creates expensive problems of control and storage. Rivers vary from raging torrents to dry beds. And if the monsoons fail in India or Southeast Asia, then there is quite simply no agriculture because there is no water.

Another fact making for poverty is that the great tropical belt stretching round the world has only limited sources of energy: no coal and not too much oil outside the Middle East, Venezuela, and Indonesia. One must conclude, therefore, that certain original differences exist in the actual endowment of resources in the advancing Northern Hemisphere and the relatively stagnant South. Nonetheless, I think the profound reason for the contrast of wealth and poverty lies in the fact that the various revolutions which have swept over the face of the Western world in the last hundred years exist at only a chaotic or embryonic stage among the poorer states.

The biological revolution of more rapid growth in population is on the way in these areas. But the other vast changes—an intellectual revolution of materialism and this-worldliness, the political revolution of equality, and above all the scientific and technological revolution which comes from the application of savings and the sciences to the whole business of daily life—are only beginning the process of transforming every idea and institution in the emergent lands. The revolution of modernization has not yet driven these states into the contemporary world. The greatest drama of our time is that they will be swept onwards. But we are still uncertain over the form these revolutions will finally take. Everywhere they have started; nowhere are they yet complete; but the trend cannot be reversed. The modernizing of the whole world is under way.

Millennia ago, hunting and food-gathering began to give way before the advance of settled agriculture. So today the transformation of society by the application of reason, science, and technology is thrusting the old static subsistence economies to the backwaters of the world. The world is, in fact, involved in a single revolutionary process of which our four dominant themes are all a part. In the wealthier lands, the first stage of this transformation has been completed in the emergence of the modern, wealthy, reasonably stable, technologically adept capitalist state. In the poorer lands, the first stage only has opened. The contrast between world wealth and world poverty largely turns upon this lag in time.

Now we must examine the impact of the four changes upon emergent lands—and we should remember again the distinction between poorer lands such as India which are at the same time rich in culture, history, and tradition, and tribal lands, whether in Africa, Australia, or Latin America, which lack even the rudiments of a developed tradition. The biological revolution brought about by a sudden acceleration of the birthrate could not take place in these countries until colonial rule abolished local wars and until modern medical science and modern sanitation began to save babies and lengthen life. That these changes were introduced *before* the establishment of a modern economy is one of the most fateful differences between East and West, and one to which we will return. But until the second half of the nineteenth century most of these lands still followed the old millennial pattern of a population rising to the limits of production and then falling back into violence, struggle, and death where the limits were surpassed. In tribal life, for instance, when the tribe had eaten up the resources available in its hunting grounds, it had no alternative but to reduce its numbers by malnutrition and starvation or break out and conquer the lands of other tribes, thereby diminishing the numbers on both sides. This cycle was one of the perennial causes of tribal war.

Even in a great settled civilization like China, history has given us a kind of physical representation of the "melancholy wheel" of fate in the pressure of population rising to the limit of resources, and there precipitating violence, despair, banditry, civil war, and invasion. Then, under tribulations of all kinds, the population falls back again to numbers which the food supply can carry, only to rise once more as peace is restored—a kind of self-perpetuating cycle in which the wheel of fate is driven by pressure of population into a constant alternation of peaceful growth and violent diminution. This, until the day before yesterday, seemed to be the fundamental fatality of man's existence.

Now let us turn to the second force: the new revolutionary emphasis on work and effort devoted to the things of *this* world, the drive of interest devoted to changing and bettering man's physical environment. In traditional or tribal societies, this force is, in the main, lacking. Very largely, the material organization of life and, above all, the natural sequence of birth and death, of the seasons, of planetary change, have been taken as given: they were not the subject of speculative activity. In primitive tribal society one can say that nature is very largely accepted as impenetrable by reason. It can be propitiated. It can be worked on by human will through magic. A flood may be diverted by drowning a male child. But no one connects the precipitation of rain at the head of the watershed with the expected annual flow and devises earthworks to avert disaster. Life is lived in the midst of mystery which cannot be manipulated, beyond very narrow limits, in answer to human needs.

In the great archaic societies—of Babylon, of Egypt, of the Indus Valley, or of the Yellow River—both the exploration of reality and the use of technology registered a formidable advance. Irrigation works such as those of ancient Egypt demanded elaborate scientific calculation, accurate observation of nature, and efficient, large-scale administration. And societies which evolved astronomy and the mathematical sciences to the levels achieved by the Persians or the Greeks achieved a penetration of matter by the human intellect unequalled until our own day. But the dynamism of our modern interest in created things was lacking. In some societies, as we shall see, the lack followed from a certain scientific indifference; in others, from a dissociation between the understanding of natural law and any idea of using the laws as tools for experimental work; and in all societies from a static concept of life in which the chief means of subsistence—agriculture—provided daily bread for the many and magnificence for the few, but was not a capital resource to be steadily extended by further

investment. And, in truth, once the limits of land and water were reached, lack of scientific experiment inhibited further expansion.

In short, the chief aims of these societies were not this-worldly in our modern sense. Take, for instance, the significant Victorian phrase "making good." We understand it in terms of making money, of achieving material success in the broadest sense. In premodern society no such meaning could possibly have been attached to any activity thought of as being 'good.' In tribal society, approved behaviour implies strict observance of tribal laws and customs. In archaic civilization, the good man, the man of wisdom, is the man who observes the rules and duties of his way of life: the rich man, in magnificence, affability, and alms-giving; the poor man, in work and respect. No group, except the despised merchant, devotes his life to accumulation. And even the merchant tends, as he did in China, to turn his wealth into land and leave the life of capital formation behind as soon as his fortune permits the change. Such societies incline of their very nature to be backward-looking, to preserve rather than to create, and to see the highest wisdom in the effort to keep things as they are. Under these conditions no underlying psychological drive impels people to work and accumulate for the future. Wisdom is to wait on Providence and follow in the ways of your forefathers, ways of life compatible with great serenity, great dignity, profound religious experience, and great art, but not with the accumulation of material wealth for society as a whole.

The lack of the third revolution—equality—has worked in the same sense. There was no concept of equality in traditional society. As one knows from still-existing tribal societies, leadership lies with the old men of the tribe. There is no way for the "young men" to claim equality. They simply have to wait for the years to pass. Seniority (as in the American Senate) also ensures that the leaders are men who respect the backward-looking traditions of the group and have a vested interest in the unequal prestige conferred by advancing years. It is the inescapable recipe for extreme conservatism.

When tribal society is left behind, the values supported by the leaders are still conservative. They are fixed by an inviolate upper order. Save in times of immense upheaval, the peasant does not reach the throne. King, warrior, landlord form a closed order to which recruitment is in the main by birth. In India the fixedness of the pattern extended to everyone. A man is born to his caste and to no other. The very idea of equality is almost meaningless since you are what you are and you cannot measure yourself against other men who are entirely different by birth and by caste. Caste thus reinforced the inability of the merchant class to achieve greater influence and status. The merchant remained a Vaishya—the merchant caste—and money-making was not considered a valuable enough occupation to warrant any increase in status or esteem. Thus the Indian merchant did not achieve the political breakthrough which launched the rising power of the middle classes in Western Europe.

Another facet of equality—a vital facet for economic growth—was lacking: since there was no national community as we understand it, competitive drives based on national equality were also absent. The tribe is a sort of tiny nation, a nation in embryo, but it cannot exercise the same economic influence as the modern nation because it is too small to be a significant market. In any case, tribal agriculture is devoted to subsistence, not to exchange.

The larger post-tribal political units were, in the main, dynastic or imperial units—one thinks of such loose structures as the India of the Guptas or of China's gigantic bureaucracy—in which there was little interconnection between the scattered cities and the great mass of people living their isolated, subsistence village lives. Certainly there was not enough economic and social coherence to define a market in such terms that a merchant would feel himself in competition with other vigorous national markets and could operate with driving energy to defend national interests against the rival national interests of others. The competitive "equality" of Western Europe's commerce was wholly absent. As one sees again and again in human history—or in daily life—people do not begin to act in new ways until they have formulated the idea of such ways in their minds. The idea of the nation was immensely reinforced—but also in part created—by the rivalry of commercial interests in Western Europe.

Now we turn to the last and most pervasive of the revolutions, the crucial revolution of science and saving. There is virtually no science in tribal society. There is a good deal of practical experience, skilled work, and early technique. It seems possible, for instance, that primitive farming developed·as a result of close observation of nature's cycle of seed and harvest and its imitation in fertility rites and religious festivals. But the idea of controlling material things by grasping the inner law of their construction is absent.

An underlying sense of the mysteriousness of things explains, as we have noticed, the use of magic. But magic depends on the force of a man's will, not upon the nature of the things upon which he tries to exercise his will. And since the human will is a very potent force, one occasionally encounters some very strange and unaccountable results which seem inexplicable in ordinary terms. Few travelers return from Africa without some sense of having brushed the uncanny fringes of a world where some of the ordinary rules do not apply. Nonetheless, primitive society lacks the sustained and purposive manipulation of matter for human ends which becomes possible once you grasp the laws to which matter responds.

In great traditional civilizations such as India and China, there certainly was enough intellectual ferment for a vast scientific breakthrough to be theoretically possible. Many of the most acute minds in those societies devoted themselves to systematic thought for generations. In the Eastern Mediterranean, among the Chaldeans and the Egyptians, some of the basic mathematical tools of science had been forged long before the Christian era. Yet the breakthrough never came. In India, there could be no obsessive research into material things since many of the finest spirits thought of the natural world as in some sense an illusion with no fundamental significance for human beings. In China, for a rather different reason, science failed to achieve the preeminence one might have expected in one of the most brilliantly intellectual societies of all time; and one in which printing—and gunpowder—were invented far ahead of the West. The reason is one more illustration of the degree to which revolutions begin—or fail to begin—in the minds of men. The Confucian gentleman who dominated the official thinking of Chinese society thought science an occupation for charlatans and fools and, therefore, not really respectable. One need hardly add that if the best brains do not think a pursuit respectable, the best brains do not devote their time to it.

The Confucians had an excuse for their prejudice. In Europe, the medieval alchemists spent much of their time and energy trying to discover the "philosopher's stone"—the catalyst which would turn base metals into gold. In the course of their futile search they made many sound experimental discoveries about the properties of metals and some people regard them as precursors of the inductive and experimental methods upon which modern science is based.

In China the "philosopher's stone" took another

form—the "elixir of life." China's emperors did not want gold. They wanted immortality and at their courts the Taoists, followers of a mystical and metaphysical religious 'way,' conducted practical experiments with plants and chemicals to see if the elixir could be produced in a test tube. To the Confucians, the folly of the aim overshadowed the potential value of the means. They turned their backs on experiment and, in doing so, on science as well. So in China, for all the ancient glory of its culture, for all the force and vitality of its intellectual tradition, the scientific breakthrough could not occur.

Primitive and archaic societies match their lack of scientific *élan* by an equal lack of sustained saving. Every society saves something. Saving is, after all, not consuming. If everything were consumed, men would be reduced to hunting and fishing—and even these occupations require rods and spears. But in settled agricultural societies, seed cord is set aside for the next harvest and men do the hedging and ditching and field-levelling needed to carry production forward year by year. Probably such saving for maintenance and repair—and more occasionally by land-clearing and irrigation, for expansion—does not surpass 4 or 5 percent of national income in any year.

The savings which make possible a general change in the techniques of productivity—more roads, more ports, more power, more education, more output on the farms, new machines in the factories—must rise dramatically above the 5 percent level. Economists fix a level of about 12 to 15 percent of national income as the range needed to cover all possible increases in population, some increase in consumption, and a high, expanding level of investment. And no traditional society ever reached this level.

One reason for this fact takes us back to the revolution of equality. The merchant in the Orient never achieved decisive political influence. There were no city corporations, no charters based on autonomous rights. As a result, the merchant never achieved full security either. The government of kings and emperors was a government above the law, depending upon the monarch's whim. There is a brilliant phrase used by one of the young gentlemen of the East India Company to describe the uncertainties of the commercial calling in India. He describes the monarch and his tax-gatherers as bird's-nesters who leave a merchant to accumulate a nestful of eggs and then come to raid them all. One can well understand that under such conditions the stimulus to sustained capital accumulation is fairly marginal. On the contrary, the tendency is to put money that is earned from trade—and a great deal of money was earned—either into hoards of currency that can be hidden or else into jewels which are easily transportable and easily hid. But neither of these reserves makes for the expansion of productive enterprise.

In short, the chief point that distinguishes tribal and traditional society is that all the internal impulses to modernization have been largely lacking. And yet today these societies are everywhere in a ferment of change. How has this come about? Where did the external stimulus come from? There is only one answer. It came, largely uninvited, from the restless, changing, rampaging West. In the last 300 years, the world's ancient societies, the great traditional civilizations of the East, together with the pre-Iberian civilizations of Latin America and the tribal societies of Africa, have all, in one way or another, been stirred up from outside by the new, bounding, uncontrollable energies of the Western powers which, during those same years, were undergoing concurrently all the revolutions—of equality, of nationalism, of rising population, and of scientific change—which make up the mutation of modernization.

The great worldwide transmitter of the modernizing tendency has been without doubt—for good and evil—Western colonialism. It is typical, I think, of the way in which the changes have come about that, again and again, Western merchants were the forerunners of upheaval. They went out to bring back the spices and silks and sophistications of the Orient to cold and uncomfortable Europe. At first, they had no intentions of conquering anything. They simply tried to establish monopoly positions for themselves—hardly surprising when you could earn a 5,000-percent profit on a shipload of nutmeg making landfall in Europe—and to drive the traders of other nations away. They fought each other ferociously at sea but on land controlled only "factories"—clusters of warehouses, port installations, and dwelling houses held on sufferance from the local ruler. And so the position might have remained. But Dutch pressure was too great for the frail political structure of Java in the seventeenth century and little by little, by backing compliant sultans and deposing sullen ones, the Dutch became political masters of all the rich "spice islands."

In the following century, the Mogul superstructure collapsed in India and in their maneuvering to destroy French influence the British found themselves assuming power by a similar route, first backing local contenders, then, saddled with them as puppets or incompetents, gradually assuming the power which slipped from their enfeebled grip. The Europeans had come out to trade. Imperial control was a by-product—and an increasingly ruinous one in commercial terms—yet as late as 1850 the nominal ruler in India was still a merchant corporation—"John Company," the East India Company.

Colonial control, developing from its origins in trade, began to set the whole revolution of modernization into motion. It launched the radical changes brought about by a rapidly increasing growth in population. Western control introduced the beginnings of medical science. It ended internal disorder. A crowding into the big cities began. There were some attempts at more modern sanitation.

Towards the close of the nineteenth century a spurt of population began throughout India and the Far East. But this spurt had a different consequence from the comparable increase in the West. Western lands were relatively underpopulated—North America absolutely so—when the processes of modernization began. The growth in numbers was a positive spur to economic growth; it brought labourers into the market and widened the market. At the same time the new machines, the new developing economy based on rising productivity, expanded the possibilities of creating wealth in a way that more than outstripped the growth in population. But in the Far East, in India, where population was already dense, the effect of the colonial impact was to increase the rate of the population's growth without launching a total transformation of the economy. More births, longer lives, sent population far beyond the capabilities of a stumbling economy. Today the grim dilemma has appeared that population is so far ahead of the means of satisfying it that each new wave of births threatens in each generation to wipe out the margin of savings necessary to sustain added numbers. The West, where growth in population acted as a spur to further expansion, has not faced this dilemma, and in the East it is not yet clear how so grave a dilemma *can* be faced.

Colonial rule brought in the sense of a this-worldly concern for the advantages of material advance by the simplest and most direct route—the "demonstration effect." The new merchants, the new administrators, lived better, lived longer, had demonstrably more materially satisfying lives. The local people saw that this was so and they began to wonder why and whether others might not live so too. Above all, the

local leaders saw vividly that the new scientific, industrial, and technological society enjoyed almost irresistible power. This, too, they naturally coveted.

At the same time, the colonial system did set in motion some definite beginnings in the processes of technical change and economic growth. There was some education of local people in the new techniques of Western life. Some merchants in the old societies, the Compradors in China, for instance, or the Gujaratis in India, began to exercise their talents as entrepreneurs in a new, settled, commercial society. Some of the preliminaries of industrialization—railways, ports, roads, some power—the preliminaries we call 'infrastructure'—were introduced to the benefit of the new colonial economy. Some export industries expanded to provide raw materials for the West. Virtually nothing was done about basic agriculture; but plantation systems did develop agricultural products—tea, pepper, ground-nuts, jute—for the growing markets of Europe.

Above all, the new political ideas streamed in. Western education gave an *élite* a first look at Magna Charta. In their school books in India the sons of Indians could read Edmund Burke denouncing the depradations of Englishmen in India. The new sense of equality, inculcated by Western education, was reinforced by the daily contrast between the local inhabitants and the colonial representatives who claimed to rule them. Personal equality fused with the idea of national equality, with the revolt educated men increasingly felt at being run by another nation. The whole national movement of anticolonialism was stirred up by Western ideas of national rights and national independence, and by the perpetual evidence that the rights were being denied.

Everywhere there was ferment; everywhere there was the beginning of change; everywhere a profound sense that the old ways were becoming inadequate, were in some way no longer valid or viable for modern man. And this feeling stirred up an equally violent reaction. Men rose up to say that the old ways were better and that the new-fangled fashions would destroy all that was valuable and profound in indigenous civilization. Between the modernizers and the traditionalists, between the young men who wanted to accept everything and the old men who wanted to reject everything, the local community threatened to be distracted by contradictory leadership. A crisis of loyalty and comprehension superimposed itself on all the other crises. It was rare for a country to achieve the national coherence that was achieved in India under the leadership of Gandhi in whom ancient vision and the modern idea of equality could coexist, and around whom old and new were thus able to unite.

The important point to remember, however, if one wishes to grasp the present contrast between the rich nations and the poor, is that all these changes, introduced pell-mell by colonialism, did not really produce a new and coherent form of society, as they had done in the West. There was no "take-off," to use Professor Rostow's phrase, into a new kind of society. The colonial impact introduced problems that seemed too large to be solved, or, at least, problems that offered immense difficulty to any solution. Take, for instance, the problem of population. You could not deny medicine; you could not resist sanitation; yet all the time life lengthened, the birthrate went on going up, and you could almost watch population beginning to outstrip resources that were not growing in proportion because saving and capital formation were still inadequate. Yet the rising population continuously made saving more difficult.

This small level of saving meant that all economic developments under colonialism—or semicolonialism—were on too small a scale to lead to a general momentum. China is a good example. After the Opium Wars the British compelled the crumbling Manchu Empire to open its ports to Western trade. In the so-called treaty ports, quite a rapid rate of economic and industrial expansion took place. Europeans brought in capital. Some Chinese entrepreneurs joined them. International trade soared. The customs, also under European control, grew to be an important source of revenue. Plans for building railways were prepared. Meanwhile, however, the desperate, overcrowded countryside where the bulk of the people lived slipped steadily down into deeper ruin. Little economic activity could spread beyond the Westernized areas; for there were no markets, no savings, no initiative—only the dead weight of rural bankruptcy.

Similarly, in India the only areas where anything like a sustained 'take-off' began to occur were in the neighbourhood of Bombay with its shrewd merchants and great port, among the Scottish jute-growers round Calcutta, and with the lively adaptable farmers of the Punjab. Elsewhere, the countryside was largely unaffected by the new economic forces.

The same patchiness affected social life and education. All over Asia the educational system began to produce an *élite* who believed in Western ideas of law, Western ideas of liberty, of constitutional government. But behind them there was little general change among the people at large and, above all, no trace of change in the vast number—80 or more percent of the population—who lived on the land where the old, unchanged, subsistence agriculture went on as before. And so there came about what one can only call a kind of dual society, in which the scattered growing points of a modern way of life were restrained almost to the pitch of immobility by enormous forces of inertia inherent in the old framework of society.

When, for instance one reads of the attempts made by small groups of Chinese merchants in the late nineteenth century to transform their economy in such a way that they could withstand the commercial and political pressure of the West, one confronts again and again the fact that the real society simply had not changed enough to go along with them. The Court was backward-looking. The Confucian bureaucracy was still utterly unchanged. Worse still, the merchants themselves were still divided in their own minds. They still hankered for the days when a successful merchant naturally put all his capital into land and became a member of the landed gentry. At every point, there were psychological blocks in men's minds when it came to completing the changes they had been ready to start. In a very real sense societies like China or India in the last century were caught between a world that had died and a new world that could not yet be born—and this is, of course, the perfect recipe for maximum psychological and social strain.

Perhaps one can best judge the extent of the inhibitions by examining the opposite example of Japan. There, an extraordinarily efficient and ruthless ruling class determined, after the forced opening of their ports by the Western powers, to transform their country completely on the modern Western model. They decided that nothing short of almost total technical transformation would give them power to resist the West. So they forced through the reform of agriculture; the imposition of savings on the people, the absolute liquidation of all forms of the feudal economy. They introduced industry, sent many men to train abroad, and set in motion a drive for universal literacy. Although, unhappily, they also borrowed from the contemporary West a spirit of imperialism also present in their own traditions, they were able to transform their society radically in about thirty years and eliminated the social blocks and psychic inhibitions which held the other societies miserably suspended between contradictory worlds.

But elsewhere throughout the uncommitted world, in the traditional societies of China and India, in large parts of Latin America, and in the primitive emergent countries of Africa, old and new remained locked in a kind of battle, stuck fast in an apparently unbreakable deadlock. And how to break out of it; how to get the forces of modernization flowing through all of society; how to change leadership; how to get the new cadres in education; how to stimulate massive saving; how to get agriculture transformed: all these urgent and irresistible problems of the new society still wait to be answered.

This is a fact which the West cannot ignore. Most of the dilemmas of the underdeveloped areas have been stirred up by Western impact. Yet I think it is not entirely untrue to say that the Western powers are not looking very hard to find answers to these dilemmas. And this, I think, is for a very good reason. They have largely forgotten about their own transition. They are not conscious of the fact that a hundred years ago, even fifty years ago, many of them were struggling with just these problems of changing leadership, of developing new social groups, giving rights to new classes, finding methods of achieving greater saving, and securing a technological breakthrough on a massive scale. We take our development so much for granted that we hardly understand the dilemmas of those who have not yet travelled so far.

Another reason for our relative indifference is that owing to the relative underpopulation of our part of the world and owing to the scale of latent resources waiting to be developed in the Atlantic world, we in the West had not too difficult a passage to modernity; certainly nothing compared with the really appalling dilemmas that are faced by the underdeveloped world today. So, although we are perhaps beginning to see that they face almost insurmountable problems, I do not think that we have worked out our response or even perhaps fully measured our responsibility. Yet there is no human failure greater than to launch a profoundly important endeavour and then leave it half done. This is what the West has done with its colonial system. It shook all the societies in the world loose from their old moorings. But it seems indifferent whether or not they reach safe harbour in the end.

This is one difficulty; but there is another, a greater one. While we face these dilemmas, another set of answers to them has been formulated—also in the West. It claims to go to the heart of all these revolutions and offer a surer route to equality, to material well-being, to the achievement of technology, science, and capital. Communism claims to be the pattern of the future and to hold the secret of the next phase of history for mankind. In one sense, the claim is serious. Communism is a sort of résumé of the revolutions that make up modernization and it offers a method of applying them speedily to societies caught fast in the dilemmas of transition. We must, therefore, admit that, at the present moment, the poor nations, the uncommitted nations, face a double challenge. They face an enormous challenge of change. But, in addition, they face an equally vast challenge of choice.

49

The Less-Developed Countries: Observations and Implications

SIMON KUZNETS

Simon Kuznets is George E. Baker Professor of Economics Emeritus at Harvard University. This selection is taken from his Nobel Memorial Lecture, December 11, 1971.

Two major groups of factors appear to have limited the spread of modern economic growth. First, such growth demands a stable, but flexible, political and social framework, capable of accommodating rapid structural change and resolving the conflicts that it generates, while encouraging the growth-promoting groups in society. Such a framework is not easily or rapidly attained, as evidenced by the long struggles toward it even in some of the presently developed countries in the nineteenth and early twentieth centuries. Japan is the only nation outside of those rooted in European civilization that has joined the group of developed countries so far. Emergence of a modern framework for economic growth may be especially difficult if it involves elements peculiar to European civilization for which substitutes are not easily found. Second, the increasingly national cast of organization in developed countries made for policies toward other parts of the world that, while introducing some modern economic and social elements, were, in many areas, clearly inhibiting. These policies ranged from the imposition of colonial status to other limitations on political freedom, and, as a result,

political independence and removal of the inferior status of the native members of the community, rather than economic advance, were given top priority.

Whatever the weight of the several factors in explaining the failure of the less-developed countries to take advantage of the potential of modern economic growth, a topic that, in its range from imperialist exploitation to backwardness of the native economic and social framework, lends itself to passionate and biased polemic, the factual findings are clear. At present, about two-thirds or more of world population is in the economically less-developed group. Even more significant is the concentration of the population at the low end of the product per capita range. In 1965, the last year for which we have worldwide comparable product estimates, the per capita Gross Domestic Product (at market prices) of 1.72 billion out of a world population of 3.27 billion, was less than \$120, whereas 0.86 billion in economically developed countries had a per capita product of some \$1,900. Even with this narrow definition of less-developed countries, the intermediate group was less than 0.7 billion, or less than 20 percent of the world total. The preponderant population was thus divided between the very low and the rather high level of per capita economic performance. Obviously, this aspect of modern economic growth deserves our greatest attention, and the fact that the quantitative data and our knowledge of the institutional structures of the less-developed countries are, at the moment, far more limited than our knowledge of the developed areas, is not reason enough for us to ignore it.

Several preliminary findings, or rather plausible impressions, may be noted. First, the group of less-developed countries, particularly if we widen it (as we should) to include those with a per capita product somewhat larger than $120 (in 1965 prices), covers an extremely wide range in size, in the relation between population and natural resources, in major inherited institutions, and in the past impact upon them of the developed countries (coming as it did at different times and from different sources). There is a striking contrast, for example, in terms of population size, between the giants like Mainland China and India, on the one hand, and the scores of tiny states in Africa and Latin America; as there is between the timing of direct Western impact on Africa and of that on many countries in Latin America. Furthermore, the remarkable institutions by which the Sinic and East Indian civilizations produced the unified, huge societies that dwarfed in size any that originated in Europe until recently, bore little resemblance to those that structured the American Indian societies or those that fashioned the numerous tribal societies of Africa.

Generalizations about less-developed countries must be carefully and critically scrutinized in the light of this wide variety of conditions and institutions. To be sure, their common failure to exploit the potential of modern economic growth means several specific common features: a low per capita product, a large share of agriculture or other extractive industries, a generally small scale of production. But the specific parameters differ widely, and because the obstacles to growth may differ critically in their substance, they may suggest different policy directions.

Second, the growth position of the less-developed countries today is significantly different, in many respects, from that of the presently developed countries on the eve of their entry into modern economic growth (with the possible exception of Japan, and one cannot be sure even of that). The less-developed areas that account for the largest part of the world population today are at much lower per

capita product levels than were the developed countries just before their industrialization; and the latter at that time were economically in advance of the rest of the world, not at the low end of the per capita product range. The very magnitudes, as well as some of the basic conditions, are quite different: no country that entered modern economic growth (except Russia) approached the size of India or China, or even of Pakistan and Indonesia; and no currently developed country had to adjust to the very high rates of natural increase of population that have characterized many less-developed countries over the last two or three decades. Particularly before World War I, the older European countries, and to some extent even Japan, relieved some strains of industrialization by substantial emigration of the displaced population to areas with more favorable opportunities—an avenue closed to the populous less-developed countries today. Of course, the stock of material and social technology that can be tapped by less-developed countries today is enormously larger than that available in the nineteenth and even early twentieth centuries. But it is precisely this combination of greater backwardness and seemingly greater backlog of technology that makes for the significant differences between the growth position of the less-developed countries today and that of the developed countries when they were entering the modern economic growth process.

Finally, it may well be that, despite the tremendous accumulation of material and social technology, the stock of innovations most suitable to the needs of the less-developed countries is not too abundant. Even if one were to argue that progress in basic science may not be closely tied to the technological needs of the country of origin (and even that may be disputed), unquestionably the applied advances, the inventions and tools, are a response to the specific needs of the country within which they originate. This was certainly true of several major inventions associated with the Industrial Revolution in England, and illustrations abound of necessity as the mother of invention. To the extent that this is true, and that the conditions of production in the developed countries differed greatly from those in the populous less-developed countries today, the material technology evolved in the developed countries may not supply the needed innovations. Nor is the social technology that evolved in the developed countries likely to provide models of institutions or arrangements suitable to the diverse institutional and population-size backgrounds of many less-developed countries. Thus, modern technology with its emphasis on labor-saving inventions may not be suited to countries with a plethora of labor but a scarcity of other factors, such as land and water; and modern institutions, with their emphasis on personal responsibility and pursuit of economic interest, may not be suited to the more traditional life patterns of the agricultural communities that predominate in many less-developed countries. These comments should not be interpreted as denying the value of many transferable parts of modern technology; they are merely intended to stress the possible shortage of material and social tools specifically fitted to the different needs of the less-developed countries.

If the observations just made are valid, several implications for the growth problems of the less-developed countries follow. I hesitate to formulate them explicitly, since the data and the stock of knowledge on which the observations rest are limited. But at least one implication is sufficiently intriguing, and seems to be illuminating of many recent events in the field, to warrant a brief note. It is that a substantial economic advance in the less-developed countries may require modifications in the available stock of material technology, and probably even greater innovations in political and social structure. It will not be a matter of merely borrowing existing tools, material and social, or of directly applying past patterns of growth, merely allowing for the difference in parameters.

The innovational requirements are likely to be particularly great in the social and political structures. The rather violent changes in these structures that occurred in those countries that have forged ahead with highly forced industrialization under Communist auspices, the pioneer entry going back over forty years (beginning with the first Five Year Plan in the U.S.S.R.), are conspicuous illustrations of the kind of social invention and innovation that may be involved. And the variants even of Communist organization, let alone those of democracy and of non-Communist authoritarianism, are familiar. It would be an oversimplification to argue that these innovations in the social and political structures were made primarily in response to the strain between economic backwardness and the potential of modern economic growth or to claim that they were inexorable effects of antecedent history. But to whatever the struggle for political and social organization is a response, once it has been resolved, the results shape significantly the conditions under which economic growth can occur. It seems highly probable that a long period of experimentation and struggle toward a viable political framework compatible with adequate economic growth lies ahead for most less-developed countries of today; and this process will become more intensive and acute as the *perceived* gap widens between what has been attained and what is attainable with modern economic growth. While an economist can argue that some aspects of growth must be present because they are indispensable components (i.e., industrialization, large scale of production, etc.), even their parameters are bound to be variable; and many specific characteristics will be so dependent upon the outcome of the social and political innovations that extrapolation from the past is extremely hazardous.